ESSAYS

ESSAYS

Kathryn A. Blake

University of Georgia

Mary Louise McBee

University of Georgia

GLENCOE PUBLISHING CO., INC.

Encino, California

Glencoe Publishing Co., Inc.
17337 Ventura Boulevard
Encino, California 91316
Collier Macmillan Canada, Ltd.

Library of Congress Catalog Card Number: 77-73252

1 2 3 4 5 6 7 8 9   81 80 79 78 77

ISBN 0-02-472160-3

ACKNOWLEDGMENTS

Acknowledgment is gratefully made to the following authors, publishers, and agents who have
granted permission to use selections from their publications.

Shana Alexander, for "The Assassination of President Kennedy" by Shana Alexander. Originally
appeared in *Redbook*, January 1976. Copyright 1976 by Shana Alexander. Reprinted with
permission.

The Atlanta Journal and Constitution Magazine, for "Are the Killer Bees Here?" by Keith Coulbourn. Originally appeared in *The Atlanta Journal and Constitution Magazine* (March 6, 1977).
Copyright 1977 by The Atlanta Journal and Constitution Magazine. Used with permission.

The Atlantic Monthly Company, for "Three Days to See" by Helen Keller. Copyright ©, by The
Atlantic Monthly Company, Boston, Mass. Reprinted with permission.

Isaac Asimov, for "The New Caves" by Isaac Asimov. Originally appeared in *American Way* (March
1976). Copyright 1976 by Isaac Asimov. Reprinted with permission.

Change Magazine, for "New Schools" by Eric Hoffer. Originally appeared in *In Our Time* (May
1976). Copyright 1976 by Eric Hoffer. Reprinted by permission of *Change* Magazine and Eric
Hoffer.

Robert Coles, for "On the Meaning of Work" by Robert Coles. Originally appeared in *Atlantic
Monthly* (October 1971). Copyright ©, 1971 by The Atlantic Monthly Company, Boston, Mass.
Reprinted with permission.

The Chronicle of Higher Education, for "The Human Use of Language" by Lawrence L. Langer.
Reprinted with permission of The Chronicle of Higher Education, January 24, 1977. Copyright ©
1977 by Editorial Projects for Education, Inc. Reprinted also by permission of Lawrence L. Langer.

Joan Daves, for "I Have a Dream" by Martin Luther King, Jr. Reprinted by permission of Joan
Daves. Copyright © 1963 by Martin Luther King, Jr.

E. P. Dutton & Co., for "Shame" by Dick Gregory with Robert Lipsyte. From *Nigger: An Autobiography* by Dick Gregory with Robert Lipsyte. Copyright © 1964 by Dick Gregory Enterprises,
Inc. Reprinted by permission of the publishers, E. P. Dutton & Co.

CONTENTS

IV. NARRATION 228

V. ESSAYS FOR INDEPENDENT ANALYSIS 286

ALTERNATE THEMATIC CONTENTS

RELATING AND RELATIONSHIPS

SELF

THE HUMAN CHARACTER

VALUES

MODERN TRENDS

PREFACE

An essay is a relatively brief prose composition expressing personal ideas. Since it is a subjective form of communication, the essay can range in topic from the concrete to the abstract, from the serious to the whimsical. And, depending on the author's purpose, its structure can be highly formal or very informal.

The essay is not a new form of literature—the earliest essay in this volume, for example, was written by Aulus Gellius in the first century A.D. However, it is generally conceded that Michel de Montaigne originated the essay as we know it about four centuries ago. Montaigne called his first works *essais*—trials. In these works, he was not concerned with presenting complete scientific or philosophical treatises, but only with communicating his own thoughts and reactions. His essays were brief, personal, and full of digressions, as he abandoned his main topic to pursue ideas as they occurred to him. His comment about his essays, "It is my selfe I pourtray," could easily be applied to many contemporary essays.

In this volume, we have collected thought-provoking and varied essays from both the past and the present. Some are short, some longer; some are formal, some informal. Except for those essays designated for independent analysis, all of the essays in the volume are classified according to one of the four modes of discourse: exposition, used to explain the nature of an object or an idea; description, used to portray a sensory experience; argument, used to convince the reader of the truth of a specific proposition; and narration, used to recount the unfolding of an event. The modes of discourse are discussed in detail in the introductions to the various parts of the book. A thematic table of contents provides an alternate approach for examining the essays.

To aid you in examining and analyzing the essays in this volume, we have included headnotes that present biographical information about the authors and questions that ask you to consider matters of form, content, and style. We have also supplied reading and writing suggestions that you can use as take-off points in writing your own essays. A Bibliography at the very back of the book provides source information to help you locate readings mentioned in the reading suggestions and the headnotes.

Two additional reference sources are included at the end of the book: a General Guide to Analyzing Essays, which is an extensive list of questions that can be used to analyze any essay—your own and those of other writers—and a Glossary, which supplies definitions for literary terms used throughout the book. Terms defined in the Glossary are marked with an asterisk.

Essays is designed to help you become a better reader and writer of essays. Your opportunity as a reader is to appreciate an essay as a work of art, to enjoy it, and to learn from it. Your challenge as a writer is to produce an essay that someone else can appreciate, enjoy, and learn from.

PART ONE

Exposition

Of the four modes of discourse—exposition, argument, narration, and description—exposition is used to present information most directly. The most widely used form of nonfiction prose, expository writing comprises much of what we read in nonfiction books, in newspapers, and in magazine articles.

The word *exposition* comes from the Latin *exponere*, "to put forth" or "to expound," and, as this Latin root suggests, exposition is a clear, straightforward presentation of ideas. Unlike argument, exposition does not try to persuade the reader to adopt a specific point of view; instead, expository writing aims for an objective approach to its subject matter. Its approach is also direct; unlike narration, it does not use a storylike form as a means of developing a theme. Exposition differs from description as well, in that it deals with ideas rather than sensory impressions of people, places, or things.

Six methods of development are most often used in expository writing. These are classification, example, definition, analysis, cause and effect, and comparison and contrast—each of which you will be examining in detail in the course of this section on exposition.

Definition

Definition is the act of pinpointing the exact meaning of a term—making clear what the object being defined is and what it is not. One way to define a term is by means of a *formal definition,* in which the writer names the genus, or class, of the word and then lists the differentiae—that is, the characteristics that distinguish the term from the other members of its class. For example, Webster's dictionary uses formal definition when it defines soccer as "a game played on a field between two teams of 11 players each with the object to propel a round ball into the opponent's goal by kicking or by hitting it with any part of the body except the hands and arms." In this definition, soccer's genus is identified as "game," and the other items of information about soccer comprise the differentiae since they distinguish soccer from other games.

Definitions can be brief, or *simple,* involving only a synonym or a formal definition like the one cited above. But if the term being defined is complex, or controversial, or if a clear understanding of the term is central to the comprehension of the essay as a whole, the writer may use an *extended definition.* An extended definition explores a term in depth, tracing its history or evolution, illustrating it with examples, or using other methods to clarify its exact meaning. In some cases, entire essays may be no more than extended definitions.

In order to use definition effectively, writers should observe the following guidelines. First, they should carefully consider the length of the definition, providing enough information to give the reader a clear picture of the term's meaning, but avoiding excessive or irrelevant information. A definition of soccer as "a game in which each of two teams attempts to propel an object into the opponent's goal" would not be sufficient, since this definition also applies to football, field hockey, and any number of other sports. On the other hand, it would not be necessary to describe all the rules of the game and the functions of the various team members in order to give a clear idea of what soccer is; such extraneous information would distract the reader from the matter at hand. Second, definitions should never be circular —that is, the name of the term should not be repeated in the definition. Defining "criticism" as "the act of criticizing" will hardly give the reader a clearer understanding of the term. Third, definitions should generally contain the genus of the term being described. Instead of writing, "Soccer is when two teams . . .," write "Soccer is a *game* in which two teams . . ." Once a reader knows the genus of a term, he or she is well on the way toward understanding its complete meaning.

OF THUMBS

Michel de Montaigne

Michel de Montaigne (1533–1592), called the father of the essay, was born to a wealthy family in the south of France and received an excellent education. After working in the legal profession for a number of years, he retired to his château to devote himself to reflection and study. It was at this time that he developed the essay form as a means to clarify and express his reflections. In "Of Thumbs," he turns his attention to the historical significance of this important digit.

Tacitus reports that amongst certain barbarian kings, their manner was, when they would make a firm obligation, to join their right hands close to one another, and intertwist their thumbs; and when, by force of straining, the blood appeared in the ends, they lightly pricked them with some sharp instrument, and mutually sucked them.

Physicians say, that the thumbs are the master fingers of the hand, and that their Latin etymology is derived from *pollere*.[1] The Greeks called them . . . another hand. And it seems that the Latins also sometimes take it in this sense for the whole hand.

> Sed nec vocibus excitata blandis,
> Molli pollice nec rogata, surgit.[2]

It was at Rome a signification of favour to depress and turn in the thumbs:

> Fautor utroque tuum laudabit pollice ludum,[3]

and of disfavour to elevate and thrust them outward:

---

1. A Latin verb meaning "to be strong."
2. Neither to be excited by soft words, or by the thumb.
3. Thy patron will applaud thy sport with both thumbs.

Converso pollice vulgi,
Quemlibet occidunt populariter,[4]

The Romans exempted from war all such as were maimed in the
thumbs, as having no more sufficient strength to hold their weapons.
Augustus confiscated the estate of a Roman knight, who had mali-
ciously cut off the thumbs of two young children he had, to excuse
them from going into the armies: and, before him, the Senate, in the
time of the Italic war, had condemned Caius Vatienus to perpetual
imprisonment, and confiscated all his goods, for having purposely
cut off the thumb of his left hand, to exempt himself from that expedition. Some one, I have forgotten who, having won a naval battle,
cut off the thumbs of all his vanquished enemies, to render them
incapable of fighting and of handling the oar. The Athenians also
caused the thumbs of the Aeginatans to be cut off, to deprive them of
the superiority in the art of navigation.

In Lacedaemon, pedagogues chastised their scholars by biting
their thumbs.

QUESTIONS

1. What purpose do the Latin references and quotations serve in this
   essay? What do they tell you about Montaigne?

2. What adjectives would you use to portray Montaigne's diction*
   and style:* concrete or abstract, general or specific, spare or wordy,
   objective or subjective, coherent or incoherent, unified or
   disunified?

3. Consider that the thumb is only one of five fingers. What do
   Montaigne's comments indicate about the nature of that particular
   digit?

4. Would people today maim themselves or their children to avoid
   military service? What would the punishment be? We often hear
   about POWs being killed, tortured, or heavily confined, yet we
   seldom hear of their being incapacitated for further warfare
   through the amputation of fingers, hands, or feet. Why do you
   think this is so?

5. Are thumbs as crucial today as they were in the past? Why, or why
   not? Which would you least like to lose—your thumbs or your
   eyes? Explain your answer.

---

4. The populace, with reverted thumbs, kill all that come before them.

*Definitions for all terms marked with an asterisk may be found in the Glossary.

READING AND WRITING SUGGESTIONS

1. Use Montaigne's approach in a brief expository essay defining the nature of the tongue. Call your essay "Of the Tongue."

2. Read a book about Helen Keller or another deaf person. Use the ideas you encounter in your reading to write a brief expository essay titled "Of Hearing."

THE WATCHER
AT THE GATES

Gail Godwin

Gail Godwin (1937–) was born in Birmingham, Alabama, and received her B.A. degree from the University of North Carolina and her M.A. and Ph.D. degrees from the University of Iowa. She has worked at such varied places as the Miami Herald, *the United States embassy in London, the University of Iowa, and the Center for Advanced Studies at the University of Illinois. Author of a number of novels, including* The Perfectionists *and* Glass People, *she has also contributed to such magazines as* Cosmopolitan, Esquire, Paris Review, *and* North American Review. *In this essay, Godwin explores the nature of an inner voice that plagues all writers—the voice of the Watcher at the Gates.*

I first realized I was not the only writer who had a restraining critic who lived inside me and sapped the juice from green inspirations when I was leafing through Freud's "Interpretation of Dreams" a few years ago. Ironically, it was my "inner critic" who had sent me to Freud. I was writing a novel, and my heroine was in the middle of a dream, and then I lost faith in my own invention and rushed to "an authority" to check whether she could have such a dream. In the chapter on dream interpretation, I came upon the following passage that has helped me free myself, in some measure, from my critic and has led to many pleasant and interesting exchanges with other writers.

Freud quotes Schiller, who is writing a letter to a friend. The friend complains of his lack of creative power. Schiller replies with an allegory. He says it is not good if the intellect examines too closely the ideas pouring in at the gates. "In isolation, an idea may be quite insignificant, and venturesome in the extreme, but it may acquire importance from an idea which follows it . . . In the case of a creative mind, it seems to me, the intellect has withdrawn its watchers from the gates, and the ideas rush in pell-mell, and only then does it review and inspect the multitude. You are ashamed or afraid of the momentary and passing madness which is found in all real creators, the longer or shorter duration of which distinguishes the thinking artist from the dreamer . . . you reject too soon and discriminate too severely."

So that's what I had: a Watcher at the Gates. I decided to get to know him better. I discussed him with other writers, who told me some of the quirks and habits of their Watchers, each of whom was as individual as his host, and all of whom seemed passionately dedicated to one goal: rejecting too soon and discriminating too severely.

It is amazing the lengths a Watcher will go to keep you from pursuing the flow of your imagination. Watchers are notorious pencil sharpeners, ribbon changers, plant waterers, home repairers and abhorrers of messy rooms or messy pages. They are compulsive looker-uppers. They are superstitious scaredy-cats. They cultivate self-important eccentricities they think are suitable for "writers." And they'd rather die (and kill your inspiration with them) than risk making a fool of themselves.

My Watcher has a wasteful penchant for 20-pound bond paper above and below the carbon of the first draft. "What's the good of writing out a whole page," he whispers begrudgingly, "if you just have to write it over again later? Get it perfect the first time!" My Watcher adores stopping in the middle of a morning's work to drive down to the library to check on the name of a flower or a World War II battle or a line of metaphysical poetry. "You can't possibly go on till you've got this right!" he admonishes. I go and get the car keys.

Other Watchers have informed their writers that:

"Whenever you get a really good sentence you should stop in the middle of it and go on tomorrow. Otherwise you might run dry."

"Don't try and continue with your book till your dental appointment is over. When you're worried about your teeth, you can't think about art."

Another Watcher makes his owner pin his finished pages to a clothesline and read them through binoculars "to see how they look from a distance." Countless other Watchers demand "bribes" for taking the day off: lethal doses of caffeine, alcoholic doses of Scotch or vodka or wine.

There are various ways to outsmart, pacify or coexist with your Watcher. Here are some I have tried, or my writer friends have tried, with success:

Look for situations when he's likely to be off-guard. Write too fast for him in an unexpected place, at an unexpected time. (Virginia Woolf captured the "diamonds in the dustheap" by writing at a "rapid haphazard gallop" in her diary.) Write when very tired. Write in purple ink on the back of a Master Charge statement. Write whatever comes into your mind while the kettle is boiling and make the steam whistle your deadline. (Deadlines are a great way to outdistance the Watcher.)

Disguise what you are writing. If your Watcher refuses to let you get on with your story or novel, write a "letter" instead, telling your "correspondent" what you are going to write in your story or next chapter. Dash off a "review" of your own unfinished opus. It will stand up like a bully to your Watcher the next time he throws obstacles in your path. If you write yourself a good one.

Get to know your Watcher. He's yours. Do a drawing of him (or her). Pin it to the wall of your study and turn it gently to the wall when necessary. Let your Watcher feel needed. Watchers are excellent critics after inspiration has been captured; they are dependable, sharp-eyed readers of things already set down. Keep your Watcher in shape and he'll have less time to keep you from shaping. If he's really ruining your whole working day sit down, as Jung did with his personal demons, and write him a letter. On a very bad day I once wrote my Watcher a letter. "Dear Watcher," I wrote, "What is it you're so afraid I'll do?" Then I held his pen for him, and he replied instantly with a candor that has kept me from truly despising him.

"Fail," he wrote back.

QUESTIONS

1. What does Godwin mean by the phrase "[the critic] sapped the juice from green inspirations"?

2. Where does Godwin get the metaphor* "Watcher at the Gates," which she uses as a title? What does this title suggest to you about Godwin's thesis?*

---

*Definitions for all terms marked with an asterisk may be found in the Glossary.

3. a. What are the characteristics of a "Watcher at the Gates"?
    b. What goal does the Watcher *seem* to be passionately dedicated to? What is the Watcher *really* doing? What is it trying to protect the writer from? Keeping in mind the price the writer must pay in terms of creativity, decide whether you think the Watcher is ultimately more helpful than harmful or vice versa.

4. Do Watchers at the Gates work for people in areas other than creative writing? Give some examples.

5. a. Name three things your own Watcher at the Gates has done to protect you from failure.
    b. In what ways, if any, has this protection from failure also kept you from achieving what you might otherwise have achieved?
    c. What are three things you can do to outsmart your Watcher at the Gates?

READING AND WRITING SUGGESTIONS

1. Write a brief expository essay defining the "courage and grace" that is exhibited when someone takes a chance and tries something really new.

2. Read accounts of the many failures experienced by a successful person—Winston Churchill or Mary Tyler Moore, for example. Use the information gathered in your reading to write a brief expository essay titled "Winners Are Losers and Losers Are Winners."

THE LOST ART OF CONVERSATION

George C. McGhee

George C. McGhee (1912–) received his undergraduate degree from the University of Oklahoma, and, after attending Oxford University as a Rhodes scholar, received a Ph.D. in the physical sciences. He has also been awarded honorary doctorates from several universities. From 1941 until his retirement in 1969, McGhee served the government in a number of capacities, including assistant secretary of state for Near Eastern, South Asian and African affairs, ambassador to Turkey, consultant to the National Security Council, under secretary of state for political affairs, and ambassador to Germany. He is currently chairman of the National Smithsonian Associates and a director of Procter and Gamble Company, Mobil Oil Corporation, Trans World Airlines, and American Security and Trust Company. In the following essay, McGhee presents the characteristics of true conversation.

What has happened to the art of conversation? By conversation I am not thinking merely of word exchanges between individuals. I am thinking of one of the highest manifestations of the use of human intelligence—the ability to transform abstractions into language; the ability to convey images from one mind to another; the ability to build a mutual edifice of ideas. In short, the ability to engage in a civilizing experience.

When the word *art* is applied to conversation, one conjures up an image of Dr. Johnson uttering words of wisdom, with a devoted Boswell taking them all down on paper. Boswell quoted Mrs. Thrale as having remarked about Johnson that his "conversation was much too strong for a person accustomed to obsequiousness and flattery; it was mustard in a young child's mouth."

But where does one find good conversation these days? Certainly not in the presence of the television set, which consumes half of the average American's non-sleeping, non-working hours. Much of the remaining free time is given to games. No matter how rewarding "bridge talk" may be, it is not conversation. Neither is chatter.

What makes good conversation? In the first place, it is essentially a mutual search for the essence of things. It is a zestful transaction, not a briefing or a lecture. Pushkin correctly identified the willingness to listen as one of the vital ingredients of any exchange. When two people are talking at the same time, the result is not conversation but a collision of decibels.

Nothing is more destructive of good talk than for one participant to hold the ball too long, like an over-zealous basketball dribbler playing to the gallery and keeping it away from everyone else. Pity the husband or wife with a garrulous mate who insists on talking long past the point where he or she has anything to say.

To be meaningful, a conversation should head in a general direction. It need not be artfully plotted to arrive at a predetermined point, but it should be gracefully kept on course—guided by many unforeseen ideas.

It has been said that if speech is silver, silence is golden. Certainly silence is preferable, under most circumstances, to inconsequential chitchat. Why is it then that so many people, when they are with others, are discomfited by the absence of human sound waves? Why are they not willing merely to sit with each other, silently enjoying the unheard but real linkages of congeniality and understanding? Why aren't people content to contemplate a lovely scene or read together in silence? "Made conversation" should not be a necessity among intimates. They know whether the weather is good or bad; both are as well or poorly informed about current events. If there is nothing to say—don't say it.

It is true that strangers meeting for the first time seem to feel uncomfortable if they do not engage in small talk to relieve their mutual awkwardness. This is the scourge of the cocktail party, but it is necessary if strangers are to size each other up. Usually, however, this is harmless. In desperation one seeks an artificial gambit. I remember one from an English girl: "Oh, I say, are you frightfully keen on cats and dogs?" Unfortunately, I wasn't.

There is a disease shared by many, particularly with new acquaintances, that leads to "dropping names" or "colleges." This is often a useful device, since a common friend or university experience can be a helpful point of departure for conversation leading to better understanding. It is, however, more often woefully abused as a means of showing off. The references are usually to the influential rather than to one's less distinguished friends: "Of course I know Ina Gottrocks. She is a very dear friend. Such a nice person [actually an awful bore].

We had lunch only yesterday [on an airplane, sitting in different class sections]." One is less inclined to refer to one's alma mater if it is Oshkosh U.

Genealogical topics should also be avoided. The danger of boring one's conversation partner and of becoming self-serving is far too great. In the first place, others don't really care about your ancestors. They know, as you should, that everyone has quite a variety ranging all the way from bums to princes. If one goes back eight generations, one has 256 forebears. How easy to pick out the one who glitters most as your claim to fame. Even the one who gave you your name is still only one in 256.

Cocktail-party necessities aside, however, some elementary rules for conversation are well worth our consideration. In the first place, certain subjects should be taboo in any general conversation. Kitchen topics—the best cleansers, recipes, and troubles with servants—should certainly be limited to interested women. Straight man-talk, such as business, golf, and hunting exploits, may be permissible in board or locker rooms but should be taboo in general discussion, along with bus schedules and all other dull or specialized things. One does not mention precise figures descriptive of one's wealth or income—not even an artful "The deal netted me something in six figures." The first digit was probably 1.

People even forget, I'm afraid, that their illnesses and operations should be outlawed as conversational topics. Only if some relative asks you on a need-to-know basis, or a doctor is interested from a professional standpoint, should you ever volunteer anything about your ailments. Everyone understands this; yet it never seems to apply to you. Remember, even if it's the most dramatic operation ever performed, it is not something to be offered gratuitously to friends at conversation time. They really don't want to hear about it.

There is also the conversationalist who must under every circumstance be right—who always has to win the game. There are those of us who want to moralize. There is the intruder into emotional subjects like religion or personalities, the malicious gossip. All should be inadmissible by any rules of good conversation. Vulgar words, even the four-letter words, can sometimes be effective—as in the English use of *bloody*. More often, however, they are in bad taste—particularly when they conjure up a revolting image at mealtime. Shouldn't there be some law against sonic pollution?

An intriguing conversational gambit was disclosed by H. Allen Smith, which could, if you got by with it, amaze your dinner partners. In preparation he boned up on traditional Chinese uses of funereal jade in the body orifices. It is best to choose a subject that would appear alien to your normal interests. A lawyer, after consulting the art histories, might break into the Pre-Raphaelite painters. A hostess at a country weekend might try: "Yes, the country is lovely here. The lower Catoctin greensand, Upper Jurassic, you know, underlies much of the Austin chalk of the valley." Stephen Potter's books on gamesmanship and one-upmanship are of course treasurehouses of this sort of off-putting play.

If conversation need not always be purposeful, it must at least be for pleasure. It should be congenial to good society—to better knowing one's conversation partner. Above all, it should be joyful and amiable, for as Addison put it: "Good nature is more agreeable in conversation than wit, and gives a certain air to the countenance which is more amiable than beauty." I do not object to enforced conversation—say, by the hostess who interrupts an after-dinner group with, "Come, we must all hear John tell us about his trip to Africa." I am less tolerant, however, of those who would arbitrarily stop a good conversation which has exciting possibilities with a flat "Come, now, let's stop all this serious talk." A good conversation is a fragile thing that must be nurtured carefully.

And, finally, I want to encourage the pixie of the conversation who can add zest and interest. Our talk too often reflects the dull things we do all day. Conversation does not always have to be in earnest. Provocation, whimsy, laughter, mockery, and flirtation all have their place in the art of good conversation, of which it has been said, "Be prompt without being stubborn, refute without argument, clothe weighty matters in a motley garb."

QUESTIONS

1. Explain the meaning of the following figures of speech:*
   —"It was mustard in a young child's mouth."
   —"If speech is silver, silence is golden."
   —"A collision of decibels."
   —"Holding the [conversational] ball too long, like an over-zealous basketball dribbler playing to the gallery and keeping it away from everyone else."
   —"It [conversation] need not be artfully plotted to arrive at a predetermined point, but it should be gracefully kept on course —guided by many unforeseen ideas."

2. Is McGhee's title accurate in the sense that conversation, as he defines it, has disappeared ?

---

*Definitions for all terms marked with an asterisk may be found in the Glossary.

3. Name at least four characteristics of true conversation.

4. Assume that McGhee's statement that conversation "must at least be for pleasure" is true.
    a. Is the nature of good conversation the same for all people? Why, or why not?
    b. Suppose someone were really interested in kitchen topics and absolutely indifferent to artistic and political topics. What would true conversation consist of for that person?
    c. Does McGhee's essay show us as much about his interests as it does about the definition of conversation? Explain your answer.

5. a. Name at least two topics that you think are conducive to true conversation and at least two more that you think are destructive to such conversation.
   b. Discuss at least two situations you've witnessed in which "everybody talked and nobody listened."

READING AND WRITING SUGGESTIONS

1. Write a brief expository essay presenting your own definition of conversation.

2. Read T. S. Eliot's play *The Cocktail Party* and write a brief expository essay discussing whether the characters in the play truly participated in conversation. Use McGhee's definition of conversation as the basis for your discussion.

ISLANDERS

Liv Ullmann

Liv Ullmann (1939–) is an internationally acclaimed actress whose stage, television, and cinema credits include Hedda Gabler, Scenes from a Marriage, Cries and Whispers, The Emigrants, The New Land, *and* Face to Face. *Recently she has written* Changing, *a collection of personal reflections on her experiences. In the following essay from her book, she explores the characteristics of a group of people she calls "islanders."*

I was searching for something on an island.

Here people lived close to the earth, close to the sea, close to that which is natural and predetermined for us.

The distinctive mark of the people I met, when the tourists had left at the end of summer, was their simplicity.

None of these men and women, I felt, could ever be humbled. They lived in harmony with their own selves, with everything that was good and evil in them. No outsiders could point at them and make them feel inferior.

People who had trust in their place on earth. They were far from uncomplicated, nor without demands, hatreds and aggressions. But they had pride, a dignity which they allowed no one to crush. They had roots which had been lodged in the same piece of earth their entire lives.

Many old people have that. They have renounced pretensions, dropped the false dream, stopped the mad rush.

They, too, are islanders in our society.

The way children are.

People who don't care to keep the mask and the façade in order. Who dare to show who they are.

Islanders.

The ones who live their thoughts. Even thoughts that may not be so remarkable.

From some of them emanates a feeling of security, a feeling of simple security, which may be the dignity of the heart.

QUESTIONS

1. Ullmann uses the terms "island" and "islander" as metaphors.*
What do these metaphors mean as Ullmann applies them?

2. Examine the style of this essay.
   a. Would you call Ullmann's style* wordy or telegraphic? Explain
   your answer.
   b. Do you think that Ullmann's use of sentence fragments—incomplete sentences—is justified? Why, or why not? Why do
   you think she uses them?

3. Consider the idea that being an islander may have something to do
with personal circumstances.
   a. Can a person who lives in the midst of many people be an
   islander?
   b. Can people be islanders if—unlike children and very old people—they are encumbered with time- and energy-consuming
   responsibilities?

4. Do you know a person who could be called an islander? How did
he or she achieve that state? Would you like to be an islander?
Explain your answer.

READING AND WRITING SUGGESTIONS

1. Identify some people you consider serene. Keeping the characteristics of these people in mind, write a brief expository essay
defining serenity.

2. Read or recall *Robinson Crusoe* and write an expository essay in
which you discuss whether or not he could be called an islander.

---

*Definitions for all terms marked with an asterisk may be found in the Glossary.

Classification

Classification is the method of development concerned with sorting members of a large group into categories on the basis of a specific criterion or principle. Suppose, for example, that you wanted to divide presidents of the United States (a large group) into two categories: great presidents and less-than-great presidents. In order to do this, you would have to develop a sorting principle or criterion—for example, great presidents are those who have led the nation successfully through a crisis. All the presidents who met this criterion could then be classified as great, and those who did not meet the criterion would be classified as less than great.

Used correctly, classification organizes facts, ideas, and experiences in a useful way by applying a system to the unsystematic. But there are three requirements which must be met if a classification is to have any value.

First, the sorting principle of classification must apply in a meaningful way to the writer's purpose in classifying the members of the group. To take an extreme example, if you were classifying all American presidents as great and less than great, it would not be meaningful to use the amount of money each president had made in private life as the principle of classification. This would reveal something about the presidents' business acumen, but it would not say much about their relative ability as leaders.

Second, the categories used in classification should, taken together, exhaust the subject. If you used the categories lawyers and plantation owners, for example, to classify the presidents of the United States in terms of occupation, you would be overlooking those presidents who were businessmen, generals, and members of other occupations, and your classification would not be complete.

Third, the categories used in classification should not overlap. You would not want to divide the presidents into the categories of scholars, bachelors, and married men, since all of the presidents who could be categorized as scholars would *also* be categorized either as bachelors or as married men. These overlapping categories would destroy the meaning and usefulness of the classification.

TO NOBLE COMPANIONS

Gail Godwin

Gail Godwin (1937–) is a contemporary author whose works in-clude The Perfectionists *and* Glass People. *(For more detailed bio-graphical information, see p. 7.) In the following essay, Godwin examines the nature of true friends and presents criteria we can use to distinguish such friends from mere acquaintances.*

What Is a True Friend?

The dutiful first answer seems programmed into us by our meager expectations: "A friend is one who will be there in times of trouble." But I believe this is a skin-deep answer to describe skin-deep friends. There is something irresistible about misfortune to human nature, and standbys for setbacks and sicknesses (as long as they are not too lengthy, or contagious) can usually be found. They can be *hired*. What I value is not the "friend" who, looming sympathetically above me when I have been dashed to the ground, appears gigantically gener-ous in the hour of my reversal; more and more I desire friends who will endure my ecstasies with me, who possess wings of their own and who will fly with me. I don't mean this as arrogance (I am too superstitious to indulge long in that trait), and I don't fly all that often. What I mean is that I seek (and occasionally find) friends with whom it is possible to drag out all those beautiful, old, outrageously *aspiring* costumes and rehearse together for the Great Roles; persons whose qualities groom me and train me up for love. It is for these people that I reserve the glowing hours, too good not to share. It is the existence of these people that reminds me that the words "friend" and "free" grew out of each other (OE *freo*, not in bondage, noble, glad; OE *freon*, to love; OE *freond*, friend.)

When I was in the eighth grade, I had a friend. We were shy and "too serious" about our studies when it was becoming fashionable with our classmates to acquire the social graces. We said little at school, but she would come to my house and we would sit down with pencils and paper, and one of us would say: "Let's start with a train whistle today." We would sit quietly together and write separate poems or stories that grew out of a train whistle. Then we would read them aloud. At the end of that school year, we, too, were transformed into social creatures and the stories and poems stopped.

When I lived for a time in London, I had a friend. He was in despair and I was in despair, but our friendship was based on the small flicker of foresight in each of us that told us we would be sorry later if we did not explore this great city because we had felt bad at the time. We met every Sunday for five weeks and found many marvelous things. We walked until our despairs resolved themselves and then we parted. We gave London to each other.

For almost four years I have had a remarkable friend whose imagination illumines mine. We write long letters in which we often discover our strangest selves. Each of us appears, sometimes prophetically, sometimes comically, in the other's dreams. She and I agree that, at certain times, we seem to be parts of the same mind. In my most sacred and interesting moments, I often think: "Yes, I must tell————." We have never met.

It is such exceptional (in a sense divine) companions I wish to salute. I have seen the glories of the world reflected briefly through our encounters. One bright hour with their kind is worth more to me than a lifetime guarantee of the services of a Job's comforter whose "helpful" lamentations will only clutter the healing silence necessary to those darkest moments in which I would rather be my own best friend.

How to Tell a Friend From an Acquaintance

This questionnaire is designed to reveal your true friends to you. Think of everyone you know who might qualify. Then simply substitute their names—one at a time—for "X." Scoring one point whenever you're able to answer a question with Yes, you can figure that a total of 24 or more indicates genuine friendship. We'd be interested to know how rare it is in your life.

	YES	NO
1 Do you know X's telephone number?	☐	☐
2. If you've been out of touch for several months, can you meet without awkwardness?	☐	☐
3. Do you know X's favorite color?	☐	☐
4. Have you ever done anything nice for X without telling him (her) about it?	☐	☐
5. Will X co-sign a loan for you?	☐	☐
6. Has a third party ever regaled you with the admiring stories X tells about you when you're not present?	☐	☐

	YES	NO
7. When X can't decide what to drink, does he (she) ask you to pick?	□	□
8. Can you list the dishes on X's ideal menu?	□	□
9. Would you trust X with your mate?	□	□
10. Can you express angry feelings about each other to each other?	□	□
11. Can X make demands on you and vice versa? (What happens if you call X up at 3 A.M.?)	□	□
12. Has X ever done anything nice for you even though he (she) stood to suffer for it?	□	□
13. Can you stand X after either of you has had three drinks?	□	□
14. If you have a bad back, does X ask you to be careful not to hurt yourself when you are playing tennis?	□	□
15. When X is badly hung over, is it you he (she) asks to join him (her) for an A.M. hair of the dog?	□	□
16. Would you let X have the keys to your house or apartment?	□	□
17. Can you borrow X's car?	□	□
18. When describing a particularly attractive member of the opposite sex does X say, "I know she'd (he'd) really like you"?	□	□
19. Does X remember your birthday?	□	□
20. Has X ever bought you an item of clothing just because he (she) thought you'd look great in it?	□	□
21. If X doesn't return your telephone calls, do you feel worried rather than insulted?	□	□
22. Do you know what kind of music X likes best? Dislikes most?	□	□
23. Can you tell X No?	□	□
24. Would you give X one of your kidneys?	□	□
25. Are you aware of the problem now on X's mind?	□	□
26. Can you list five books X would like to have on a desert island?	□	□
27. Does X tell you when he (she) thinks you're acting like a fool, and you are?	□	□
28. Will X lend you money? Clothes?	□	□
29. Has X always kept your confidence?	□	□
30. Has X confessed an irrational fear to you?	□	□
31. Do you know what X would like as a birthday present?	□	□
32. Can you spend time together comfortably without talking?	□	□
33. Has X ever brought you chicken soup when you were sick?	□	□
34. Can you say anything that comes into your head when you're with X?	□	□
35. If, contrary to your advice, X marries Y, will he (she) want to retain your friendship?	□	□

QUESTIONS

1   a. What does the expression "fair-weather friend" mean? Are the
       people that Godwin describes the opposite of "fair-weather
       friends"?
    b. What is "a Job's comforter"? What is the source of the image,
       "helpful lamentations of a Job's comforter"? Does Godwin
       classify such people as true friends?

2. Why does Godwin use the questionnaire? Do you think it presents
   valid criteria for sorting people into the groups "true friends" and
   "acquaintances"?

3. Godwin writes about three people she considers to be true friends.
   What did she share with each one? What characteristic does she
   use to classify people—that is, what is her grouping, or sorting,
   criterion?

4. Which do you feel is easier: to find people who help in times of
   trouble or to find people who share joy and growth? What type of
   friend would you rather have? Why? What type would you rather
   be? Why?

5. Consider the sentence " 'Helpful lamentations' . . . clutter the
   healing silence necessary to those darkest moments in which I
   would rather be my own best friend." Which is better: to work
   things out for ourselves or to get the sympathy of others? Is there
   only one constructive way to deal with misfortune, or should the
   method used depend on the person using it?

READING AND WRITING SUGGESTIONS

1. Think about Godwin's metaphor, "friends with whom it is possible to drag out all those beautiful, old, outrageously *aspiring* costumes and rehearse together for the Great Roles." Take as your
   thesis that such people are true friends. Write a brief classification
   essay that defines the characteristics of people who have joined
   you in such growth experiences and that describes what these
   people meant to you.

2. Read *Ellen Terry and George Bernard Shaw: A Correspondence,* which
   is a collection of the letters exchanged between these two people.
   Author George Bernard Shaw and actress Ellen Terry never met
   each other; they had a friendship similar to the one Godwin describes in her next-to-last paragraph. Choose a person you would

like as a friend but do not know personally. Write a brief expository essay describing the characteristics you think would bind you together as friends and include two letters of the type you might write to this person.

JUSTICE FOR <u>HUSTLER</u>

Arthur Kretchmer

Arthur Kretchmer (1940–), a native of New York City, received his B.A. degree from City University of New York. He was the managing editor of Cavalier *Magazine from 1964 to 1966, took a position with* Playboy *Magazine in 1966, and became executive editor of that magazine in 1971. He is listed in* Who's Who in America *and is a member of the Society of Magazine Editors. In this article he comments on an issue that directly affects him as executive editor of* Playboy—*the controversy over the kinds of material that should be classified as obscene.*

As the editorial director of the magazine that is credited with having "started it all " I've been under pressure lately to take a stand against Larry Flynt and *Hustler* magazine. Interviewers seem to find it deliciously provocative to ask if the editor of *Playboy* isn't perhaps a little, um, offended by *Hustler*. Well . . . yes. I don't have delicate sensibilities, but *Hustler* has succeeded more than once in shocking them. Flynt's magazine is as shamelessly vulgar as its reputation suggests. It is not merely sexually explicit, it is perverse; the magazine thrives on gross, racist and scatological humor. Its overt aim is to shock one and all.

Having admitted the affront to my taste, however, I must add that it is a far greater affront to my sensibilities that Larry Flynt was jailed and that he faces a prolonged stay behind bars. Flynt's conviction has confirmed my fears that the Supreme Court's 1973 obscenity decision could be used to enable any community to punish the publisher of any journal whose standards are less fastidious than its own. He is the victim of a vindictive prosecution that was aimed not at protecting the community but at destroying the man. The case stands as a clear warning to others.

Offensive Grandstanding

Flynt is an exhibitionist *provocateur*. His grandstanding and chutzpah have offended his enemies far beyond what has appeared in the magazine. To a responsible businessman, his judgment has been terrible. No one with any sense would have mailed, as Flynt did, photographs of maimed Vietnam veterans throughout Cincinnati where his trial was to be held. Flynt's stated point was that "violence, not sex, is the real obscenity." The photos, also published in the December *Hustler*, were enough to make strong men sick. But do you put a man in jail for provoking the gag reflex?

One of the more scandalous aspects of the community-standards apparatus that's been used to bury Flynt is that it makes no provision for an appeal from people who might constitute a "community" of opposing views. The man, after all, has an audience. But where is the government agency that should seek to protect the rights of Larry Flynt's fans? If *Hustler* is childish and rude, perhaps the audience is also rude. Or perhaps it has fantasies of being rude. Don't such people have a right to protest the deprivation inflicted upon them by the presumably genteel folk in Hamilton County, Ohio? One of the principles of the Constitution is that the majority shall not destroy the rights of the minority. One person's notions of probity and sanctity are not to be imposed on us all. As Justice Holmes said, freedom of thought is "freedom for the thought that we hate."

Flynt has been convicted of incorrigible bad taste. The good citizens of Cincinnati have acted like embarrassed parents trying to shush a fresh child. The reference to children is required because all discussions of censorship lead directly to concerns about children even though it is a well-established legal precedent that suitability for children is not a permissible standard for judging literature intended for adults.

What Children See

One of the jurors in the *Hustler* case said she found Flynt guilty because " . . . magazines like that shouldn't be around. Younger kids can get hold of them."

I have two children, ages 3 and 5. On a recent evening when I was to make an appearance on a local news show, the kids sat in front of the TV and watched a man walk a banker down the street with a shotgun at his head; the aftermath of a murder-robbery at a local store; an essay on child abuse; and the gory recap of a train disaster. I called my wife and told her to get the kids away from the set and give each a copy of *The Joy of Sex*.

My kids have grown up face-to-face with sexual images that are available to them in dad's magazine. My 8-year-old spent an entire afternoon recently avidly perusing five years' worth of *Playboy*. When I got home he told me that he really likes the drawings in the magazine—the kind where a perfectly rendered pretzel, on closer inspection, turns out to be a map of China. I'm convinced that when he is old enough to show a stronger interest in the erotic images in *Playboy*, he will be at an age when that interest is running full-tilt anyway. There'll be no sense in raising his temperature even higher by trying to censor his reading matter.

What children are allowed to see is a parental, not a state, problem. Nevertheless, I would be the first to admit that there are images in *Hustler* so violent and lurid that they are beyond explaining to children. But there are laws about what can and cannot be sold to minors. Adults who worry about erotic material being seen by children are expressing anxieties of their own. There is a fear of sex buried deep in the American psyche that emerges as the belief that a more open sexuality leads to social decay. This supposition is, at best, arguable. What is certain is that freedom of expression is easily destroyed once we allow its erosion to begin.

Weighted Juries

What about *Playboy*? Does the conviction of Larry Flynt make the editor of *Playboy* vulnerable? Indeed, in this era of hand-picked juror rolls, prosecutors can weight the jury-selection process according to ethnic, economic and political backgrounds and literally hunt down any publisher on charges of obscenity. Under the "community standards" doctrine, if there are only twelve people in the country who might find *Playboy* obscene, and the prosecutor manages to get them all into the same courtroom, I've had it. Juries are not told to establish what they think the standards of the community might be, they are robed in the immodest notion that they *are* the community.

The more I think about Flynt sitting in a cage for publishing an infantile magazine, the more outraged I become. He committed no crime against person or property. He did not murder, maim, rape or plunder. There's a strong temptation, even among the less benighted, to say that what he published exceeded the limits of free expression, but once you place *any* limit on free expression—even a responsible one—you no longer have it. If you don't like Flynt's manners, don't invite him into the house; don't buy his magazine. But don't leave his fate to a dozen people with the impudent thought that their taste is so exalted and so wise that any man who would offend it should spend 25 years in jail.

QUESTIONS

1. What do the connotations* of the words *vulgar, gross, racist, scatological, perverse, sadomasochistic, macabre, Gothic, prurient, obscene,* and *pornographic* have in common?

2. Consider whether censorship should be a public or a private responsibility.
    a. One relevant issue is the criterion or criteria that should be used to classify material as obscene and unlawful.
       —According to Kretchmer, what is the U.S. Supreme Court's position?
       —What is Flynt's position?
       —What is the Cincinnati juror's position?
       —What is Kretchmer's position?
    b. Through the centuries, even on the walls of prehistoric cave dwellings, we have had sexual, scatological, and sadomasochistic jokes, stories, publications, and pictures. In the twentieth century we have also been exposed to such elements in movies and on TV.
       —Does Kretchmer maintain that people should be free to enjoy these materials?
       —What does he say about children's exposure to such materials?
       —In his last paragraph, Kretchmer suggests one way to censor material. What is his suggestion?

3. Consider what materials you would classify as obscene and appropriate to ban.
    a. Would you classify any of the following as obscene?
       —Michelangelo's statue, *David*
       —James Dickey's novel, *Deliverance*
       —*Playboy* Magazine
       —Pictures of the My Lai killings; pictures of Vietnamese children running down a road with their clothes, bodies, and hair on fire from napalm.

---

*Definitions for all terms marked with an asterisk may be found in the Glossary.

      —Pictures or detailed descriptions of an accident that resulted in disfigurement or dismemberment.

      —Pictures or written material depicting consenting adults in sexual or scatological situations; descriptions of one adult subjecting another to dismemberment, disfigurement, or whipping.

      —Pictures or written material depicting children, or children with adults, in sexual or scatological situations; descriptions of an adult subjecting a child to dismemberment, disfigurement, or whipping.

      —Pictures or written material encouraging an adult to sexually assault or physically injure another adult.

      —Pictures or written material encouraging an adult to sexually assault or physically injure a child.

  b. What do your answers indicate about your criteria for classifying material as obscene?

  c. Answer questions 4a and 4b again, this time considering whether such material should be banned from public display. Are your criteria different from those you established for determining whether material is obscene?

4. Decide whether you feel there should be any limit at all to freedom of expression.

  a. Kretchmer quotes Justice Holmes as saying, "Freedom of thought is 'freedom for the thought that we hate.' " Do you agree? Why, or why not?

  b. Justice Holmes also said, "We do not have the freedom to shout 'fire' in a crowded theatre." What does this quotation mean? What would it suggest that we do if we had evidence that certain kinds of material led some people to commit acts of violence by showing them how, by exciting them to the point where they needed to commit such acts, or by giving them the idea that such acts were acceptable?

READING AND WRITING SUGGESTIONS

1. Write a brief classification essay about one of the following groups: adults who are too closed minded about sexual or scatological material or about material depicting atrocities; adults who are too open minded about such material.

2. Collect information about societies in which book burning and other forms of censorship have taken place. Write a brief classification essay describing the characteristics of such societies.

THE MEDICAL PROGNOSIS: FAVORABLE, TREATABLE, CURABLE

Michael E. DeBakey

Michael E. Debakey (1908–), a pioneer in open-heart surgery, is president of Baylor College of Medicine and chairman of its Department of Surgery. He is also the director of the Cardiovascular Research and Training Center at Houston's Methodist Hospital. He has written extensively in the area of medicine. Here Dr. DeBakey explores some of the advances we can expect in the medical sciences in the near future, classifying these advances into several categories and explaining each category.

"There are no such things as incurables," said Bernard Baruch. "There are only things for which man has not found a cure." A lifetime in medical practice, education, and research has convinced me, too, that we need not accept disease as an inescapable human destiny, despite our lack of information about many forms of human illness. If we are willing to invest the time, effort, and money, we can find not only cures but also causes of currently enigmatic illness, and once we have learned causes, we will have a basis for prevention. Although death may remain inevitable, it need not occur prematurely or be preceded by acute or protracted suffering.

It is human nature to wonder about the future and to imagine what the world will be like 50 or 100 years hence. Our dreams and aspirations for the future, however, need not be idle fantasies; they can, and often do, serve as an impetus for new inquiries and new discoveries. It is true, as Horace Walpole said, that "prognostics do not always prove prophecies," but a few predictions about the future of medicine can be made with relative safety, based, as they are, on a Janus-like look at the past and the future.

The organization and administration of the practice of medicine, for one thing, will be far more efficient than it is today, with more coordinated use of regional resources, facilities, and personnel. Primary, secondary, and tertiary health care will be organized in units specifically designed for these respective purposes so that the medical needs of the population will be met in a prescribed region for urban as well as suburban and rural groups. Primary units will serve that part of the population which needs immediate, but not specialized, care. Secondary units will be available for patients requiring hospitalization, for example, for general health problems. Finally, tertiary units, or highly sophisticated medical centers, will be used by patients referred for conditions that require special attention. Health-care delivery of high quality will thus be distributed in a stepwise fashion to all people without concern of cost, through an effective form of national health insurance. Citizens will be much better informed about the physiological functions and mechanisms of their bodies and, through a regular and continuing program of public-health education beginning at the primary school level, will more readily recognize premonitory signs of disturbances in health.

Just as many of today's routine methods of diagnosis and treatment were unimaginable 50 years ago, so the techniques of the twenty-first century seem only visionary today.

Replacement of bodily parts and organs, by cadaver or artificial substitutes, will continue to become more refined and more effective. Bio-engineers will probably design an implantable hearing aid for the deaf and will perfect an instrument to permit the blind to "see." Genetic engineering should result in the reduction, if not the elimination, of congenital deformities, and reconstructive surgery will be able to transform into normal-appearing human beings those few babies born with defects. Effective treatment, and eventually cure, can be expected for such crippling disorders as multiple sclerosis, muscular dystrophy, emphysema, and arthritis. The riddle of schizophrenia and psychosis will be unlocked. Considerable emphasis will be directed toward gerontological research; ways will be explored, and found, of making the elderly healthier, happier, and more productive.

As the public becomes better informed about the methods, the directions, and the benevolent purposes of medical research, a higher national priority will be ordered for this activity. The current skepticism and wariness that some display in regard to science, engendered partly by the intemperate publicity given to the relatively few exploiters and offenders and the exaggerated accounts of their misdeeds, will be replaced by confidence in the humanitarian purpose of scientists and by a renewed dedication to the conquest of human disease. Society will come to realize that the health of the nation's people mirrors the state of medical knowledge and will understand that no matter how efficient the *delivery* of health care becomes, its *effectiveness* will remain at a plateau until new knowledge is acquired—and this can be achieved only through research.

The fiscal wisdom will thus become increasingly evident of investing in the search for the *causes* and *prevention* of human illnesses rather than continuously supporting the more costly treatment or repair of disorders once they occur. The discovery of antibiotics, for example, by reducing hospitalization and absenteeism and thus increasing productivity of thousands of workers each year, has been an economic asset. Costly hospitalization for poliomyelitis and prolonged incapacitation from tuberculosis, both previously an economic drain on patient and family, have been virtually eliminated by the fruits of medical research. Effective drugs for diabetes and hypertension have restored countless numbers of people to employment. Dramatic new operations directly on the heart and blood vessels have prolonged and improved the lives of thousands of people who would previously have been doomed to a life of disability, if not to death. Treatment for man's most frightening disease, cancer, has seen remarkable progress, including the excellent anticipation of cure for Wilm's tumor of the kidney in children, choriocarcinoma (a form of cancer) in women, Burkitt's lymphoma, and Hodgkin's disease. The outlook for children with leukemia is much more encouraging now than ever before. Numerous other therapeutic innovations originating in the research laboratory have transformed hosts of people from welfare recipients into taxpayers.

The practice of medicine today, although advanced in many ways, remains largely *retrospective*, with emphasis on cure or palliation once disease occurs. Future attention will shift to prevention as the search intensifies for the causes of illness.

Heart Disease

The cause of most forms of heart disease, which remains responsible for the greatest toll on human life, is still unknown. Although we have made significant strides in understanding and treating specific forms of heart disease, we have yet to discover the precise cause of arteriosclerosis, or atherosclerosis—the basis for 95 percent of heart ailments. Observations thus far suggest that we are dealing, not with a single entity, as implied by the composite "heart disease," but with a number of distinct entities arising from different causes. Increasing evidence has now accumulated to show that arteriosclerosis assumes distinctive patterns, both in anatomic-pathological features of the lesions and in rate of progression. In some patterns, for example, the disease is highly localized, often no more than half an inch in extent, with the remainder of the arterial tree being relatively normal, whereas in others the disease is extensive and diffuse, involving many parts of the arterial tree. Moreover, the rate of progression of these different clinical patterns varies widely, from little or no progression for many years to rapid progression within a few years or less, suggesting an acute and fulminating process. Of particular interest is the fact that no significant correlation has been found between such highly ballyhooed presumptive causative factors as diet, cholesterol, obesity, exercise, and the like, on the one hand, and these various distinctive patterns of the disease on the other. Happily, medical scientists are now beginning to direct their attention to a better understanding of the pathogenesis of these different forms of the disease, and a national network of arteriosclerotic research centers is now being developed to intensify and accelerate research on this most important subject. Research will now focus heavily on discovering the specific *cause* or causes of these different forms of arteriosclerosis rather than on peripheral aspects, such as associated risks.

Cancer

Cancer, perhaps the most feared of all diseases, remains unconquered, primarily because its genesis is not fully understood. Among the causative concepts today is the genetic transmission of cancer; that is, "master cancer genes," normally repressed in cells, are inserted into the genetic apparatus from "oncogenic (or cancer producing) viruses." Such genes are believed to be responsible for activation of "slave genes," which effect growth, invasiveness, and metastasis. Chemical carcinogens, such as cigarettes, have been implicated, as have radiation (particularly X-radiation) and specific hormonal factors. It is not yet known whether the susceptibility to cancer of hormonally responsive tissues, such as the breast, uterus, prostate, colon, and skin, is due to a decrease in immune protection with advancing age or to the repeated bombardment of cells by chemical and physical stimuli.

The nucleolus, a small body in the nucleus that produces about 85 percent of all the RNA of the cell, is of special interest in cancer chemotherapy because its function is blocked by specific anticancer antibiotics, including actinomycin D, daunomycin, and the important new antibiotic adriamycin. The attack on the nucleolus, like many other chemotherapeutic attacks on cancer, is specific only for growth. In the future, an attack must be made on specific features of cancer, either the "master cancer genes" or other important genes that are non-operative in normal tissues.

We can look forward to the prevention of some neoplasms by implementation of appropriate environmental controls. If viruses prove to be causative for specific types of cancer, preventive vaccines or effective anti-viral therapy can be developed. More sensitive tests for early detection of the disease will certainly be devised.

Genetics

The relative incidence of inherited and genetic defects in hospitalized patients has risen in the United States because of advances in diagnosis and treatment of acquired diseases, as well as increased recognition of the genetic origin of some diseases. Man cannot avoid the ill effects of his genetic composition as easily as he can avoid acquired diseases. Important goals of medical geneticists are, therefore, the improvement of recognition of high-genetic-risk patients or families, the provision of means of avoiding the genetic high risk, the amelioration of the severe effects of genetic diseases, and the correction of the defect of the inherited disease.

Some severe genetic diseases can be prevented by means now available. Physicians can provide genetic counseling to couples planning to have children, prenatal diagnostic techniques can identify many severe or lethal diseases *in utero*, and transmission of many inherited diseases can be prevented by carrier-detection screening. For example, normal-appearing couples who may produce a child with Tay-Sachs disease can be identified by a biochemical blood test. Normal-appearing carriers of sickle cell anemia are also readily detectable by biochemical methods. Practicable medical approaches, such as artificial insemination and implantation of ova in surrogate mothers, can further reduce the risk of genetic disease. Although these approaches have obvious social and ethical implications, both have been extensively used on lower animals without ill effects. Artificial insemination (fertilization), for example, can eliminate a genetic risk if the father has a disease that can be directly transmitted to his offspring (autosomal dominant), and it can reduce the risk to a minimum for other inherited diseases (autosomal recessive).

Methods of treatment of inherited diseases are steadily improving.

Dietary therapy, for example, has proved beneficial for phenyl-
ketonuria, a genetic disease producing mental retardation. Treatment
of sickle cell anemia with cyanate is yielding encouraging results. We
can expect future progress in the prevention of diseases that require
both a primary genetic factor and a secondary factor (diet, drugs,
social behavior, habit, environment) for the manifestation of the
abnormal gene as a disease. Pulmonary emphysema associated with
alpha-1-antitrypsin (a body enzyme) deficiency, for example, is
strongly affected by the smoking of tobacco. Genetic factors may be
important in determining who will have a myocardial infarction as a
result of certain contributory environmental elements or who will
acquire cancer of the lung from smoking. Research may well lead to
positive identification of the second factor responsible for expression
of otherwise-silent defective genes, and avoidance of the factor by a
genetically different person may prevent development of the disease.

Correction of genetic defects is a direct but difficult approach to
treatment of inherited diseases. Two concepts are practical now. The
replacement of abnormal or absent circulating proteins has been successful in patients with such diseases as diabetes mellitus (insulin),
Burton's agammaglobulinemia (gamma globulin), and hemophilia
(factor VIII). It is not yet certain that a component needed inside the
cell can be successfully replaced, although some favorable results of
research in this field have been reported. A transplantation approach
to some inherited diseases has also proved fruitful. Immune-
competent cells, for example, have been successfully transplanted to
children with inherited immune deficiency, and renal transplantation has proved effective for a variety of inherited diseases of the
kidney. An interesting outgrowth of renal transplantation is the possibility that in Fabry's disease the normal donor kidney may provide
a continuing source of normal enzyme for other body tissues that are
enzyme deficient. The transplanted normal tissue, thus, not only may
replace the diseased organ but also may improve the function of other
tissues. An obvious long-term goal is correction of cellular defects in
genes.

Computers

Recent years have seen a surge of technological developments in
medical research and practice. Of particular importance has been the
introduction of the digital computer into daily medical practice. Long
used for its computational capability in medical research, the computer has emerged from this traditional role as a major tool in record

storage and retrieval, monitoring and control of physiological functions, education of students in basic science, assessment of extensive
data to uncover hidden characteristics of a specific population, and
has even proved of value in the doctor-patient encounter.

What can we expect in the way of further developments? The
digital-computer market is in an extremely dynamic state today,
with the primary activity focused on mini-computers and micro-
computers. Spurred by a rapidly expanding technological development known as large-scale integration, which can place thousands of
components in an area smaller than a dime, the application of these
"small" machines has been expanding rapidly, while their cost has
been falling.

Whereas the use of small computers in medical care can be
expected to increase, they are unlikely to replace the traditional
functions of large computers—central file control and large-scale
computational support for clinical and basic research and for national
medical data banks to serve the needs of an increasingly mobile
population. We may expect to see primary-care physicians expand
their use of automation in diagnosis and care of patients. Ventures
that have already proved successful are automated processing of
the electrocardiogram, evaluation and warning systems for multiple
drug interactions, and development of a variety of "computer-
consultants" to support specialized therapy through dialogue between physician and computer. Such an approach affords uniformity
of care and rapid application of recent discoveries at the bedside.
These same "computer-consultants," which are actually sophisticated programs that detail the thinking of experts in a given field, will
also provide a uniform foundation for training newly graduated physicians in various disciplines. The primary-care physician may also
benefit from adoption of computer-stored patient records, which permit the transfer of information frequently needed in group practice
and health-maintenance organizations.

During the past few years, a variety of experiments has demonstrated the utility of the digital computer in caring for critically ill
patients. Moderate success has been achieved, but much more work
is required before the best approach to this problem can be selected.
In some instances, the major deterrent to progress is the lack of a
suitable measuring device (transducer) for needed clinical information. Once this device has been found, the optimum array of measurements must be determined for each patient. The computer has
already proved feasible for measurements, formulation of therapeutic
decisions, and, in some environments, direct intervention in patient
care.

Implantable Prosthetics

Research into various implantable prosthetics, notably artifical hearts, shows promise of clinical application in the future. These prospective devices, in addition to currently available clinical instruments, such as pacemakers, will be improved by the ability to alter performance in response to changing physiologic conditions. At present, the sensor and control systems of currently available clinical instruments, such as pacemakers, are limited to relatively simple functions by requirements for size and power. The continuing reduction in size of integrated circuit devices, coupled with expected micropower operation, however, will make implantable digital computers an eventual reality. Rather than being dependent on simple assessment of rate and pressure, a computer-controlled artificial heart, equipped with appropriate transducers, may be programmed to respond to blood chemical changes with or without residual neural input from vagal or baroreceptor sites, the arterial pressure receptor. Long-term implantation will be aided by future developments in bioelectric power sources, which will obviate the need, or reduce the requirement, for battery-power sources.

Ultrasound

Recently, another exciting development of great diagnostic potential has received considerable attention—the use of low-energy ultrasound for non-invasive estimation of size, shape, and motion of internal structures of the body. Initially limited to single crystals, which provided only a pencil-thin view of internal structures, newly developed transducers permit simultaneous views along a number of paths. The digital computer will play an important role in managing the high information rates as arrays of ultrasound transducers become more and more complex. It is feasible now, and will become commonplace in the future, to obtain images of the quality of modern roentgenograms through the judicious combination of ultrasonic transducers and digital computers. By using the organizational capabilities of the digital computer, scientists will construct three-dimensional images of the organ to be analyzed, which the clinician can view from various perspectives.

Multi-phasic Screening

Large-scale, multi-phasic screening, already in active use in clinical practice, will soon become commonplace, primarily as a result of a national shift of emphasis in medicine to early detection and prevention of disease. Acceleration of the flow of patients through such elaborate screening facilities will require that a digital computer manage and control routine tasks of data-gathering and record entry, as well as automation of many tests. By providing immediate data entry on completion of individual tests of the screening protocol, the computer enables the patient's pathway through the facility to be guided by a few preliminary results. Under these circumstances, the computer will simultaneously collect and analyze data, make a preliminary diagnosis, schedule facilities, guide the patient, and produce a report that the attending physician can use to discuss the diagnosis with the patient and select appropriate treatment for the disorder before the patient leaves the facility.

Simulated Physiological Systems

As indicated earlier, considerable development in transducers is necessary for further advancement in this field. The physiological systems of the body are complex and interrelated multi-variate control systems. Many electrical, chemical, chromatic, acoustic, and other manifestations within each system reflect that system's operation. Although we have made great strides in understanding a few of these variables, our knowledge of all the complex interrelations between the physiological functions of the various systems remains extremely limited. One application of computers that may assist in the assessment of these interrelations is modeling, or creating a simulation of physiological systems. Using a background of knowledge, the modeler may manipulate functions of the system so that he can determine their effects on the organism's performance.

Medical Data Banks

In the medium-to-large computers, national data banks will be created to fulfill both clinical and research needs. By making available a medical record of a patient who is unable to provide such data to an unfamiliar physician, the computer allows the physician to provide more immediate care, based on better information, to accident victims or others suddenly disabled away from home. These same data banks, or elaborations of them, will also provide the basis for establishing the character or patterns of diseases and the association of these diseases with controllable environmental, personal, and social factors. Maintenance in these data banks of the identity of special-risk patients, such as pacemaker-wearers or persons sensitive to air pollution, enables initiation of warning mechanisms to reduce the risk to these people. In general, as the volume of medical data increases and the pressures for quantitative medicine continue to grow, the computer will become an extension of the physician's mind, just as the scalpel is an extension of the surgeon's hand.

My faith in human virtue and human wisdom reassures me of man's future on earth. His remarkable ingenuity will meet the challenge of finding other sources of nutrition as conventional food resources become taxed. The confusing state of our current knowledge regarding proper diet will be clarified. The problems created by pollution will be conquered by devising new ways of providing energy.

Moral and ethical problems, inevitable accompaniments of advancing scientific knowledge and technology, will be resolved by the pooling of wisdom and judgment of the savants and the man-on-the-street. Despite the speculation and fears that accompany unsettling new scientific knowledge, whether it be organ transplantation, genetic manipulation, or birth control, history has proved that once the public recognizes and understands that such discoveries can be used to the benefit of society, the fears will be replaced by reasoned concern, unemotional discussion, and eventually humanistic resolution. Even if new laws are required for the application of new scientific knowledge, the public will promote such legislation and will even support the reversal of previous legislation that may have become obsolete or injudicious in light of the new knowledge. We have witnessed evolutionary changes in attitudes and mores that few could have anticipated, and we will continue to adapt our mores as circumstances dictate. The innate humanity and morality of the majority of the people will triumph over the peccancy and ignominy of the few. We can, therefore, have faith in the ultimate wisdom of society to cope—intellectually, psychologically, and ethically—with moral and social issues arising from scientific discoveries, even though those decisions may sometimes seem slow in coming.

QUESTIONS

1. DeBakey maintains that we can make some medical predictions with relative accuracy because they are based on a "Janus-like look at the past and the future."
   a. Who was the god Janus?
   b. What is a Janus-like look? Why does it suggest an accurate prediction?

2. Consider the title of DeBakey's article.
   a. What does the term *medical prognosis* mean? What does the suffix* -*able* mean?
   b. The term *prognosis* followed by the three adjectives with the suffix -*able* portrays both a meaning and a feeling. What is the meaning? What is the feeling?
   c. What two-letter prefix* could entirely change the meaning and feeling portrayed in the title?

3 DeBakey writes that medical practice today is mostly "retrospective, with emphasis on cure and palliation once disease occurs." He also writes that, in the future, "attention will shift to prevention as the search intensifies for the causes of illness."
   a. Name at least one advance in each of the following categories: replacement of bodily parts, public acceptance of medical research, understanding of the origins of heart disease and cancer, genetics, computers, implantable prosthetics, ultrasound, multi-phasic screening, and medical data banks.
   b Explain why the terms "retrospective," "cure," and "palliation" are an accurate description of modern medicine's approach to the treatment of heart disease.
   c. Why is knowledge about the cause of illnesses so important to prevention? When we do not know about cause, why must we content ourselves with retrospection, cure, and palliation?

4. Do DeBakey's comments about implantable prosthetics suggest that we might eventually be able to produce bionic people? In what categories presented in DeBakey's article would advances be required in order to produce a real bionic woman or bionic man similar to the fictional characters on TV?

5 a. DeBakey suggests that it would be fiscally sound to invest more money in research on causes and prevention of medical problems than in treatment and repair of disorders once they occur. Do you agree? Explain your answer.
   b. Find out how much money the federal government allocated last year to the Department of Defense, the Department of the Interior, the Department of Agriculture, and the National Institutes of Health within the Department of Health, Education, and Welfare. Rank the agencies in terms of the amount of money they received. Do you agree with the way the money

---

*Definitions for all terms marked with an asterisk may be found in the Glossary.

was parceled out? Why, or why not? What changes, if any, would you make?

READING AND WRITING SUGGESTIONS

1. As we conduct further medical research, there is a possibility that we might run into some serious problems. For example, work with DNA might lead to the creation of fast-growing, harmful forms of life. Write a brief expository essay describing the category *dangerous life form* and discussing safeguards we might use against the possibility of creating such life forms.

2. The issue of the quantity, or length, of life versus the quality, or goodness, of life has long been a subject for debate. Examples of literature on this issue are Aldous Huxley's *After Many a Summer Dies the Swan* and the story of Cybele, the mythological goddess who first made the gods agree to let her live almost indefinitely and then begged them to let her die. Read some literature that relates to this issue and write a brief expository essay that deals both with research we need on how to live a *better* life and research we need on how to live a *longer* life.

from UNBOUGHT AND UNBOSSED

Shirley Chisholm

Shirley Chisholm (1924–) is a member of Congress from New York's Twelfth Congressional District who has had a great deal of positive influence in Congress, in the black liberation movement, and in the women's liberation movement. She ran unsuccessfully for the 1972 Democratic presidential nomination. In this excerpt from her book Unbought and Unbossed, *Chisholm decries the tendency to respond to people in terms of meaningless stereotypes and categories. She also weighs her two major "handicaps"—being black and being female.*

There are 435 members of the House of Representatives and 417 are white males. Ten of the others are women and nine are black. I belong to both of these minorities, which makes it add up right. That makes me a celebrity, a kind of side show attraction. I was the first American citizen to be elected to Congress in spite of the double drawbacks of being female and having skin darkened by melanin.

When you put it that way, it sounds like a foolish reason for fame. In a just and free society it would be foolish. That I am a national figure because I was the first person in 192 years to be at once a congressman, black, and a woman proves, I would think, that our society is not yet either just or free.

Sometimes the media make me feel like a monkey in a cage. As soon as I was elected, the newspapers and networks started to besiege me. The first question was almost always, "How does it feel?" Naturally, it feels good. I am proud and honored that the people of my district believed in me enough to choose me to represent them. My Twelfth Congressional District of Brooklyn is mostly composed of poor neighborhoods with all the problems of poverty in an aggravated form: slum housing, high unemployment, too few medical services, high crime rate, neglected schools—the whole list. About 69 percent of my people are black and Puerto Rican. The rest are Jewish, Polish, Ukrainian, and Italian. Speaking for them at this moment in history is a great responsibility because they have been unrepresented and ignored for so long and their needs are so many and so urgent.

But I hope if I am remembered it will finally be for what I have done, not for what I happen to be. And I hope that my having made it, the hard way, can be some kind of inspiration, particularly to women. The number of women in politics has never been large, but now it is getting even smaller.

Women are a majority of the population, but they are treated like a minority group. The prejudice against them is so widespread that, paradoxically, most persons do not yet realize it exists. Indeed, most women do not realize it. They even accept being paid less for doing the same work as a man. They are as quick as any male to condemn a woman who ventures outside the limits of the role men have assigned to females: that of toy and drudge.

Of my two "handicaps," being female put many more obstacles in my path than being black. Sometimes I have trouble, myself, believing that I made it this far against the odds. No one, not even my father, whose hopes for me were extravagant, would ever have dared to predict it.

QUESTIONS

1. Chisholm uses the terms *toy* and *drudge* to describe the role of women. What do these terms mean? Do they accurately describe the role of women in today's society? Explain your answer.

2. In the title of her book, *Unbought and Unbossed,* Chisholm uses two negative prefixes*, parallel structure*, and alliteration*. Would the title *An Independent Congressperson* have been as compelling? Why, or why not?

3. Chisholm names three groups that she has been classified a member of. What are these three? What does Chisholm want to be remembered for: what she is or what she does?

4. It is possible to classify people into a great number of categories: black/white, hardworking/lazy, male/female, intelligent/not intelligent, and so on.
   a. What sorting criteria would be useful in helping to determine the members of the House of Representatives who are valuable and those who are not valuable? What criteria would you use to classify good and poor teachers? Good and poor social workers?
   b. Is it ever useful or accurate to judge people's value on the basis of their race, sex, national origin, or any other condition of birth? Why, or why not?
   c. Chisholm states, "That I am a national figure because I was the first person in 192 years to be at once a congressman, black, and a woman proves, I would think, that our society is not yet either just or free." What does the nation's response to the kind of classifications Chisholm is referring to have to do with our having a just and free society?

5. Chisholm can be classified as a black person, a female, a member of Congress, a national figure, a contributor to her constituents' welfare, and so on.
   a. Name at least ten groups into which you could be classified.
   b. Are you particularly admired or valued for your membership in any of these groups? If so, is this admiration justified? Why, or why not? Do you feel particularly proud of your membership in any of these groups? Explain your answer.

READING AND WRITING SUGGESTIONS

1. Chisholm maintains that she has achieved national prominence because of the juxtaposition of three groups into which she is

classified—that is, because she is simultaneously a woman, black, and a member of Congress. Write a brief expository essay in which you explore how people might react to a person who belongs to two categories which are seldom juxtaposed—for example, a blind physician.

2. Read a book, such as Laura K. Hobson's *Gentlemen's Agreement*, which describes what happens when people respond negatively to a person on the basis of his or her social class, race, religion, or nationality instead of responding to the person's character and accomplishments. Write a brief essay in which you discuss the results of such negative reactions.

Example

One of the most powerful ways to make an abstraction meaningful to a reader is to illustrate it by means of an example. The right to a trial by jury may seem a dry abstraction to some, but a few concrete examples of events that took place during the Spanish Inquisition or of the brutal lynchings that occurred in the early American West make this right seem much more vital and necessary.

There are a number of requirements that must be met if the examples used in an essay are to be effective. First—and most basically—an example should be a true illustration of the proposition or subject it is supporting. In a discussion of the mating behavior of fish, an example describing the mating behavior of a particular species of frog will only cause the reader confusion.

Second, examples should represent a fair cross section of the subject under discussion. If the only people named as examples in an essay on great scientists are Marie Curie, Louis Pasteur, and Andre Ampere, the reader might get the false impression that all great scientists are French.

Finally, there are many examples available to illustrate almost any abstraction, but, since a writer can use only a few examples in an essay, these must be selected with care. The writer must choose examples that conform with the level of the essay's complexity; a highly technical essay requires highly technical examples, whereas an essay intended for a general audience demands examples that are easily understood by the average reader. The examples will also be far more effective if they are interesting to the reader; an example that captures a reader's imagination can have great impact on the reader's response to the essay as a whole.

CONFESSIONS
OF A NONBELIEVER

Dan Greenburg

Dan Greenburg (1931–) is an author whose writing credits include How to Be a Jewish Mother, Scoring, *and* Something's There, *as well as a large number of magazine articles on subjects of current interest. He has also worked as a reporter for newspapers and scientific publications and is the publisher of a newsletter entitled* Science and Government Report. *In this essay Greenburg gives examples of paranormal experiences he has had—experiences that defy explanations in terms of the real world as we know it.*

I have something to tell you and I don't know how you're going to take it. I don't really know how to take it myself, if you want to know the truth.

What I have to tell you is that, all those years when we used to giggle at anything having to do with the occult—with ghosts and clairvoyants and faith healers and voodoo and mind-over-matter and whatnot—well, maybe we were wrong to giggle.

Look, I'm a rational, logical, linear-thinking, sensible fella, same as yourself, and if about two years ago I started running around with witches and mediums and practitioners of ceremonial magic, it was mostly because I figured they'd be fun to write about. Have a little chuckle at their expense, and where's the harm, you know? I certainly never expected to encounter anything I couldn't explain away with my rational, logical, linear-thinking, sensible, old belief system, but that is what seems to have happened.

It didn't happen in the melodramatic situations I found my way into either—it didn't happen in the spooky home of a black magician next to Loch Ness, Scotland, and it didn't happen in the coven of teen-age witches I hung out with in Brooklyn, and it didn't happen during the sinister voodoo ceremonies I got into in Haiti. Where it happened was in perfectly ordinary apartments in perfectly ordinary places like Chicago and New York City and Toronto. There was no

44

weird chanting, no voodoo drums, no whooshes of fire, nothing like that.

Seeing Is Believing?

The first thing that happened was that a psychic named Alex Tanous asked me and a ladyfriend to participate in a little experiment. He went into a room adjacent to the one we were in, found a magazine, opened it at random so none of us could see it and put it face down on a bed. Then he came back into the room we were in and, in a semi-meditative process, guided us into trying to"see" it. He asked us to describe the picture in the other room and, not believing there was the remotest chance of doing so, we took a whack at it.

We each described entirely different images: the young lady described a small black-and-white portrait of a woman with a broad-brimmed hat. I described a religious painting, dark in color, with a three-quarter-inch white border around it and a glare on the page. We went into the other room and turned over the magazine. On one page was a small black-and-white portrait of a woman with a broad-brimmed hat. On the facing page was a religious painting, dark in color, with a three-quarter-inch white border around it and a glare on the page.

Our reaction was giddy laughter. It didn't seem possible. It didn't seem frightening either. It was just fooling around.

Paranormal Shenanigans

The next time something happened I was fooling around too. While watching a ghastly old movie on TV, I half-seriously suggested to my companion that I was going to hurl an invisible bolt at the screen and shut the set off. I hurled. The set shut off. We laughed that time too, but maybe not as loudly.

The next thing involved a psychic in Chicago named Olof Jonsson, who did the by now famous ESP tests with astronaut Edgar Mitchell from the moon. When I met Olof he had me hold a deck of ordinary playing cards in my hand and, although he never came within 15 feet of me, he caused a card in the deck I held to dematerialize.

I've described this incident to a number of stage magicians. They all assure me it's the oldest trick in the book, but when I ask them how it was done the best they can do is mumble something about how I only *thought* Olof was 15 feet away from me. All I can tell you is that he *was* 15 feet away. I mean, I was there and the magicians weren't. (Olof did something else that day of an eerie nature, but I'll tell you about that in a moment.)

Now then, if it isn't satisfying to describe such incidents to stage magicians, it's even less so to tell them to physicists. Most physicists say they don't believe in paranormal shenanigans any more than you do, but don't get them started talking shop or before you know it they'll be telling you about things like tachyons, which are subatomic particles which travel faster than the speed of light and arrive at their destinations almost before they start out. And don't talk shop with astronomers or they'll tell you about black holes, which are collapsed stars with magnetic fields so strong they swallow up even light waves. And biologists are no better because they'll tell you about eels that can smell a thimbleful of rose scent diluted in a lake covering 14,000 square miles.

Anyway, what I did about all this was write a book called *Something's There* and, although it's come out, I haven't stopped my research. I have even tentatively called myself a psychic investigator a couple of times, just to see how it sounds.

I must confess that I have also been doing a lot of chuckling at all my old, rational, logical, linear-thinking, sensible friends who don't believe in the occult—they're obviously threatened by it. Not like us hip, open-minded psychic investigators.

Eerie Nature

Funny thing, though, about us hip, open-minded psychic investigators—sometimes we don't act so hip. Remember my saying that Olof did something else of an eerie nature when I met him? What he did was he had me think of a short phrase, and then he read my mind. Not once, but three times in succession. I'm so hip and open-minded that, the moment it happened, I blocked it out of my mind until long after it was too late to put it into my book.

So I guess I'm pretty threatened by the paranormal after all. There's only one problem about this field, though—I've come too far and seen too much to go back to my comfortable old beliefs. But I have gone back to giggling a little at the occult. Laughter is still the best method I know of dealing with fright.

QUESTIONS

1. Greenburg sets a certain tone* in the introductory paragraph. What is it? What does it lead you to expect?

---

*Definitions for all terms marked with an asterisk may be found in the Glossary.

2. What is a "rational, logical, linear-thinking, sensible" belief system? Do the four adjectives mean the same thing? Would one adjective be sufficient to express Greenburg's meaning? Why does he use four?

3. Consider the two groups of words that follow: *paradox, black holes,* and *tachyons; black magic, covens,* and *voodoo.* How are the concepts in the two groups alike? How are they different?

4. What generalization does Greenburg make about paranormal events? Do you agree? Why, or why not? What examples does Greenburg give to support his generalization? Do you accept the validity of these examples? Explain your answer.

5. Do you ever experience the urge to giggle about paranormal events? Have you seen people use laughter to deal with similar phenomena? Do you agree with Greenburg that laughter is the best way to deal with threatening experiences? Explain.

READING AND WRITING SUGGESTIONS

1. Choose a topic such as ESP, UFOs, events in the Bermuda Triangle, or another topic dealing with phenomena that have not been fully explained. Do some reading in the area you choose, and decide whether you think the phenomena discussed are natural or supernatural. Write a brief expository paper presenting examples that support the generalizations you make.

2. Read a novel, such as William P. Blatty's *The Exorcist,* Ira Levin's *Rosemary's Baby,* or Henry James's *The Turn of the Screw,* which deals with supernatural events. Decide whether you think people can be possessed by supernatural forces. Write a brief expository essay presenting examples that support your generalization.

ECCENTRICITIES
OF FAMOUS MEN

Cesare Lombroso

Cesare Lombroso (1836–1909) was born in Venice, Italy, and be-
came a professor of psychiatry at the University of Turin. His essays
on the pathology of genius, in which he implies that genius is a
diseased or abnormal condition, resulted in considerable controversy
in the latter part of the nineteenth century. In this essay about
people of genius, Lombroso gives examples of both the char-
acteristics and the problems that this group shares.

Forgetfulness is one of the characteristics of genius. It is said that
Newton once rammed his niece's finger into his pipe; when he left
his room to seek for anything he usually returned without bringing
it. Rouelle generally explained his ideas at great length, and when he
had finished, he added: "But this is one of my arcana which I tell to
no one." Sometimes one of his pupils rose and repeated in his ear
what he had just said aloud; then Rouelle believed that the pupil had
discovered the arcanum by his own sagacity, and begged him not to
divulge what he had himself just told to two hundred persons. One
day, when performing an experiment during a lecture, he said to his
hearers: "You see, gentlemen, this caldron over the flame? Well, if I
were to leave off stirring it, an explosion would at once occur which
would make us all jump." While saying these words, he did not fail to
forget to stir, and the prediction was accomplished; the explosion
took place with a fearful noise: the laboratory windows were all
smashed, and the audience fled to the garden. Sir Everard Home
relates that he once suddenly lost his memory for half an hour, and
was unable to recognize the house and the street in which he lived;
he could not recall the name of the street, and seemed to hear it for the
first time. It is told of Ampere that when traveling on horseback in
the country he became absorbed in a problem; then, dismounting,
began to lead his horse, and finally lost it; but he did not discover his
misadventure until, on arrival, it attracted the attention of his

friends. Babinet hired a country house, and after making the pay-
ments returned to town; then he found that he had entirely forgotten
both the name of the place and from what station he had started.

One day Buffon, lost in thought, ascended a tower and slid down
by the ropes, unconscious of what he was doing, like a som-
nambulist. Mozart, in carving meat, so often cut his fingers, accustomed only to the piano, that he had to give up this duty to other
persons. Of Bishop Munster, it is said that, seeing at the door of his
own antechamber the announcement: "The master of the house is
out," he remained there awaiting his own return. Of Toucherel, it is
told by Arago, that he once even forgot his own name. Beethoven, on
returning from an excursion in the forest, often left his coat on the
grass, and often went out hatless. Once, at Neustadt, he was arrested
in this condition, and taken to prison as a vagabond; here he might
have remained, as no one would believe that he was Beethoven, if
Herzog, the conductor of the orchestra, had not arrived to deliver
him. Gioia, in the excitement of composition, wrote a chapter on the
table of his bureau instead of on paper. The Abbe Beccaria, absorbed
in his experiments, said during mass: "Ite! experientia facta est."[1] St.
Dominic, in the midst of a princely repast, suddenly struck the table
and exclaimed: "Conclusum est contra manicheos."[2] It is told of
Ampere that having written a formula, with which he was preoccupied, on the back of a cab, he started in pursuit as soon as the cab
went off. Diderot hired vehicles which he then left at the door and
forgot, thus needlessly paying coachmen for whole days. He often
forgot the hour, the day, the month, and even the person to whom he
was speaking; he would then speak long monologues like a som-
nambulist. Rossini, conducting the orchestra at the rehearsal of his
"Barbiere," which was a fiasco, did not perceive that the public, and
even the performers, had left him alone in the theatre until he
reached the end of an act.

Hagen notes that originality is the quality that distinguishes genius from talent. And Jurgen-Meyer: "The imagination of talent re-
produces the stated fact; the inspiration of genius makes it anew. The
first disengages or repeats; the second invents or creates. Talent aims
at a point which appears difficult to reach; genius aims at a point

---

1. The Abbe absentmindedly substituted the words "Go! The experiment is com-
pleted," for "Go! The Mass is ended," which is the traditional conclusion of the
Roman Catholic Mass.

2. "The decision has been made against the Manicheans." The Manicheans were
members of a religious sect considered heretical by Roman Catholics.

which no one perceives. The novelty, it must be understood, resides not in the elements, but in their shock." Novelty and grandeur are the two chief characters which Bettinelli attributes to genius; "for this reason," he says, "poets call themselves troubadours or trouveres." Cardan conceived the idea of the education of deaf mutes before Harriot; he caught a glimpse of the application of algebra to geometry and geometric constructions before Descartes. Giordano Bruno divined the modern theories of cosmology and of the origin of ideas. Cola di Rienzi conceived Italian unity, with Rome as capital, four hundred years before Cavour and Mazzini. Stoppani admits that the geological theory of Dante, with the regard to the formation of seas, is at all points in accordance with the accepted ideas of today.

Genius divines facts before completely knowing them; thus Goethe described Italy very well before knowing it; and Schiller, the land and people of Switzerland, without having been there. And it is on account of those divinations which all precede common observation, and because genius, occupied with lofty researches, does not possess the habits of the many, and because, like the lunatic and unlike the man of talent, he is often disordered, the man of genius is scorned and misunderstood. Ordinary persons do not perceive the steps which have led the man of genius to his creation, but they see the difference between his conclusions and those of others, and the strangeness of his conduct. Rossini's "Barbiere," and Beethoven's "Fidelio" were received with hisses; Boito's "Mefistofele" and Wagner's "Lohengrin" have been hissed at Milan. How many academicians have smiled compassionately at Marzolo, who has discovered a new philosophic world! Bolyai, for his invention of the fourth dimension in anti-Euclidian geometry, has been called the geometrician of the insane, and compared to a miller who wishes to make flour of sand. Everyone knows the treatment accorded to Fulton and Columbus and Papin, and, in our own days, to Piatti and Praga and Abel, and to Schliemann, who found Ilium, where no one else had dreamed of looking for it, while learned academicians laughed. "There never was a liberal idea," wrote Flaubert, "which has not been unpopular; never an act of justice which has not caused scandal; never a great man who has not been pelted with potatoes or struck by knives. 'The history of human intellect is the history of human stupidity,' as M. de Voltaire said."

In this persecution, men of genius have no fiercer or more terrible enemies than the men of academies, who possess the weapons of talent, the stimulus of vanity, and the prestige by preference accorded to them by the vulgar, and by governments which, in large part, consist of the vulgar. There are, indeed, countries in which the ordinary level of intelligence sinks so low that the inhabitants come to hate, not only genius, but even talent.

QUESTIONS

1. Lombroso uses the word *eccentricities* in his title. What is the denotative* meaning of this word? What is its connotative* meaning? What are some euphemisms* we could substitute for the word *eccentricities?*

2. Lombroso's very serious purpose in this essay is to give examples of the nature of that class of people called geniuses and examples of the problems they have. How does he introduce this serious topic? Why do you think he uses this method of introduction?

3. Give at least two examples of differences between the genius group and the talented group. Why are geniuses sometimes ridiculed, or persecuted, or both?

4. Is there a difference between absentmindedness and such great concentration on the problem at hand that commonsense behavior is not practiced? If so, how would you define the difference? Does absentmindedness due to great concentration mean that a person is mentally diseased or abnormal? Explain your answer.

5. Consider whether people have changed since Lombroso wrote this essay.
   a. In today's world, who gets more attention and money: the star football player or the astronomer who identifies a new planet? Why is this the case?
   b. Look back at Greenburg's essay on paranormal events and note his tone of half-apology. Are people sometimes ridiculed or rejected when they espouse new ideas, such as ESP? Why?

READING AND WRITING SUGGESTIONS

1. Think about a person you know, or have known, who was different from others. Write a brief expository essay about that person, giving examples of ways he or she was unusual.

2. Read a book, such as *Flowers for Algernon* by Daniel Keyes, which concerns a person who is different in a major way from most people. Develop a generalization about the ways people treat those

---

*Definitions for all terms marked with an asterisk may be found in the Glossary.

who differ a great deal—for example, people who are exceptionally intelligent or mentally retarded. Then write a brief expository essay, giving examples that support your generalization. You should consider whether the nature of the treatment accorded to such people depends more on the *extent* to which they are different or on the *ways* in which they are different.

THE BLOOD LUST

Eldridge Cleaver

Eldridge Cleaver (1935–) was born in Wabbaseka, Arkansas, the son of a dining car waiter and a janitor. His first job was shining shoes. As a youth, he was sent to reform school for selling marijuana, and in 1956 he began the first of his many terms in California state prisons, including San Quentin, Folsom, and Soledad. It was in Folsom prison that he began the work which resulted in his most famous book, Soul on Ice. *His writings also include* Eldridge Cleaver: Post-Prison Writings and Speeches, *and* Eldridge Cleaver's Black Papers. *In this essay he explores the temper of the American character, supporting his point of view with some highly graphic examples.*

The boxing ring is the ultimate focus of masculinity in America, the two-fisted testing ground of manhood, and the heavyweight champion, as a symbol, is the real Mr. America. In a culture that secretly subscribes to the piratical ethic of "every man for himself"—the social Darwinism of "survival of the fittest" being far from dead, manifesting itself in our ratrace political system of competing parties, in our dog-eat-dog economic system of profit and loss, and in our adversary system of justice wherein truth is secondary to the skill and connections of the advocate—the logical culmination of this ethic, on a person-to-person level, is that the weak are seen as the natural and just prey of the strong. But since this dark principle violates our democratic ideals and professions, we force it underground, out of a perverse national modesty that reveals us as a nation of peep freaks who prefer the bikini to the naked body, the white lie to the black truth, Hollywood smiles and canned laughter to a soulful Bronx cheer. The heretical mailed fist of American reality rises to the surface in the velvet glove of our every institutionalized endeavor, so that each year we, as a nation, grind through various cycles of attrition, symbolically quenching the insatiable appetite of the *de facto* jungle law underlying our culture, loudly and unabashedly proclaiming to the world that "competition" is the law of life, getting confused, embarrassed, and angry if someone retorts: "Competition is the Law of the Jungle and Cooperation is the Law of Civilization."

Our mass spectator sports are geared to disguise, while affording expression to, the acting out in elaborate pageantry of the myth of the fittest in the process of surviving. From the Little League to the major leagues, through the orgiastic climax of the World Series; from high school football teams, through the college teams, to the grand finale of the annual bowl washouts; interspersed with the subcycles of basketball, track, and field meets—all of our mass spectator sports give play to the basic cultural ethic, harnessed and sublimated into national-communal pagan rituals.

But there is an aspect of the crystal of our nature that eschews the harness, scorns sublimation, and demands to be seen in its raw nakedness, crying out to us for the sight and smell of blood. The vehemence with which we deny this obvious fact of our nature is matched only by our Victorian hysteria on the subject of sex. Yet, we deny it in vain. Whether we quench our thirst from the sight of a bleeding Jesus on the Cross, from the ritualized sacrifice in the elevation of the Host and the consecration of the Blood of the Son, or from bullfighting, cockfighting, dogfighting, wrestling, or boxing, spiced with our Occidental memory and heritage of the gladiators of Rome and the mass spectator sport of the time of feeding Christians and other enemies of society to the lions in the Coliseum—whatever the mask assumed by the impulse, the persistent beat of the drum over the years intones the chant: Though Dracula and Vampira must flee the scene with the rising of the sun and the coming of the light, night has its fixed hour and darkness must fall. And all the lightbulbs ever fashioned, and all the power plants generating electricity, have absolutely no effect on the primeval spinning of the earth in its orbit.

In America, we give maximum expression to our blood lust in the mass spectator sport of boxing. Some of us are Roman enough to admit our love and need of the sport. Others pretend to look the other way. But when a heavyweight championship fight rolls around, the nation takes a moral holiday and we are all tuned in—some of us peeping out of the corner of our eye at the square jungle and the animal test of brute power unfolding there.

Every institution in America is tainted by the mystique of race, and the question of masculinity is confused by the presence of both a "white" man and a "black" man here. One was the master and the other was the slave until a moment ago when they both were declared to be equal "men"; which leaves American men literally without a unitary, nationally viable self-image. Whatever dim vision of masculinity they have is a rough-and-ready, savage mishmash of violence and sexuality, a dichotomized exercise and worship of physical force/submission to and fear of physical force—which is only one aspect of the broken-down relationship between men and women in America. This is an era when the models of manhood and womanhood have been blasted to dust by social upheaval, as the most alienated males and females at the bottom of society move out of "their places" and bid for their right to be "man" and "woman" on an equal basis with the former masters and mistresses. These, in turn, are no longer seen by themselves and others as supermen and superwomen, but only as men and women like all others. And in this period of social change and sexual confusion, boxing, and the heavyweight championship in particular, serves as the ultimate test of masculinity, based on the perfection of the body and its use.

QUESTIONS

1. Cleaver uses personification* in the phrase "symbolically quenching the insatiable appetite of the *de facto* jungle law underlying our culture."
   a. What does this figurative* expression mean?
   b. Find another example of the same type of figurative language in the essay.

2. Consider how well the title "Blood Lust" represents the content of the essay.
   a. How does Cleaver develop the idea of blood lust in the essay?
   b. What relation does this idea have to the idea of social Darwinism—that is, the survival of the fittest in society?
   c. Are the ideas of blood lust and the survival of the fittest the same?
   d. Does Cleaver need to develop both ideas in order to make his point?

---

*Definitions for all terms marked with an asterisk may be found in the Glossary.

3. Cleaver uses the national love of boxing and other spectator sports as examples to support a generalization about American character. What generalization is he making? Do you agree with it?

4. a. What is the general tone* of the essay? Does it differ from the tone of DeBakey's essay on p. 28? If so, how does it differ?
   b. Does Cleaver see the American character in a positive or a negative light?
   c. Consider Cleaver's background and suggest a reason why he views the American character as he does.

5. Make a generalization that you think applies to the American character and give two examples that support your generalization.
   a. How do your generalization and examples differ from Cleaver's?
   b. What experiences in your background led you to your generalization?

READING AND WRITING SUGGESTIONS

1. Make a generalization about the American character that is opposite to Cleaver's and write a brief expository essay presenting this point of view. Be certain to support the generalization you make with concrete examples.

2. Read accounts of blood sports practiced in the past, in the present, and in a number of different cultures. Hemingway's essay "Bull Fighting" (p. 62) is a good example of such an account. Use the ideas you read as examples to support or attack the generalization, "Blood lust is present in some people in all cultures."

---

*Definitions for all terms marked with an asterisk may be found in the Glossary.

THE "BEHAVIOR MOD" SQUAD

Albert Rosenfeld

Albert Rosenfeld (1925–) was the science editor of Life *magazine for many years and now serves in the same capacity for* Saturday Review. *He is also an adjunct assistant professor in the Department of Human Biological Chemistry and Genetics at the University of Texas Medical Branch at Galveston. Here Rosenfeld discusses a method of shaping and controlling behavior called behavior modification, giving examples of the ways this technique is being misused.*

The scientific technique called behavior modification has lately fallen into disfavor—and deserves to. Not that it has ever been deemed particularly reprehensible to modify behavior. What else is the time-honored purpose of all persuasion and all education? We constantly seek to induce others to behave as they "ought" or as we would wish them to. And we accept that others freely and routinely do the same to us.

But scientists like to deal with circumstances they can control—at least in part. If you put Mr. X in a situation and have him do *this* and say *that*, how does Mr. Y react? Scientists did not, of course, invent this kind of tampering. Shakespeare's plots, for instance, are full of such artifice. We see behavior modification in our daily lives. But customarily it is done through individual whim and caprice, and the capacity for mischief is thus limited and erratic. Science, on the other hand, proceeds in a calculated, systematic manner, measuring and monitoring all the way—and generally does so, these days, with public funds.

As one example, a recent U.S. Navy program was designed to train better qualified race-relations officers. Civilians from a number of navy bases were put through "creative racial confrontation," where they were deliberately provoked to anger and their deepest racial emotions were stirred. The program was canceled before its completion because some of the participants protested.

In medicine, human experimentation requires informed consent. One problem in behavioral experiments is that if the subject is informed, then he will not react spontaneously—and the experiment will be ruined. Take Stanley Milgram's morbidly fascinating experiments at Yale, described in his recent book, *Obedience to Authority.* Milgram's subjects *were* informed that they were participating in a scientific experiment—but they didn't know that they were the *subjects.* He wanted to see how willing ordinary people would be to administer electric shocks to make-believe subjects—actually actors pretending to be involved in a complex learning exercise. He found that an appalling number of people were all too willing to keep administering what they believed to be severe shocks, even when warned that the "subject" had heart trouble—as long as the scientist gave the command and took the responsibility. Only later did the shockers become the shocked on learning that they were the unwitting subjects of the investigation. Many question the ethics of such experiments, regardless of how revealing they may be.

People really worry about "behavior mod," as it is familiarly known, when human subjects are treated as if they were experimental animals, to be manipulated and monitored in detail, even made acutely uncomfortable and exposed to physical and psychological cruelties, in order to "improve" their behavior. (B. F. Skinner would never treat his pigeons that way.) This has been carried forward most excessively among convicts.

It was only last year, on reading several blisteringly critical chapters in Jessica Mitford's *Kind and Usual Punishment,* that I became aware of the extent to which behavior mod was practiced in the prisons—and the details of *how* it was practiced. Her descriptions made it clear that what Anthony Burgess and Stanley Kubrick intended as futuristic satire in the film *A Clockwork Orange* had already become sober (and sobering) current reality in the American prison system.

Bodily deprivations of all sorts went along with a total assault on the psyche. Communist brainwashing techniques were deliberately employed, with the rationalization that this time it was in a good cause: to replace the criminal mentality with a more amenable personality. To this end, some felt free to use electroshock, psychosurgery, and aversion therapy. Among the drugs considered employable were *cyproterone acetate,* the so-called castration drug; *apomorphine,* which causes violent vomiting for fifteen minutes at a stretch; *anectine,* a derivative of curare, which can cause the subject to lose all muscular control and even briefly to stop breathing; *prolixin,* a powerful tranquilizer, with serious and sometimes irreversible side effects. The treatments often only made angry men a whole lot angrier.

These are the more flagrant abuses, of course. And it may be that prison officials, seeing a new way of managing their troublesome cases, took more advantage of the opportunity than the scientists originally had intended. But such experiments *were* carried out—and by respected scientists, often under university auspices and government grants. And, let's face it, with our tacit approval—for don't we really believe that when a "criminal" vanishes behind those walls, he loses his human rights? Fortunately, a lot of hell has been raised about all this over the past many months.

As a result of the unfavorable publicity, the more objectionable programs have been canceled. From now on, it appears that informed consent by volunteers only will be a requirement for all behavioral experiments. But this, too, needs careful monitoring. For one still-planned project, an official mentioned that he would seek volunteers among those coming up soon for parole. It might be hard to refuse to volunteer under those circumstances. All this has nothing to do with "coddling criminals," but rather with saving our own humanity.

Behavior mod has its more benevolent aspects and has been used in gentler ways, with more or less success (and usually with some controversy), in industry and in the school system. Now and then it can even provide us with a good laugh. Take the story—told in a recent issue of *Psychology Today*—of the junior high school in Visalia, California, where all the teachers were complimenting one special teacher on the marvelous job he had done in improving the behavior and scholarship of their most difficult "problem children." But what that special teacher finally confessed he had been doing was teaching the kids to use behavior-mod techniques on their *teachers*. (For instance, they used compliments as positive reinforcement, just as Professor Skinner might have advised.) As a result, they got a better quality of teaching and all-around treatment.

On the other hand, no one got the prior informed consent of the subjects. What are the ethics of *that?* Maybe the story isn't as hilarious as I first thought.

QUESTIONS

1. It has been said that, in many circumstances, behavior modification has become "the tail that wags the dog." What does this statement mean in the context of Rosenfeld's essay?

2. In this essay, Rosenfeld gives only examples which support his thesis.*

---

*Definitions for all terms marked with an asterisk may be found in the Glossary.

a. Look up "Left-out information" in the glossary. How might this logical error apply to Rosenfeld's essay?

b. Give two examples of the use of behavior modification that do not support Rosenfeld's theory.

3. Rosenfeld objects to the use of behavior modification on ethical grounds.

a. What is the ethical principle underlying Rosenfeld's objections?

b. What examples of violations of this ethical principle does Rosenfeld cite?

c. Give at least two other examples of similar ethical violations which you have encountered in your personal experience or your reading.

d. Users of behavior modification in situations like the ones Rosenfeld describes would probably argue that a good end justifies the use of whatever means are necessary to bring about that end. Take a position on this issue and give one example that supports your position and one that contradicts it.

4. Behavior modification is a technique for changing behavior by rewarding people when they behave as we think they ought to and ignoring or punishing them when they do not behave in a way we approve of.

a. Give two examples of occasions when your parents, teachers, or friends used behavior modification on you. Give two examples of situations in which you used behavior modification on other people. Was the ethical violation discussed by Rosenfeld committed in any of these cases?

b. Did Rosenfeld set science up as a straw man?* In answering this question, consider the fact that we are shaped and manipulated by many forces in our lives without our knowledge and consent. Is science any more systematic and calculating than the school system? The church? The advertising industry? The media? If so, in what ways is this true?

5. Give two examples of a use of behavior modification that you would approve of and two that you would disapprove of. Examine these examples. What general principles can you draw from them that would guide your use of behavior modification?

---

*Definitions for all terms marked with an asterisk may be found in the Glossary.

READING AND WRITING SUGGESTIONS

1. Behavior modification is a neutral tool; the problem lies in how it is used. Consider another neutral tool—something concrete, like a hammer, or something more abstract, like advertising. Write a brief expository essay that contains examples of how this neutral tool can be used both wisely and unwisely.

2. Read a book, such as B. F. Skinner's *Walden Two*, which demonstrates the positive uses of behavior modification. Write a brief expository essay which contains examples of how behavior management techniques can be used for good purposes.

Analysis

Analysis is a means of examining a subject by breaking it down into parts and studying the relationships between those parts. One of the most efficient ways of examining the nature of the U.S. government, for example, is to divide it into its three main branches—the executive, the judicial, and the legislative—and to examine the functions of each branch, exploring the system of checks and balances that defines the relationships between the branches.

Process analysis is a special form of analysis which shows how to perform an action, how something works, or how something happens by presenting the process in a series of sequential steps. Consider, for example, a technical manual which shows how to repair a complex piece of machinery. The manual shows technicians how to dismantle each section of the machine in order to reach the affected part, how to make the repair correctly, and how to reassemble the machine. The important elements here—as in all process analysis used for technical purposes—are that the sequence of steps be presented in the correct order and that each necessary step be included and precisely described so that the process can be clearly understood and accurately performed.

In essays, writers sometimes adhere strictly to sequence in the same way that technical manuals do. But remember that essays are, by definition, personal reflections on a subject. If their purpose requires it, therefore, essay writers sometimes use process analysis in a way that is less dry and rigid, presenting only the broad outline of the sequence they are describing.

BULL FIGHTING

Ernest Hemingway

Ernest Hemingway (1899–1961) began writing as a newspaper reporter shortly after his graduation from high school. His life was full of action and adventure: he enjoyed big game hunting and sports fishing and participated in three wars—World War I, the Spanish Civil War, and World War II. This aspect of his life is reflected in the subject matter of many of his works and in the emphasis on physical bravery that pervades his writing. His many books include For Whom the Bell Tolls, The Sun Also Rises, A Moveable Feast, *and* The Old Man and the Sea. *In the following essay, Hemingway presents the sequence of events that comprises a classic bull fight.*

The bull ring or Plaza de Toros was a big, tawny brick amphitheatre standing at the end of a street in an open field. The yellow and red Spanish flag was floating over it. Carriages were driving up and people getting out of buses. There was a great crowd of beggars around the entrance. Men were selling water out of big terra cotta water bottles. Kids sold fans, canes, roasted salted almonds in paper spills, fruit and slabs of ice cream. The crowd was gay and cheerful but all intent on pushing toward the entrance. Mounted civil guards with patent leather cocked hats and carbines slung over their backs sat their horses like statues, and the crowd flowed through.

Inside they all stood around in the bull ring, talking and looking up in the grandstand at the girls in the boxes. Some of the men had field glasses in order to look better. We found our seats and the crowd began to leave the ring and get into the rows of concrete seats. The ring was circular—that sounds foolish, but a boxing ring is square—with a sand floor. Around it was a red board fence—just high enough for a man to be able to vault over it. Between the board fence, which is called the barrera, and the first row of seats ran a narrow alley way. Then came the seats which were just like a football stadium except that around the top ran a double circle of boxes.

Every seat in the amphitheatre was full. The arena was cleared. Then on the far side of the arena out of the crowd, four heralds in medieval costume stood up and blew a blast on their trumpets. The band crashed out, and from the entrance on the far side of the ring four horsemen in black velvet with ruffs around their necks rode out into the white glare of the arena. The people on the sunny side were baking in the heat and fanning themselves. The whole sol side was a flicker of fans.

Behind the four horsemen came the procession of the bull fighters. They had been all formed in ranks in the entrance way ready to march out, and as the music started they came. In the front rank walked the three espadas or toreros, who would have charge of the killing of the six bulls of the afternoon.

They came walking out in heavily brocaded yellow and black costumes, the familiar "toreador" suit, heavy with gold embroidery, cape, jacket, shirt and collar, knee breeches, pink stockings, and low pumps. Always at bull fights afterwards the incongruity of those pink stockings used to strike me. Just behind the three principals— and after your first bull fight you do not look at their costumes but their faces—marched the teams or cuadrillas. They are dressed in the same way but not as gorgeously as the matadors.

Back of the teams ride the picadors. Big, heavy, brown-faced men in wide flat hats, carrying lances like long window poles. They are astride horses that make Spark Plug look as trim and sleek as a King's Plate winner. Back of the pics come the gaily harnessed mule teams and the red-shirted monos or bull ring servants.

The bull fighters march in across the sand to the president's box. They march with easy professional stride, swinging along, not in the least theatrical except for their clothes. They all have the easy grace and slight slouch of the professional athlete. From their faces they might be major league ball players. They salute the president's box and then spread out along the barrera, exchanging their heavy brocaded capes for the fighting capes that have been laid along the red fence by the attendants.

We leaned forward over the barrera. Just below us the three matadors of the afternoon were leaning against the fence talking. One lighted a cigaret. He was a short, clear-skinned gypsy, Gitanillo, in a wonderful gold brocaded jacket, his short pigtail sticking out under his black cocked hat.

"He's not very fancy," a young man in a straw hat, with obviously American shoes, who sat on my left, said.

"But he sure knows bulls, that boy. He's a great killer."

"You're an American, aren't you?" asked Mike.

"Sure," the boy grinned. "But I know this gang. That's Gitanillo. You want to watch him. The kid with the chubby face is Chicuelo.

They say he doesn't really like bull fighting, but the town's crazy about him. The next to him is Villalta. He's the great one."

I had noticed Villalta. He was straight as a lance and walked like a young wolf. He was talking and smiling at a friend who leaned over the barrera. Upon his tanned cheekbone was a big patch of gauze held on with adhesive tape.

"He got gored last week at Malaga," said the American.

The American, whom later we were to learn to know and love as the Gin Bottle King, because of a great feat of arms performed at an early hour of the morning with a container of Mr. Gordon's celebrated product as his sole weapon in one of the four most dangerous situations I have ever seen, said: "The show's going to begin."

Out in the arena the picadors had galloped their decrepit horses around the ring, sitting straight and stiff in their rocking chair saddles. Now all but three had ridden out of the ring. These three were huddled against the red painted fence of the barrera. Their horses backed against the fence, one eye bandaged, their lances at rest.

In rode two of the marshals in the velvet jackets and white ruffs. They galloped up to the president's box, swerved and saluted, doffing their hats and bowing low. From the box an object came hurtling down. One of the marshals caught it in his plumed hat.

"The key to the bull pen," said the Gin Bottle King.

The two horsemen whirled and rode across the arena. One of them tossed the key to a man in torero costume, they both saluted with a wave of their plumed hats, and had gone from the ring. The big gate was shut and bolted. There was no more entrance. The ring was complete.

The crowd had been shouting and yelling. Now it was dead silent. The man with the key stepped toward an iron barred, low, red door and unlocked the great sliding bar. He lifted it and stepped back. The door swung open. The man hid behind it. Inside it was dark.

Then, ducking his head as he came up out of the dark pen, a bull came into the arena. He came out all in a rush, big, black and white, weighing over a ton and moving with a soft gallop. Just as he came out the sun seemed to dazzle him for an instant. He stood as though he were frozen, his great crest of muscle up, firmly planted, his eyes looking around, his horns pointed forward, black and white and sharp as porcupine quills. Then he charged. And as he charged I suddenly saw what bull fighting is all about.

For the bull was absolutely unbelievable. He seemed like some great prehistoric animal, absolutely deadly and absolutely vicious. And he was silent. He charged silently and with a soft galloping rush. When he turned he turned on his four feet like a cat. When he charged the first thing that caught his eye was a picador on one of the wretched horses. The picador dug his spurs into the horse and they galloped away. The bull came on in his rush, refused to be shaken off, and in full gallop crashed into the animal from the side, ignored the horse, drove one of his horns high into the thigh of the picador, and tore him, saddle and all, off the horse's back.

The bull went on without pausing to worry the picador lying on the ground. The next picador was sitting on his horse braced to receive the shock of the charge, his lance ready. The bull hit him sideways on, and horse and rider went high up in the air in a kicking mass and fell across the bull's back. As they came down the bull charged into them. The dough-faced kid, Chicuelo, vaulted over the fence, ran toward the bull and flopped his cape into the bull's face. The bull charged the cape and Chicuelo dodged backwards and had the bull clear in the arena.

Without an instant's hesitation the bull charged Chicuelo. The kid stood his ground, simply swung back on his heels and floated his cape like a ballet dancer's skirt into the bull's face as he passed.

"Olé!"—pronounced Oh-Lay!—roared the crowd.

The bull whirled and charged again. Without moving Chicuelo repeated the performance. His legs rigid, just withdrawing his body from the rush of the bull's horns and floating the cape out with that beautiful swing.

Again the crowd roared. The Kid did this seven times. Each time the bull missed him by inches. Each time he gave the bull a free shot at him. Each time the crowd roared. Then he flopped the cape once at the bull at the finish of a pass, swung it around behind him and walked away from the bull to the barrera.

"He's the boy with the cape all right," said the Gin Bottle King. "That swing he did with the cape's called a Veronica."

The chubby faced Kid who did not like bull fighting and had just done the seven wonderful Veronicas was standing against the fence just below us. His face glistened with sweat in the sun but was almost expressionless. His eyes were looking out across the arena where the bull was standing making up his mind to charge a picador. He was studying the bull because a few minutes later it would be his duty to kill him, and once he went out with his thin, red-hilted sword and his piece of red cloth to kill the bull in the final set it would be him or the bull. There are no drawn battles in bull fighting.

I am not going to describe the rest of that afternoon in detail. It was the first bull fight I ever saw, but it was not the best. The best was in the little town of Pamplona high up in the hills of Navarre, and came weeks later. Up in Pamplona, where they have held six days of bull fighting each year since 1126 A.D., and where the bulls race through the streets of the town each morning at six o'clock with half the town running ahead of them. Pamplona, where every man and boy in town is an amateur bull fighter and where there is an amateur fight each morning that is attended by 20,000 people in which the amateur fighters are all unarmed and there is a casualty list at least equal to a Dublin election. But Pamplona, with the best bull fight and the wild tale of the amateur fights, comes in the second chapter.

I am not going to apologize for bull fighting. It is a survival of the days of the Roman Coliseum. But it does need some explanation. Bull fighting is not a sport. It was never supposed to be. It is a tragedy. A very great tragedy. The tragedy is the death of the bull. It is played in three definite acts.

The Gin Bottle King—who, by the way, does not drink gin—told us a lot of this that first night as we sat in the upstairs room of the little restaurant that made a specialty of roast young suckling pig, roasted on an oak plank and served with a mushroom tortilla and vino rojo. The rest we learned later at the bull fighters' pensione in the Via San Jeronimo, where one of the bull fighters had eyes exactly like a rattlesnake.

Much of it we learned in the sixteen fights we saw in different parts of Spain from San Sebastian to Granada.

At any rate bull fighting is not a sport. It is a tragedy, and it symbolizes the struggle between man and the beasts. There are usually six bulls to a fight. A fight is called a corrida de toros. Fighting bulls are bred like race horses, some of the oldest breeding establishments being several hundred years old. A good bull is worth about $2,000. They are bred for speed, strength and viciousness. In other words a good fighting bull is an absolutely incorrigible bad bull.

Bull fighting is an exceedingly dangerous occupation. In sixteen fights I saw there were only two in which there was no one badly hurt. On the other hand it is very remunerative. A popular espada gets $5,000 for his afternoon's work. An unpopular espada though may not get $500. Both run the same risks. It is a good deal like Grand Opera for the really great matadors except they run the chance of being killed every time they cannot hit high C.

No one at any time in the fight can approach the bull at any time except directly from the front. That is where the danger comes. There are also all sorts of complicated passes that must be done with the cape, each requiring as much technique as a champion billiard player. And underneath it all is the necessity for playing the old tragedy in the absolutely custom bound, law-laid-down way. It must all be done gracefully, seemingly effortlessly and always with dignity. The worst criticism the Spaniards ever make of a bull fighter is that his work is "vulgar."

The three absolute acts of the tragedy are first the entry of the bull when the picadors receive the shock of his attacks and attempt to protect their horses with their lances. Then the horses go out and the second act is the planting of the banderillos. This is one of the most interesting and difficult parts but among the easiest for a new bull fight fan to appreciate in technique. The banderillos are three-foot, gaily colored darts with a small fish hook prong in the end. The man who is going to plant them walks out into the arena alone with the bull. He lifts the banderillos at arm's length and points them toward the bull. Then he calls "Toro! Toro!" The bull charges and the banderillero rises to his toes, bends in a curve forward and just as the bull is about to hit him drops the darts into the bull's hump just back of his horns.

They must go in evenly, one on each side. They must not be shoved, or thrown or stuck in fron the side. This is the first time the bull has been completely baffled, there is the prick of the darts that he cannot escape and there are no horses for him to charge into. But he charges the man again and again and each time he gets a pair of the long banderillos that hang from his hump by their tiny barbs and flop like porcupine quills.

Last is the death of the bull, which is in the hands of the matador who has had charge of the bull since his first attack. Each matador has two bulls in the afternoon. The death of the bull is most formal and can only be brought about in one way, directly from the front by the matador who must receive the bull in full charge and kill him with a sword thrust between the shoulders just back of the neck and between the horns. Before killing the bull he must first do a series of passes with the muleta, a piece of red cloth he carries about the size of a large napkin. With the muleta the torero must show his complete mastery of the bull, must make the bull miss him again and again by inches, before he is allowed to kill him. It is in this phase that most of the fatal accidents occur.

The word "toreador" is obsolete Spanish and is never used. The torero is usually called an espada or swordsman. He must be proficient in all three acts of the fight. In the first he uses the cape and does veronicas and protects the picadors by taking the bull out and away from them when they are spilled to the ground. In the second act he plants the banderillos. In the third act he masters the bull with the muleta and kills him.

Few toreros excel in all three departments. Some, like young

Chicuelo, are unapproachable in their cape work. Others like the late Joselito are wonderful banderilleros. Only a few are great killers. Most of the greatest killers are gypsies.

QUESTIONS

1. "Beauty is in the eye of the beholder." "Taste cannot be disputed." What do these two maxims mean? Use them as the basis for a discussion of the very different adjectives that a torero, a meat packer and a Sunday hiker would use to describe a "good" bull.

2. What adjectives would you use to describe Hemingway's diction* and style?*

3. What steps in the bull-fighting process does Hemingway list?

4. Consider how Hemingway's view of bull fighting relates to essays by other authors.
   a. Does the liking for a blood sport indicate a blood lust? Judging from his essay on p. 52, what would Eldridge Cleaver say? What do you think Hemingway would say?
   b. What do you think bull fighting symbolizes? What would Cleaver say? What does Hemingway say?
   c. Is bull fighting an obscenity? What would Larry Flynt, the publisher of *Hustler* Magazine, say? (See Arthur Kretchmer's essay, "Justice for 'Hustler,' " on p. 23.)

5. What is your opinion of blood sports? Are they desirable entertainment? Why, or why not? Do they serve a useful purpose? Explain your answer.

READING AND WRITING SUGGESTIONS

1. Using Hemingway's essay as a model, write a brief process analysis of a fishing trip.

2. Consult an encyclopedia or another reliable source about fox hunting. Using Hemingway's essay as a guide, write a brief process analysis of the blood sport of fox hunting.

---

*Definitions for all terms marked with an asterisk may be found in the Glossary.

WANT A JOB?

Kirby W. Stanat

Kirby W. Stanat (1933–) was a personnel recruiter in industry for thirteen years; he estimates that during this period he hired about eight thousand people. In addition, he served as placement director at the University of Wisconsin at Milwaukee for seven years. In his book, Job Hunting Secrets and Tactics, *Stanat presents the entire procedure that a person should follow in order to get a good job. The following essay focuses on a specific aspect of this process—how to succeed in the campus job interview.*

The college placement center is like an auto showroom where recruiters are constantly shopping for sporty new models.

The recruiters want to talk to students, and they have jobs for them, jobs they must fill. If you're in your last year of college and if you want a job after you graduate, the placement center is a must for you. It's your best shot.

The typical recruiter on the college circuit may interview from 70 to 100 people for four or five jobs. Why is he doing that at all? Why is his company spending money to send him around to talk to a bunch of green college seniors?

No mystery—to save money. College seniors become "entry level personnel," and entry level people come cheap. They're a real bargain for the employer . . .

So companies need you. Or, rather, a company needs perhaps 10 entry level people. And 300 are interested in working for that company. That gets to the heart of your problem. And the recruiter's problem. How are you going to convince the recruiter that you're what he needs? What does he have going for him to help him decide which 10 of the 300 students are the right 10?

What the campus recruiter has to work with is some data and his own intuition. That is not much. And that is what college recruiters feel is the dark side of the job—that they have to make professionally binding decisions on evidence that is dangerously thin.

Look at the information they have to go on. Almost every student the recruiter talks to is going to get a degree. The degree, therefore, is a common denominator, and any statistician knows that a common denominator is no good as a selector.

The most obvious variable statistic for a college student is grade point average. Some employers consider grade point a good indicator of ability to do well on a job, but others consider it meaningless.

There are other hard facts, such as age, marital status, extra-curricular activities, summer and part-time work, but the differences among candidates in those areas are usually insignificant. The result is that the recruiter is going to recommend the candidate he likes best, the one who impressed him most in the interview, based on all the minor details of appearance, manners, general bearing, speech and awareness of the work. It's that simple: the one he likes best.

To succeed in campus job interviews, you have to know where that recruiter is coming from. The simple answer is that he is coming from corporate headquarters.

That may sound obvious, but it is a significant point that too many students do not consider. The recruiter is not a free spirit as he flies from Berkeley to New Haven, from Chapel Hill to Boulder. He's on an invisible leash to the office, and if he is worth his salary, he is mentally in corporate headquarters all the time he's on the road.

If you can fix that in your mind—that when you walk into that bare-walled cubicle in the placement center you are walking into a branch office of Sears, Bendix or General Motors—you can avoid a lot of little mistakes and maybe some big ones.

If, for example, you assume that because the interview is on cam-pus the recruiter expects you to look and act like a student, you're in for a shock. A student is somebody who drinks beer, wears blue jeans and throws a Frisbee. No recruiter has jobs for student Frisbee whizzes.

A cool spring day in late March, Sam Davis, a good recruiter who has been on the college circuit for years, is on my campus talking to candidates. He comes out to the waiting area to meet the student who signed up for an 11 o'clock interview. I'm standing in the doorway of my office taking in the scene.

Sam calls the candidate: "Sidney Student." There sits Sidney. He's at a 45 degree angle, his feet are in the aisle, and he's almost lying down. He's wearing well-polished brown shoes, a tasteful pair of brown pants, a light brown shirt, and a good looking tie. Unfortu-nately, he tops off this well–co-ordinated outfit with his Joe's Tavern Class A Softball Championship jacket, which has a big woven em-blem over the heart.

If that isn't bad enough, in his left hand is a cigarette and in his right hand is a half-eaten apple.

When Sam calls his name, the kid is caught off guard. He ditches the cigarette in an ashtray, struggles to his feet, and transfers the apple from the right to the left hand. Apple juice is everywhere, so Sid wipes his hand on the seat of his pants and shakes hands with Sam.

Sam, who by now is close to having a stroke, gives me that what-do-I-have-here look and has the young man follow him into the interviewing room.

The situation deteriorates even further—into pure Laurel and Hardy. The kid is stuck with the half-eaten apple, doesn't know what to do with it, and obviously is suffering some discomfort. He carries the apple into the interviewing room with him and places it in the ashtray on the desk—right on top of Sam's freshly lit cigarette.

The interview lasts five minutes . . .

Let us move in for a closer look at how the campus recruiter operates.

Let's say you have a 10 o'clock appointment with the recruiter from the XYZ Corporation. The recruiter gets rid of the candidate in front of you at about 5 minutes to 10, jots down a few notes about what he is going to do with him or her, then picks up your resume or data sheet (which you have submitted in advance) . . .

Although the recruiter is still in the interview room and you are still in the lobby, your interview is under way. You're on. The recruiter will look over your sheet pretty carefully before he goes out to call you. He develops a mental picture of you.

He thinks, "I'm going to enjoy talking with this kid," or "This one's going to be a turkey." The recruiter has already begun to make a screening decision about you.

His first impression of you, from reading the sheet, could come from your grade point. It could come from misspelled words. It could come from poor erasures or from the fact that necessary information is missing. By the time the recruiter has finished reading your sheet, you've already hit the plus or minus column.

Let's assume the recruiter got a fairly good impression from your sheet.

Now the recruiter goes out to the lobby to meet you. He almost shuffles along, and his mind is somewhere else. Then he calls your name, and at that instant he visibly clicks into gear. He just went to work.

As he calls your name he looks quickly around the room, waiting for somebody to move. If you are sitting on the middle of your back, with a book open and a cigarette going, and if you have to rebuild yourself to stand up, the interest will run right out of the recruiter's face. You, not the recruiter, made the appointment for 10 o'clock, and the recruiter expects to see a young professional come popping out of that chair like today is a good day and you're anxious to meet him.

At this point, the recruiter does something rude. He doesn't walk across the room to meet you halfway. He waits for you to come to him. Something very important is happening. He wants to see you move. He wants to get an impression about your posture, your stride, and your briskness.

If you slouch over him, sidewinderlike, he is not going to be impressed. He'll figure you would probably slouch your way through your workdays. He wants you to come at him with lots of good things going for you. If you watch the recruiter's eyes, you can see the inspection. He glances quickly at shoes, pants, coat, shirt; dress, blouse, hose—the whole works.

After introducing himself, the recruiter will probably say, "Okay, please follow me," and he'll lead you into his interviewing room.

When you get to the room, you may find that the recruiter will open the door and gesture you in—with him blocking part of the doorway. There's enough room for you to get past him, but it's a near thing.

As you scrape past, he gives you a closeup inspection. He looks at your hair; if it's greasy, that will bother him. He looks at your collar; if it's dirty, that will bother him. He looks at your shoulders; if they're covered with dandruff, that will bother him. If you're a man, he looks at your chin. If you didn't get a close shave, that will irritate him. If you're a woman, he checks your makeup. If it's too heavy, he won't like it.

Then he smells you. An amazing number of people smell bad. Occasionally a recruiter meets a student who smells like a canal horse. That student can expect an interview of about four or five minutes.

Next the recruiter inspects the back side of you. He checks your hair (is is combed in front but not in back?), he checks your heels (are they run down?), your pants (are they baggy?), your slip (is it showing?), your stockings (do they have runs?).

Then he invites you to sit down.

At this point, I submit, the recruiter's decision on you is 75 to 80 per cent made.

Think about it. The recruiter has read your resume. He knows who you are and where you are from. He knows your marital status, your major and your grade point. And he knows what you have done with your summers. He has inspected you, exchanged greetings with you and smelled you. There is very little additional hard information that he must gather on you. From now on it's mostly body chemistry.

Many recruiters have argued strenuously with me that they don't make such hasty decisions. So I tried an experiment. I told several recruiters that I would hang around in the hall outside the interview room when they took candidates in.

I told them that as soon as they had definitely decided not to recommend (to department managers in their companies) the candidate they were interviewing, they should snap their fingers loud enough for me to hear. It went like this.

First candidate: 38 seconds after the candidate sat down: Snap!

Second candidate: 1 minute, 42 seconds: Snap!

Third candidate: 45 seconds: Snap!

One recruiter was particularly adamant, insisting that he didn't rush to judgment on candidates. I asked him to participate in the snapping experiment. He went out in the lobby, picked up his first candidate of the day, and headed for an interview room.

As he passed me in the hall, he glared at me. And his fingers went "Snap!"

QUESTIONS

1. Give at least three adjectives which describe Stanat's diction* and style.*

2. What simile* does Stanat use as an introduction? What does it mean?

3. The end of the process Stanat describes is to succeed in the campus job interview—to convince the recruiter that you are what he or she needs.
   a. Does Stanat present the steps directly? What device does he use to get his ideas across to the reader?
   b. Compress Stanat's essay into a set of numbered steps that a recruiter might use to size up a student.

4. Translate the set of numbered steps you developed in question 3b into a list of the positive steps students can take in preparing for and participating in an interview.

―――――――

*Definitions for all terms marked with an asterisk may be found in the Glossary.

5. a. Make a list of the errors students might make at each stage of the recruitment process.

   b. Consider which errors you might make yourself and record your conclusions by writing yes or no beside each error on the list you made.

   c. List a set of steps you can take to avoid practicing those of your habits which might cause you to make a poor impression during a recruitment interview.

READING AND WRITING SUGGESTIONS

1. Many professions have a particular personal style—for example, a banker's style differs a great deal from a journalist's style. Needless to say, you will be more satisfied and more effective in a job if your personal style matches that of the profession you choose. Write a brief process analysis describing how you can identify the styles of the different professions.

2. Read a book or an article on how to be a successful student. Then write a brief process analysis describing the steps you can take to improve your method of study.

SURVIVING THIN AIR

Dee B. Crouch

Dee B. Crouch, (1942–) received his medical degree from the University of Colorado Medical School and is currently providing emergency medical services at Community Hospital in Boulder, Colorado. In 1976 Dr. Crouch was a member of the American Bicentennial Everest Expedition. The team began its climb in August, and Crouch was one of the small group that reached the summit in October. In this essay, he describes some of the physical and psychological traumas to which Everest climbers are susceptible.

After spending time on Everest, humans are weaker and less fit in every respect. One problem is acute mountain sickness, caused by ascending too rapidly; this can lead to cerebral and pulmonary edema (excess fluid in the brain and lungs). But the main problem at high altitude is chronic hypoxemia: not enough oxygen reaches the body's tissues. If men climb Everest without extra oxygen, they risk severe brain damage as well as loss of fingers and toes secondary to frostbite. Even with oxygen supplies, living in thin air for several weeks causes a decrease in blood oxygen and eventual deterioration.

We used oxygen starting at 24,000 feet, the usual altitude for such assistance. We had two oxygen regulating systems, both able to lower one's altitude at the summit by more than a vertical mile. But the more complex system (similar to those used in military aircraft) was vulnerable to icing and freezing. It failed Ang Phurba at the summit. In addition to climbing oxygen, we used sleeping oxygen to prevent insomnia, a major problem above 24,000 feet. While sleeping, one's breathing normally slows, which effectively raises one's physiological altitude by several thousand feet. At Everest altitudes, the sleeper dreams of suffocating, wakes up gasping, and the cycle is repeated. The insomnia is worsened by the persistent cold. At 21,000 feet, we regularly measured temperatures as low as minus 25 degrees Fahrenheit. At the col and above, they may have hit minus 40 degrees. In such weather, the blood simply does not have enough oxygen to keep the body fires going.

To nobody's surprise, we also developed nausea and resisted eating. At altitude, hypoxemia causes a significant decrease in digestive enzymes, which prevents essential proteins and fats from being absorbed into the bloodstream. As a result, one cannot maintain usual muscle strength, and persistent muscle wasting occurs in direct logarithmic relationship to the altitude. The wasting may not be evident to the climber himself; heavy clothing conceals the condition from others. Only after we returned to Base Camp after 43 days above 17,500 feet did we perceive our state of semistarvation. The weight loss averaged 20 pounds per man. Most of the climbers then became so hungry again that they devoured six or eight meals a day. The exceptions were the two summit climbers, whose ordeal left them so fatigued that they could not eat for several days.

We know that the brain is exceedingly susceptible to hypoxic damage. How vulnerable are Everest climbers? Before and after the climb, four expedition members were carefully tested in the neurological laboratory at the University of Colorado Medical Center; they will be retested every six months. Whatever the results, most of the expedition members, especially those high on the mountain, reported various psychological effects—impaired memory, errors in judgment, mental lassitude, indifference, slowness in reasoning. All this may be temporary. But certainly it compounds what I called "postexpedition syndrome," the confusions of returning from an extreme situation to the slow pace of one's ordinary life. We were uncommon men climbing an uncommon mountain in an uncommon land. Now we must return to face ourselves, the common man, and we may have difficulty. Most expedition members underrated their experience immediately upon descent from the mountain. With each passing day, however, they considered it more and more significant. Some of them may leave it at that: a thing to be cherished. But others may ultimately change their values, their occupations, even their lifestyles.

QUESTIONS

1. In this essay, Crouch uses the common and useful writing technique of defining technical words in context. Analyze the context to find the definition of the following terms: cerebral and pulmonary edema, chronic hypoxemia, hypoxic brain damage, and postexpedition syndrome.

2. What is the tone* of most of the essay? How does that tone change in the last six sentences?

3. Crouch states that "after spending time on Everest, humans are weaker and less fit in every respect." Judging from the general information Crouch gives in this essay, what steps can be taken to prevent or combat cerebral and pulmonary edema, chronic hypoxemia, hypoxic brain damage, and postexpedition syndrome?

4. An activity like climbing Mt. Everest is expensive, dangerous, and physically and psychologically stressful.
   a. In your opinion, what are the benefits? Why do people subject themselves to such difficulties?
   b. In a TV report on the expedition, Crouch said that his motive in climbing Everest was to find the limits of what he could do both physically and psychologically. What is your opinion of such self-testing to gain greater knowledge about oneself?

5. Some of the climbers in the Bicentennial Everest Expedition were college students or recent graduates. Crouch had just finished medical school.
   a. If you had a choice, would you go on such an expedition? Why, or why not?
   b. If you did go, what steps would you take to prepare yourself physically and psychologically for the ordeal?

READING AND WRITING SUGGESTIONS

1. Consider an activity you have participated in which is physically stressful, psychologically stressful, or both. Write a process analysis essay describing the way the activity wears your mind or body down and listing the steps you take to deal with these stresses.

2. Find and read material which describes how people are prepared for an extreme physical and psychological challenge—for example, how athletes are trained for the Olympics, how military personnel are trained for survival, or how astronauts are prepared for space travel. Write a brief process analysis paper showing the major steps taken in the activity you read about.

---

*Definitions for all terms marked with an asterisk may be found in the Glossary.

BIOFEEDBACK: AN EXERCISE IN "SELF-CONTROL"

Barbara Brown

Barbara B. Brown (1917–), a pioneer researcher in the area of biofeedback, received her undergraduate degree at Ohio State University and her Ph.D. in pharmacology from the University of Cincinnati. She has taught at the University of California and is currently working at the Veterans Administration hospital in Sepulveda, California. Her publications include New Mind, New Body—Bio-Feedback: New Directions for the Mind *and numerous articles published in scientific journals. Here Brown presents a general analysis of the phenomenon of biofeedback, and, within that general analysis, a more specific analysis of how biofeedback may be used to combat a number of medical problems.*

Most biomedical discoveries are about bits and pieces of man's mind or body. It is not that these discoveries are not important; they have saved society the sadness of much disease and salvaged injured bodies and damaged minds. Significant as medical progress has been, it has not slaked the nagging feeling, the intuition, of most people that the occasional brilliance and power of man's mind in conquering nature could as well be turned to promoting the well-being of mind and body by action of the mind alone. As sophisticated as society has become, today's robust resurgence of interest in spiritual healing and psychic surgery is graphic testimony of a wide-spread belief in mind power.

From the beginning of history, mentalists have challenged scientific authority, just as convinced that mind power controls the universe as scientists are that physical order controls man's destiny. Science has always won, for it is far easier to be convincing with demonstrations of physical cause and effect on your side. On its side, mind power has not been systematically corralled nor put to effective use. Mind power has not existed for most scientific authority, even when it fathomed mysteries or became engulfed in momentous ideologic conflicts.

Then suddenly, in the Sixties, like a series of underground nuclear explosions, experiments began rumbling throughout the country that presaged perhaps the greatest medical discoveries of all time. In the frantic research activity that has followed, it has become clear that man may, after all, have a mind resource to control his own being, down to the most minute fragments of his physical structure. Including his brain.

The simplest statement of the discovery is revolutionary: Given information about how any one of the internal physiological systems is operating, the ordinary human being can learn to control the activity of the system. It can be heartbeat, blood pressure, gastric acid, brain waves, or bits of muscle tissue; it does not seem to make much difference what function of the body it is as long as information about how it is behaving is made available. And generally, the more the information, the easier it is to learn to control the body function.

Most people can control what they do with arms and legs, with eye, face, or other muscles, using the kind of body control called voluntary. But until recently, medical science has believed and taught that nearly all other body functions, such as blood flow, body temperature, brain waves, or even residual muscle tension itself, were under automatic regulation and beyond voluntary control. Almost without warning this dictum has collapsed. The new research has shown that people can learn to control even these kinds of body function.

The discovery of this ability of mind is abbreviated in the term *biofeedback*, an ideograph that describes the phenomenon of control over internal biological functions occurring when information about the function is "fed back" to the person whose biologic activity it is. It is a compound of a technology and a training procedure, using specially designed electronic instruments to detect and monitor physiologic activities (such as heart rate or brain waves). The individual practices to control the action of the monitor by manipulating his mental and internal activities, and the result is a learned, voluntary control over the physiologic functions monitored. It is a technique for extending the capabilities of the mind to control the body— and the mind.

The discovery occurred when researchers began giving information about body activities directly *to* people rather than recording it to be filed away for their own research or medical uses. It is the return of information to the individual that is crucial to the biofeedback process. For centuries medical men have laid claim to the increasing volumes of information about human bodies, but never before have they shared it. Somehow medical opinion had decided that information about the workings of one's own body could be hazardous to one's health. But medical opinion was wrong.

The implications of biofeedback are revolutionary and perplexing, because biofeedback research itself is dramatic and mystifying. In Dr. John Basmajian's neuroanatomy laboratory, for example, ordinary people are shown oscilloscope tracings of the spontaneous electrical activity of various small groups of their own muscle cells, activity detected by sensors on the skin over a muscle. With almost psychic power, these ordinary people begin to control, selectively, the minute electrical activity of different groups of muscle cells—voluntarily—just as they can voluntarily control the whole muscle when they want to move it. However, now they are activating as few as three muscles *cells* simply by deciding to do so.

Basmajian further taxes our capacity to conceptualize such mind control by demonstrating that the site of control actually occurs in single motoneuron cells in the spinal cord. His subjects (and the subjects of many other investigators) learn to activate these single cells within as short a time as 15 minutes, sometimes much less. The precision of the control is extraordinary: To activate one cell independently means that other related cells, normally involved in muscle movement, must simultaneously be suppressed. Yet despite the facility in learning the control, and its complexity and precision, the human mind appears to be at a complete loss to explain how it accomplishes this extraordinary feat. The reports of most people are that they know they *can* do it, but they do not know *how* they do it.

Or, as in the laboratories of Brener and Hothersall, it was discovered that human beings could—unconsciously—learn to control a body function traditionally believed to function automatically: the rate of the beating heart.

Like so many other experimental psychological studies, this one sounds more like a practical joke than research: yet the results are impressive and interesting. Volunteer subjects were asked to make a device produce different pitches of tones "by purely mental means." A red-light signal was a request to make high tones, and a green light was a request to make low tones. Presumably the subjects did not know that they were, in fact, directly wired to the tone-producing device and that it was the amplified electrical energy of their own heartbeats that activated the tones. When the heart accelerated, the tones were high; when the heart slowed, the tones were low. With a little practice, the subjects learned to manipulate the tones. Incredibly, they remained unaware that their own heartbeats turned on the tones and that it was their unconsciously learned control of heart rate that caused the tones to change.

In the brief span of time during which biofeedback has been with us, there have been more reports confirming its validity than for almost any previous biological discovery in an equivalent period of time. Its implications for both theory and applications are almost limitless, for when we come right down to it, there is little about the functioning of human beings that does not in some way depend upon the feeding back of biological information to the generator of that information. The excitement that biofeedback has brought is the discovery that man's mind can process and understand even his own cellular information and use it to extend his control of self far beyond that ever before believed possible.

Take the role of biofeedback in tension and anxiety as the simplest example, but one with perhaps the farthest-reaching potential. The majority of emotional problems, and perhaps a good many medical problems as well, stem from the excessive tension and anxiety of today's fast-paced world, and the tensions are directly and immediately manifest as muscle tension.

In medical science the vast therapeutic benefits of relaxation have been known since the early days of this century. Although remarkably successful in many emotional and medical problems, the medical use of relaxation has been limited because it is time-consuming and requires more patience and persistence than most ill patients can summon. This relative impracticability has led therapists to neglect the fact that it is the intimate relationship between muscles and mind that becomes distorted under mental and emotional tension, that somehow this affects other body functions, and that effective relaxation can relieve those emotionally caused illnesses called psychosomatic.

To many relaxation theorists, anxiety (emotional tension) and relaxation are mutually exclusive. Certainly it has been learned, both medically and psychologically, that where there is anxiety, there is muscle tension, and that when muscle tension is relieved, so is anxiety.

Physiologic studies suggest why this may be true. The tension of muscle cells is adjusted by means of a feedback control loop operating between tension sensors in muscle cells and brain areas concerned with effective muscle movement. The control system, operating something like the household thermostat, compares actual tension with what it should be for a given situation and initiates activation of appropriate adjustments. This linear mechanism is ideal for moving muscles and for mobilizing muscles as a first line of defense. The system does not, however, cope well with the way human beings react to social pressures. By social custom physical action is tempered, submerging the defense posture into an unconscious intention to be ready for action, to be alert and tensed. When emotional tension and its muscle-tensing effect are prolonged, the system undergoes adaptation and the control becomes set to higher and higher levels of tolerated muscle tension. It is an insidious accommodation that leads to the muscles' becoming set into patterns of tenseness. Its continuous-loop nature feeds upon itself, anxiety tenses the muscles, and the increased tension of muscles keeps the mind apprehensive. But because it is a continuous loop, intervention can be either in the mind or in the muscles. Effective psychotherapy can relieve muscle tension, and effective relaxation procedures can relieve anxiety.

Biofeedback-assisted relaxation is so reasonable that it is surprising it has taken so long to discover. With its ability to amplify a hundredfold, it detects that muscle tension persisting even when the muscles appear at complete rest, the tension built up from social pressures. This residual tension is amplified and converted to a form of electrical energy that can operate meters or any other convenient signal. Because a signal like a meter constantly reads and displays the tension, it can be perceived as it fluctuates over time. Although this is a new form of muscle information, the brain uses it to exert voluntary control over the otherwise-imperceptible tension level in the same way that it uses internally sensed information from muscle sensors to move muscles.

In much the same way, symbols of the body's other functions are used to bring them under voluntary control. The diversity of functions—such as peripheral blood flow, blood pressure, heart rate, intestinal contractions and secretions, skin electrical activity, and brain waves—that are responsive to this learning paradigm sharply implicates the intervention of complex mental activity in the automatic regulation of the body.

A strange blindness has prevailed in modern science about the role of the mind in the catalog of human abilities. The failure of the mind sciences to conjecture meaningfully about mind capabilities is easily seen in their indifferent attitude about the way the mind-brain can supervene in what we take to be the automaticity of reflexes. Take blinking and winking, two simple, related, but quite different acts: one automatic, the other learned. Nearly every physiologic system of the body has a similar automatic mode for its fundamental operation, and now biofeedback has shown that each automatic control system can be additionally influenced by higher mental activities. Yet until this discovery, science had put little thought to what brain activity might occur when ordinary reflexes are controlled mentally, as when blinking is done intentionally and becomes winking. There is little, if any, concrete neurophysiologic knowledge about how volition turns into action.

There are other unacknowledged dimensions of voluntary control. Because intention can select and direct *any* physiologic action, it can be deduced that the decision to intervene actively and specifically in an otherwise automatic biologic activity may be a function of mind relatively independent of specific physiologic systems. This possibility is reminiscent of metaphysical thought: If intention—the will—can be mentally evoked and applied to a variety of biological actions with molecular specificity, it is necessary to postulate other mental actions of similar relative independence. The *decision* to do something must be implemented; it needs mechanisms to select the body system and to direct or carry out the intent.

As a matter of fact, the biofeedback phenomenon has already rather startlingly revealed a semi-independent role for sensory information. Bundles of sensory information once believed to play a subsidiary role in directing various physiologic activities can, instead, be mobilized to assume a primary role, as when visual information is used to control muscle tension or is substituted for visceral information to control heart rate. This unexpected substitution of sensory information is a sophisticated action of the mind-brain and one that begs for experimental clarification by its implications for extending mind abilities.

Until biofeedback and the recognition that higher, complex mental processes could alter automatic functions, the concept of intention, or voluntary control, was considered exclusively in terms of control of muscular activity. Yet despite a century of research, the decision-making part of brain activity has eluded physiological and anatomical definition. The paucity of information about the purely mental activities of the brain is not generally appreciated by mind scientists. The brain scientist becomes enmeshed in the complexities of neural and biochemical elements, while the experimental psychologist attempts to define mental capabilities largely in terms of behavioral responses to changes in the environment.

So the authorities on the functions of mind have data chiefly for reductionist theories to describe the abilities of the mind, theories circumscribed by the physical nature of the brain and physical responses to physical stimuli. Any experiencer of hallucinogens, or any religious mystic, could give more recognition to the existence of mind and its unique place in nature than could any mind scientist. It is as if laboratory-man, no less than primitive man, fears the unknown. Rather than seeking to learn and to use the non-ordinary capacities of mind, mind scientists (who are mainly brain scientists) have worked to keep the awesome power of mind within the limits of its physical confines.

I do not argue that ultimately the brain scientists may not prove out their theories; what I argue is that they have dogmatized rigid inhibitions for using mind, and these have captured our social standards. We have set limits and norms for intelligence and creativity and outlawed flights of mind. It was less science than a changing social conscience that allowed some minds to see the ability of mind to control itself and its body in experiments that were little different from hundreds of earlier experiments that had discouraged such thoughts.

Through biofeedback we now know, as perhaps we should have always known, that the mind-body cannot direct the activities of the body unless it has information about what is going on in the environment of the body, its tissues, and its cells. And we should have known, too, that if the mind-brain cannot operate without information from the body, and the body cannot operate without information from the mind-brain, then mind-brain and body are not merely connected, they exist and function as a unit. There are volumes of experimental and medical documentation confirming the inseparability of mind and body; yet professional therapists, by tradition, by certification, and probably by economic considerations, assume responsibility for only one aspect: mind *or* body. Even with the development of psychiatry, medical science continues to impose a schizophrenic therapy on the problems of illness. The capacity of mind to regulate and heal the body, and itself, has been shortshrifted almost out of existence; problems of mind especially are nearly always first attacked by salving minds with drugs.

The unexpectedness of the biofeedback phenomenon stimulates more philosophic scientific conjecture than does any previous psychophysiologic research. It has taken some time for most researchers to realize that this "new" capacity of mind is most likely an extension of the inherent capability of man, and animals, to exert voluntary control over their own beings. Just how we voluntarily control anything about ourselves is still a mystery, but no matter how the phenomenon is viewed, it proceeds from a sophisticated action of the mind-brain. The fact that learning to control physiologic activities occurs without obvious use of conscious effort and without conscious understanding of how the control is accomplished is a dramatic confirmation of the remarkable capabilities of mind.

It has been, of course, disturbing to find that subjective knowledge of how individuals accomplish control of body functions could rarely be defined in conscious awareness. If the sensation of manipulating distant body activities is so elusive as to escape descriptions that can be communicated, then one is led to conjecture that a non-conscious awareness guides the entire process. And a complicated process it is, one that involves sense perception of abstract information (such as a meter reading) about a physiologic activity, one that organizes, associates, and integrates the information, then disperses correct directions to be transmitted neurally to the organs to change their activity according to a pre-determined effective objective.

The non-verbalizable aspects of consciousness are a no-man's-land, uncharted and unpartitioned, without physical landmarks or guideposts. The scientist hesitates to enter such a strange land; yet the obvious facility of the mind to learn control over even the most vital of the body's functions can provide the scientist with physical indices for marking the action of the subconscious mind. To chart this long-hidden expanse of mind is one of the most exciting future uses of biofeedback.

The biofeedback phenomenon also generates new conjecture about the structural capabilities of the body. The rapidity and ease of biofeedback learning is difficult to account for by known theory and literally mandates new insights for study of those internally generated mental abilities that shape what our minds and bodies do. If people can so quickly learn to control events in their bodies that they scarcely knew existed, are they reactivating a lost ability, or are they evolving a new capacity of mind? Either conjecture is provocative. The fact that we, and our animal relatives, do voluntarily control our major life's activities suggests that the control ability has always existed. If it were a new, evolving capacity, chances are it would be manifest as an erratic, fumbling attempt to control the microcosms of our bodies. But if, as in Basmajian's experiments with single cells buried deep in the spinal cord, the human mind can learn full control in a matter of minutes, is it because the ability to control single cells has always existed? If it has always existed, has our reluctance to recognize it been because the idea that mind can alter physical nature has been too overwhelming conceptually to our primitive understanding of the physical order of the universe, or too God-defying, to bring into conscious appreciation? Is it possible that man has suppressed a higher level of mental function, one that regulates every cell of the body?

And will the extraordinary potential of the biofeedback breakthrough be realized, or will the tradition that requires substantive proof of the limits of mind continue to restrain explorations of the endowments of mind claimed by artists, musicians, mathematical geniuses, inventors, mystics, and drug-takers?

The sticky point is that our society has accepted a good bit of scientific theory about the mind as fact, accepting definitions of mind as bounded and limited by the physical nature of the brain. The concept that the mind functions one-to-one with brain processes, a theory for which there is really very little data, should not be accepted as an unwritten limit to the faculties of the mind. Rather, because science is a long way from defining mind, it should be just as valid to explore the mind subjectively as it is to explore it by means of the objective measures currently used that are admittedly inadequate, meager, and often inappropriate.

We should by this time be well aware of the powerful consequences of untracking the mind and breaking its limits by means of drugs, the musical experience, or the emotional overloading of unorthodox experiential psychological techniques. While scientists themselves avoid recognizing the powerful impact of awareness-raising, consciousness-expanding, creative explosions that have marked the non-scientific society since the early Sixties, there can be no doubt about the revolutions in thought and conscience and consciousness that have occurred. New attitudes have developed about war, about social responsibility, about life values, about the environment. These are powerful changes in mind function, which have, in fact, significantly altered our notions of reality.

And yet, as a member of the scientific community, I watch reports of new research that purport to explore the principle of biofeedback, and I see the security blanket of traditional methodology and concept smothering the vital mechanism of a "new" mind, shaping experimental forays and conclusions to conform to concepts of mind that yet other evidence suggests may be illusory. It is like the Western attitude toward yogis. Until biofeedback, appropriate scientific experts refused to acknowledge the possibility of control of the physical body by mental disciplines. Now that biofeedback has shown that similar control can be attained through technologic aids, the conclusion is drawn that the yogic process is a biofeedback process and that the biofeedback process is little more than rote learning. That such conclusions are drawn without data is ignored; it seems obvious to these experts that the similarities must exist and, more comfortingly, that the model for explaining human behavior can be preserved intact. And they continue to forget that the model does not explain why and how we select our goals, or what intention and creativity are.

For the immediate, practical applications of biofeedback, it may make little difference how the nature of the phenomenon is viewed, that is, whether one views it as a mechanical learning contingent upon rewards or as a capactiy of mind in which complex mental processes can be marshalled by other complex mental processes that give rise to intent and direction. It will make no difference how the effect occurs, for the ability of the mind to exert voluntary control over body functions can be used effectively to relieve a startling number of distressing conditions of body and mind. Biofeedback has been successful in an unbelievable array of problems of health: tension and migraine headaches, cardiac irregularities, high blood pressure, peripheral vascular disease, gastric ulcer, insomnia, epilepsy, asthma, spastics, learning problems in children, and a host of other troublesome medical and psychological problems in human beings. And along the way it is opening the door to a more holistic approach to therapy.

The future of biofeedback is uncertain only because no one knows the limits of mental control of mind and body. A wide variety of physical and emotional illnesses are certain to be relieved. We should be able to learn how to keep our bodies and minds in states of good health because we now have the means to become aware of their best operating conditions. We have only now begun to explore what all of our brain waves mean to human mental activity, and in the future it seems likely that we will be able to control many of the numerous specific brain waves as well as patterns of brain waves that reflect the activities of our minds and states of consciousness. We should be able to become so aware of the best states of minds and bodies that we can achieve both internal harmony and harmony with the universe.

QUESTIONS

1. Examine Brown's use of metaphors* and explain what she means by the following phrases:
   a. "like a series of underground nuclear explosions, experiments began rumbling through the country that presaged perhaps the greatest medical discoveries of all time"
   b. "the security blanket of traditional methodology . . . smothering the vital mechanisms of a 'new' mind"

2. Brown uses a number of conventions commonly found in scientific writing. Where does she get the evidence to support her assertions? What is her tone?* Her point of view?*

3. What steps are used to achieve biofeedback-assisted relaxation?

4. Brown refers to "awareness-raising, consciousness-expanding, creative explosions that have marked the non-scientific society since the early sixties."
   a. What are some of the creative explosions she is referring to?
   b. We can raise and expand consciousness by the use of many processes. Name two processes which can be helpful to the body and two processes which can be harmful.

---

*Definitions for all terms marked with an asterisk may be found in the Glossary.

5. Can everyone use biofeedback to control muscle tension or blood pressure? Do you think that an ability to concentrate and a belief in the process are prerequisites to the effective use of biofeedback?

6. Read or reread Michael DeBakey's essay on p. 28. Both Brown's and DeBakey's essays were written at about the same time and are concerned with scientific advances which could hold great promise for humanity.
   a. Do the styles of the two essays reflect their relative similarity in subject matter? How do the essays differ? In your opinion, why do they differ?
   b. Which approach to health maintenance and care do you think will be more productive? Why? Is there room in medical research for both approaches? Should we give money and other forms of support to both approaches? Why or why not?

READING AND WRITING SUGGESTIONS

1. Devise a way to deal with tension and fear in a threatening situation, such as a test you are not prepared for. Write a brief process analysis explaining how to use that procedure.

2. Read a book or article concerned with methods of relaxing, such as Herbert Benson's *The Relaxation Response*. Write a brief process analysis summarizing the procedure the author suggests.

Cause and Effect

Cause-and-effect analysis can move in one of two directions: it can either involve the examination of events or circumstances which led to a particular situation, or be concerned with the results that follow from a particular cause. In the first type of analysis, the *effect* is known, and it is the causes leading up to that effect which are being examined. Questions such as why the sky is blue, why Hitler was able to gain power in Germany, and even why a person chose a particular career all lend themselves to this kind of analysis. The second type of analysis is the reverse of the first type; here the *cause* is known, and it is the effects stemming from that cause that are being sought. Questions that would invite this type of analysis are: What was the effect of World War I on the British poetry of the period? What effect will the dwindling supply of natural fuels have on the American way of life?

It is essential that writers who use cause-and-effect analysis differentiate between real and apparent causes; the fact that one event precedes another does not mean that the first event was a cause of the second. A classic example of this type of confusion is illustrated by the case of the man who drank scotch with water and got drunk. He then drank bourbon with water and again got drunk. Finally, he experimented with rye and water and again found himself totally intoxicated. At this point, he concluded that water made him drunk.

When using cause-and-effect analysis, writers must also make a distinction between necessary and sufficient conditions. For example, a student must study for a given amount of time if he or she is to pass a test. This is a *necessary* condition, but it is not *sufficient* to ensure that the student will pass. The student must also study the right material, absorb a sufficient amount of it, and successfully convey an understanding of the material while taking the test.

Finally, writers must always keep in mind that few complex situations have a single cause. It is essential that the writer search out all the causes of a specific event, even those that are not readily apparent.

THREE REASONS ASSIGNED BY PHILOSOPHERS FOR THE PUNISHMENT OF CRIMES

Aulus Gellius

Aulus Gellius (c. 780), one of the earliest precursors of the modern essayists, was probably born in or near Rome. He assembled his and others' writings in a twenty-volume collection entitled Attic Nights. *In this essay, Gellius shows us that both the problem of crime and its solutions are hardly new.*

It is usually supposed that there are three proper reasons for punishing crimes; the one is "admonition" when a rebuke is administered for the sake of correction and improvement, that he who has committed an accidental offense may become more regular and attentive. The second is that which they who distinguish nicely between terms call "retribution." This mode of noticing an offense takes place when the dignity and authority of him against whom it is committed is to be defended, lest the passing by the crime should give rise to contempt or a diminution of respect; therefore they suppose this word to signify the vindication of honor. The third mode of punishment is called by the Greeks παραδειγμα (example) and is applied when punishment is necessary for the sake of example, that others may be deterred from similar offenses against the public by the dread of similar punishment. Therefore did our ancestors also denominate the heaviest and most important punishments, examples. When, therefore, there is either great hope that he who has offended will without punishment voluntarily correct himself, or, on the contrary, there is no hope that he can be amended and corrected; or that it is not necessary to fear any loss of that dignity, against which he has offended; or the offense is of that kind, the example of which it is not necessary to impress with particular terror; in this case, and with respect to every such offense, there does not seem to exist the necessity of being eager to inflict punishment. These three modes of vengeance, other philosophers in various places, and our Taurus in the first book of his Commentaries on the "Gorgias" of Plato, has set down. But Plato himself has plainly said that there only exist two causes for punishment. The one, which we have first mentioned, for correction; the other, which we have spoken of in the third place, to deter by example. These are the words of Plato: "It is proper for every one who is punished by him who punishes from a proper motive, that he should become better and receive advantage; or that he should be an example to others, that others, seeing him suffer, may from terror be rendered better."

In these lines it is evident that Plato used the word τιμορια[1] not, as I have before remarked some people have, but in its common and general sense, for all kinds of punishment. But whether, because he passed over as too insignificant and really contemptible, the inflicting punishment to avenge the injured dignity of man; or rather that he omitted it as not being necessary to the question he was discussing, as he was writing of punishments which were to take place not in this life among men, but after death, this I leave to others to determine.

QUESTIONS

1. According to this essay, Plato differs from other philosophers in his assessment of the proper causes for punishment. How does his view differ?

2. Using a dictionary, if necessary, define the following words: *admonition, diminution, retribution, vindication, mode, contemptible.*

3. What were considered to be the three desired effects of punishment when Gellius wrote his essay? Do these desired effects differ from those accepted in the earlier period when Plato wrote on the subject? Do we desire different effects today?

4. Just before being hanged, one murderer said about the means of his punishment: "If I was wrong, how can you be right?" How would you have answered him? How does your answer jibe with the reasons Gellius lists for the punishment of crimes?

5. a. In your opinion, which is the most desirable effect of punishing crimes? The least desirable?
   b. Do you agree with Gellius and Plato on this issue? If not, why do you disagree?

---

1. A Greek word meaning punishment or retribution.

c. Does the threat of punishment keep you from committing a
   crime? If so, how?

READING AND WRITING SUGGESTIONS

1. In dealing with New York City's financial problems, city officials
   had to choose whether to make the larger percentage cut in the
   school budget or in the police, court, and prison budget. Decide
   what your choice would be and write a brief cause-and-effect essay
   about why your solution would be more effective in reducing
   crime than the alternative choice would.

2. Read some literature on the value of capital punishment. Then take
   a position on whether we should abolish capital punishment and
   write a brief cause-and-effect paper explaining why your position
   would be more effective in reducing crime than its alternative
   would.

HAPPINESS
AND GOOD-NATURE

Oliver Goldsmith

*Oliver Goldsmith (1728–1774) was born in County Langford,
Ireland. He took a B.A. degree at Trinity College in Dublin and
studied medicine at the University of Edinburgh in Scotland. After
traveling throughout Europe on foot—supporting himself by playing
the flute—he returned penniless to London, where he worked at
writing and practiced medicine. Goldsmith's writing includes comedy, poetry, fiction, and essays. He is best remembered for his novel,*
The Vicar of Wakefield, *a long poem,* "The Deserted Village," *and
a comedy,* She Stoops to Conquer. *In this essay, Goldsmith considers the most effective way of dealing with adversity.*

When I reflect on the unambitious retirement in which I passed the
earlier part of my life in the country, I can not avoid feeling some pain

in thinking that those happy days are never to return. In that retreat all nature seemed capable of affording pleasure: I then made no refinements on happiness, but could be pleased with the most awkward efforts of rustic mirth; thought cross-purposes the highest stretch of human wit, and questions and commands the most rational amusement for spending the evening. Happy could so charming an illusion still continue! I find age and knowledge only contribute to sour our dispositions. My present enjoyments may be more refined, but they are infinitely less pleasing. The pleasure Garrick[1] gives can no way compare to that I have received from a country wag who imitated a Quaker's sermon. The music of Matei[2] is dissonance to what I felt when our old dairymaid sung me into tears with "Johnny Armstrong's Last Good-Night," or "The Cruelty of Barbara Allen."

Writers of every age have endeavored to show that pleasure is in us, and not in the objects offered for our amusement. If the soul be happily disposed, everything becomes a subject of entertainment, and distress will almost want a name. Every occurrence passes in review like the figures of a procession: some may be awkward, others ill dressed; but none but a fool is for this enraged with the master of the ceremonies.

I remember to have once seen a slave in a fortification in Flanders, who appeared no way touched with his situation. He was maimed, deformed, and chained; obliged to toil from the appearance of day till nightfall, and condemned to this life; yet, with all these circumstances of apparent wretchedness, he sung, would have danced, but that he wanted a leg, and appeared the merriest, happiest man of all the garrison. What a practical philosopher was here! a happy constitution supplied philosophy, and though seemingly destitute of wisdom, he was really wise. No reading or study had contributed to disenchant the fairyland around him. Every thing furnished him with an opportunity of mirth; and though some thought him from his insensibility a fool, he was such an idiot as philosophers might wish in vain to imitate.

They who, like him, can place themselves on that side of the world in which everything appears in a ridiculous or pleasing light will find something in every occurrence to excite their good humor. The most calamitous events, either to themselves or others, can bring no new affliction; the whole world is to them a theatre, on which comedies

---

1. David Garrick, an eighteenth-century English actor.
2. Any of several Italian musicians of similar name who were in England in the seventeenth and eighteenth centuries.

only are acted. All the bustle of heroism, or the rants of ambition, serve only to heighten the absurdity of the scene, and make the humor more poignant. They feel, in short, as little anguish at their own distress, or the complaints of others, as the undertaker, though dressed in black, feels sorrow at a funeral.

Of all the men I ever read of, the famous Cardinal de Retz possessed this happiness of temper in the highest degree. As he was a man of gallantry, and despised all that wore the pedantic appearance of philosophy, wherever pleasure was to be sold he was generally foremost to raise the auction. Being a universal admirer of the fair sex, when he found one lady cruel he generally fell in love with another, from whom he expected a more favorable reception; if she too rejected his addresses, he never thought of retiring into deserts, or pining in hopeless distress,—he persuaded himself that instead of loving the lady, he only fancied he had loved her, and so all was well again. When Fortune wore her angriest look, when he at last fell into the power of his most deadly enemy, Cardinal Mazarin, and was confined a close prisoner in the castle of Vincennes, he never attempted to support his distress by wisdom or philosophy, for he pretended to neither. He laughed at himself and his persecutor, and seemed infinitely pleased at his new situation. In this mansion of distress, though secluded from his friends, though denied all the amusements, and even the conveniences of life, teased every hour by the impertinence of wretches who were employed to guard him, he still retained his good humor, laughed at all their little spite, and carried the jest so far as to be revenged by writing the life of his gaoler.

All that philosophy can teach is to be stubborn or sullen under misfortunes. The Cardinal's example will instruct us to be merry in circumstances of the highest affliction. It matters not whether our good humor be construed by others into insensibility, or even idiotism; it is happiness to ourselves, and none but a fool would measure his satisfaction by what the world thinks of it.

Dick Wildgoose was one of the happiest silly fellows I ever knew. He was of the number of those good-natured creatures that are said to do no harm to any but themselves. Whenever Dick fell into any misery, he usually called it seeing life. If his head was broke by a chairman, or his pocket picked by a sharper, he comforted himself by imitating the Hibernian dialect of the one, or the more fashionable cant of the other. Nothing came amiss to Dick. His inattention to money matters had incensed his father to such a degree that all the intercession of friends in his favor was fruitless. The old gentleman was on his deathbed. The whole family, and Dick among the number, gathered round him. "I leave my second son Andrew," said the expiring miser, "my whole estate, and desire him to be frugal." Andrew, in a sorrowful tone, as is usual on these occasions, "prayed Heaven to prolong his life and health to enjoy it himself." "I recommend Simon, my third son, to the care of his elder brother, and leave him beside four thousand pounds." "Ah, father!" cried Simon, (in great affliction to be sure), "may Heaven give you life and health to enjoy it yourself!" At last, turning to poor Dick, "As for you, you have always been a sad dog, you'll never come to good, you'll never be rich; I'll leave you a shilling to buy a halter." "Ah, father!" cries Dick, without any emotion, "may Heaven give you life and health to enjoy it yourself!" This was all the trouble the loss of fortune gave this thoughtless, imprudent creature. However, the tenderness of an uncle recompensed the neglect of a father; and Dick is not only excessively good-humored, but competently rich.

The world, in short, may cry out at a bankrupt who appears at a ball; at an author, who laughs at the public which pronounces him a dunce; at a general, who smiles at the reproach of the vulgar; or the lady who keeps her good-humor in spite of scandal; but such is the wisest behavior they can possibly assume. It is certainly a better way to oppose calamity by dissipation than to take up the arms of reason or resolution to oppose it: by the first method we forget our miseries, by the last we only conceal them from others. By struggling with misfortunes, we are sure to receive some wounds in the conflict; the only method to come off victorious is by running away.

QUESTIONS

1. How does Goldsmith use the metaphors* of a parade (a procession) and a theatre to illustrate what the response of the "happily disposed soul" is toward life?

2. In this essay, Goldsmith considers the very different effects of letting happiness depend on external events and allowing it to depend on a positive state of mind. According to Goldsmith:
   a. What are the effects of letting happiness depend on things that happen to us?
   b. What are the effects of letting happiness depend on our inner selves?
   c. Which is the "better way to oppose calamity"?
   d. What is the effect of struggling with misfortune?
   e. What is the effect of running away from misfortune?

*Definitions for all terms marked with an asterisk may be found in the Glossary.

f. Should people care what the world thinks of their behavior in times of trouble?

3. The Greek philosophers posed the following question: One wise man lost his health, his money and property, his family, and his friends. The other wise man kept all of these things. Which wise man was the happier? (That is, what is the effect of misfortune on the first wise man and the effect of good fortune on the second wise man?)
   a. How would Goldsmith answer the question?
   b. How would you answer the question?
   (The Greek philosophers' answer was that both men were equally happy because they were both wise, and, for wise people, the source of happiness is internal virtue, which they can control, not external circumstance, which they cannot control. That is, fortune —good or bad—does not affect a truly wise person.)

4. Consider someone you know who has a problem that he or she cannot change.
   a. What are two ways the person can seek diversion while getting on with the business of life?
   b. What are two ways the person can fight the problem with reason, or resolution, or both?
   c. Which approach do you think would result in greater happiness for the person? Which approach would be more admired by other people?
   d. Should the person be more concerned with personal happiness or with other people's opinions?

READING AND WRITING SUGGESTIONS

1. Goldsmith's essay deals with misfortunes which people can do nothing about. Write a brief cause-and-effect essay about the effects of applying Goldsmith's suggestions to problems that people *can* do something about.

2. Read or recall the book *Pollyanna* by Eleanor Porter. Then write a brief cause-and-effect essay considering whether Pollyanna's approach to dealing with problems would have the positive effect that Goldsmith's essay suggests it would have.

The question of whether government should be totally candid or judiciously selective in releasing information to the public is a difficult one to answer. In the two essays that follow, David B. Wilson and Shana Alexander give very different opinions on this issue.

IS CANDOR ALWAYS ADVISABLE?

David B. Wilson

David B. Wilson (1927–) was born in Brooklyn, New York. After earning a bachelor's degree from Harvard in 1948, he went to work as a copyboy for the New York Herald Tribune. *Since then he has served in a number of capacities with some of the country's largest newspapers. For the past twelve years he has been with the* Boston Globe.

Suppose that in the months of shock and panic immediately following the assassination of John F. Kennedy, it had been discovered and disclosed that Lee Harvey Oswald was an authorized, conscious agent of Fidel Castro.

Or suppose that irrefutable evidence of such a relationship should be developed today and made public. What would the reaction be? And what would the reaction have been in December of 1963?

The questions are entirely theoretical. This column has no evidence that Castro had anything to do with the Kennedy assassination and neither, on the record, does the American government.

The questions are asked to illustrate the agonizing choices presented to the policymakers of a democratic society in a world of instantaneous mass communications in which conspiratorial terrorism has become commonplace.

Now most of the abundant and dubious Kennedy assassination literature darkly hints that the President was gunned down by a conspiracy of the Right determined to prevent the extension of the New Frontier and the realization of Camelot.

This kind of speculation nourishes existing prejudices and, in the absence of proof, is harmless if despicable.

Should proof develop there would be political ramifications; but the criminal justice system quite probably could operate to slake the national thirst for retribution.

The report of the Senate Selection Committee on Intelligence Activities implies that the Central Intelligence Agency ignored or avoided pursuing the possibility that there was a connection between U.S. plots to kill Castro and the assassination in Dallas.

Given Oswald's activities on behalf of the Fair Play for Cuba Committee, widely publicized at the time, it is difficult to believe that the investigating agencies were unaware of the possibility.

It is also difficult to believe that the CIA, given its skills and resources, could not have obtained the death of the Cuban dictator whenever it wanted to, whatever contingency plans it may have considered.

What is impossible to believe is that the United States would not, in 1963, have embarked on a popular, punitive war against Cuba had the public become convinced that Castro had deliberately caused the death of the President.

Demands for vengeance would have been irresistible. Indeed, should Castro be perceived today beyond a reasonable doubt to have been responsible for the Dallas assassination, war with Cuba would certainly be a most likely result.

The killing of John F. Kennedy came a little more than a year after the Cuban missile crisis. As part of the deal for dismantling the Soviet missile bases, the President agreed to respect the territorial integrity of Cuba.

The sheer terror of those crisis days, the practical possibility of transpolar nuclear holocaust, remains fresh in the memories of those who lived them.

War with the Soviet Union would have been entirely probable had the United States invaded Cuba in retaliation for Dallas, whether or not Castro was in fact responsible.

It is all very well, post-Watergate, to insist on absolute candor in the relationship between the electorate and the elected. And it is presumably unexceptionable to state that the public has a right o know who was responsible for President Kennedy's murder.

Yet, if a disclosure credibly threatens to provoke a war that certainly would cost millions of lives and reduce civilization to ashes, ought that disclosure to be made in defense of a noble but frequently and casually violated principle?

There seems no ready solution to this dilemma, which is faced in less awesome terms on a day-to-day basis by the individuals charged with the harsh duty of governing.

How many innocent must suffer to punish the guilty or right ancient wrongs? How many jobs equal one cancer death? Is disclosure of sexual or fiscal impropriety justified when the result is destruction of an otherwise admirable career? Is "covert activity" less or more moral than warfare? Is bribery never, ever justified?

THE ASSASSINATION OF PRESIDENT KENNEDY:
Real Gardens, Real Toads— Some Speculations on Secrecy— and the Dark Night of the CIA

Shana Alexander

Shana Alexander (1925–) is a writer and TV commentator. A former editor of McCall's *Magazine, she has represented the liberal viewpoint on the "Point-Counterpoint" segment of the TV show "60 Minutes." She is the author of* The Feminine Eye, Shana Alexander's State Guide to Women's Rights, *and many articles.*

The letter was forwarded to me by CBS News. Underneath a demurely garlanded *O* traced in Wedgwood blue the letter read:

June 8, 1975

Dear Ms. Alexandria:

There was indeed a conspiracy in November 1963 in which my young son Lee Harvey Oswald was allowed to take the blame.

Sincerely,
Marguerite C. Oswald

How swiftly she swam up from the depths of my memory—a pathetic, clownish eccentric in glasses and a funny hat. A publicity seeker and flinger of wild charges. A nutty, slightly sinister, big-nurse type. Not a woman to take seriously.

That was 12 years ago. Today one feels differently. Twelve years ago I believed the Warren Commission Report, believed that President Kennedy had been killed by a single, deranged assassin acting alone, believed that this man in turn had been killed by another deranged assassin acting alone—Jack Ruby. I do not necessarily believe that now. But my belief survived for a dozen years—survived the assassinations of Robert Kennedy and of Martin Luther King and the shooting of George Wallace; survived Vietnam and Cambodia and Chicago '68 and Jackson and Kent State; and lasted even through much of Watergate. My belief held steadfast much longer than most people's.

Three years after President Kennedy's assassination, the Gallup and Harris polls reported that two thirds of the American people refused to accept the conclusions of the Warren Commission. But like most professional journalists, I did accept them. I wrote off the skeptics and doubters as a pack of conspiracy nuts, assassination buffs, loonies and paranoids babbling about a second gun, a third Oswald, conjuring up James Bond plots and secrét links between Cuba, the CIA and Cosa Nostra—flaky people, like Mother Oswald, not to be taken seriously.

Then the CIA revelations began to surface, leading first to the formation of the Rockefeller Commission and later to the inquiries directed by Senator Frank Church and Congressman Otis Pike. This was different. I took the spook stuff seriously from the very beginning; and as time passed I began to wonder why.

What was I looking for? I knew the intelligence establishment was overgrown and overblown. I knew it tapped phones, read mail, engaged in dirty tricks; that it mixed in the internal affairs of other nations, propped up "friendly" governments and tried to "destabilize" others. I knew that for a generation or more Congress had preferred to look the other way rather than exercise the appropriate and necessary control, and I knew the dangers to democracy when police power is allowed to range unchecked.

In short, I knew that there was little in these new CIA headlines that we didn't already know. So why the eagerness for the morning paper, the thirst for the nightly news? At first it was the magnetism of the subject matter, the pull toward secrecy itself. To think the unthinkable, discuss the unmentionable, poke around the untouchable, is a pleasure very hard to come by in these days of bared souls, spread-eagled account books, full-political-disclosure laws and full-frontal-nudity art. Very few forbidden subjects remain. The secret world of the secret agent is the last taboo place left.

Marianne Moore once described poetry as the art of creating imaginary gardens with real toads in them. The secret agent lives in exactly the opposite landscape—real gardens, imaginary toads. What can it be like in there?

As the year wore on I found myself temporarily distracted from these speculations about gardens and toads by new doubts about the Warren Commission Report. More accurately, I found myself wondering why it was that so many "rational, responsible" reporters like myself, including nearly all my professional colleagues and friends, had so long refused to listen to the assassination nuts and conspiracy freaks. Who and what were *we* afraid to take seriously? Ourselves? I voiced my doubts to James J. Kilpatrick, the syndicated newspaper columnist who is my opposite in our weekly "Point-Counterpoint" exchange on the CBS-TV program *60 Minutes*. It was these comments that triggered the instant response from Lee Harvey Oswald's mother.

Admittedly my new doubts were based on old and circumstantial evidence: suggestions that Oswald may at one time have been an undercover FBI agent, that a so-called "second Oswald" may have been operating in New Orleans and Mexico City, that more than one set of fingerprints had been found in the Texas School Book Depository; evidence that at the time of the President's murder the CIA was already heavily into the assassination business in Latin America and elsewhere, sometimes with the helping hand—the Black Hand—of the Mafia; evidence that some original information about Lee Harvey Oswald had been hushed up by the Dallas police, and that other information about him had been deliberately withheld from the Warren Commission by the FBI and the CIA.

I was not the only person with newfound doubts. The recent CIA revelations had convinced even a member of the Warren Commission staff, Ohio Judge Burt Griffin, that back then the country had been told something less than the truth. The climate of sheer puppy-dog belief that existed ten years ago in America is almost inconceivable today. In 1965 Life magazine had headlined an insider's account of the Warren Commission's findings: MOTHER'S MYTH: OSWALD WAS A PAID U.S. AGENT. Implying that Marguerite Oswald was in fact a 100-per-cent nutball, the writer boasted that the commission had "the sworn denials . . . of men like FBI Director J. Edgar Hoover and Secretary of State Dean Rusk. We quizzed personnel from the U.S. Embassy in Moscow," the article continued. "We sent our own men into the agencies involved to study their old personnel files. We were, and we are now, convinced that Oswald was never an agent for the U.S. Government." The author of these staunch reassurances was Michigan Congressman Gerald R. Ford.

In the past bloody decade the FBI, the CIA, the White House and Government itself have lost credibility. Recent history forces one to consider that maybe the conspiracy buffs were right. Personally I'd hate to discover that last year's paranoid nut is next year's Pulitzer Prize-winning investigative reporter, but that's a chance recent history forces us to take. Ten years ago it was difficult to doubt the conclusions of the Warren Report. Now new studies of the Report are under way in both the House and Senate. The very same items we were once unable to doubt we are now unable to believe.

Read the Warren Report again.

• It is difficult today to believe that all 52 witnesses were mistaken who testified that at least some of the shots came not from the Texas Book Depository behind the car in which the President was riding, but from the grassy knoll in front of him.

• It is difficult today to believe the so-called "magic bullet" theory: that one single shot struck President Kennedy in the back, came out his neck and hit Governor John Connally in the back, smashed through Connally's rib, came out his chest, struck him in the wrist, wound up in his thigh, and was later conveniently discovered on the Governor's stretcher in the hospital.

• It is difficult today to believe Oswald could have hit the moving target at all from the book depository window. He had been a poor shot in the Marine Corps. He was right-handed and the clumsy old single-shot, Mannlicher-Carcano rifle had a left-handed scope. None of the three National Rifle Association marksmen hired by the Warren Commission to re-create the shooting was able to hit even a level, stationary target within the required 5.6 seconds, the interval that movie films proved had elapsed between the first and the third, fatal shot.

• It is difficult today to accept it that within three years of the assassination 17 witnesses to the murders of Kennedy, Oswald and Dallas Police Officer Tippit would die under curious circumstances. Five died of "natural causes"; 12 were victims of murder, suicide or fatal accidents. The actuarial odds against this happening have been reckoned at 100 *trillion* to one!

• It is difficult today to accept that the President's brain, removed after autopsy and preserved in formalin because the pattern of its wounds was crucial to proving the "magic bullet" theory, has innocently disappeared from the National Archives building.

• It is difficult today to accept that the two photographs of Oswald holding a rifle, which the Dallas police say they found in his garage the day of the shooting, are photographs of the same man, or even photographs of Oswald at all. The man in one picture is six inches taller than the man in the other.

• It is almost impossible today to accept the Commission's murder timetable: that Oswald was able to rearrange the shield of boxes he had set up around the sixth-floor window from which it was said he shot, wipe his fingerprints off the rifle, hide it, run down four flights of stairs to the second-floor Coke machine and be found there by the police calmly sipping Coke only 80 seconds later.

The truth is, today it is difficult to accept *any* FBI or CIA testimony or evidence at face value. Remember, the Warren Commission had no investigative staff of its own; all its field work was done by FBI or CIA agents. Remember that J. Edgar Hoover admitted withholding certain files from the Commission. Remember that while then-CIA Director Allen Dulles claimed he was telling the truth when he denied Oswald had ever been a CIA agent, he also admitted that, yes, he would lie under oath to protect the CIA. So indeed would any CIA man! Then what was truth? Real gardens, imaginary toads.

Marianne Moore's toads are truths, of course, which is why the world of the secret agent must be just the opposite of the poet's. The spy lives in a real garden with imaginary toads—a world of double agents, dealers of doubt, smugglers of truth, speculators in rumor, hoarders of dirt, spendthrifts of lies. It is a garden whose only signs read KEEP OUT, NO ENTRY, BEWARE THE DOG! The public is emphatically *not* invited. Nor are the public's representatives welcome—that is, the Congress—save to rubber-stamp what's going on anyway.

Inside this garden the gardeners make their own rules, sit in judgment on their own crimes, write and break their own laws with no accountability to anyone save to their one god: "national security." But even this god is at least sometimes false. The recent nose-to-nose confrontation between Congress and the White House questioned the value and competence of secret intelligence reports, notably on the eve of the Tet offensive and later of the 1973 Yom Kippur war, when the President was wrongly assured that there was no danger of attack.

It seems obvious here that former CIA Director William Colby was struggling to protect not national security but the CIA cover-up of its own incompetence, as well as various abuses of power by intelligence officials. Deadly poisons were stockpiled in the garden in direct contravention of Presidential orders; frightening, sometimes-fatal drug experiments were carried out; mail was opened, phones were tapped, civilians were spied on illegally and in wholesale batches; underworld liaisons and assassination plots were commonplace—and all this has been kept continually watered with billions of dollars of uncounted and unaccountable tax-payer dollars.

Looking back at the Warren Commission Report from this CIA-conditioned vantage point, one finds there such a volume of evidence to contradict the conclusions of the Warren Commission that one can see the Report itself as a kind of conspiracy by the Government and its investigative agencies to suppress or ignore any evidence of a conspiracy by assassin or assassins unknown. Not evidence that in any way linked the FBI or the CIA with the assassination of President Kennedy, but evidence of numerous shadowy links that appeared to exist between these agencies and Lee Harvey Oswald and between the FBI and Jack Ruby.

Whether these links did in fact exist is no longer of major importance. What is new and important is not the evidence but the doubts about it. What has changed is the climate. What has cracked here is belief itself—belief in all institutions, not just in the thoroughness and—yes—*honesty* of the 888-page Warren Report, handsomely bound and reassuringly stamped with the trusty U.S. seal. From its inception the purpose of the Report was double. First, it was necessary to find out exactly what had happened. Second, it was necessary to reassure the nation that the moment of danger had passed. This twofold purpose was always the flaw, the crack in the credibility of the Report: One document could not reasonably be expected to be a thorough job of police work and a giant security blanket for the nation.

The crack that began in 1963 had widened and become a chasm by 1975, a Grand Canyon of doubts. At the bottom of a tangled bone yard of shattered beliefs lie the decade's news events: the assassinations of the President's brother Robert Kennedy and of Martin Luther King; the attempts on the lives of other leaders, from George Wallace to President Ford; increasing doubts about the wisdom of the Vietnam War, doubts that finally forced President Johnson to give up his office, doubts that led directly to the massive disaffection of the people, and especially the young, and helped the "turn on, tune in, drop out" drug culture to flourish; doubts that led to active revolution —the Weathermen, the bombings, the urban despair that became riots in Watts, Newark, Detroit, Boston; outbursts of psychopathic violence such as the Manson murders and the Symbionese Liberation Army's hokey, confused politics of idealistic anarchy, which began with the murder of School Superintendent Marcus Foster, accelerated with the kidnaping of Patricia Hearst, triggered the assault by the Los

Angeles police against the SLA holdouts in a burning house and will end God knows where. By the time the Vietnam war had "wound down" through Cambodia and the Christmas bombing, the national honor itself seemed to teeter on the brink of the chasm. With Watergate it fell in. From now on everything was poisoned, nobody could be believed, anything was possible.

I think it no accident that the politician most popular today among his constituents is California's Governor Edmund G. Brown, Jr. Brown is an austere, icy figure who seems to me to understand the national illness better than any other politician. He understands that the fundamental problem in this country is that the people have lost confidence in all the institutions that traditionally nourish and protect them, including that overarching institution called *government*. He understands that the only way to restore that necessary measure of equilibrium which will permit our institutions to function again is to recover the regard of the major political constituency in this country—all those people who have become so turned off, they don't even bother to vote; that crucial majority (56 per cent in the last California election) which Brown calls "the constituency of no confidence."

There is only one way to regain that confidence, and that one way is through truth. Turn over every rock, ask every question, examine every toad. Don't just reopen the investigation of President Kennedy's death. Test the "second gun" theory in the Robert Kennedy assassination. Look again into the killing of Martin Luther King, and ask anew where convict James Earl Ray got his money and how he could have acted alone. Ask how it was that dim and dippy Arthur Bremer was able to shoot down George Wallace. Find out how Lynette "Squeaky" Fromme, who appears to be everybody's next-door psychopath, could creep so frighteningly close to President Ford; how Sara Jane Moore, a woman of some concern to the San Francisco Police Department, could be free in a crowd to fire a pistol at him. Ask every question. Open up the garden; examine all the toads. Ask *yourself* what you can believe.

A member of the Senate Foreign Relations Committee once told me that whenever a witness testifying in closed session told the senators he had the information but couldn't reveal it, he was automatically assumed to be either faking or lying. This is a pretty solid assumption, too seldom made by most of us. We are too easily cowed by self-proclaimed experts. "If *you* only knew what I know," they murmur, and we nod gravely. "Ah, if *we* only knew what *they* know . . ." (about Vietnam, about the atom bomb)—*we* being the public and *they* being the experts, the Secretary of Defense, the Joint Chiefs, the CIA, the President.

Except that the hindsight of history tells us that they didn't, entirely, know. As one comes to realize that most executive command decisions of necessity are made on the basis of incomplete or inaccurate or misleading intelligence information, the more one dares to question, to turn over toads.

"Secrecy itself frequently gets in the way of rational examination of our intelligence," says Representative Otis Pike, drawing on his 14 years' experience on the Armed Services Committee. It gets in the way at every level, top to bottom. Secret organizations are run on a "need-to-know" basis. Each man knows only as much as he needs to know to carry out his bit of the operation. But when the spooks apply the need-to-know rule to the man at the top, to the President, to protect him from knowing the dirty work his own men are up to, that's trouble.

The man at the top has an overriding need and duty to know everything because he's in charge. The buck stops here, as President Truman said, or you face the horrifying prospect that it doesn't stop anywhere, that free-lance assassins are loose, mad dogs out of their masters' control. Something like this may already have occurred in the Caribbean, Latin America, Africa, perhaps elsewhere. Though, of course, one doesn't know. The man and woman at the bottom have an overriding duty too—to explore the garden, look at toads.

What does the secret life do to the man? Isn't the secret a terrible burden to have to carry? Sometimes I imagine the man as a kind of stone urn or stoppered jar, and the secrets as a powerful liquid that eventually must corrode and eat away at the jar itself. On TV, the CIA's Colby, Helms & Co. looked to me like men who have contained the acid too long. And in the tight face of James J. Angleton, the former head of the CIA's counterintelligence group, one saw a man not only self-contained but also self-embalmed.

When a man becomes an initiate, part of a select company chosen to serve a select cause, he acquires certain privileges not accorded outsiders. He is removed from ordinary accountability. He can lie and the lie is morally justified. He can assassinate. Membership in the secrets society becomes so compelling that people who are not evil in themselves begin to do bad things to stay in the inner group. Acceptance of the group's methods is the price of belonging, and that price keeps rising.

The weight of forbidden secrets can warp a man's loyalties. We are told that Dr. Nathan Gordon, a former "middle-level CIA employee," decided "on his own" to preserve a deadly medicine cabinetful of shellfish toxin, cobra venom and heaven knows what other horrors. Richard Helms, then chief of the CIA, says well, yes, he did give an "oral order" in 1970 to destroy the stuff, as President Nixon had directed. But it appears obvious that the real reason the deadly vials were preserved was that a man in Dr. Gordon's position can come to believe that the highest authority is neither the law of the land nor the President of the United States. It is the Secret Organization itself —and that is very bad news indeed, because it means there is no authority at all.

Presidential aide John Dean told his boss Richard Nixon there was a cancer growing on the Presidency. Recent CIA revelations suggest that for years a cancer has been growing on this whole country. The intelligence community was a secret, dark garden, and what appears to have been growing there under cover of such rubrics as "national security" was nothing less than the roots and tentacles of a genuine police state. Of course we need to keep some secrets. Of course we need to maintain an intelligence capability—though far less, I suspect, than the present intelligence community and the White House would have us believe.

Once you set up something so secret that nobody else can look at it, nobody else can oversee it. You no longer have to ask yourself: How dirty a trick is "too dirty"? You can use any damned trick you want. One is free to lie. One is also free to cheat, embezzle or steal without fear of ordinary criminal prosecution. This is the very antithesis of our system of checks and balances. What were the punishments for murders, attempted murders, botched murder plots? No way to tell.

Another things about secrets: They don't seem to last as long as they used to. They ooze; they leak; they degenerate and decay into history almost before our eyes. The official secrets closet today, I suspect, is a threadbare place full of obsolete codes, moldy disguises, broken ciphers, bulging files on plots long dead. It was in recognition of this modern truth that Congress recently amended the Freedom of Information Act, over President Ford's veto. This amendment provides the public with a tool to pry no-longer-critical information out of the Government.

What is to be done? It is all so massive and so sinister, one is tempted to make the radical suggestion to abolish the CIA altogether. Or at the very least, cut the monster into two pieces—surveillance and operations—and put each one under separate Government control. Or if the CIA has grown too fat in its 30-year history, too Hydra-headed to be cut in two, or if the dirty tricks have been too dirty too long to clean up now, perhaps we should let the dear old monster go the way of the brontosaurus. Consider it obsolete and start over. Only time and vigorous continuing Congressional investigations will tell. I hope they tell plenty.

I think we need to hear a lot more about the value and durability of secrets in the post-Vietnam, pan-nuclear age. We also need to give some thought to the distinction between *data* and *intelligence*. The Warren Commission Report, in hindsight, appears to be mostly data, and incomplete data at that. But what is the nature of "intelligence" in a world where, as someone in Washington recently testified, "the lead time on World War Three is fifteen minutes"?

I don't know the answers—only that we all must begin to ask ourselves these questions. We all must pick up the toads and handle them. Self-government in the dark is not possible. The central secret of democracy may be that there *can be* no enduring secrets, that the people must know, that to opt for the democratic form of government is to forfeit forever one of life's sweetest comforts: the right not to know.

QUESTIONS

1. Alexander uses several metaphors* in her essay. Explain what she means by the following: puppy-dog belief, real toads, imaginary toads, real gardens, and imaginary gardens.

2. What is the central thesis* of Alexander's essay?

3. To develop her thesis, Alexander presents information about the Kennedy assassination and the congressional investigations of the CIA and FBI.
   a. What other events in the recent past could she have used to make the same point?
   b. What *current* events could she have used to illustrate the same point?
   c. Could she have made her point by using only one of the examples as illustration?
   d. Give at least one reason why she uses both examples.

4. In her title and subtitle, Alexander suggests four subject areas that she will discuss.
   a. What are these four areas?
   b. Explain how these subject areas are developed and connected in the essay.
   c. What do you think Alexander accomplishes by naming so many subject areas in the title?

---

*Definitions for all terms marked with an asterisk may be found in the Glossary.

5. What device does Alexander use as an introduction to her essay? What does this device accomplish? Does it foreshadow* the thesis? Does it attract the reader's interest?

6. During his presidency, John F. Kennedy purportedly had a liaison with a woman who, at the same time, was engaged in a liaison with a Mafia leader. The Kennedy liaison was halted when J. Edgar Hoover showed the president the FBI file on the matter and pointed out the dangers of the situation for internal and external U.S. affairs. The FBI did not make the files public. Should they have done so? Explain your answer.

7. During their tenure in office, John and Robert Kennedy gave the FBI permission to wiretap and use other surveillance techniques on Martin Luther King, Jr. The Federal Courts have ruled that the material collected must be put under seal and not divulged to the public. Should absolute candor be practiced in this case? Should the files be made public? Why, or why not?

8. At the time that Alexander wrote her essay, information about the Kennedy/FBI situation and the King/FBI situation were in the public domain. Why do you think Alexander did not cite these incidents as examples of how FBI secrecy can hamper our ability to govern ourselves wisely?
   a. On "60 Minutes," Alexander represents the liberal viewpoint in a weekly confrontation with conservative James J. Kilpatrick. Might her liberal background cause her to be uncritical of a Democratic president and a civil rights leader but highly critical of the FBI and CIA? Might authors' value systems cause them to select certain examples and omit others?
   b. Should an author give only the evidence that supports his or her thesis, or should an author give all the evidence available, whether it aids the author in making a point or not? To what extent is an author's bias acceptable?

9. What does Wilson contend would have happened if the public had been given evidence that Cubans assassinated Kennedy?

10. The early 1960s was a period of strong anti-Communist feeling and a time of great belief in the invincibility of the United States. Imagine that, during that period, you were a member of a small committee that knew Kennedy actually was assassinated by

---

*Definitions for all terms marked with an asterisk may be found in the Glossary.

Cubans acting under orders from their government. Given the temper of the times and the possibility of nuclear war with Russia, would you have advised that the truth be published? Why, or why not?

11. Alexander says that in order for a democratic system of government to work there can be no enduring secrets. On the other hand, Wilson points out that publishing the truth can sometimes lead to undesirable and destructive results.
    a. Should a truth be told if that truth would cause harm to innocent people?
    b. Should a truth be told if its publication might cause world-wide nuclear war?
    c. Should a truth be told if it would jeopardize the career of an individual who would have a great potential for benefiting society if allowed to continue working? Consider, for example, the Kennedy/Hoover exchange or the King/FBI situation.
    d. On a more personal level, do you sometimes tell "white lies" to protect people? Should you?

READING AND WRITING SUGGESTIONS

1. Alexander characterized the right *not* to know as "one of life's sweetest comforts." Someone else has made the same point by saying, "The truth shall set you free, but freedom will break your heart." Write a brief cause-and-effect essay about a situation in which telling the truth caused pain and decide whether the truth should have been withheld in that particular situation.

2. Read some books or articles describing the affair of Lucy Mercer and Franklin D. Roosevelt, for example, *Eleanor and Franklin*, by Joseph Lash. The affair occurred in the 1925–1940 period but was not revealed until the '60s and '70s. Write a brief cause-and-effect essay in which you speculate on how revealing the truth about the affair would have affected Roosevelt's career, and, in turn, the history of the United States, and the history of the world.

THE HUMAN USE
OF LANGUAGE

Lawrence Langer

Lawrence Langer (1929–), a professor of English at Simmons College, received his undergraduate degree at City College of New York and his M.A. and Ph.D. degrees at Harvard University. He is the author of The Holocaust and the Literary Imagination. *In this essay, Langer shows how the misuse of language complicates the already difficult task of communicating.*

A friend of mine recently turned in a paper to a course on behavior modification. She had tried to express in simple English some of her reservations about this increasingly popular approach to education. She received it back with the comment: "Please rewrite this in behavioral terms."

It is little wonder that human beings have so much trouble saying what they feel, when they are told that there is a specialized vocabulary for saying what they think. The language of simplicity and spontaneity is forced to retreat behind the barricades of an official prose developed by a few experts who believe that jargon is the most precise means of communication. The results would be comic, if they were not so poisonous; unfortunately, there is an attitude toward the use of language that is impervious to human need and drives some people back into silence when they realize the folly of risking human words on insensitive ears.

The comedy is easy to come by. Glancing through my friend's textbook on behavior modification, I happened on a chapter beginning with the following challenging statement: "Many of the problems encountered by teachers in the daily management of their classes could be resolved if. . . ." Although I was a little wary of the phrase "daily management," I was encouraged to plunge ahead, because as an educator I have always been interested in ideas for improving learning. So I plunged. The entire sentence reads: "Many of the problems encountered by teachers in the daily management of their classes could be resolved if the emission of desirable student behaviors was increased."

Emission? At first I thought it was a misprint for "omission," but the omission of desirable student behaviors (note the plural) hardly seemed an appropriate goal for educators. Then I considered the possibility of metaphor, both erotic and automotive, but these didn't seem to fit, either. A footnote clarified the matter: " 'Emission' is a technical term used in behavioral analysis. The verb, 'to emit,' is used specifically with a certain category of behavior called 'operant behavior.' Operant behaviors are modified by their consequences. Operant behaviors correspond closely to the behavior colloquially referred to as voluntary." Voluntary? Is jargon then an attack on freedom of the will?

Of course, this kind of abuse of language goes on all the time— within the academic world, one regrets to say, as well as outside it. Why couldn't the author of this text simply say that we need to motivate students to learn willingly? The more I read such non-human prose, and try to avoid writing it myself, the more I am convinced that we must be in touch with ourselves before we can use words to touch others.

Using language meaningfully requires risk; the sentence I have just quoted takes no risks at all. Much of the discourse that poses as communication in our society is really a decoy to divert our audience (and often ourselves) from that shadowy plateau where our real life hovers on the precipice of expression. How many people, for example, have the courage to walk up to someone they like and actually *say* to them: "I'm very fond of you, you know"?

Such honesty reflects the use of language as revelation, and that sort of revelation, brimming with human possibilities, is risky precisely because it invites judgment and rebuff. Perhaps this is one reason why, especially in academe, we are confronted daily with so much neutral prose: Our students are not yet in touch with themselves; not especially encouraged by us, their instructors, to move in that direction; they are encouraged indeed to expect judgment and hence perhaps rebuff, too, in our evaluation of them. Thus they instinctively retreat behind the anonymity of abstract diction and technical jargon to protect themselves against us—but also, as I have suggested, against themselves.

This problem was crystallized for me recently by an encounter only peripherally related to the issue. As part of my current research, I have been interviewing children of concentration-camp survivors. One girl I have been meeting with says that her mother does not like to talk about the experience, *except with other survivors*. Risk is diminished when we know in advance that our audience shares with us a sympathy for our theme. The nakedness of pain *and* the nakedness of love require gentle responses. So this survivor is reticent, except with fellow victims.

But one day a situation arose which tempted her to the human use of language although she could not be sure, in advance, of the reception her words would receive. We all recognize it. This particular woman, at the age of 40, decided to return to school to get a college degree. Her first assignment in freshman composition was to write a paper on something that was of great importance to her personally. The challenge was immense; the risk was even greater. For the first time in 20 years, she resolved to confront a silence in her life that she obviously needed to rouse to speech.

She was 14 when the Germans invaded Poland. When the roundup of the Jews began a year later, some Christian friends sent their young daughter to "call for her" one day, so that they might hide her. A half hour later, the friends went themselves to pick up her parents, but during that interval, a truck had arrived, loaded aboard the Jewish mother and father—and the daughter never saw them or heard from them again. Their fate we can imagine. The girl herself was eventually arrested, survived several camps, and after the war came to America. She married, had children of her own, and except for occasional reminiscences with fellow survivors, managed to live adequately without diving into her buried personal past. Until one day her instructor in English composition touched a well-insulated nerve, and it began to throb with a painful impulse to express. I present verbatim the result of that impulse, a paper called "People I Have Forgotten":

> Can you forget your own Father and Mother? If so—how or why?
>
> I thought I did. To mention their names, for me is a great emotional struggle. The brutal force of this reality shakes my whole body and mind, wrecking me into ugly splinters; each crying to be mended anew. So the silence I maintain about their memory is only physical and valid as such but not true. I could never forget my parents, nor do I want to do it. True, I seldom talk about them with my husband or my children. How they looked, who they were, why they perished during the war. The love and sacrifices they have made for me during their lifetime, never get told.
>
> The cultural heritage to which each generation is entitled to have access to seems to be nonexistant [sic], since I dare not talk about anything relating to my past, my parents.
>
> This awful, awesome power of not-remembering, this heart-breaking sensation of the conspiracy of silence is my dilemma.

> Often, I have tried to break through my imprisoning wall of irrational silence, but failed: now I hope to be able to do it.
>
> Until now, I was not able to face up to the loss of my parents, much less talk about them. The smallest reminder of them would set off a chain reaction of results that I could anticipate but never direct. The destructive force of sadness, horror, fright would then become my master. And it was this subconscious knowledge that kept me paralyzed with silence, not a conscious desire to forget my parents.
>
> My silent wall, my locked shell existed only of real necessity; I needed time.
>
> I needed time to forget the tragic loss of my loved ones, time to heal my emotional wound so that there shall come a time when I can again remember the people I have forgotten.

The essay is not a confrontation, only a prelude, yet it reveals qualities which are necessary for the human use of language: In trying to reach her audience, the author must touch the deepest part of herself. She risks self-exposure—when we see the instructor's comment, we will realize how great was her risk—and she is prepared for judgment and perhaps even rebuff, although I doubt whether she was prepared for the form they took. This kind of prose, for all its hesitant phraseology, throws down a gauntlet to the reader, a challenge asking him to understand that life is pain as well as plenty, chaos as well as form. Its imagery of locked shells and imprisoning walls hints at a silent world of horror and sadness far less enchanting than the more familiar landscape of love where most of us dwell. Language is a two-edged tool, to pierce the wall which hides that world, or build high abstract barriers to protect us from its threats.

The instructor who graded the paper I have just read preferred walls to honest words. At the bottom of the last page she scrawled a large "D-minus," emphatically surrounded by a circle. Her only comment was: "Your theme is not clear—you should have developed your 1st paragraph. You talk around your subject." At this moment, two realms collide: a universe of unarticulated feeling seeking expression (and the courage and encouragement to express) and a nature made so immune to feeling by heaven-knows-what that she hides behind the tired, tired language of the professional theme-corrector.

Suddenly we realize that reading as well as writing requires risks, and that the metaphor of insulation, so central to the efforts of the Polish woman survivor to re-establish contact with her past, is a metaphor governing the response of readers, too. Some writing, like "the emission of desirable student behaviors," thickens the insulation that already separates the reader from the words that throw darts at his armor of indifference. But even when language unashamedly reveals the feeling that is hidden behind the words, it must contend with a different kind of barrier, the one behind which our instructor lies concealed, unwilling or unable to hear a human voice and return a human echo of her own.

Ironically, the victor in this melancholy failure at communication is the villain of the piece, behavior modification. For the Polish survivor wrote her next theme on an innocuous topic, received a satisfactory grade, and never returned to the subject of her parents. The instructor, who had encountered a problem in the daily management of her class in the form of an essay which she could not respond to in a human way, altered the attitude of her student by responding in a non-human way, thus resolving her problem by increasing the emission of desirable student behavior. The student now knows how vital it is to develop her first paragraph, and how futile it is to reveal her first grief.

Even more, she has learned the danger of talking around her subject: She not only refuses to talk *around* it now, she refuses to talk *about* it. Thus the human use of language leads back to silence—where perhaps it should have remained in the first place.

QUESTIONS

1. What does the title of the essay tell you about the thesis* and central conflict in the narrative?

2. Langer uses two well-developed examples to illustrate his thesis. How does he connect each with the thesis? How does he make the transition between them?

3. What sentence did the author of the textbook on behavior modification use to convey the idea that "we need to motivate students to learn more willingly"? What is your judgment of the textbook author's sentence?

4. Langer uses figurative language frequently. Identify five instances.

5. a. Briefly summarize the concentration-camp survivor's paper. What grade and comment did the instructor write on the paper? Can you think of a reason other than the one Langer gives

---

*Definitions for all terms marked with an asterisk may be found in the Glossary.

that explains why the instructor responded to the paper in this way?

b. What effect did the instructor's response have? What did the student do in later themes? What might have happened if the instructor had written "A , a beautiful story. I'm proud of you and honored to know you"? What might the student's next theme have been like?

c. Should we praise students when they express their true feelings, no matter how awkwardly they do so? Should we praise instructors when they forget mechanics and concentrate on recognizing students' deep feelings with tenderness and respect? Should we criticize instructors who are insensitive to students? What might be some effects of such praise and reproof?

6. The main idea of behavior modification is to use rewards and punishment to get people to act in a way that is considered desirable. In answering question 5, you probably came out in favor of expressing praise for a student's openness and an instructor's responsiveness and expressing reproof for an instructor's insensitivity. If you did so, you were advocating something very similar to behavior modification.

a. Are you in favor of using behavior modification to obtain what you consider desirable effects?

b. Langer says that "the victor in this melancholy failure at communication is the villain of the piece, behavior modification." Which is the villain—behavior modification or the instructor's values and goals, which, in Langer's opinion, are misguided? Can a neutral tool be a villain, or is the villain the person who misuses such a tool?

READING AND WRITING SUGGESTIONS

1. Write a brief cause-and-effect essay showing how someone's failure to understand kept you from taking a chance and sharing something you really felt deeply about. Describe the effect this failure in understanding had on you.

2. Read a book about language usage, such as Edwin Newman's *Strictly Speaking: Will America Be the Death of English?* Write a brief cause-and-effect essay about words that interfere with communication between people.

Comparison and Contrast

Comparisons show how two or more things are similar; *contrasts,* the reverse of comparisons, show how things are different. Comparison and contrast has three main uses. First, it can be used to explain the nature of a thing more fully. For example, it is easier to comprehend what the term "female" means when it is compared and contrasted with the term "male." The second purpose for which comparison and contrast is used is to determine the superiority of one thing over another. In deciding whether to buy a Ford Pinto or a Ford LTD, for example, it would be advisable to compare and contrast the two cars in terms of such features as cost, gas mileage, durability, and safety in order to decide which of the two would best suit your needs. Third, it is sometimes possible to use comparison and contrast to suggest the causes of a condition or an event. If you wanted to discover why children were being born with a specific birth defect, you would probably begin your search by comparing and contrasting the backgrounds of such children's parents—examining their family histories, finding out what medication the mothers took during pregnancy, etc. You would, of course, be looking for a common element in the backgrounds of the parents, because this might be a cause of the birth defect.

Comparison-and-contrast essays may be organized in two ways: subject by subject or point by point. If you were using the subject-by-subject pattern, you would first give all the information about one of the subjects of the essay and then all the information about the next subject. For example, you would discuss all the pros and cons of the Ford Pinto and then present all the corresponding information about the LTD. In a point-by-point essay, you would deal consecutively with each point of comparison, showing how the subjects of the essay compared and contrasted in each area. If you were discussing the relative merits of the two cars, you would first compare and contrast their cost, then discuss how they compared in gas mileage, and so on.

There are five special requirements for using comparison and contrast effectively. First, the subjects being weighed against each other must relate in a meangful way to the purpose of the essay. If you were attempting to determine which of two cars was the better buy, it would be useless to compare a Pinto and a bicycle. But this *would* be a useful comparison if you were weighing the virtues and drawbacks of different *forms of transportation.*

Second, the points of comparison also should bear a direct relationship to the purpose of the essay. If you were considering which of three cars was most economical, you would want to use original cost, maintenance costs, and probable resale value as points of comparison—not the beauty or comfort of the cars.

Third, when using comparison and contrast to determine the cause of a condition or an event, you should try to ascertain whether the similarities between the things being compared are logically related to the cause. If, for example, you were comparing the backgrounds of parents of children with birth defects and you discovered that all the parents had eaten hamburgers at one time or another, you should not automatically assume that this similarity meant that the hamburgers were the cause of the problem.

Fourth, all conclusions arrived at through a comparison must be accurately qualified. If Pintos are as comfortable as LTDs—but only for persons under six feet tall—this qualification should be clearly noted.

Fifth, subjects should be compared on all relevant points of comparison. If the point of your paper is to show that car X is more economical than car Y, it would be unfair to quote only car X's lower purchase price, omitting the fact that the maintenance costs for car X are higher than those for car Y.

Analogy is a specific type of comparison which explains a difficult or inaccessible thing by comparing it with a simpler, more familiar thing. For example, the role of the president of the United States has often been compared with the role of a ship's captain. Needless to say, the two roles are not identical, but it is easier to visualize the more abstract role of the president when we imagine him at the helm, steering the ship of state through the rough seas of national crisis. However, it is essential that analogies not be carried too far; the fact that two things are similar in some ways does not mean that they are similar in all respects. The passengers of the ship of state, for example, cannot be unloaded in a foreign port like the passengers on a sailing vessel.

THE WHISTLE

Benjamin Franklin

*Benjamin Franklin (1706–1790), one of the most distinguished fig-
ures in American history, was a man of numerous and varied talents.
Among many other accomplishments, he founded America's first
circulating library, studied lightning, electricity, earthquakes, and
the Gulf Stream, and gained fame as an inventor and writer. He also
had a distinguished political career, becoming one of the signers of
the Declaration of Independence.* Poor Richard's Almanac *is his
best-known work. In "The Whistle," he uses a childhood experience
as an analogy to comment on the relative value of the things people
desire and seek in life.*

When I was a child, at seven years old, my friends on a holiday filled
my pockets with coppers. I went directly to a shop where they sold
toys for children; and, being charmed with the sound of a whistle,
that I met by the way in the hands of another boy, I voluntarily
offered him all my money for one. I then came home, and went
whistling all over the house, much pleased with my whistle, but
disturbing all the family. My brothers and sisters and cousins, understanding the bargain I had made, told me I had given four times as
much for it as it was worth. This put me in mind what good things I
might have bought with the rest of the money; and they laughed at
me so much for my folly that I cried with vexation; and the reflection
gave me more chagrin than the whistle gave me pleasure.

This, however, was afterwards of use to me, the impression continuing on my mind, so that often, when I was tempted to buy some
unnecessary thing, I said to myself, "Don't give too much for the
whistle"; and so I saved my money.

As I grew up, came into the world, and observed the actions of
men, I thought I met with many, very many, who gave too much for
the whistle.

When I saw any one too ambitious of court favor, sacrificing his
time in attendance on levees[1], his repose, his liberty, his virtue, and

---

1. Receptions.

perhaps his friends, to attain it, I have said to myself, "This man gave too much for his whistle."

If I knew a miser, who gave up every kind of comfortable living, all the pleasure of doing good to others, all the esteem of his fellow-citizens, and the joys of benevolent friendship, for the sake of accumulating wealth; "Poor man," says I, "you do indeed pay too much for your whistle."

When I meet a man of pleasure, sacrificing every laudable improvement of the mind, or of his fortune, to mere corporeal sensations; "Mistaken man," says I, "you are providing pain for yourself instead of pleasure; you give too much for your whistle."

If I see one fond of fine clothes, fine furniture, fine equipages, all above his fortune, for which he contracts debts, and ends his career in prison; "Alas," says I, "he has paid dear, very dear, for his whistle."

When I see a beautiful, sweet-tempered girl, married to an ill-natured brute of a husband; "What a pity it is," says I, "that she has paid so much for a whistle."

In short, I conceived that great part of the miseries of mankind were brought upon them by the false estimates they had made of the value of things, and by their giving too much for their whistles.

QUESTIONS

1. *Gullible, innocent, inexperienced,* and *dumb* are all terms that can be used to describe someone who "paid too much for a whistle." Some of these terms are harsh and some are not. Choose two harsh terms and two euphemisms* for these terms.

2. What sentence in the essay contains Franklin's thesis statement?* What phrase signals that this is a thesis statement?

3. Franklin uses his experience with the whistle as an analogy.*
   a. What idea does he use this analogy to portray?
   b. To what other situations does he apply this idea?

4. Franklin thought he paid too much for the toy that he bought.
   a. Did he really pay too much, or did he acquire something else along with the whistle that made the purchase worthwhile?
   b. Tell about two times when you (or someone you know) appeared to make a mistake that turned out to be a blessing in disguise.

---

*Definitions for all terms marked with an asterisk may be found in the Glossary.

5. Consider Franklin's comments about the ambitious person, the miser, the man of pleasure, the materialist, and the young wife.
   a. If the people described valued the things they bartered for, did they really pay too much for their whistles?
   b. Is the worth of something absolute? That is, does worth depend on what the buyer values and wants—the buyer's value system?

READING AND WRITING SUGGESTIONS

1. Write a brief essay using an analogy to tell about a time when you (or someone you know) paid more than something was worth. Describe whether the experience had positive or negative effects on the subsequent behavior of the person involved.

2. Reread or recall the story of *Jack and the Beanstalk*. Take one of the following statements as your thesis: Jack paid too much for his whistle, or Jack's whistle was worth the price he paid. Write a brief essay on the subject, using an analogy to develop your thesis.

<u>HAYWIRE</u>: A REVIEW

Lois Gould

Lois Gould, a contemporary novelist and essayist, is the author of Such Good Friends, Necessary Objects, Final Analysis, *and* A Sea-Change. *She has also written two nonfiction books, and is a frequent contributor to the* New York Times, *to* New York *and* Ms. *magazines, and to other publications. In the following review of Brooke Hayward's* Haywire, *Gould contrasts the fantasy life a woman tried to create for her children with the realities that finally pierced that fantasy.*

Here we are, home again, in the land of our beautiful and damned. Again raking over the golden surface, so bright that it blinds the heart. Again probing, deep within, for the sources of pain. By now we all admit what we are doing here—why we can never resist another true account of how bad it was, how few survived. We never cease to marvel at the scars. Hollywood was our life-forming habit. Those of us born before the 1960's were all casualties of make-believe —those who made it no less than those who merely believed it.

Haywire is a Hollywood childhood memoir, a glowing tapestry spun with equal parts of gold and pain. As a book it is an absolute beauty—a Hollywood beauty, to be precise—with all the charm that term implies, the deceptive simplicity, the complex hidden machinery and, above all, the terrible cost.

Its author, Brooke Hayward, is one of the star-crossed children that Hollywood, the land of our beautiful and damned, produced in its most flamboyantly glamorous time—the late 1930's and 40's. Her mother was the actress Margaret Sullavan, an angel of light with straight gold bangs, an irresistible crooked grin, a husky voice with a breaking heart in it, and more talent and drive than she ever dared let loose. Father was Leland Hayward, the "gentleman agent" and later Broadway producer, who taught Fred Astaire how to dress and whom Katharine Hepburn called "the most wonderful man in the world"—even after he ended their romance to marry Margaret Sullavan. In the manner of show-biz types (before the rest of us began doing it too), Margaret Sullavan had been married before to Henry Fonda and William Wyler, and after Hayward she married Kenneth Wagg, an English businessman. Hayward married five times altogether. But this book is not about the love lives of the stars. Nor is it about how the rich and famous are different from you and me. It is, rather, about the need for simple truth instead of magic between people who love each other, especially parents and children. Without such truths, the senses dull, time warps, and in the gathering twilight people begin to mistake one another for gods.

It is the children of such twilight gods whom we meet and fall in love with in the course of *Haywire*. With Brooke, the eldest, the rebel; with Bridget, her exquisite porcelain sister; and with their reckless baby brother Bill—"tiger cubs, tumbling in a heap on the mossy floor of some exotic jungle." By the time Brooke is 23, Bridget is dead at 21, possibly by her own hand; their incandescent mother is dead, too— also, possibly, a suicide; Bill is a scarred veteran of mental institutions; and Brooke herself is sifting through the glittering shards of their beautiful lost life together—searching for clues to how such a family could have destroyed itself.

The clues, of course, were everywhere, but nowhere so tellingly as in the battle Margaret Sullivan fought to play a perfect wife-and-mother instead of a star. So terrified was she of the price of public life that she turned her private life—and that of her husband and children —into a glorious light comedy that should have run forever. Unfortunately, life does not imitate art, after all.

One of the most poignant moments in the book occurs when her teen-aged children finally meet the dangerous woman from whom Margaret Sullavan has so fiercely guarded them—herself. The confrontation takes place on opening night of *The Deep Blue Sea* in 1952. She was returning, triumphantly, to Broadway after nine years of self-imposed exile. As Brooke recalls it:

"We were unprepared. We had no idea, no idea at all. She was absolutely wonderful. . . . Exposed to every nuance, every trick in her performances at home, we were primed to pick her performance on stage to pieces. Set on a stage all the tricks fell into place. Gestures, movements, voice inflections that might seem a shade too broad, too histrionic for the business of everyday life were totally right when mounted on a proscenium, bathed in intense light, and viewed from a distance of thirty-odd feet. We were shocked that she had ever given up—for whatever reason, even if it happened to be us —a profession at which she excelled.

" 'Damn,' I growled out of the corner of my mouth at intermission, 'it works better here than in life.' Bridget jabbed at my ribs with her elbow. But it was true. I resented Mother for alleging that her talent was less important than the happiness of her three children. Given a choice, we would have been just as happy all these years if we could have cued her and watched her go out where she belonged."

Later, Brooke tells her mother this, to her face. "Now we feel gypped," she says. Her mother replies:

" '*Gypped!*' She swung around, her voice cracking with amusement.

" 'Well,' I gulped, thoroughly excited by my daring—'cheated. You are Margaret Sullavan. What's wrong with that?' "

What was wrong was that Margaret Sullavan didn't trust it—not did she trust her family to survive and prosper if she, their mother, were free to be her own woman and they were free to know who that woman really was. In withholding that one essential truth, even from herself, she played them all false.

The irony is that her sacrifice should have backfired so devastatingly. The harder she tried to cast everyone in their assigned roles —to deny their individual needs to be Leland Hayward, Brooke, Bridget and Bill, or Margaret Sullavan—the more fiercely each was forced to fight for freedom, self-definition, survival. Their need to break out of her fantasy of family life erupted in quirky, bizarre or savagely self-destructive ways. Leland Hayward, man-about-

Hollywood, bon vivant, "Toscanini of the telephone," was badly miscast in the role of home-loving country squire. But Margaret moved the family out of unwholesome California, settled them in rustic Connecticut, and forbade Leland to conduct his beloved business during family time. As Jules Stein, founder of MCA, the talent agency, and an old friend, told Brooke, years later: ". . . [your mother] insisted that he could not have any telephone calls, and he just couldn't stand it . . . he used to go to the . . . country store, maybe half a mile away, and call up the office to find out what was going on. The theatrical world and the agency world was his world. It was his life. I was amused by your mother's attempts to keep Leland in line. I think if she hadn't done that she still would have been married to him until he died." Uprooted and trapped inside a long-running, family-fun-filled production of *Life With Father*, Leland developed violent allergies to the flowers, the isolation, the fresh country air, everything in that wholesome alien environment—including, inevitably, his wife.

Margaret Sullavan had difficulty admitting her mistakes. She was so certain about what life should be, and particularly what her children's lives should be, that she could not even acknowledge the signs of serious trouble when they began: Bridget withdrew into ever-lengthening silences, refusing to eat, refusing to play, refusing to be what she was "expected" to be. Bill smeared his walls with toothpaste, his floor with Vaseline; lied his way to 13 successive spankings over a single incident; set small fires; he was cutting small jagged holes in that hermetically sealed world, if only to breathe.

Yet the things their mother wanted for them were the stuff of fairytales and American dreams. She wanted to give them a world of love and beauty, homemade by her own hands. She took charge of their education on the ground that "the entire California school system was inadequate." A private tutor was summoned daily to the house, and, says Brooke, "we cut our teeth on the most beautiful books she and Mother could find, such as 'Tanglewood Tales' and 'Sinbad the Sailor'. . . . My entire concept of what the world looked like and what life promised was shaped by the sensuous textures and sinuous lines of [Edmond] Dulac's fantasies, the exotic blues and purples and thick-lipped heavy-lidded sentinels of slender youth that populated Maxfield Parrish's visions. Bridget and I learned to read quickly and voraciously."

A visit to New York City's Museum of Natural History expressed in microcosm the Hayward children's introduction to reality through their mother's eyes, voice and spellbinding sense of theater: " 'Now, look—look!' she exclaimed, her eyes widening with excitement and her magical voice stretching until it seemed it might snap and carry us with it, so that we sighted down her outstretched hand, with its crimson enameled nails glistening like Fabergé charms, at the room that danced before us and at the gold-inscribed sarcophagi. . . ."

The one thing Mother could not teach them, however, was how to declare their independence from her—to strike out on their own. At mealtimes, everyone was expected to have "perfect manners, excellent appetites and stimulating non-stop conversation." Even being sick in bed had to be fun. Mother would hop into bed with them and read aloud until she was hoarse, or show them how to crayon and finger-paint. Life was perceived as "an exciting game, invented, explained and directed by Mother." The catch was that if they refused to play by Mother's rules, the game didn't work at all. Then too, there were moments when no one felt like playing—moments that grew increasingly frequent and bitter as time wore on. After Father left, creating the first irreparable crack in that perfect world, the children began to see how fragile the place was, after all, and how dangerous it would be to go on believing in it.

Father remarried; Mother did too. Bridget and Bill left their mother at ages 16 and 14. The parting was agonizingly bitter, and no one ever repaired that either. Bridget succumbed to a recurrent, unexplained illness marked by epileptic seizures and bouts of severe depression. Bill, rebellious and failing at school, was sent to one psychiatric clinic, then another. Brooke grew up to be a beauty, married and divorced twice, had two children, fooled around with modeling and acting, and finally discovered she was a writer.

Long after her parents' divorce and the younger children's heartbreaking defection, but not long before the sudden, shocking deaths, nine months apart, of Margaret Sullavan and Bridget, Brooke and her parents met in the driveway of her mother's Connecticut home, for a brief reunion. Bridget and Bill were both hospitalized, but there was still a sense of hope. Standing there, watching her parents, Brooke recalls another moment, 14 years earlier, on a summer evening when she was eight. She and Bill and Bridget had run away from home, armed with hard-boiled eggs and Cokes, and like most children, were ready to come back just in time for dinner. Now, she conjures up that homecoming, as she does a thousand other small buried treasures of her fairy-tale childhood—every color and taste with its joy intact, every stab of pain with the authentic sting of fresh tears:

"I climbed onto Father's gleaming shoes with my bare feet, and we swung clumsily across the grass, circling faster and faster until my legs flew out from under me and I howled at him, between convulsions of laughter, to stop or I'd wet my pants.

"The screen door banged; everyone else was going in to dinner. Father gradually lowered me toward the grass.

" 'Now make a wish,' he said, pointing my head toward the moon.

" 'What's yours?' I asked, rapidly discarding one idea after another.

" 'I've narrowed it down,' said Father. 'We stay here, right here in this very spot—here and now—for the rest of our lives.' "

Like most wishes it never came true. Brooke, one of the last two survivors of that lovely, lost family, blames emotional extravagance and extraordinary "carelessness," in a conscious echo of F. Scott Fitzgerald's *The Great Gatsby*. Perhaps she is right, but I did not read it that way. Margaret Sullavan, a woman—far more than a star—of her time, cared, if anything, too much. So much that she built them a make-believe world in which to escape, not only from Hollywood, but from her own brilliant secret self. She wanted to spare them all the mortal risk of being truer to the self than to one another. No one could have escaped. No one ever does.

QUESTIONS

1. Explain what the following expressions mean as Gould uses them:
   —"a glowing tapestry spun with equal parts of gold and pain"
   —"as a book it is . . . a Hollywood beauty"
   —"she played them all false"

2. In this essay, Gould contrasts the artificial world that Margaret Sullavan tried to create for her family with the reality of their characters and their lives.
   a. What were the things that Margaret Sullavan wished to give her children?
   b. What roles did she want her husband and children to play?
   c. What role did she want to play?
   d. Compare and contrast these roles with reality. What was each member of the family really like? How did each finally react to the role he or she was forced to play?

3. Describe a role that you have seen a person act out. How did the role contrast with the real character and situation of that person?

4. Think about a time when you acted a role, behaving as others expected you to behave. Compare and contrast this experience with a time when you acted in a way consistent with your own character.
   a. Were there differences in the way you responded to other people?

b. Which made you happier—acting a role or being yourself?

c. Did you get more tense when you played the role? How long could you have kept it up?

READING AND WRITING SUGGESTIONS

1. Consider the phrase, "the mortal risk of being truer to the self than to one another." Write a brief essay comparing and contrasting the lives of people who are essentially "true to themselves" with the lives of people who are more essentially "true to one another."

2. Gould writes, "Margaret Sullavan, a woman of her time, cared, if anything, too much." Read Betty Friedan's *The Feminine Mystique*, which shows the attitudes about women, motherhood, family, and togetherness that were prevalent in the 1940s and the 1950s. Write a brief essay describing the attitudes that Margaret Sullavan was trying to embody and comparing these attitudes to those of the 1960s and 1970s.

FROM POPPING THE QUESTION TO POPPING THE PILL

Margaret Mead

Margaret Mead (1901–), a respected cultural anthropologist, holds honorary degrees from twelve universities. She is in demand as a speaker and lecturer and has taught at some of the country's great universities, including Stanford, the University of California, Harvard, and Yale. Mead is the author or editor of twenty-nine books, of which Coming of Age in Samoa, *published in 1928, is generally considered her classic work. In recent years, having turned her attention to problems and changes in American culture, she has become an authority on life in contemporary society. Here Mead examines the customs surrounding modern courtship and marriage, comparing these rituals with the customs of the past.*

There have been major changes in attitudes toward courtship and marriage among those middle-class, educated Americans who are celebrated in the media and who are style setters for American life. Courtship was once a regular part of American life; it was a long period, sometimes lasting for many years, and also a tentative one, during which a future husband or wife could still turn back but during which their relationship became more and more exclusive and socially recognized. Courtship both preceded the announcement of an engagement and followed the announcement, although a broken engagement was so serious that it could be expected to throw the girl into a depression from which she might never recover.

There were definite rules governing the courtship period, from the "bundling" permitted in early New England days, when young couples slept side by side with all their clothes on, to strict etiquette that prescribed what sort of gifts a man might give his fiancée in circles where expensive presents were customary. Gifts had to be either immediately consumable, like candy or flowers, or indestructible, like diamonds—which could be given back, their value unimpaired, if there was a rift in the relationship. Objects that could be damaged by use, like gloves and furs, were forbidden. A gentleman might call for a lady in a cab or in his own equipage, but it was regarded as inappropriate for him to pay for her train fare if they went on a journey.

How much chaperoning was necessary, and how much privacy the courting couple was allowed, was a matter of varying local custom. Long walks home through country lanes after church and sitting up in the parlor after their elders had retired for the night may have been permitted, but the bride was expected to be a virgin at marriage. The procedure for breaking off an engagement, which included the return of letters and photographs, was a symbolic way of stating that an unconsummated relationship could still be erased from social memory.

The wedding day was the highest point in a girl's life—a day to which she looked forward all her unmarried days and to which she looked back for the rest of her life. The splendor of her wedding, the elegance of dress and veil, the cutting of the cake, the departure amid a shower of rice and confetti, gave her an accolade of which no subsequent event could completely rob her. Today people over 50 years of age still treat their daughter's wedding this way, prominently displaying the photographs of the occasion. Until very recently, all brides' books prescribed exactly the same ritual they had prescribed 50 years before. The etiquette governing wedding presents—gifts that were or were not appropriate, the bride's maiden initials on her linen—was also specified. For the bridegroom the wedding represented the end of his free, bachelor days, and the bachelor dinner the right before the wedding symbolized this loss of freedom. A woman who did not marry—even if she had the alibi of a fiancé who had been killed in war or had abilities and charm and money of her own—was always at a social disadvantage, while an eligible bachelor was sought after by hostess after hostess.

Courtship ended at the altar, as the bride waited anxiously for the bridegroom who might not appear or might have forgotten the ring. Suppliant gallantry was replaced overnight by a reversal of roles, the wife now becoming the one who read her husband's every frown with anxiety lest she displease him.

This set of rituals established a rhythm between the future husband and wife and between the two sets of parents who would later become co-grandparents. It was an opportunity for mistakes to be corrected; and if the parents could not be won over, there was, as a last resort, elopement, in which the young couple proclaimed their desperate attraction to each other by flouting parental blessing. Each part of the system could be tested out for a marriage that was expected to last for life. We have very different ways today.

Since World War I, changes in relationships between the sexes have been occurring with bewildering speed. The automobile presented a challenge to chaperonage that American adults met by default. From then on, except in ceremonial and symbolic ways, chaperonage disappeared, and a style of premarital relationship was set up in which the onus was put on the girl to refuse inappropriate requests, while each young man declared his suitability by asking for favors that he did not expect to receive. The disappearance of chaperonage was facilitated by the greater freedom of middle-aged women, who began to envy their daughters' freedom, which they had never had. Social forms went through a whole series of rapid changes: The dance with formal partners and programs gave way to occasions in which mothers, or daughters, invited many more young men than girls, and the popular girl hardly circled the dance floor twice in the same man's arms. Dating replaced courtship—not as a prelude to anything but rather as a way of demonstrating popularity. Long engagements became increasingly unfashionable, and a series of more tentative commitments became more popular. As college education became the norm for millions of young people, "pinning" became a common stage before engagement. The ring was likely to appear just before the wedding day. And during the 1950's more and more brides got married while pregnant—but they still wore the long white veil, which was a symbol of virginity.

In this conservative, security-minded decade love became less important than marriage, and lovers almost disappeared from parks and riverbanks as young people threatened each other: "Either you marry me now, or I'll marry someone else." Courtship and dating were embraced by young people in lower grades in school, until children totally unready for sex were enmeshed by the rituals of pairing off. Marriage became a necessity for everyone, for boys as well as for girls: Mothers worried if their sons preferred electronic equipment or chess to girls and pushed their daughters relentlessly into marriage. Divorce became more and more prevalent, and people who felt their marriages were failing began to worry about whether they ought to get a divorce, divorce becoming a duty to an unfulfilled husband or to children exposed to an unhappy marriage. Remarriage was expected, until finally, with men dying earlier than women, there were no men left to marry. The United States became the most married country in the world. Children, your own or adopted, were just as essential, and the suburban life-style—each nuclear family isolated in its own home, with several children, a station wagon and a country-club membership—became the admired life-style, displayed in magazines for the whole world to see.

By the early sixties there were signs of change. We discovered we were running out of educated labor, and under the heading of self-fulfillment educated married women were being tempted back into the labor market. Young people began to advocate frankness and honesty, rebelling against the extreme hypocrisy of the 1950s, when religious and educational institutions alike connived to produce pregnancies that would lead to marriage. Love as an absorbing feeling for another person was rediscovered as marriage as a goal for every girl and boy receded into the background.

A series of worldwide political and ecological events facilitated these changes. Freedom for women accompanied agitation for freedom for blacks, for other minorities, for the Third World, for youth, for gay people. Zero-population growth became a goal, and it was no longer unfashionable to admit one did not plan to have children, or perhaps even to marry. The marriage age rose a little, the number of children fell a little. The enjoyment of pornography and use of obscenity became the self-imposed obligation of the emancipated women. Affirmative action catapulted many unprepared women into executive positions. Men, weary of the large families of the '50s, began to desert them; young mothers, frightened by the prospect of being deserted, pulled up stakes and left their suburban split-levels to try to make it in the cities. "Arrangements," or public cohabitation of young people with approval and support from their families, college deans and employers, became common.

By the early 1970s the doomsters were proclaiming that the family was dead. There were over 8,000,000 single-parent households, most of them headed by poorly paid women. There were endless discussions of "open marriages," "group marriages," communes in which the children were children of the group, and open discussion of previously taboo subjects, including an emphasis on female sexuality. Yet most Americans continued to live as they always had, with girls still hoping for a permanent marriage and viewing "arrangements" as stepping-stones to marriage. The much-publicized behavior of small but conspicuous groups filtered through the layers of society, so that the freedoms claimed by college youth were being claimed five years later by blue-collar youth; "swinging" (mate swapping) as a pastime of a bored upper-middle-class filtered down.

Perhaps the most striking change of all is that courtship is no longer a prelude to consummation. In many levels of contemporary society, sex relations require no prelude at all; the courtship that exists today tends to occur between a casual sex encounter and a later attempt by either the man or the woman to turn it into a permanent relationship. Courtship is also seen as an act in which either sex can take the lead. Women are felt to have an alternative to marriage, as once they had in the Middle Ages, when convent life was the choice of a large part of the population. Weddings are less conventional, although new conventions, like reading from Kahlil Gibran's *The Prophet,* spread very quickly. There is also a growing rebellion against the kind of town planning and housing that isolate young couples from the help of older people and friends that they need.

But the family is not dead. It is going through stormy times, and millions of children are paying the penalty of current disorganization, experimentation and discontent. In the process, the adults who should never marry are sorting themselves out. Marriage and parenthood are being viewed as a vocation rather than as the duty of every human being. As we seek more human forms of existence, the next question may well be how to protect our young people from a premature, pervasive insistence upon precocious sexuality, sexuality that contains neither love nor delight.

The birthrate is going up a little; women are having just as many babies as before, but having them later. The rights of fathers are being discovered and placed beside the rights of mothers. Exploitive and commercialized abortion mills are being questioned, and the Pill is proving less a panacea than was hoped. In a world troubled by economic and political instability, unemployment, highjacking, kid-napping and bombs, the preoccupation with private decisions is shifting to concern about the whole of humankind.

Active concern for the world permits either celibacy *or* marriage, but continuous preoccupation with sex leaves no time for anything else. As we used to say in the '20s, promiscuity, like free verse, is lacking in structure.

QUESTIONS

1. "Popping the question" and "popping the pill" are both idioms.*
   What does each phrase mean? What way of life does each idiom connote?*

2. Mead uses amusing parallelism* in her title.
   a. Give a more serious title that would describe the content of her essay.
   b. Why did she use the title she did?
   c. Which title—yours or her own—would she be more likely to use if she submitted her essay to the *Journal of Anthropological Research* or *Scientific American?*
   d. Which title would attract more people to her essay?
   e. Is it fair practice to use a catchy title to get people to read a serious work? Why, or why not?

3. Mead maintains that, over several generations, major changes have occurred in attitudes toward courtship and marriage and the customs that surround these two institutions.
   a. What are some attitudes and customs that have stayed the same?
   b. What are some attitudes and customs that have changed?
   c. Name some events that have facilitated, or at least accompanied, changes that have occurred.

4. One question that follows naturally from this essay is whether changes of various kinds make a difference in the quality of life.
   a. Now that the changes in courtship and marriage customs that Mead describes have occurred, are we better off? Worse off? About the same?
   b. Read Michael DeBakey's essay on page 28 about new developments in medicine. If the new developments he describes occur, will humanity be better off? Worse off? About the same?

---

*Definitions for all terms marked with an asterisk may be found in the Glossary.

   c. Did your answers to questions 4a and 4b differ? If they did, how did they differ? Why do you think they did?

5. Consider the trends that Mead presents in relation to your own generation's courtship and marriage experiences.
   a. Will your experiences differ from your parents' experiences? How?
   b. Will your experiences differ from your grandparents' experiences? How?
   c. Which set of experiences would you rather have: your generation's, your parents', or your grandparents'? Explain your answer.

READING AND WRITING SUGGESTIONS

1. Write a brief essay comparing and contrasting courtship and marriage attitudes and customs in three settings: the United States, another Western nation, and an Eastern nation. Do some research on the subject so that you can present your ideas in detail.

2. Read a book about life in the future, such as Alvin Toffler's *Future Shock*. Relate the information in Mead's essay about the present and the past with your reading about the future and write a brief essay comparing and contrasting courtship and marriage customs in the three periods of time.

THE GRADUATE STUDENT WHO BECAME A CHICANO

Richard Rodriguez

Richard Rodriguez (1944–) was teaching English at the University of California at Berkeley when he published this essay, which was adapted from an essay he submitted to a contest on graduate school experiences sponsored by the Wright Institute at Berkeley. In the essay, Rodriguez compares the Mexican culture he abandoned as a child with the mainstream American culture he adopted in its stead.

Today I am only technically the person I once felt myself to be—a Mexican-American, a Chicano. Partly because I had no way of comprehending my racial identity except in this technical sense, I gave up long ago the cultural consequences of being a Chicano.

The change came gradually but early. When I was beginning grade school, I noted to myself the fact that the classroom environment was so different in its styles and assumptions from my own family environment that survival would essentially entail a choice between both worlds. When I became a student, I was literally "remade"; neither I nor my teachers considered anything I had known before as relevant. I had to forget most of what my culture had provided, because to remember it was a disadvantage. The past and its cultural values became detachable, like a piece of clothing grown heavy on a warm day and finally put away.

Strangely, the discovery that I have been inattentive to my cultural past has arisen because others—student colleagues and faculty members—have started to assume that I am a Chicano. The ease with which the assumption is made forces me to suspect that the label is not meant to suggest cultural, but racial, identity. Nonetheless, as a graduate student and a prospective university faculty member, I am routinely expected to assume intellectual leadership *as a member of a racial minority*. Recently, for example, I heard the moderator of a panel discussion introduce me as "Richard Rodriguez, a Chicano intellectual." I wanted to correct the speaker—because I felt guilty representing a non-academic cultural tradition that I had willingly abandoned. So I can only guess what it would have meant to have retained my culture as I entered the classroom, what it would mean for me to be today a "Chicano intellectual." (The two words juxtaposed excite me; for years I thought a Chicano had to decide between being one or the other.)

Does the fact that I barely spoke any English until I was nine, or that as a child I felt a surge of self-hatred whenever a passing teenager would yell a racial slur, or that I saw my skin darken each summer— do any of these facts shape the ideas which I have or am capable of having? Today, I suspect they do—in ways I doubt the moderator who referred to me as a "Chicano intellectual" intended. The peculiar status of being a "Chicano intellectual" makes me grow restless at the thought that I have lost at least as much as I have gained through education.

I remember when, 20 years ago, two grammar-school nuns visited my childhood home. They had come to suggest—with more tact than was necessary, because my parents accepted without question the church's authority—that we make a greater effort to speak as much English around the house as possible. The nuns realized that my brothers and I led solitary lives largely because we were barely able to comprehend English in a school where we were the only Spanish-speaking students. My mother and father complied as best they could. Heroically, they gave up speaking to us in Spanish—the language that formed so much of the family's sense of intimacy in an alien world—and began to speak a broken English. Instead of Spanish sounds, I began hearing sounds that were new, harder, less friendly. More important, I was encouraged to respond in English.

The change in language was the most dramatic and obvious indication that I would become very much like the "gringo"—a term which was used descriptively rather than pejoratively in my home— and unlike the Spanish-speaking relatives who largely constituted my preschool world. Gradually, Spanish became a sound freighted with only a kind of sentimental significance, like the sound of the bedroom clock I listened to in my aunt's house when I spent the night. Just as gradually, English became the language I came not to *hear* because it was the language I used every day, as I gained access to a new, larger society. But the memory of Spanish persisted as a reminder of the society I had left. I can remember occasions when I entered a room and my parents were speaking to one another in Spanish; seeing me, they shifted into their more formalized English. Hearing them speak to me in English troubled me. The bonds their voices once secured were loosened by the new tongue.

This is not to suggest that I was being *forced* to give up my Chicano past. After the initial awkwardness of transition, I committed myself, fully and freely, to the culture of the classroom. Soon what I was learning in school was so antithetical to what my parents knew and did that I was careful about the way I talked about myself at the evening dinner table. Occasionally, there were moments of childish cruelty: a son's condescending to instruct either one of his parents about a "simple" point of English pronunciation or grammar.

Social scientists often remark, about situations such as mine, that children feel a sense of loss as they move away from their working-class identifications and models. Certainly, what I experienced, others have also—whatever their race. Like other generations of, say, Polish-American or Irish-American children coming home from college, I was to know the silence that ensues so quickly after the quick exchange of news and the dwindling of common interests.

In addition, however, education seemed to mean not only a gradual dissolving of familial and class ties but also a change of racial identity. The new language I spoke was only the most obvious reason for my associating the classroom with "gringo" society. The society I knew as Chicano was barely literate—in English *or* Spanish—and so impatient with either prolonged reflection or abstraction that I found the academic environment a sharp contrast. Sharpening the contrast was the stereotype of the Mexican as a mental inferior. (The fear of this stereotype has been so deep that only recently have I been willing to listen to those, like D. H. Lawrence, who celebrate the "noncerebral" Mexican as an alternative to the rational and scientific European man.) Because I did not know how to distinguish the healthy non-rationality of Chicano culture from the mental incompetency of which Chicanos were unjustly accused, I was willing to abandon my non-mental skills in order to disprove the racist's stereotype.

I was wise enough not to feel proud of the person education had helped me to become. I knew that education had led me to repudiate my race. I was frequently labeled a *pocho*, a Mexican with gringo pretentions, not only because I could not speak Spanish but also because I would respond in English with precise and careful sentences. Uncles would laugh good-naturedly, but I detected scorn in their voices. For my grandmother, the least assimilated of my relations, the changes in her grandson since entering school were especially troubling. She remains today a dark and silently critical figure in my memory, a reminder of the Mexican-Indian ancestry that somehow my educational success has violated.

Nonetheless, I became more comfortable reading or writing careful prose than talking to a kitchen filled with listeners, withdrawing from situations to reflect on their significance rather than grasping for meaning at the scene. I remember, one August evening, slipping away from a gathering of aunts and uncles in the backyard, going into a bedroom tenderly lighted by a late sun, and opening a novel about life in nineteenth-century England. There, by an open window, reading, I was barely conscious of the sounds of laughter outside.

With so few fellow Chicanos in the university, I had no chance to develop an alternative consciousness. When I spent occasional weekends tutoring lower-class Chicano teenagers or when I talked with Mexican-American janitors and maids around the campus, there was a kind of sympathy—a sense, however privately held—that we knew something about one another. But I regarded them all primarily as people from my past. The maids reminded me of my aunts (similarly employed); the students I tutored reminded me of my cousins (who also spoke English with barrio accents).

When I was young, I was taught to refer to my ancestry as Mexican-American. *Chicano* was a word used among friends or relatives. It implied a familiarity based on shared experience. Spoken casually, the term easily became an insult. In 1968 the word *Chicano* was about to become a political term. I heard it shouted into microphones as Third World groups agitated for increased student and faculty representation in higher education. It was not long before I *became* a Chicano in the eyes of students and faculty members. My racial identity was assumed for only the simplest reasons: my skin color and last name.

On occasion I was asked to account for my interests in Renaissance English literature. When I explained them, declaring a need for cultural assimilation on the campus, my listener would disagree. I sensed suspicion on the part of a number of my fellow minority students. When I could not imitate Spanish pronunciations or the dialect of the barrio, when I was plainly uninterested in wearing ethnic costumes and could not master a special handshake that minority students often used with one another, they knew I was different. And I was. I was assimilated into the culture of a graduate department of English. As a result, I watched how in less than five years nearly every minority graduate student I knew dropped out of school, largely for cultural reasons. Often they didn't understand the value of analyzing literature in professional jargon, which others around them readily adopted. Nor did they move as readily to lofty heights of abstraction. They became easily depressed by the seeming uselessness of the talk they heard around them. "It's not for real," I still hear a minority student murmur to herself and perhaps to me, shaking her head slowly, as we sat together in a class listening to a discussion on punctuation in a Renaissance epic.

I survived—thanks to the accommodation I had made long before. In fact, I prospered, partly as a result of the political movement designed to increase the enrollment of minority students less assimilated than I in higher education. Suddenly grants, fellowships, and teaching offers became abundant.

In 1972 I went to England on a Fulbright scholarship. I hoped the months of brooding about racial identity were behind me. I wanted to concentrate on my dissertation, which the distractions of an American campus had not permitted. But the freedom I anticipated did not last for long. Barely a month after I had begun working regularly in the reading room of the British Museum, I was surprised, and even frightened, to have to acknowledge that I was not at ease living the rarefied life of the academic. With my pile of research file cards growing taller, the mass of secondary materials and opinions was making it harder for me to say anything original about my subject. Every sentence I wrote, every thought I had, became so loaded with qualifications and footnotes that it said very little. My scholarship became little more than an exercise in caution. I had an accompanying suspicion that whatever I did manage to write and call my dissertation would be of little use. Opening books so dusty that they must not have been used in decades, I began to doubt the value of writing what only a few people would read.

Obviously, I was going through the fairly typical crisis of the American graduate student. But with one difference: After four years of involvement with questions of racial identity, I now saw my problems as a scholar in the context of the cultural issues that had been raised by my racial situation. So much of what my work in the British Museum lacked, my parents' culture possessed. They were people not afraid to generalize or to find insights in their generalities. More important, they had the capacity to make passionate statements, something I was beginning to doubt my dissertation would ever allow me to do. I needed to learn how to trust the use of "I" in my writing the way they trusted its use in their speech. Thus developed a persistent yearning for the very Chicano culture that I had abandoned as useless.

Feelings of depression came occasionally but forcefully. Some days I found my work so oppressive that I had to leave the reading room and stroll through the museum. One afternoon, appropriately enough, I found myself in an upstairs gallery containing Mayan and Aztec sculptures. Even there the sudden yearning for a Chicano past seemed available to me only as nostalgia. One morning, as I was

reading a book about Puritan autobiography, I overheard two Spaniards whispering to one another. I did not hear what they said, but I
did hear the sound of their Spanish—and it embraced me, filling my
mind with swirling images of a past long abandoned.

I returned from England, disheartened, a few months later. My
dissertation was coming along well, but I did not know whether I
wanted to submit it. Worse, I did not know whether I wanted a career
in higher education. I detested the prospect of spending the rest of
my life in libraries and classrooms, in touch with my past only
through the binoculars nostalgia makes available. I knew that I could
not simply re-create a version of what I would have been like had I
not become an academic. There was no possibility of going back. But
if the culture of my birth was to survive, it would have to animate my
academic work. That was the lesson of the British Museum.

I frankly do not know how my academic autobiography will end.
Sometimes I think I will have to leave the campus, in order to recon-
cile my past and present. Other times, more optimistically, I think
that a kind of negative reconciliation is already in progress, that I can
make creative use of my sense of loss. For instance, with my sense of
the cleavage between past and present, I can, as a literary critic,
identify issues in Renaissance pastoral—a literature which records
the feelings of the courtly when confronted by the alternatives of rural
and rustic life. And perhaps I can speak with unusual feeling about
the price we must pay, or have paid, as a rational society for confessing seventeenth-century Cartesian faiths. Likewise, because of
my sense of cultural loss, I may be able to identify more readily than
another the ways in which language has meaning simply as sound
and what the printed word can and cannot give us. At the very least, I
can point up the academy's tendency to ignore the cultures beyond
its own horizons.

February 1974

On my job interview the department chairman has been listening
to an oral version of what I have just written. I tell him he should be
very clear about the fact that I am not, at the moment, confident
enough to call myself a Chicano. Perhaps I never will be. But as I say
all this, I look at the interviewer. He smiles softly. Has he heard what
I have been trying to say? I wonder. I repeat: I have lost the ability to
bring my past into my present; I do not know how to be a Chicano
reader of Spenser or Shakespeare. All that remains is a desire for the
past. He sighs, preoccupied, looking at my records. Would I be interested in teaching a course on the Mexican novel in translation? Do I

understand that part of my duties would require that I become a counselor of minority students? What was the subject of that dissertation I did in England? Have I read the book on the same subject that was just published this month?

Behind the questioner, a figure forms in my imagination: my grandmother, her face solemn and still.

QUESTIONS

1. Rodriguez is the son of Mexican parents. Why does he use the word *became* in the title?

2. What is a *pocho?* How does a *pocho* correspond to an *Uncle Tom* or an *Oreo Cookie?* What is a *gringo?* How does a *gringo* correspond to a *honky?*

3. Examine the phrase "in touch with my past only through the binoculars nostalgia makes available." What does this figure of speech* suggest?

4. Rodriguez refers twice to his grandmother. What is he trying to express through the use of her image?

5. A sense of loss permeates this essay as Rodriguez compares and contrasts the two cultures and identifies valuable features of the Mexican culture he gave up.
   a. How was the change Rodriguez made deeper than just a change in language and in literacy? What fundamental contrast does he make between the Mexican-Indian consciousness and the North American-European consciousness?
   b. Consider the contrast between the two types of consciousness in terms of the author's statement, "And perhaps I can speak with unusual feeling about the price we must pay, or have paid, as a rational society for confessing seventeenth-century Cartesian faiths." (One of Descartes's main tenets was "I think, therefore I am.")

      Does being a rational (thinking) society keep us from being a sentient (feeling) society? Can we be both? Is it better to give more importance to feeling than to thinking? Why, or why not?

6. a. Why did Rodriguez change his racial identity when he was a child? Why did he become conscious of being a Chicano and of the need to rediscover his Mexican identity as an adult?

---

*Definitions for all terms marked with an asterisk may be found in the Glossary.

   b. Suppose that a Caucasian-American child was born and reared in Mexico under conditions similar to those Rodriguez experienced in the United States. Do you think that the child would respond in the same way that Rodriguez did? Would he or she experience the same conflicts? Explain your answer.

7. Does the department chairman depicted at the end of the essay understand at all what Rodriguez is trying to say? Have you ever told people about something very important to you and found that they were responding in terms of their own interests, without understanding your message? How did it make you feel?

READING AND WRITING SUGGESTIONS

1. Although a commonly held image of the United States has been that of the melting pot, and although the motto of the nation is *e pluribus unum*, Rodriguez and others are suggesting the importance of maintaining cultural diversity. Write a brief essay comparing and contrasting the two ideals—unity and diversity—in terms of their advantages and disadvantages.

2. Read a book about ethnic identity, such as Alex Haley's *Roots* or Arthur Laurent's *The Way We Were*, and explore the theme of Rodriguez's essay as it applies to a different ethnic group. Write a brief essay comparing and contrasting what the characters in the book you read have gained and lost as they moved between cultures.

PART TWO

Description

The word *description* comes from the Latin *describere,* meaning "to write about." Because the ability to describe is an essential part of all writing, description is a tool of the other forms of discourse as well as a mode of discourse in its own right. The function of description is to depict an object, a place, an event, or a person as it is perceived through the five senses—smell, taste, vision, hearing, and touch.

There are two types of description. *Objective* description, sometimes called *realistic* description, depicts a subject as a camera would —as impartially and concretely as possible. For example, a chair might be described objectively as "the family's battered old wooden rocking chair, which was covered with chipped red paint." The writer of *subjective* or *impressionistic* description, on the other hand, can be compared more exactly to a painter who interprets and expresses a response to the object which is being portrayed. The chair described above could be depicted subjectively as well: "It was obvious that the rocking chair had served the family well. Its seat and back were battered by the endless succession of children and parents and grandparents who had sought comfort in its gentle motion, and its coating of red paint, which had once brightened the corner of the kitchen where the chair stood, was now chipped and dull." As you might expect, most descriptive essays include both subjective and objective passages.

Figurative language, which stimulates and appeals to the imagination, is an essential ingredient of effective description. The most common figures of speech are similes, metaphors, alliteration, and personification. *Similes* use the words "like" or "as" to make direct comparisons: *He was as sly and secretive as a cat. Metaphors* make comparisons without the use of prepositions or conjunctions by suggesting a likeness or analogy between one object and another: *She was a large bulldog of a woman. Alliteration* is the repetition of sounds at the beginning of two or more consecutive words to make the sound of a sentence more pleasing or emphatic: *They entered the brilliant, bustling room. Personification* endows inanimate objects or abstract ideas with human attributes: *The restless sea tossed sleeplessly.* In the essays that follow, you will see many examples of these figures of speech.

THE SPARROW

Ivan Sergeyevich Turgenev

Ivan Sergeyevich Turgenev (1818–1883), one of the great Russian writers of the nineteenth century, was born in Orel, Russia. His father was a retired cavalry officer, and his mother was a wealthy landowner whose ill-treatment of her servants and her children impressed him deeply. Turgenev was educated, as a child, by private tutors, studied at Moscow University, and later graduated from St. Petersburg University. Although he started his literary career as a poet, it was a collection of essays that established his reputation. This collection, entitled A Sportsman's Notebook, *depicted life in Russia in the 1840s. Turgenev also wrote novels, several of which are commentaries on social problems in Russia. His essay "The Sparrow" demonstrates the simplicity of his style as well as his talent for observing and recording details with great precision.*

I returned home from the chase, and wandered through an alley in my garden. My dog bounded before me.

Suddenly he checked himself, and moved forward cautiously, as if he scented game.

I glanced down the alley, and perceived a young sparrow with a yellow beak, and down upon its head. He had fallen out of the nest (the wind was shaking the beeches in the alley violently), and lay motionless and helpless on the ground, with his little, unfledged wings extended.

The dog approached it softly, when suddenly an old sparrow, with a black breast, quitted a neighboring tree, dropped like a stone right before the dog's nose, and, with ruffled plumage, and chirping desperately and pitifully, sprang twice at the open, grinning mouth.

He had come to protect his little one at the cost of his own life. His little body trembled all over, his voice was hoarse, he was in an agony —he offered himself.

The dog must have seemed a gigantic monster to him. But, in spite of that, he had not remained safe on his lofty bough. A Power stronger than his own will had forced him down.

Treasure stood still and turned away. . . . It seemed as if he also felt this Power.

I hastened to call the discomfited dog back, and went away with a feeling of respect.

Yes, smile not! I felt a respect for this heroic little bird, and for the depth of his paternal love.

Love, I reflected, is stronger than death and the fear of death; it is love alone that supports and animates all.

QUESTIONS

1. Even in this brief essay, Turgenev makes extensive use of sensory details. Name three or four places in the essay where he describes a sight or sound of the scene with particular vividness.

2. What is the central thesis* of the essay? Where is it most clearly stated? Why do you think Turgenev chooses that particular point in the essay to state his thesis?

3. What device does Turgenev use in paragraph six to dramatize the bravery of the old sparrow?

4. What does the author mean by the sentence, "A Power stronger than his own will had forced him down"?

5. Do you think this account of a bird's love for its young is typical of parental love and protection in all species, including the human race? Describe any instances you know of—concerning either people or animals—that seem to portray a failure of this kind of instinctual love.

READING AND WRITING SUGGESTIONS

1. Write a brief description of a parent's display of extraordinary love and sacrifice for a child.

2. Write an essay about a dog or cat you have known, describing its appearance, its special traits, and one event which shows its distinctive personality.

3. Read Sheila Burnford's book, *The Incredible Journey*, the story of two dogs and a cat who look after one another, share scarce food, and encourage each other on a 250-mile trek across the Canadian wilderness. Write a brief description of the bond of affection these three animals share.

---

*Definitions for all terms marked with an asterisk may be found in the Glossary.

MARY WHITE

William Allen White

William Allen White (1868–1944) was owner and editor of the Emporia Gazette *from 1895 until his death. He is the author of several novels and biographies, but he is best known for his contributions to newspapers and magazines. One editorial, "To an Anxious Friend," won him a Pulitzer Prize in 1922. The essay "Mary White," which appeared in the Emporia* Gazette *March 15, 1921, is a description of White's daughter, who was killed in a fall from a horse.*

The Associated Press reports carrying the news of Mary White's death declared that it came as the result of a fall from a horse. How she would have hooted at that! She never fell from a horse in her life. Horses have fallen on her and with her—"I'm always trying to hold 'em in my lap," she used to say. But she was proud of few things, and one was that she could ride anything that had four legs and hair. Her death resulted not from a fall, but from a blow on the head which fractured her skull, and the blow came from the limb of an overhanging tree on the parking.

The last hour of her life was typical of its happiness. She came home from a day's work at school, topped off by a hard grind with the copy on the High School Annual, and felt that a ride would refresh her. She climbed into her khakis, chattering to her mother about the work she was doing, and hurried to get her horse and be out on the dirt roads for the country air and radiant green fields of the spring. As she rode through the town on an easy gallop she kept waving at passers-by. She knew everyone in town. For a decade the little figure with the long pig-tail and the red hair ribbon has been familiar on the streets of Emporia, and she got in the way of speaking to those who nodded at her. She passed the Kerrs, walking the horse, in front of the Normal Library, and waved at them; passed another friend a few hundred feet further on, and waved at her. The horse was walking and, as she turned into North Merchant Street she took off her cowboy hat, and the horse swung into a lope. She passed the Tripletts and waved her cowboy hat at them, still moving gaily north on Merchant Street. A Gazette carrier passed—a High School boy friend —and she waved at him, but with her bridle hand; the horse veered quickly; plunged into the parking where the low-hanging limb faced her, and, while she still looked back waving, the blow came. But she did not fall from the horse; she slipped off, dazed a bit, staggered and fell in a faint. She never quite recovered consciousness.

But she did not fall from the horse, neither was she riding fast. A year or so ago she used to go like the wind. But that habit was broken, and she used the horse to get into the open to get fresh, hard exercise, and to work off a certain surplus energy that welled up in her and needed a physical outlet. That need has been in her heart for years. It was back of the impulse that kept the dauntless, little brown-clad figure on the streets and country roads of this community and built into a strong, muscular body what had been a frail and sickly frame during the first years of her life. But the riding gave her more than a body. It released a gay and hardy soul. She was the happiest thing in the world. And she was happy because she was enlarging her horizon. She came to know all sorts and conditions of men; Charley O'Brien, the traffic cop, was one of her best friends. W. L. Holtz, the Latin teacher, was another. Tom O'Connor, farmer-politician, and Rev. J. H. J. Rice, preacher and police judge, and Frank Beach, music master, were her special friends, and all the girls, black and white, above the track and below the track, in Pepville and Stringtown, were among her acquaintances. And she brought home riotous stories of her adventures. She loved to rollick; persiflage was her natural expression at home. Her humor was a continual bubble of joy. She seemed to think in hyperbole and metaphor. She was mischievous without malice, as full of faults as an old shoe. No angel was Mary White, but an easy girl to live with, for she never nursed a grouch five minutes in her life.

With all her eagerness for the out-of-doors she loved books. On her table when she left her room were a book by Conrad, one by Galsworthy, *Creative Chemistry* by E. E. Slossom, and a Kipling book. She read Mark Twain, Dickens and Kipling before she was ten—all of their writings. Wells and Arnold Bennett particularly amused and diverted her. She was entered as a student in Wellesley in 1922; was assistant editor of the High School Annual this year, and in line for election to the editorship of the Annual next year. She was a member of the executive committee of the High School YWCA.

Within the last two years she had begun to be moved by an ambition to draw. She began as most children do by scribbling in her school books, funny pictures. She bought cartoon magazines and took a course—rather casually, naturally, for she was, after all, a child with no strong purposes—and this year she tasted the first fruits of success by having her pictures accepted by the High School Annual. But the thrill of delight she got when Mr. Ecord, of the Normal Annual, asked her to do the cartooning for that book this spring, was too beautiful for words. She fell to her work with all her enthusiastic heart. Her drawings were accepted, and her pride—always repressed by a lively sense of the ridiculousness of the figure she was cutting— was a really gorgeous thing to see. No successful artist ever drank a deeper draught of satisfaction than she took from the little fame her work was getting among her school-fellows. In her glory, she almost forgot her horse—but never her car.

For she used the car as a jitney bus. It was her social life. She never had a "party" in all her nearly seventeen years—wouldn't have one; but she never drove a block in the car in her life that she didn't begin to fill the car with pick-ups! Everybody rode with Mary White— white and black, old and young, rich and poor, men and women. She liked nothing better than to fill the car full of long-legged High School boys and an occasional girl, and parade the town. She never had a "date," nor went to a dance, except once with her brother, Bill, and the "boy proposition" didn't interest her—yet. But young people— great spring-breaking, varnish-cracking, fender-bending, door-sagging carloads of "kids" gave her great pleasure. Her zests were keen. But the most fun she ever had in her life was acting as chairman of the committee that got up the big turkey dinner for the poor folks at the county home; scores of pies, gallons of slaw; jam, cakes, pre-serves, oranges and a wilderness of turkey were loaded in the car and taken to the county home. And, being a practical turn of mind, she risked her own Christmas dinner by staying to see that the poor folks actually got it all. Not that she was a cynic; she disliked to tempt folks. While there she found a blind colored uncle, very old, who could do nothing but make rag rugs, and she rustled up from her school friends rags enough to keep him busy for a season. The last en-gagement she tried to make was to take the guests at the county home out for a car ride. And the last endeavor of her life was to try to get a rest room for colored girls in the High School. She found one girl reading in the toilet, because there was no better place for a colored girl to loaf, and it inflamed her sense of injustice and she became a nagging harpy to those who, she thought, could remedy the evil. The poor she had always with her, and was glad of it. She hungered and thirsted for righteousness; and was the most impious creature in the world. She joined the Congregational Church without consulting her parents; not particularly for her soul's good. She never had a thrill of piety in her life, and would have hooted at a "testimony." But even as a little child she felt the church was an agency for helping people to more of life's abundance, and she wanted to help. She never wanted help for herself. Clothes meant little to her. It was a fight to get a new rig on her; but eventually a harder fight to get it off. She never wore a jewel and had no ring but her High School class ring, and never asked for anything but a wrist watch. She refused to have her hair up; though she was nearly seventeen. "Mother," she protested, "you don't know how much I get by with, in my braided pigtails, that I could not with my hair up." Above every other passion of her life was her passion not to grow up, to be a child. The tom-boy in her, which was big, seemed to loathe to be put away forever in skirts. She was a Peter Pan, who refused to grow up.

Her funeral yesterday at the Congregational Church was as she would have wished it; no singing, no flowers save the big bunch of red roses from her Brother Bill's Harvard classmen—Heavens, how proud that would have made her! And the red roses from the Gazette force—in vases at her head and feet. A short prayer, Paul's beautiful essay on "Love" from the Thirteenth Chapter of First Corinthians, some remarks about her democratic spirit by her friend, John H. J. Rice, pastor and police judge, which she would have deprecated if she could, a prayer sent down for her by her friend, Carl Nau, and opening the service the slow, poignant movement from Beethoven's Moonlight Sonata, which she loved, and closing the service a cutting from the joyously melancholy first movement of Tschaikowski's Pathetic Symphony, which she liked to hear in certain moods on the phonograph; then the Lord's Prayer by her friends in the High School.

That was all.

For her pall-bearers only her friends were chosen: her Latin teacher, W. L. Holtz; her High School principal, Rice Brown; her doctor, Frank Foncannon; her friend, W. W. Finney; her pal at the Gazette office, Walter Hughes; and her brother, Bill. It would have made her smile to know that her friend, Charley O'Brien, the traffic cop, had been transferred from Sixth and Commercial to the corner near the church to direct her friends who came to bid her good-by.

A rift in the clouds in a gray day threw a shaft of sunlight upon her coffin as her nervous, energetic little body sank to its last sleep. But the soul of her, the glowing, gorgeous, fervent soul of her, surely was flaming in eager joy upon some other dawn.

QUESTIONS

1. Define the following words: *rollick, persiflage, harpy, loathe, deprecate, poignant, fervent, riotous.*

2. What qualities and characteristics of Mary White are illustrated in the second and third paragraphs of the essay?

3. In the opening paragraph, White emphasizes and reemphasizes the fact that Mary White did not fall from her horse. Why do you think he is so concerned about this distinction between Mary's *falling* from the horse and her *slipping off* the horse after receiving a blow to her head?

4. Make a list of the figurative* words and phrases White uses to paint a picture of What Mary was like.

5. In what way does the description of Mary's funeral parallel the description of Mary presented earlier in the essay?

6. Comment on the function and the effectiveness of the last paragraph. How does it fit with the image of Mary that White has created?

READING AND WRITING SUGGESTIONS

1. All of us, at one point or another, are faced with the death of a family member or close friend. In a brief essay, describe such an experience in your own life. Use the experience, as White did, not as an end in itself, but as a way to characterize the life of the essay's subject.

2. Read *Death Be Not Proud* by John Gunther, the story of his son's death after a long and heroic bout with cancer. Write a brief essay describing in your own words the ways the family dealt with the tragedy.

---

*Definitions for all terms marked with an asterisk may be found in the Glossary.

A PEASANT'S PHILOSOPHY

Laurence Sterne

Laurence Sterne (1713–1768) was born at Clonmel, Ireland, where his father, an English army officer, was stationed. At the age of ten Sterne was sent to England to school, and after graduating from Cambridge he became a minister in the English Established Church. Sterne achieved fame in 1760 with the publication of his great novel, Tristram Shandy. *Eight years later he published* A Sentimental Journey, *a series of vignettes describing his travels through France and Italy. In the following essay, which is taken from* A Sentimental Journey, *Sterne describes an evening spent with a peasant family.*

A shoe coming loose from the forefoot of the thill horse, at the beginning of the ascent of Mount Taurira, the postilion dismounted, twisted the shoe off, and put it in his pocket. As the ascent was of five or six miles, and that horse our main dependence, I made a point of having the shoe fastened on again as well as we could; but the postilion had thrown away the nails, and the hammer in the chaise box being of no great use without them, I submitted to go on. He had not mounted half a mile higher, when, coming to a flinty piece of road, the poor devil lost a second shoe, and from off his other forefoot. I then got out of the chaise in good earnest; and seeing a house about a quarter of a mile to the left hand, with a great deal to do I prevailed upon the postilion to turn up to it. The look of the house, and of everything about it, as we drew nearer, soon reconciled me to the disaster. It was a little farmhouse, surrounded with about twenty acres of vineyard, and about as much corn; and close to the house on one side was a *potagerie* of an acre and a half, full of everything which could make plenty in a French peasant's house; and on the other side was a little wood, which furnished wherewithal to dress it. It was about eight in the evening when I got to the house; so I left the postilion to manage his point as he could,—and for mine, I walked directly into the house.

The family consisted of an old gray-headed man and his wife, with five or six sons and sons in law and their several wives, and a joyous genealogy out of them. They were all sitting down together to their lentil soup; a large wheaten loaf was in the middle of the table; and a flagon of wine at each end of it promised joy through the stages of the repast; 'twas a feast of love. The old man rose up to meet me, and with a respectful cordiality would have me sit down at the table; my heart was set down the moment I entered the room, so I sat down at once like a son of the family; and to invest myself in the character as speedily as I could, I instantly borrowed the old man's knife, and, taking up the loaf, cut myself a hearty luncheon; and as I did it, I saw a testimony in every eye, not only of an honest welcome, but of a welcome mixed with thanks that I had not seemed to doubt it. Was it this,—or tell me, Nature, what else it was,—that made this morsel so sweet; and to what magic I owe it, that the draught I took of their flagon was so delicious with it, that they remain upon my palate to this hour? If the supper was to my taste, the grace which followed it was much more so.

When supper was over, the old man gave a knock upon the table with the haft of his knife, to bid them prepare for the dance. The moment the signal was given, the women and girls ran all together into a back apartment to tie up their hair, and the young men to the door to wash their faces and change their sabots; and in three minutes every soul was ready, upon a little esplanade before the house, to begin. The old man and his wife came out last, and, placing me betwixt them, sat down upon a sofa of turf by the door. The old man had some fifty years ago been no mean performer upon the vielle; and at the age he was then of, touched it well enough for the purpose. His wife sung now and then a little to the tune, then intermitted, and joined her old man again as their children and grandchildren danced before them.

It was not till the middle of the second dance, when, for some pauses in the movement, wherein they all seemed to look up, I fancied I could distinguish an elevation of spirit different from that which is the cause or the effect of simple jollity. In a word, I thought I beheld Religion mixing in the dance; but as I had never seen her so engaged, I should have looked upon it now as one of the illusions of an imagination which is eternally misleading me, had not the old man, as soon as the dance ended, said that this was their constant way; and that all his life long he had made it a rule, after supper was over, to call out his family to dance and rejoice; believing, he said, that a cheerful and contented mind was the best sort of thanks to Heaven that an illiterate peasant could pay. Or a learned prelate either, said I.

QUESTIONS

1. Define the following words: *thill, postilion, potagerie, genealogy, lentil, flagon, repast, draught, haft, sabots, esplanade, vielle, prelate.*

2. In the second paragraph of his essay, Sterne poses a rhetorical question*. Is this an effective device? Who or what is the "Nature" referred to in the sentence?

3. What is the thesis* of the essay? Where is it most clearly stated?

4. Do you agree that maintaining a "cheerful and contented mind" is a way of conveying gratitude? Why, or why not?

5. What meaning does this essay have for you?

6. How would a farm family in this country today differ from the family described in this essay?

7. Description is based on an appeal to one or more of the senses. How many of the five senses does Sterne appeal to in this descriptive essay?

READING AND WRITING SUGGESTIONS

1. Write a brief description of a visit you made to someone's home which left you with a warm and welcome feeling. Focus on the setting, the people present, and the specific acts which resulted in your feeling of belonging.

2. Read *Colonial America* by Stanley N. Katz or a similar book describing family life and activities in the early history of this country. Write a brief essay in which you describe what an evening spent with a colonial family might have been like.

---

*Definitions for all terms marked with an asterisk may be found in the Glossary.

ON THE FAR SIDE OF PAIN

George A. Sheehan

George A. Sheehan (1918–) is a graduate of the State University of New York's College of Medicine in Brooklyn and is now a practicing physician in Red Bank, New Jersey. His specialty is internal medicine. In this essay, Sheehan describes the pain which trained athletes must endure in order to excel at their sport.

For the trained athlete, pain is his major enemy. Already disciplined to the long training schedule, the curtailment of social life and the separation from other interests, the athlete even at the top of his powers still must endure pain beyond his imagination and capacity if he wishes to get maximal performance.

"Your stomach feels as though it's going to fall out," writes Don Schollander, "every kick hurts like hell—and suddenly you hear a shrill internal scream. Then you have a choice. Most swimmers back away. If you push through the pain barrier into real agony, you're a champion."

Runners have told of the same tortures. The muscles gradually hardening up into painful leaden stumps. The breath shortening to convulsive gasps. The chest filled with dry fire. The stomach threatening to explode in agony.

And again the difference between athletes is the peculiar ability— Roger Bannister describes it as a capacity for mental excitement— which enables the runner to ignore or overcome discomfort and pain.

"It is this psychological factor—beyond the ken of physiology— which sets the razor's edge between victory and defeat," Bannister says, "and which determines how closely an athlete comes to the absolute limits of performance."

QUESTIONS

1. Give four examples of figurative language* in the essay.

---

*Definitions for all terms marked with an asterisk may be found in the Glossary.

2. Explain what the following phrases mean:
   —"beyond the ken of physiology"
   —"If you push through the pain barrier into real agony, you're a champion"
   —"suddenly you hear a shrill internal scream"

3. Why are athletes willing to curtail their social lives, to subject themselves to rigorous training schedules, and even to endure pain? Is it for self-satisfaction? The glory of their alma mater? The money? The chance to get ahead?

4. Sheehan's essay describes the agony athletes endure to excel in sports. Do you think athletes should receive special treatment as a reward for their efforts? Should they be paid?

5. The most tangible symbol of a nonprofessional athlete's success is often a medal or trophy. Read the following quotation and discuss the way it relates to Sheehan's essay: "A medal is a label by which we distinguish the man who is unnatural enough to put the needs of civilization before the needs of survival. A medal is an award, not a reward." –A. T. W. Simeons

6. To excel in any activity or calling—whether it be art, music, law, sports, or business—a person must make certain sacrifices. What sacrifices do you think you will be asked to make in your chosen profession?

READING AND WRITING SUGGESTIONS

1. Write a brief essay describing your peak experience in athletics. It can be an event at which you were a spectator or one in which you were a participant. Describe your impressions of the spectators, the athletes, and the excitement and emotion of the contest.

2. Read *Tarkenton* by Jim Klobuchar and Fran Tarkenton or another book about a famous athlete, and write a paper describing the individual's achievements. Describe in detail the personal qualities of the athlete and the sacrifices he or she made to get to the top.

THE APPLE TREE

John Galsworthy

John Galsworthy (1867–1933), a well-known novelist, play-wright, and social critic, was born in England and attended Harrow and Oxford. He was admitted to the bar, and for a time he worked and traveled for his father's company. In the course of his life, Gals-worthy published about twenty novels, over two dozen plays, and several collections of essays and poems. He is best known for The Forsyte Saga, *the history of an upper-middle-class family. In 1932, Galsworthy received the Nobel Prize for literature. The following passage, in which he describes an orchard at night, was first pub-lished in 1916.*

It was nearly eleven that night when Ashurst put down the pocket *Odyssey* which for half an hour he had held in his hands without reading, and slipped through the yard down to the orchard. The moon had just risen, very golden, over the hill, and like a bright, powerful, watching spirit peered through the bars of an ash tree's half-naked boughs. In among the apple trees it was still dark, and he stood making sure of his direction, feeling the rough grass with his feet. A black mass close behind him stirred with a heavy grunting sound, and three large pigs settled down again close to each other, under the wall. He listened. There was no wind, but the stream's burbling, whispering chuckle had gained twice its daytime strength. One bird, he could not tell what, cried "Pip—pip," "Pip—pip," with perfect monotony; he could hear a night-jar spinning very far off; an owl hooting. Ashurst moved a step or two, and again halted, aware of a dim, living whiteness all round his head. On the dark, unstirring trees innumerable flowers and buds all soft and blurred were being bewitched to life by the creeping moonlight. He had the oddest feeling of actual companionship, as if a million white moths or spirits had floated in and settled between dark sky and darker ground, and were opening and shutting their wings on a level with his eyes. In the bewildering, still, scentless beauty of that moment he almost lost memory of why he had come to the orchard. The flying glamour which had clothed the earth all day had not gone now that night had fallen, but only changed into this new form. He moved on through the thicket of stems and boughs covered with that live, powdering whiteness, till he reached the big apple tree. No mistaking that, even in the dark, nearly twice the height and size of any other, and leaning out towards the open meadows and the stream. Under the thick branches he stood still again, to listen. The same sounds exactly, and a faint grunting from the sleepy pigs. He put his hands on the dry, almost warm tree trunk, whose rough, mossy surface gave forth a peaty scent at his touch. Would she come—would she? And among these quivering, haunted, moon-witched trees he was seized with doubts of everything! All was unearthly here, fit for no earthly lovers; fit only for god and goddess, faun and nymph—not for him and this little country girl. Would it not be almost a relief if she did not come? But all the time he was listening. And still that unknown bird went "Pip—pip," "Pip—pip," and there rose the busy chatter of the little trout stream, whereon the moon was flinging glances through the bars of her tree-prison. The blossom on a level with his eyes seemed to grow more living every moment, seemed with its mysterious white beauty more and more a part of his suspense. He plucked a fragment and held it close—three blossoms. Sacrilege to pluck fruit-tree blossom—soft, sacred, young blossom—and throw it away! Then suddenly he heard the gate close, the pigs stirring again and grunting; and leaning against the trunk, he pressed his hands to its mossy sides behind him, and held his breath. She might have been a spirit threading the trees, for all the noise she made! Then he saw her quite close—her dark form part of a little tree, her white face part of its blossom; so still, and peering towards him. He whispered: "Megan!" and held out his hands.

QUESTIONS

1. Define the following words: *peaty, faun, nymph, sacrilege, burbling.*

2. Find examples in the essay of especially effective word choices that help set the tone* of the essay as a whole.

3. What particular words or sentences do you think contribute to a sense of excitement or expectancy in the essay?

4. What is the essay's thesis?* Is it stated or implied?

---

*Definitions for all terms marked with an asterisk may be found in the Glossary.

5. Do you think that this account of the meeting of a young man and woman is outdated? Would such a meeting happen in the same way today? Why, or why not?

6. Does this essay call to mind an experience from your past—for example, your first date, or a secret meeting at night in childhood? If so, describe the experience.

READING AND WRITING SUGGESTIONS

1. Write a brief narrative in which you pick up where "The Apple Tree" leaves off, describing a scene that might have transpired between the two characters in the essay.

2. Write a brief narrative essay describing a secret rendezvous between two young lovers today. Where might they meet? What book might the young man be reading? What sounds might he hear while waiting?

3. Read William John Fielding's *Strange Customs of Courtship and Marriage*, Ernest S. Turner's *A History of Courting*, or a similar book about the customs of courtship, and write a brief essay describing how these customs have changed through the years.

THE MOUNTAIN OF MISERIES

Joseph Addison

Joseph Addison (1672–1719), one of England's greatest essayists, exerted a strong influence on English public opinion in the eighteenth century. After graduating with honors from Oxford, Addison entered politics, and he eventually became secretary of state. The son of a clergyman, he was recognized as a man of lofty character who was concerned about purity and uprightness. Many of his essays depict the virtue, simplicity, and good nature which Addison demonstrated in his own life and which he valued in others. Addi-

son's fame rests primarily on his contributions to the Tatler *and the*
Spectator, *two newspapers which carried political, social, and lit-*
erary news of the period. In the following essay, which is taken from
the Spectator, *Addison describes the scene that might transpire if*
people were given a chance to trade their own miseries for the
miseries of others.

> *Qui fit, Maecenas, ut nemo, quam sibi sortem*
> *Seu ratio dederit, seu fors objecerit, illa*
> *Contentus vivat: laudet diversa sequentes?*
> —Hor. Sat. i., Lib. I. 1

> Whence is't, Maecenas, that so few approve
> The state they're placed in, and incline to rove;
> Whether against their will by fate impos'd,
> Or by consent and prudent choice espous'd?
> —Horneck

It is a celebrated thought of Socrates, that if all the misfortunes of
mankind were cast into a public stock, in order to be equally distributed among the whole species, those who now think themselves the
most unhappy would prefer the share they are already possessed of
before that which would fall to them by such a division. Horace has
carried this thought a great deal further in the motto of my paper,
which implies that the hardships or misfortunes we lie under are
more easy to us than those of any other person would be, in case we
could change conditions with him.

As I was ruminating upon these two remarks, and seated in my
elbow chair, I insensibly fell asleep; when, on a sudden, methought
there was a proclamation made by Jupiter that every mortal should
bring in his griefs and calamities, and throw them together in a heap.
There was a large plain appointed for this purpose. I took my stand in
the centre of it, and saw with a great deal of pleasure the whole
human species marching one after another, and throwing down their
several loads, which immediately grew up into a prodigious mountain, that seemed to rise above the clouds.

There was a certain lady of a thin airy shape, who was very active
in this solemnity. She carried a magnifying glass in one of her hands,
and was clothed in a loose flowing robe, embroidered with several
figures of fiends and spectres, that discovered themselves in a thousand chimerical shapes, as her garment hovered in the wind. There
was something wild and distracted in her looks. Her name was
Fancy. She led up every mortal to the appointed place, after having

very officiously assisted him in making up his pack, and laying it upon his shoulders. My heart melted within me to see my fellow-creatures groaning under their respective burdens, and to consider that prodigious bulk of human calamities which lay before me.

There were, however, several persons who gave me great diversion upon this occasion. I observed one bringing in a fardel very carefully concealed under an old embroidered cloak, which, upon his throwing it into the heap, I discovered to be Poverty. Another, after a great deal of puffing, threw down his luggage, which, upon examining, I found to be his wife.

There were multitudes of lovers saddled with very whimsical burdens composed of darts and flames; but, what was very odd, though they sighed as if their hearts would break under these bundles of calamities, they could not persuade themselves to cast them into the heap, when they came up to it; but, after a few faint efforts, shook their heads, and marched away as heavy laden as they came. I saw multitudes of old women throw down their wrinkles, and several young ones who stripped themselves of a tawny skin. There were very great heaps of red noses, large lips, and rusty teeth. The truth of it is, I was surprised to see the greatest part of the mountain made up of bodily deformities. Observing one advancing towards the heap with a larger cargo than ordinary upon his back, I found upon his near approach that it was only a natural hump, which he disposed of, with great joy of heart, among this collection of human miseries. There were likewise distempers of all sorts, though I could not but observe that there were many more imaginary than real. One little packet I could not but take notice of, which was a complication of all the diseases incident to human nature, and was in the hand of a great many fine people: this was called the spleen. But what most of all surprised me was, a remark I made, that there was not a single vice or folly thrown into the whole heap; at which I was very much astonished, having concluded within myself that every one would take this opportunity of getting rid of his passions, prejudices, and frailties.

I took notice in particular of a very profligate fellow, who I did not question came loaded with his crimes; but upon searching into his bundle I found that instead of throwing his guilt from him, he had only laid down his memory. He was followed by another worthless rogue, who flung away his modesty instead of his ignorance.

When the whole race of mankind had thus cast their burdens, the phantom which had been so busy on this occasion, seeing me an idle Spectator of what had passed, approached towards me. I grew uneasy at her presence, when of a sudden she held her magnifying glass full before my eyes. I no sooner saw my face in it, but was startled at the shortness of it, which now appeared to me in its utmost aggravation. The immoderate breadth of the features made me very much out of humor with my own countenance, upon which I threw it from me like a mask. It happened very luckily that one who stood by me had just before thrown down his visage, which it seems was too long for him. It was indeed extended to a most shameful length; I believe the very chin was, modestly speaking, as long as my whole face. We had both of us an opportunity of mending ourselves; and all the contributions being now brought in, every man was at liberty to exchange his misfortunes for those of another person. But as there arose many new incidents in the sequel of my vision, I shall reserve them for the subject of my next paper.

> *Quid causae est, merito quin illis Jupiter ambas*
> *Iratus buccas inflet, neque se fore posthac*
> *Tam facilem dicat, votis ut prabeat aurem?*
> > –Hor. Sat. i., Lib. I., 20.

> Were it not just that Jove, provok'd to heat,
> Should drive these triflers from the hallow'd seat,
> And unrelenting stand when they entreat?
> > —Horneck.

In my last paper I gave my reader a sight of that mountain of miseries which was made up of those several calamities that afflict the minds of men. I saw with unspeakable pleasure the whole species thus delivered from its sorrows; though at the same time, as we stood round the heap, and surveyed the several materials of which it was composed, there was scarcely a mortal in this vast multitude, who did not discover what he thought the pleasures of life, and wondered how the owners of them ever came to look upon them as burdens and grievances.

As we were regarding very attentively this confusion of miseries, this chaos of calamity, Jupiter issued out a second proclamation, that every one was now at liberty to exchange his affliction, and to return to his habitation with any such other bundle as should be delivered to him.

Upon this, Fancy began again to bestir herself, and, parceling out the whole heap with incredible activity, recommended to every one his particular packet. The hurry and confusion at this time was not to be expressed. Some observations, which I made upon this occasion, I shall communicate to the public. A venerable gray-headed man, who had laid down the colic, and who, I found, wanted an heir to his estate, snatched up an undutiful son that had been thrown into the heap by his angry father. The graceless youth, in less than a quarter of an hour, pulled the old gentleman by the beard, and had liked to have knocked his brains out; so that meeting the true father, who came towards him with a fit of the gripes, he begged him to take his son again, and give him back his colic; but they were incapable either of them to recede from the choice they had made. A poor galley slave, who had thrown down his chains, took up the gout in their stead, but made such wry faces, that one might easily perceive he was no great gainer by the bargain. It was pleasant enough to see the several exchanges that were made, for sickness against poverty, hunger against want of appetite, and care against pain.

The female world were very busy among themselves in bartering for features: one was trucking a lock of gray hairs for a carbuncle, another was making over a short waist for a pair of round shoulders, and a third cheapening a bad face for a lost reputation; but on all these occasions there was not one of them who did not think the new blemish, as soon as she had got it into her possession, much more disagreeable than the old one. I made the same observation on every other misfortune or calamity which every one in the assembly brought upon himself in lieu of what he had parted with. Whether it be that all the evils which befall us are in some measure suited and proportioned to our strength, or that every evil becomes more supportable by our being accustomed to it, I shall not determine.

I could not from my heart forbear pitying the poor hump-backed gentleman mentioned in the former paper, who went off a very well-shaped person with a stone in his bladder; nor the fine gentleman who had struck up this bargain with him, that limped through a whole assembly of ladies, who used to admire him, with a pair of shoulders peeping over his head.

I must not omit my own particular adventure. My friend with a long visage had no sooner taken upon him my short face, but he made such a grotesque figure in it that as I looked upon him I could not forbear laughing at myself, insomuch that I put my own face out of countenance. The poor gentleman was so sensible of the ridicule that I found he was ashamed of what he had done; on the other side, I found that I myself had no great reason to triumph, for as I went to touch my forehead I missed the place, and clapped my finger upon my upper lip. Besides, as my nose was exceeding prominent, I gave it two or three unlucky knocks as I was playing my hand about my face, and aiming at some other part of it. I saw two other gentlemen by me who were in the same ridiculous circumstances. These had made a foolish swop between a couple of thick bandy legs and two long trapsticks that had no calves to them. One of these looked like a man walking upon stilts, and was so lifted up into the air, above his ordinary height, that his head turned round with it; while the other made such awkward circles, as he attempted to walk, that he scarcely knew how to move forward upon his new supporters. Observing him to be a pleasant kind of fellow, I stuck my cane in the ground, and told him I would lay him a bottle of wine that he did not march up to it on a line, that I drew for him, in a quarter of an hour.

The heap was at last distributed among the two sexes, who made a most piteous sight, as they wandered up and down under the pressure of their several burdens. The whole plain was filled with murmurs and complaints, groans and lamentations. Jupiter at length, taking compassion on the poor mortals, ordered them a second time to lay down their loads, with a design to give every one his own again. They discharged themselves with a great deal of pleasure; after which, the phantom who had led them into such gross delusions was commanded to disappear. There was sent in her stead a goddess of a quite different figure; her motions were steady and composed, and her aspect serious but cheerful. She every now and then cast her eyes towards heaven, and fixed them upon Jupiter; her name was Patience. She had no sooner placed herself by the Mount of Sorrows, but, what I thought very remarkable, the whole heap sunk to such a degree that it did not appear a third part so big as it was before. She afterwards returned every man his own proper calamity, and, teaching him how to bear it in the most commodious manner, he marched off with it contentedly, being very well pleased that he had not been left to his own choice as to the kind of evils which fell to his lot.

Besides the several pieces of morality to be drawn out of this Vision, I learnt from it never to repine at my own misfortunes, or to envy the happiness of another, since it is impossible for any man to form a right judgment of his neighbor's sufferings; for which reason also I have determined never to think too lightly of another's complaints, but to regard the sorrows of my fellow-creatures with sentiments of humanity and compassion.

QUESTIONS

1. Define the following words: *prudent, espoused, ruminating, prodigious, fiends, spectres, chimerical, officiously, fardel, profligate, visage, bandy, lamentations, commodious, Jupiter.*

2. Decide which sentence in the essay most clearly states Addison's thesis* and restate the thesis in your own words.

3. What examples of personification* can you find in the essay? What effect does this device produce?

4. In the essay, Addison combines humor with a critical view of humanity. Which element predominates—the humor or the criticism? Cite examples in the essay which support your point of view.

5. Were you surprised to find that in Addison's view the greatest part of the "mountain of miseries" was made up of physical deformities? Why, or why not?

6. Why do you think there was "not a single vice or folly thrown into the whole heap"? Is Addison suggesting that we don't recognize these weaknesses in ourselves, or that we simply don't want to give them up?

7. How does the symbolic figure of the goddess Patience relate to the events described in this essay?

READING AND WRITING SUGGESTIONS

1. In his essay, Addison brings to life the old adage that our own misfortunes are easier to bear than the misfortunes of others by describing what would happen if people were given the chance to trade away their miseries. Using Addison's essay as a model, write a brief essay describing what would happen if the following idea became a reality: If we could read the thoughts of the people around us, we would act very differently than we do now.

2. Read a biography of a well-known person who suffered from a lifelong misfortune such as poverty, physical disability, or extreme ugliness. Describe the way the person dealt with suffering, and speculate on how the person's life would have been different if the misfortune had been removed.

---

*Definitions for all terms marked with an asterisk may be found in the Glossary.

THREE DAYS TO SEE

Helen Keller

*Helen Keller (1880–1968) came to be known the world over for her
achievements, despite the fact that an early childhood illness left her
blind and deaf. Her teacher and lifelong companion, Anne Sullivan,
helped Keller's world come alive by teaching her to communicate.
Keller's courage in overcoming her handicaps has been recorded in
her books* The Story of My Life *and* The World I Live In *and on the
stage and screen in* The Miracle Worker. *The following essay is a
moving account of what Keller thinks she would experience if she
were given three days to see.*

All of us have read thrilling stories in which the hero had only a
limited and specified time to live. Sometimes it was as long as a year;
sometimes as short as twenty-four hours. But always we were interested in discovering just how the doomed man chose to spend his last
days or his last hours. I speak, of course, of free men who have a
choice, not condemned criminals whose sphere of activities is strictly
delimited.

Such stories set us thinking, wondering what we should do under
similar circumstances. What events, what experiences, what associations should we crowd into those last hours as mortal beings? What
happiness should we find in reviewing the past, what regrets?

Sometimes I have thought it would be an excellent rule to live each
day as if we should die tomorrow. Such an attitude would emphasize
sharply the values of life. We should live each day with a gentleness,
a vigor, and a keenness of appreciation which are often lost when
time stretches before us in the constant panorama of more days and
months and years to come. There are those, of course, who would
adopt the epicurean motto of "Eat, drink, and be merry," but most
people would be chastened by the certainty of impending death.

In stories, the doomed hero is usually saved at the last minute by
some stroke of fortune, but almost always his sense of values is
changed. He becomes more appreciative of the meaning of life and its
permanent spiritual values. It has often been noted that those who

live, or have lived, in the shadow of death bring a mellow sweetness to everything they do.

Most of us, however, take life for granted. We know that one day we must die, but usually we picture that day as far in the future. When we are in buoyant health, death is all but unimaginable. We seldom think of it. The days stretch out in an endless vista. So we go about our petty tasks, hardly aware of our listless attitude toward life.

The same lethargy, I am afraid, characterizes the use of all our faculties and senses. Only the deaf appreciate hearing, only the blind realize the manifold blessings that lie in sight. Particularly does this observation apply to those who have lost sight and hearing in adult life. But those who have never suffered impairment of sight or hearing seldom make the fullest use of these blessed faculties. Their eyes and ears take in all sights and sounds hazily, without concentration and with little appreciation. It is the same old story of not being grateful for what we have until we lose it, of not being conscious of health until we are ill.

I have often thought it would be a blessing if each human being were stricken blind and deaf for a few days at some time during his early adult life. Darkness would make him more appreciative of sight; silence would teach him the joys of sound.

Now and then I have tested my seeing friends to discover what they see. Recently I was visited by a very good friend who had just returned from a long walk in the woods, and I asked her what she had observed. "Nothing in particular," she replied. I might have been incredulous had I not been accustomed to such responses, for long ago I became convinced that the seeing see little.

How was it possible, I asked myself, to walk for an hour through the woods and see nothing worthy of note? I who cannot see find hundreds of things to interest me through mere touch. I feel the delicate symmetry of a leaf. I pass my hands lovingly about the smooth skin of a silver birch, or the rough shaggy bark of a pine. In spring I touch the branches of trees hopefully in search of a bud, the first sign of awakening Nature after her winter's sleep. I feel the delightful, velvety texture of a flower, and discover its remarkable convolutions, and something of the miracle of Nature is revealed to me. Occasionally, if I am fortunate, I place my hand gently on a small tree and feel the happy quiver of a bird in full song. I am delighted to have the cool waters of a brook rush through my open fingers. To me a lush carpet of pine needles or spongy grass is more welcome than the most luxurious Persian rug. To me the pageant of seasons is a thrilling and unending drama, the action of which streams through my finger tips.

At times my heart cries out with longing to see all these things. If I can get so much pleasure from mere touch, how much more beauty must be revealed by sight. Yet, those who have eyes apparently see little. The panorama of color and action which fills the world is taken for granted. It is human, perhaps, to appreciate little that which we have and to long for that which we have not, but it is a great pity that in the world of light the gift of sight is used only as a mere convenience rather than as a means of adding fullness to life.

If I were the president of a university I should establish a compulsory course in "How to Use Your Eyes." The professor would try to show his pupils how they could add joy to their lives by really seeing what passes unnoticed before them. He would try to awake their dormant and sluggish faculties.

Perhaps I can best illustrate by imagining what I should most like to see if I were given the use of my eyes, say, for just three days. And while I am imagining, suppose you, too, set your mind to work on the problem of how you would use your own eyes if you had only three more days to see. If with the oncoming darkness of the third night you knew that the sun would never rise for you again, how would you spend those three precious intervening days? What would you most want to let your gaze rest upon?

I, naturally, should want most to see the things which have become dear to me through my years of darkness. You, too, would want to let your eyes rest long on the things that have become dear to you so that you could take the memory of them with you into the night that loomed before you.

If, by some miracle I were granted three seeing days, to be followed by a relapse into darkness, I should divide the period into three parts.

On the first day, I should want to see the people whose kindness and gentleness have made my life worth living. First I should like to gaze long upon the face of my dear teacher, Mrs. Anne Sullivan Macy, who came to me when I was a child and opened the outer world to me. I should want not merely to see the outline of her face, so that I could cherish it in my memory, but to study that face and find in it the living evidence of the sympathetic tenderness and patience with which she accomplished the difficult task of my education. I should like to see in her eyes that strength of character which has enabled her to stand firm in the face of difficulties, and that compassion for all humanity which she has revealed to me so often.

I do not know what it is to see into the heart of a friend through that "window of the soul," the eye. I can only "see" through my finger tips the outline of a face. I can detect laughter, sorrow, and many other obvious emotions. I know my friends from the feel of their faces. But I cannot really picture their personalities by touch. I know their personalities, of course, through other means, through the thoughts they express to me, through whatever of their actions are revealed to me. But I am denied that deeper understanding of them which I am sure would come through sight of them, through watching their reactions to various expressed thoughts and circumstances, through noting the immediate and fleeting reactions of their eyes and countenance.

Friends who are near to me I know well, because through the months and years they reveal themselves to me in all their phases; but of casual friends I have only an incomplete impression, an impression gained from a handclasp, from spoken words which I take from their lips with my finger tips, or which they tap into the palm of my hand.

How much easier, how much more satisfying it is for you who can see to grasp quickly the essential qualities of another person by watching the subtleties of expression, the quiver of a muscle, the flutter of a hand. But does it ever occur to you to use your sight to see into the inner nature of a friend or acquaintance? Do not most of you seeing people grasp casually the outward features of a face and let it go at that?

For instance, can you describe accurately the faces of five good friends? Some of you can, but many cannot. As an experiment, I have questioned husbands of long standing about the color of their wives' eyes, and often they express embarrassed confusion and admit they do not know. And, incidentally, it is a chronic complaint of wives that their husbands do not notice new dresses, new hats, and changes in household arrangements.

The eyes of seeing persons soon become accustomed to the routine of their surroundings, and they actually see only the startling and spectacular. But even in viewing the most spectacular sights the eyes are lazy. Court records reveal every day how inaccurately "eyewitnesses" see. A given event will be "seen" in several different ways by as many witnesses. Some see more than others, but few see everything that is within the range of their vision.

Oh, the things that I should see if I had the power of sight for just three days!

The first day would be a busy one. I should call to me all my dear friends and look long into their faces, imprinting upon my mind the outward evidences of the beauty that is within them. I should let my eyes rest, too, on the face of a baby, so that I could catch a vision of the eager, innocent beauty which precedes the individual's consciousness of the conflicts which life develops.

And I should like to look into the loyal, trusting eyes of my dogs—the grave, canny little Scottie, Darkie, and the stalwart, understanding Great Dane, Helga, whose warm, tender, and playful friendships are so comforting to me.

On that busy first day I should also view the small simple things of my home. I want to see the warm colors in the rugs under my feet, the pictures on the walls, the intimate trifles that transform a house into home. My eyes would rest respectfully on the books in raised type which I have read, but they would be more eagerly interested in the printed books which seeing people can read, for during the long night of my life the books I have read and those which have been read to me have built themselves into a great shining lighthouse, revealing to me the deepest channels of human life and the human spirit.

In the afternoon of that first seeing day, I should take a long walk in the woods and intoxicate my eyes on the beauties of the world of Nature, trying desperately to absorb in a few hours the vast splendor which is constantly unfolding itself to those who can see. On the way home from my woodland jaunt my path would lie near a farm so that I might see the patient horses plowing in the field (perhaps I should see only a tractor!) and the serene content of men living close to the soil. And I should pray for the glory of a colorful sunset.

When dusk had fallen, I should experience the double delight of being able to see by artificial light, which the genius of man has created to extend the power of his sight when Nature decrees darkness.

In the night of that first day of sight, I should not be able to sleep, so full would be my mind of the memories of the day.

The next day—the second day of sight—I should arise with the dawn and see the thrilling miracle by which night is transformed into day. I should behold with awe the magnificent panorama of light with which the sun awakens the sleeping earth.

This day I should devote to a hasty glimpse of the world, past and present. I should want to see the pageant of man's progress, the kaleidoscope of the ages. How can so much be compressed into one day? Through the museums, of course. Often I have visited the New York Museum of Natural History to touch with my hands many of the objects there exhibited, but I have longed to see with my eyes the condensed history of the earth and its inhabitants displayed there—animals and the races of men pictured in their native environment; gigantic carcasses of dinosaurs and mastodons which roamed the earth long before man appeared, with his tiny stature and powerful brain, to conquer the animal kingdom; realistic presentations of the processes of evolution in animals, in man, and in the implements which man has used to fashion for himself a secure home on this planet; and a thousand and one other aspects of natural history.

I wonder how many readers of this article have viewed this panorama of the face of living things as pictured in that inspiring museum. Many, of course, have not had the opportunity, but I am sure that many who have had the opportunity have not made use of it. There, indeed, is a place to use your eyes. You who see can spend many fruitful days there, but I, with my imaginary three days of sight, could only take a hasty glimpse, and pass on.

My next stop would be the Metropolitan Museum of Art, for just as the Museum of Natural History reveals the material aspects of the world, so does the Metropolitan show the myriad facets of the human spirit. Throughout the history of humanity the urge to artistic expression has been almost as powerful as the urge for food, shelter, and procreation. And here, in the vast chambers of the Metropolitan Museum, is unfolded before me the spirit of Egypt, Greece, and Rome, as expressed in their art. I know well through my hands the sculptured gods and goddesses of the ancient Nile-land. I have felt copies of Parthenon friezes, and I have sensed the rhythmic beauty of charging Athenian warriors. Apollos and Venuses and the Wingèd Victory of Samothrace are friends of my finger tips. The gnarled, bearded features of Homer are dear to me, for he, too, knew blindness.

My hands have lingered upon the living marble of Roman sculpture as well as that of later generations. I have passed my hands over a plaster cast of Michelangelo's inspiring and heroic Moses; I have sensed the power of Rodin; I have been awed by the devoted spirit of Gothic wood carving. These arts which can be touched have meaning for me, but even they were meant to be seen rather than felt, and I can only guess at the beauty which remains hidden from me. I can admire the simple lines of a Greek vase, but its figured decorations are lost to me.

So on this, my second day of sight, I should try to probe into the soul of man through his art. The things I knew through touch I should now see. More splendid still, the whole magnificent world of painting would be opened to me, from the Italian Primitives, with their serene religious devotion, to the Moderns, with their feverish visions. I should look deep into the canvases of Raphael, Leonardo da Vinci, Titian, Rembrandt. I should want to feast my eyes upon the warm colors of Vernonese, study the mysteries of El Greco, catch a new vision of Nature from Corot. Oh, there is so much rich meaning and beauty in the art of the ages for you who have eyes to see!

Upon my short visit to this temple of art I should not be able to review a fraction of that great world of art which is open to you. I should be able to get only a superficial impression. Artists tell me that for a deep and true appreciation of art one must educate the eye. One must learn through experience to weigh the merits of line, of composition, of form and color. If I had eyes, how happily would I embark upon so fascinating a study! Yet I am told that, to many of you who have eyes to see, the world of art is a dark night, unexplored and unilluminated.

It would be with extreme reluctance that I should leave the Metropolitan Museum, which contains the key to beauty—a beauty so neglected. Seeing persons, however, do not need a Metropolitan to find this key to beauty. The same key lies waiting in smaller museums, and in books on the shelves of even small libraries. But naturally, in my limited time of imaginary sight, I should choose the place where the key unlocks the greatest treasures in the shortest time.

The evening of my second day of sight I should spend at a theater or at the movies. Even now I often attend theatrical performances of all sorts, but the action of the play must be spelled into my hand by a companion. But how I should like to see with my own eyes the fascinating figure of Hamlet, or the gusty Falstaff amid colorful Elizabethan trappings! How I should like to follow each movement of the graceful Hamlet, each strut of the hearty Falstaff! And since I could see only one play, I should be confronted by a many-horned dilemma, for there are scores of plays I should want to see. You who have eyes can see any you like. How many of you, I wonder, when you gaze at a play, a movie, or any spectacle, realize and give thanks for the miracle of sight which enables you to enjoy its color, grace, and movement?

I cannot enjoy the beauty of rhythmic movement except in a sphere restricted to the touch of my hands. I can vision only dimly the grace of a Pavlova, although I know something of the delight of rhythm, for often I can sense the beat of music as it vibrates through the floor. I can well imagine that cadenced motion must be one of the most pleasing sights in the world. I have been able to gather something of this by tracing with my fingers the lines in sculptured marble; if this static grace can be so lovely, how much more acute must be the thrill of seeing grace in motion.

One of my dearest memories is of the time when Joseph Jefferson allowed me to touch his face and hands as he went through some of the gestures and speeches of his beloved Rip Van Winkle. I was able to catch thus a meager glimpse of the world of drama, and I shall never forget the delight of that moment. But, oh, how much I must miss, and how much pleasure you seeing ones can derive from watching and hearing the interplay of speech and movement in the unfolding of a dramatic performance! If I could see only one play, I should know how to picture in my mind the action of a hundred plays which I have read or had transferred to me through the medium of the manual alphabet.

So, through the evening of my second imaginary day of sight, the great figures of dramatic literature would crowd sleep from my eyes.

The following morning, I should again greet the dawn, anxious to discover new delights, for I am sure that, for those who have eyes which really see, the dawn of each day must be a perpetually new revelation of beauty.

This, according to the terms of my imagined miracle, is to be my third and last day of sight. I shall have no time to waste in regrets or longings; there is too much to see. The first day I devoted to my friends, animate and inanimate. The second revealed to me the history of man and Nature. Today I shall spend in the workaday world of the present, amid the haunts of men going about the business of life. And where can one find so many activities and conditions of men as in New York? So the city becomes my destination.

I start from my home in the quiet little suburb of Forest Hills, Long Island. Here, surrounded by green lawns, trees, and flowers, are neat little houses, happy with the voices and movements of wives and children, havens of peaceful rest for men who toil in the city. I drive across the lacy structure of steel which spans the East River, and I get a new and startling vision of the power and ingenuity of the mind of man. Busy boats chug and scurry about the river—racy speed boats, stolid, snorting tugs. If I had long days of sight ahead, I should spend many of them watching the delightful activity upon the river.

I look ahead, and before me rise the fantastic towers of New York, a city that seems to have stepped from the pages of a fairy story. What an awe-inspiring sight, these glittering spires, these vast banks of stone and steel—structures such as the gods might build for themselves! This animated picture is a part of the lives of millions of people every day. How many, I wonder, give it so much as a second glance? Very few, I fear. Their eyes are blind to this magnificent sight because it is so familiar to them.

I hurry to the top of one of those gigantic structures, the Empire State Building, for there, a short time ago, I "saw" the city below through the eyes of my secretary. I am anxious to compare my fancy with reality. I am sure I should not be disappointed in the panorama spread out before me, for to me it would be a vision of another world.

Now I begin my rounds of the city. First, I stand at a busy corner, merely looking at people, trying by sight of them to understand something of their lives. I see smiles, and I am happy. I see serious determination, and I am proud. I see suffering, and I am compassionate.

I stroll down Fifth Avenue. I throw my eyes out of focus so that I see no particular object but only a seething kaleidoscope of color. I am certain that the colors of women's dresses moving in a throng must be a gorgeous spectacle of which I should never tire. But perhaps if I had sight I should be like most other women—too interested in styles and the cut of individual dresses to give much attention to the splendor of color in the mass. And I am convinced, too, that I should become an inveterate window shopper, for it must be a delight to the eye to view the myriad articles of beauty on display.

From Fifth Avenue I make a tour of the city—to Park Avenue, to the slums, to factories, to parks where children play. I take a stay-at-home trip abroad by visiting the foreign quarters. Always my eyes are open wide to all the sights of both happiness and misery so that I may probe deep and add to my understanding of how people work and live. My heart is full of the images of people and things. My eye passes lightly over no single trifle; it strives to touch and hold closely each thing its gaze rests upon. Some sights are pleasant, filling the heart with happiness; but some are miserably pathetic. To these latter I do not shut my eyes, for they, too, are part of life. To close the eye on them is to close the heart and mind.

My third day of sight is drawing to an end. Perhaps there are many serious pursuits to which I should devote the few remaining hours, but I am afraid that on the evening of that last day I should again run away to the theater, to a hilariously funny play, so that I might appreciate the overtones of comedy in the human spirit.

At midnight my temporary respite from blindness would cease, and permanent night would close in on me again. Naturally in those three short days I should not have seen all I wanted to see. Only when darkness had again descended upon me should I realize how much I had left unseen. But my mind would be so crowded with glorious memories that I should have little time for regrets. Thereafter the touch of every object would bring a flowing memory of how that object looked.

Perhaps this short outline of how I should spend three days of sight does not agree with the program you would set for yourself if you knew that you were about to be stricken blind. I am, however, sure that if you actually faced that fate your eyes would open to things you had never seen before, storing up memories for the long night ahead. You would use your eyes as never before. Everything you saw would become dear to you. Your eyes would touch and embrace every object that came within your range of vision. Then, at last, you would really see, and a new world of beauty would open itself before you.

I who am blind can give one hint to those who see—one admonition to those who would make full use of the gift of sight: Use your eyes as if tomorrow you would be stricken blind. And the same method can be applied to the other senses. Hear the music of voices, the song of a bird, the mighty strains of an orchestra, as if you would be stricken deaf tomorrow. Touch each object you want to touch as if tomorrow your tactile sense would fail. Smell the perfume of flowers, taste with relish each morsel, as if tomorrow you could never smell and taste again. Make the most of every sense; glory in all the facets of pleasure and beauty which the world reveals to you through the several means of contact with Nature provides. But of all the senses, I am sure that sight must be the most delightful.

QUESTIONS

1. Is the central thesis* of Keller's essay stated or implied? State the thesis in your own words.

2. How many of the early paragraphs in the essay are actually part of the introduction? What is the value of the introductory paragraphs in setting the tone* of the essay?

3. Imagine that you are in the same situation as Helen Keller and, after a life of blindness, have only three days to see. How would you spend your three days? Would your priorities differ from hers? If so, how?

4. Define the following words: *impairment, panorama, subleties, tactile, facets, dormant.*

5. Which do you consider the most valuable of your five senses? How would your life have been different if you had been born without the use of that sense?

6. Analyze the effect of the author's two closing paragraphs. What is she attempting to do? How effective is she in achieving her aim?

---

*Definitions for all terms marked with an asterisk may be found in the Glossary.

7. Helen Keller uses figurative language* throughout the essay. List examples of this colorful language and, keeping in mind Keller's physical limitations, explain the effect it has on the essay as a whole.

8. Keller speaks of the joy of being able to see the faces of friends, and then questions whether many people with sight can describe accurately the faces of five good friends. See if you can do this.

READING AND WRITING SUGGESTIONS

1. Helen Keller indicated that she would use her first day of seeing to look upon those whose "kindness and gentleness and companionship have made my life worth living." Describe the person who has played the single most significant role in your life—the person to whom you feel most indebted.

2. Read a book about the life of Franklin D. Roosevelt or some other individual of national or international reputation who has achieved success and fame in spite of a physical handicap. Write a brief essay describing the individual's handicap and giving examples of the spirit and determination which helped the individual succeed in life.

---

*Definitions for all terms marked with an asterisk may be found in the Glossary.

AN OLD COUNTRYHOUSE
AND AN OLD LADY

Henry Mackenzie

Henry Mackenzie (1745–1831), an essayist and novelist, was born in Edinburgh, Scotland. He became the editor of the Lounger, *a periodical of his day. Mackenzie was among the first to recognize the genius of the great Scottish poet, Robert Burns, and the* Lounger *carried Burns's work. Mackenzie's novels include* The Man of the World *and* The Man of Feeling. *"An Old Countryhouse and an Old Lady," taken from the* Lounger, *presents a good example of Mackenzie's gift for imagery and figurative language.*

I have long cultivated a talent very fortunate for a man of my disposition, that of traveling in my easy-chair; of transporting myself, without stirring from my parlor, to distant places and to absent friends; of drawing scenes in my mind's eye, and of peopling them with the groups of fancy, or the society of remembrance. When I have sometimes lately felt the dreariness of the town, deserted by my acquaintance; when I have returned from the coffeehouse, where the boxes were unoccupied, and strolled out from my accustomed walk, which even the lame beggar had left, I was fain to shut myself up in my room, order a dish of my best tea (for there is a sort of melancholy which disposes one to make much of oneself), and calling up the powers of memory and imagination, leave the solitary town for a solitude more interesting, which my younger days enjoyed in the country, which I think, and if I am wrong I do not wish to be undeceived, was the most Elysian spot in the world.

'Twas at an old lady's, a relation and godmother of mine, where a particular incident occasioned my being left during the vacation of two successive seasons. Her house was formed out of the remains of an old Gothic castle, of which one tower was still almost entire; it was tenanted by kindly daws and swallows. Beneath, in a modernized part of the house, resided the mistress of the mansion. The house was skirted by a few majestic elms and beeches, and the stumps of several others showed that once they had been more numerous. To the west a clump of firs covered a rugged rocky dell, where the rooks claimed a prescriptive seigniory. Through this a dashing rivulet forced its way, which afterwards grew quiet in its progress, and gurgling gently through a piece of downy meadow ground, crossed the bottom of the garden, where a little rustic paling inclosed a washing green, and a wicker seat, fronting the south, was placed for the accommodation of the old lady, whose lesser tour, when her fields did not require a visit, used to terminate in this spot. Here, too, were ranged the hives for her bees, whose hum, in a still warm sunshine, soothed the good old lady's indolence, while their proverbial industry was sometimes quoted for the instruction of her washers. The brook ran brawling through some underwood on the outside of the garden, and soon after formed a little cascade, which fell into the river that winded through a valley in front of the house. When haymaking or harvest was going on, my godmother took her long stick in her hand, and overlooked the labors of the mowers or reapers; though I believe there was little thrift in the superintendency, as the visit generally cost her a draught of beer or a dram, to encourage their diligence.

Within doors she had so able an assistant, that her labor was little. In that department an old manservant was her minister, the father of my Peter, who serves me not the less faithfully that we have gathered nuts together in my godmother's hazel bank. This old butler (I call him by his title of honor, though in truth he had many subordinate offices) had originally enlisted with her husband, who went into the army a youth (though he afterwards married and became a country gentleman), had been his servant abroad, and attended him during his last illness at home. His best hat, which he wore on Sundays, with a scarlet waistcoat of his master, had still a cockade in it.

Her husband's books were in a room at the top of a screw staircase, which had scarce been opened since his death; but her own library, for Sabbath or rainy days, was ranged in a little book press in the parlor. It consisted, so far as I can remember, of several volumes of sermons, a Concordance, Thomas à Kempis, Antoninus's *Meditations*, the works of the author of the *Whole Duty of Man*, and a translation of Boethius; the original editions of the Spectator and Guardian, Cowley's *Poems* (of which I had lost a volume soon after I first came about her house), Baker's *Chronicle*, Burnet's *History of His Own Times*, Lamb's *Royal Cookery*, Abercromby's *Scots Warriors*, and Nisbet's *Heraldry*.

The subject of the last-mentioned book was my godmother's strong ground; and she could disentangle a point of genealogy beyond any one I ever knew. She had an excellent memory for anecdotes, and her stories, though sometimes long, were never tiresome; for she had been a woman of great beauty and accomplishment in her youth, and had kept such company as made the drama of her stories respectable and interesting. She spoke frequently of such of her own family as she remembered when a child, but scarcely ever of those she had lost, though one could see that she thought of them often. She had buried a beloved husband and four children. Her youngest, Edward, "her beautiful, her brave," fell in Flanders, and was not entombed with his ancestors. His picture, done when a child, an artless red and white portrait, smelling at a nosegay, but very like withal, hung at her bedside, and his sword and gorget were crossed under it. When she spoke of a soldier, it was in a style above her usual simplicity; there was a sort of swell in her language, which sometimes a tear (for her age had not lost the privilege of tears) made still more eloquent. She kept her sorrows, like her devotions that solaced them, sacred to herself. They threw nothing of gloom over her deportment; a gentle shade only, like the fleckered clouds of summer, that increase, not diminish, the benignity of the season.

She had few neighbors, and still fewer visitors; but her reception of such as did visit her was cordial in the extreme. She pressed a little too much, perhaps; but there was so much heart and good-will in her importunity, as made her good things seem better than those of any other table. Nor was her attention confined only to the good fare of her guests, through it might have flattered her vanity more than that of most exhibitors of good dinners, because the cookery was generally directed by herself. Their servants lived as well in her hall, and their horses in her stable. She looked after the airing of their sheets, and saw their fires mended if the night was cold. Her old butler, who rose betimes, would never suffer anybody to mount his horse fasting.

The parson of the parish was her guest every Sunday, and said prayers in the evening. To say truth, he was no great genius, nor much of a scholar. I believe my godmother knew rather more of divinity than he did; but she received from him information of another sort,—he told her who were the poor, the sick, the dying of the parish, and she had some assistance, some comfort for them all.

I could draw the old lady at this moment! dressed in gray, with a clean white hood nicely plaited (for she was somewhat finical about the neatness of her person), sitting in her straight-backed elbowchair, which stood in a large window, scooped out of the thickness of the ancient wall. The middle panes of the window were of painted glass—the story of Joseph and his brethren. On the outside waved a honeysuckle tree, which often threw its shade across her book or her work; but she would not allow it to be cut down. "It has stood there many a day," said she, "and we old inhabitants should bear with one another." Methinks I see her thus seated, her spectacles on, but raised a little on her brow for a pause of explanation, their shagreen case laid between the leaves of a silver-clasped family Bible. On one side, her bell and snuffbox; on the other, her knitting apparatus in a blue damask bag. Between her and the fire an old Spanish pointer, that had formerly been her son Edward's, teased, but not teased out of his gravity, by a little terrier of mine. All this is before me, and I am a hundred miles from town, its inhabitants, and its business. In town I may have seen such a figure; but the country scenery around, like the tasteful frame of an excellent picture, gives it a heightening, a relief, which it would lose in any other situation.

Some of my readers, perhaps, will look with little relish on the portrait. I know it is an egotism in me to talk of its value; but over this dish of tea, and in such a temper of mind, one is given to egotism. It will be only adding another to say that when I recall the rural scene of the good old lady's abode, her simple, her innocent, her useful employments, the afflictions she sustained in this world, the conforts she drew from another, I feel a serenity of soul, a benignity of affections, which I am sure confer happiness, and, I think, must promote virtue.

QUESTIONS

1. Define the following words: *Elysian, Gothic, daws, seigniory, indolence, proverbial, cockade, genealogy, gorget, benignity, importunity, shagreen.*

2. What is the central thesis around which Mackenzie's essay is built? Where is this thesis most clearly stated?

3. Explain the meaning of the following phrases:
   a. "for there is a sort of melancholy which disposes one to make much of oneself"
   b. "for her age had not lost the privilege of tears"

4. From what point of view* is the essay written? Is the author consistent in his description of the house and the old lady? How does the author bring the house and the old lady into sharp focus?

5. We hear a great deal today about the plight of older people—about their loneliness and isolation in current society. To what extent

---

*Definitions for all terms marked with an asterisk may be found in the Glossary.

does the picture of the old lady painted in this essay reflect the lives of many of today's older people? What essential changes have taken place in our society regarding the aged in the time since Mackenzie's essay was written?

READING AND WRITING SUGGESTIONS

1. Write an essay describing some of the significant moments in your childhood. Consider writing about your home, your playmates, your family, or any other aspect of your childhood that evokes strong memories.

2. Write a brief essay describing one of your grandparents. Introduce some dialogue which will sharpen the picture you paint of your grandparent and of your mutual relationship.

3. Read *The Adventures of Huckleberry Finn,* Mark Twain's great novel about youthful adventure. Choose some character or scene in the book that seems particularly striking to you and write a descriptive essay giving as many details as you can about your subject.

THE END OF ALL PERFECTION

Lydia H. Sigourney

Lydia H. Sigourney (1791–1865) was born Lydia Huntley in Norwich, Connecticut. She taught school until her marriage in 1819 to Charles Sigourney, and later, when her husband suffered financial setbacks, she began writing to assist him. Her essays, poems, and stories were well received, and she became a celebrated writer of the early nineteenth century. Among her books are Letters to Young Ladies, Gleanings, The Man of Uz and Other Poems, *and* Lucy Howard's Journal. *In this essay, Sigourney describes the "end of perfection," which she sees as an inevitable element of the human condition.*

I have seen a man in the glory of his days, and in the pride of his strength. He was built like the strong oak, that strikes its root deep in the earth—like the tall cedar, that lifts its head above the trees of the forest. He feared no danger—he felt no sickness—he wondered why any should groan or sigh at pain. His mind was vigorous like his body; he was perplexed at no intricacy, he was daunted at no obstacle. Into hidden things he searched, and what was crooked he made plain. He went forth boldly upon the face of the mighty deep. He surveyed the nations of the earth. He measured the distances of the stars, and called them by their names. He gloried in the extent of his knowledge, in the vigor of his understanding, and strove to search even into what the Almighty had concealed. And when I looked upon him, I said with the poet, "What a piece of work is man! how noble in reason! how infinite in faculties! in form and moving, how express and admirable! in action how like an angel! in apprehension how like a god!"

I returned—but his look was no more lofty, nor his step proud. His broken frame was like some ruined tower. His hairs were white and scattered, and his eye gazed vacantly upon the passers-by. The vigor of his intellect was wasted, and of all that he had gained by study, nothing remained. He feared when there was no danger, and where was no sorrow he wept. His decaying memory had become treacherous. It showed him only broken images of the glory that had departed. His house was to him like a strange land, and his friends were counted as enemies. He thought himself strong and healthful, while his feet tottered on the verge of the grave. He said of his son, "He is my brother"; of his daughter, "I know her not." He even inquired what was his own name. And as I gazed mournfully upon him, one who supported his feeble frame, and ministered to his many wants, said to me, "Let thine heart receive instruction, for thou hast seen an end of all perfection!"

I have seen a beautiful female, treading the first stages of youth, and entering joyfully into the pleasures of life. The glance of her eye was variable and sweet, and on her cheek trembled something like the first blush of the morning. Her lips moved, and there was melody, and when she floated in the dance, her light form, like the aspen, seemed to move with every breeze.

I returned—she was not in the dance. I sought her among her gay companions, but I found her not. Her eye sparkled not there—the music of her voice was silent. She rejoiced on earth no more. I saw a train—sable and slow-paced. Sadly they bore towards an open grave what once was animated and beautiful. As they drew near, they paused, and a voice broke the solemn silence: "Man that is born of a woman is of few days and full of misery. He cometh up, and is cut down like a flower, he fleeth as it were a shadow, and never continueth in one stay." Then they let down into the deep, dark pit, that maiden whose lips but a few days since were like the half-blown rosebud. I shuddered at the sound of clods falling upon the hollow coffin. Then I heard a voice saying, "Earth to earth, ashes to ashes, dust to dust." They covered her with the damp soil, and the uprooted turf of the valley, and turned again to their own homes. But one mourner lingered to cast himself upon the tomb. And as he wept he said, "There is no beauty, nor grace, nor loveliness, but what vanisheth like the morning dew. I have seen an end of all perfection!"

I saw an infant, with a ruddy brow, and a form like polished ivory. Its motions were graceful, and its merry laughter made other hearts glad. Sometimes it wept—and again it rejoiced,—when none knew why. But whether its cheek dimpled with smiles, or its blue eyes shone more brilliant through tears, it was beautiful. It was beautiful because it was innocent. And careworn and sinful men admired, when they beheld it. It was like the first blossom which some cherished plant has put forth, whose cup sparkles with a dewdrop, and whose head reclines upon the parent stem.

Again I looked. It had become a child. The lamp of reason had beamed into its mind. It was simple, and single-hearted, and a follower of the truth. It loved every little bird that sang in the trees, and every fresh blossom. Its heart danced with joy as it looked around on this good and pleasant world. It stood like a lamb before its teachers —it bowed its ear to instruction—it walked in the way of knowledge. It was not proud, nor stubborn, nor envious, and it had never heard of the vices and vanities of the world. And when I looked upon it, I remembered our Savior's words, "Except ye become as little children, ye cannot enter into the kingdom of heaven."

I saw a man, whom the world calls honorable. Many waited for his smile. They pointed to the fields that were his, and talked of the silver and gold which he had gathered. They praised the stateliness of his domes, and extolled the honor of his family. But the secret language of his heart was, "By my wisdom have I gotten all this." So he returned no thanks to God, neither did he fear or serve him. As I passed along, I heard the complaints of the laborers, who had reaped his fields—and the cries of the poor, whose covering he had taken away. The sound of feasting and revelry was in his mansion, and the unfed beggar came tottering from his door. But he considered not that the cries of the oppressed were continually entering into the ears of the Most High. And when I knew that this man was the docile child whom I had loved, the beautiful infant on whom I had gazed with delight, I said in my bitterness, "Now have I seen an end of all perfection!" And I laid my mouth in the dust.

QUESTIONS

1. Sigourney makes extensive use of figurative language.* Point out examples of alliteration,* similes,* and metaphors* in her essay.

2. Is the central thesis* of the essay stated or implied? State the thesis in your own words.

3. Sigourney gives three examples to illustrate the "end of all perfection." How are the three people she describes different, and how are they alike?

4. To what purpose does the author use a quotation from the Bible in the next-to-last paragraph?

5. Give the meaning of the essay's ending and explain how this ending relates in tone* to the rest of the essay.

6. What do you think the author is saying in this essay? That there is no perfection? That perfection is tied to youth, to strength, to beauty, and to honor—and that it ends when these are gone?

7. How do you react personally to the essay? Do you feel that the author is justified in her pessimistic view of the human condition?

READING AND WRITING SUGGESTIONS

1. The author gives three examples which illustrate "the end of perfection." Choose another example that would fit Sigourney's thesis and, using her essay as a model, write a brief essay of your own describing a person's perfection and decline.

2. Read Hannah Arendt's *The Human Condition,* Vance Packard's *The Hidden Persuaders,* or a similar book about the problems that plague modern society. Write a summary of the problems as the author sees them and describe some solutions that could be applied to these problems.

---

*Definitions for all terms marked with an asterisk may be found in the Glossary.

PART THREE

Argument

The purpose of argument as a mode of discourse is to persuade the reader to accept the writer's viewpoint on an issue. There are two forms of argument: *logical argument,* which appeals to the reason or intellect of the reader, and *persuasive argument,* which appeals primarily to the reader's emotions. Needless to say, many strong arguments are wrought by combining these two forms in a single essay.

Logical argument uses three methods to develop a strong and convincing position—induction, deduction, and analogy. *Induction* presents a series of facts or truths that lead to a larger general truth. If, for example, you wanted to argue inductively that the Loch Ness Monster does not exist, you would begin your essay by stating the facts supporting your position: that no one has ever seen Nessie at close range, that photographs and films purporting to show the monster are blurred and indistinct, and that a recent scientific expedition using sophisticated equipment failed to detect any sign of the creature. You would then close your argument with the generalization that the Loch Ness Monster does not, therefore, exist.

Deduction, on the other hand, begins with a generalization about an entire class and applies that generalization to a specific member of the class. For example, you might begin a deductive argument by stating and attempting to prove the generalization that no monsters exist on earth. Once you had shown that Nessie is, indeed, a monster, you could then argue that the creature does not exist. The problems inherent in this type of argument are apparent in this example; to prove your point you would have to show not only that Nessie is a monster, but also that your generalization—no monsters exist on earth—is true.

Analogy, the third method of development, employs the reasoning that if two or more things share certain proven similarities, then they will probably be similar in other respects. To use the monster example once again, you might say that since King Kong and Nessie are both monsters, and King Kong does not exist, then Nessie also does not exist. As this example illustrates, however, analogy can easily be misused, for few ideas or things are exactly alike. If the two things being compared are only superficially similar, the analogy may be false, leading to an unreliable or untenable conclusion.

As mentioned earlier, *persuasive argument,* unlike logical argument, appeals to the emotions of the reader. Rather than depending on a specific type of reasoning, persuasive argument relies particularly on strength of language to convince the reader of the truth of a proposition. Persuasive argument is seldom effective, however, if it is not supported by logic; even the most elegant of phrases will not convince the reader who sees that the argument simply does not make sense.

The force of an argument always depends on the nature of the evidence given to support the proposition; this evidence must be both accurate and sufficient to prove the point, and the authorities quoted in support of the argument must be qualified in the subject area being discussed. Writers—and readers—of argument must be aware of logical fallacies which weaken a discussion; the most common of these are non sequiturs, post hoc ergo propter hoc reasoning, ad hominem attacks, begging the question, overgeneralization, and special pleading. If you are not aware of these logical fallacies, consult the Glossary for definitions.

I HAVE A DREAM

Martin Luther King, Jr.

Martin Luther King, Jr. (1929–1968), a Baptist minister and the president of the Southern Christian Leadership Conference, was the leader of the nationwide movement toward equal rights for blacks until his assassination in 1968. King was born in Atlanta, Georgia, and was educated at Morehouse College, Crosier Theological Seminary, Boston University, and Chicago Theological Seminary. He held honorary degrees from numerous colleges and universities and, in 1964, was awarded the Nobel Peace Prize. Some of his best-known books are Stride Toward Freedom, Strength to Love, *and* Why We Can't Wait. *In the following address, which is typical of King's rhetorical power and eloquence, he presents his dream of freedom and equality for all Americans.*

I am happy to join with you today in what will go down in history as the greatest demonstration for freedom in the history of our nation.

Five score years ago, a great American, in whose symbolic shadow we stand today, signed the Emancipation Proclamation. This momentous decree came as a great beacon light of hope to millions of Negro slaves who had been seared in the flames of withering injustice. It came as a joyous daybreak to end the long night of their captivity. But one hundred years later, the Negro still is not free. One hundred years later, the life of the Negro is still sadly crippled by the manacles of segregation and the chains of discrimination. One hundred years later, the Negro lives on a lonely island of poverty in the midst of a vast ocean of material prosperity. One hundred years later, the Negro is still anguished in the corners of American society and finds himself in exile in his own land. And so we have come here today to dramatize a shameful condition.

In a sense we have come to our nation's capital to cash a check. When the architects of our republic wrote the magnificent words of the Constitution and the Declaration of Independence, they were signing a promissory note to which every American was to fall heir. This note was the promise that all men—yes, Black men as well as white men—would be guaranteed the inalienable rights of life, liberty, and the pursuit of happiness.

It is obvious today that America has defaulted on this promissory note insofar as her citizens of color are concerned. Instead of honoring this sacred obligation, America has given the Negro people a bad check, a check which has come back marked "insufficient funds." But we refuse to believe that the bank of justice is bankrupt. We refuse to believe that there are insufficient funds in the great vaults of opportunity of this nation; and so we have come to cash this check, a check that will give us upon demand the riches of freedom and the security of justice.

We have also come to this hallowed spot to remind America of the fierce urgency of *now*. This is no time to engage in the luxury of cooling off or to take the tranquilizing drug of gradualism. *Now* is the time to make real the promises of democracy. *Now* is the time to rise from the dark and desolate valley of segregation to the sunlit path of racial justice. *Now* is the time to lift our nation from the quicksands of racial injustice to the solid rock of brotherhood. *Now* is the time to make justice a reality for all of God's children.

It would be fatal for the nation to overlook the urgency of the moment. This sweltering summer of the Negro's legitimate discontent will not pass until there is an invigorating autumn of freedom and equality. Nineteen Sixty-three is not an end, but a beginning. And those who hope that the Negro needed to blow off steam and will now be content will have a rude awakening if the nation returns to business as usual. There will be neither rest nor tranquility in America until the Negro is granted his citizenship rights. The whirlwinds of revolt will continue to shake the foundations of our nation until the bright day of justice emerges.

But there is something that I must say to my people who stand on the warm threshhold which leads into the palace of justice. In the process of gaining our rightful place, we must not be guilty of wrongful deeds. Let us not seek to satisfy our thirst for freedom by drinking from the cup of bitterness and hatred. We must forever conduct our struggle on the high plane of dignity and discipline. We must not allow our creative protest to degenerate into physical violence. Again and again we must rise to the majestic heights of meeting physical force with soul force. And the marvelous new militancy which has engulfed the Negro community must not lead us to a distrust of all white people; for many of our white brothers, as evidenced by their presence here today, have come to realize that their destiny is tied up with our destiny, and they have come to realize that their freedom is inextricably bound to our freedom.

We cannot walk alone. And as we walk we must make the pledge that we shall always march ahead. We cannot turn back. There are those who are asking the devotees of civil rights, "When will you be satisfied?" We can never be satisfied as long as the Negro is the victim of the unspeakable horrors of police brutality. We can never be satisfied as long as our bodies, heavy with the fatigue of travel, cannot gain lodging in the motels of the highways and the hotels of the cities. We cannot be satisfied as long as the Negro's basic mobility is from a smaller ghetto to a larger one. We can never be satisfied as long as our children are stripped of their selfhood and robbed of their dignity by signs stating "For Whites Only." We cannot be satisfied as long as the Negro in Mississippi cannot vote and a Negro in New York believes he has nothing for which to vote. No, no, we are not satisfied, and we will not be satisfied until justice rolls down like waters and righteousness like a mighty stream.

I am not unmindful that some of you have come here out of great trials and tribulations. Some of you have come fresh from narrow jail cells. Some of you have come from areas where your quest for freedom left you battered by the storms of persecution and staggered by the winds of police brutality. You have been the veterans of creative suffering. Continue to work with the faith that unearned suffering is redemptive.

Go back to Mississippi, and go back to Alabama. Go back to South Carolina. Go back to Georgia. Go back to Louisiana. Go back to the slums and ghettos of our Northern cities, knowing that somehow this situation can and will be changed. Let us not wallow in the valley of despair.

I say to you today, my friends, even though we face the difficulties of today and tomorrow, I still have a dream. It is a dream deeply rooted in the American dream. I have a dream that one day this nation will rise up and live out the true meaning of its creed: "We hold these truths to be self-evident, that all men are created equal." I have a dream that one day, on the red hills of Georgia, sons of former slaves and the sons of former slave owners will be able to sit down together at the table of brotherhood. I have a dream that one day even the state of Mississippi, a state sweltering with the heat of injustice, sweltering with the heat of oppression, will be transformed into an oasis of freedom and justice. I have a dream that my four little children will one day live in a nation where they will not be judged by the color of their skin, but by the content of their character.

I have a dream today. I have a dream that one day down in Alabama—with its vicious racists, with its governor's lips dripping with the words of interposition and nullification—one day right there in

Alabama, little Black boys and Black girls will be able to join hands with little white boys and white girls as sisters and brothers.

I have a dream today. I have a dream that one day every valley shall be exalted and every hill and mountain shall be made low, the rough places will be made plain and the crooked places will be made straight, and the glory of the Lord shall be revealed, and all flesh shall see it together.

This is our hope. This is the faith that I go back to the South with. And with this faith we will be able to hew out of the mountain of despair a stone of hope. With this faith we will be able to transform the jangling discords of our nation into a beautiful symphony of brotherhood. With this faith we will be able to work together, to play together, to struggle together, to go to jail together, to stand up for freedom together, knowing that we will be free one day.

And this will be the day—this will be the day when all of God's children will be able to sing with new meaning:

> My country, 'tis of thee,
> Sweet land of liberty,
>   Of thee I sing;
> Land where my fathers died,
> Land of the Pilgrims' pride,
> From every mountainside
>   Let freedom ring.

And if America is to be a great nation, this must become true.

And so let freedom ring from the prodigious hilltops of New Hampshire. Let freedom ring from the mighty mountains of New York. Let freedom ring from the heightening Alleghenies of Pennsylvania. Let freedom ring from the snow-capped Rockies of Colorado. Let freedom ring from the curvaceous slopes of California.

But not only that. Let freedom ring from Stone Mountain of Georgia. Let freedom ring from Lookout Mountain of Tennessee. Let freedom ring from every hill and molehill of Mississippi. "From every mountainside let freedom ring."

And when this happens—when we allow freedom to ring, when we let it ring from every village and every hamlet, from every state and every city—we will be able to speed up that day when all of God's children, Black men and white men, Jews and Gentiles, Protestants and Catholics, will be able to join hands and sing in the words of the old Negro spiritual: "Free at last! Free at last! Thank God Almighty. We are free at last!"

QUESTIONS

1. Define the following words: *manacles, gradualism, redemptive, interposition, nullification.*

2. List five or six of the figures of speech* King uses in his essay. How does this figurative language aid him in the presentation of his ideas?

3. King uses repetition and parallel structure* as means of heightening the appeal of his argument. Locate examples of these devices and comment on their effectiveness.

4. Would you classify the overall tone* of King's speech as rational or emotional? Cite passages to support your answer.

5. Why do you think King refers to the Emancipation Proclamation? The Constitution? The Declaration of Independence? What effect is he attempting to achieve by quoting the words of the song, "America"?

6. What are your reactions to "I Have a Dream"? Do you feel sympathy? Anger? Do you think that King's dream for black people is justified?

READING AND WRITING SUGGESTIONS

1. Over a decade has passed since King described his dream in this speech. To what extent have his hopes for his people been realized? Write a brief essay presenting specific examples to support your point of view.

2. Questions still surround King's assassination; some think that James Earl Ray acted alone, while others believe that King's death was part of a larger conspiracy. Read about the investigations that have been made into this matter and formulate your own opinion about the assassination. Then write an essay in which you present your conclusions, supporting them with concrete, factual details.

3. Read King's book, *Stride Toward Freedom,* which was published in 1958. Write a brief paper in which you describe how his positions on various issues differ from those expressed in this essay.

---

*Definitions for all terms marked with an asterisk may be found in the Glossary.

THE RIGHT TO DIE

Norman Cousins

Norman Cousins (1912–) was born in New Jersey. After studying at Columbia University, he began his career as the education editor of the New York Evening Post. *For many years, he was the literary and managing editor of the* Saturday Review of Literature, *and he is best known for his weekly editorials on a great variety of subjects. Cousins is the author and editor of a number of books, including collections of* Saturday Review *essays, many of which he wrote. Here he presents a brief and compassionate argument in support of the right to choose one's own time of death.*

The world of religion and philosophy was shocked recently when Henry P. Van Dusen and his wife ended their lives by their own hands. Dr. Van Dusen had been president of Union Theological Seminary; for more than a quarter-century he had been one of the luminous names in Protestant theology. He enjoyed world status as a spiritual leader. News of the self-inflicted death of the Van Dusens, therefore, was profoundly disturbing to all those who attach a moral stigma to suicide and regard it as a violation of God's laws.

Dr. Van Dusen had anticipated this reaction. He and his wife left behind a letter that may have historic significance. It was very brief, but the essential point it made is now being widely discussed by theologians and could represent the beginning of a reconsideration of traditional religious attitudes toward self-inflicted death. The letter raised a moral issue: does an individual have the obligation to go on living even when the beauty and meaning and power of life are gone?

Henry and Elizabeth Van Dusen had lived full lives. In recent years, they had become increasingly ill, requiring almost continual medical care. Their infirmities were worsening, and they realized they would soon become completely dependent for even the most elementary needs and functions. Under these circumstances, little dignity would have been left in life. They didn't like the idea of taking up space in a world with too many mouths and too little food.

They believed it was a misuse of medical science to keep them technically alive.

They therefore believed they had the right to decide when to die. In making that decision, they weren't turning against life as the highest value; what they were turning against was the notion that there were no circumstances under which life should be discontinued.

An important aspect of human uniqueness is the power of free will. In his books and lectures, Dr. Van Dusen frequently spoke about the exercise of this uniqueness. The fact that he used his free will to prevent life from becoming a caricature of itself was completely in character. In their letter, the Van Dusens sought to convince family and friends that they were not acting solely out of despair or pain.

The use of free will to put an end to one's life finds no sanction in the theology to which Pitney Van Dusen was committed. Suicide symbolizes discontinuity; religion symbolizes continuity, represented at its quintessence by the concept of the immortal soul. Human logic finds it almost impossible to come to terms with the concept of non-existence. In religion, the human mind finds a larger dimension and is relieved of the ordeal of a confrontation with non-existence.

Even without respect to religion, the idea of suicide has been abhorrent throughout history. Some societies have imposed severe penalties on the families of suicides in the hope that the individual who sees no reason to continue his existence may be deterred by the stigma his self-destruction would inflict on loved ones. Other societies have enacted laws prohibiting suicide on the grounds that it is murder. The enforcement of such laws, of course, has been an exercise in futility.

Customs and attitudes, like individuals themselves, are largely shaped by the surrounding environment. In today's world, life can be prolonged by science far beyond meaning or sensibility. Under these circumstances, individuals who feel they have nothing more to give to life, or to receive from it, need not be applauded, but they can be spared our condemnation.

The general reaction to suicide is bound to change as people come to understand that it may be a denial, not an assertion, of moral or religious ethics to allow life to be extended without regard to decency or pride. What moral or religious purpose is celebrated by the annihilation of the human spirit in the triumphant act of keeping the body alive? Why are so many people more readily appalled by an unnatural form of dying than by an unnatural form of living?

"Nowadays," the Van Dusens wrote in their last letter, "it is difficult to die. We feel that this way we are taking will become more usual and acceptable as the years pass.

"Of course, the thought of our children and our grandchildren makes us sad, but we still feel that this is the best way and the right way to go. We are both increasingly weak and unwell and who would want to die in a nursing home?

"We are not afraid to die. . . ."

Pitney Van Dusen was admired and respected in life. He can be admired and respected in death. "Suicide," said Goethe, "is an incident in human life which, however much disputed and discussed, demands the sympathy of every man, and in every age must be dealt with anew."

Death is not the greatest loss in life. The greatest loss is what dies inside us while we live. The unbearable tragedy is to live without dignity or sensitivity.

QUESTIONS

1. What is the central thesis* of this essay? Where is it most clearly stated?

2. Define the following words: *quintessence, stigma, abhorrent.*

3. Why is attempted suicide against the law in some states? In your opinion, are legal prohibitions against suicide justified?

4. On what arguments does Cousins base his conclusion that suicide is an acceptable end to life?

5. What do you think Goethe meant when he said that suicide "in every age must be dealt with anew"?

6. How do you feel about the issue of mercy killing? Under what conditions, if any, do you feel that mercy killing is justified?

7. What are your views on suicide? Why do you think you hold these views? Explain why you agree or disagree with Cousins's conclusion about suicide.

---

*Definitions for all terms marked with an asterisk may be found in the Glossary.

READING AND WRITING SUGGESTIONS

1. Suicide is the second highest cause of death among college students. Give this fact some thought, and write a brief essay explaining why you think this is the case.

2. Every society has its own way of dealing with death. Read a book on the subject, such as Elizabeth Kübler-Ross's *On Death and Dying,* and write an argumentative essay defending or attacking America's way of dealing with death. Discuss such aspects of the subject as: the cost of funerals, the custom of displaying the corpse, and the construction of elaborate memorial monuments.

3. "Living wills" are under considerable discussion these days. In such a document, a person requests in advance that mercy death be allowed if he or she develops an irreversible illness. Do you agree or disagree with the idea of allowing people to draw up "living wills"? Write a brief essay setting forth your arguments for or against such documents.

THE NEW CAVES

Isaac Asimov

Isaac Asimov (1920–) was born in Russia, was brought to the United States when he was three, and became an American citizen at the age of eight. He earned his B.S., M.A., and Ph.D. degrees at Columbia University. Since 1949 he has been a member of the biochemistry faculty at the Boston University School of Medicine. One of the country's most prolific contemporary writers, Asimov is the author of sixty-five books—six under his pseudonym, Paul French—and the editor of five others. He wrote his first book, Pebble in the Sky, *in 1950, and since then he has written on a variety of subjects, including science, chemistry, the human body, and outer space. In this essay, written in 1973, Asimov presents some interesting arguments for moving the earth's cities and cultures underground.*

During the ice ages, human beings exposed to the colder temperatures of the time would often make their homes in caves. There they found greater comfort and security than they would have in the open.

We still live in caves called houses, again for comfort and security. Virtually no one would willingly sleep on the ground under the stars. Is it possible that someday we may seek to add further to our comfort and security by building our houses underground—in new, man-made caves?

It may not seem a palatable suggestion, at first thought. We have so many evil associations with the underground. In our myths and legends, the underground is the realm of evil spirits and of the dead, and is often the location of an afterlife of torment. (This may be because dead bodies are buried underground, and because volcanic eruptions make the underground appear to be a hellish place of fire and noxious gases.)

Yet there are advantages to underground life, too, and something to be said for imagining whole cities, even mankind generally, moving downward; of having the outermost mile of the Earth's crust honeycombed with passages and structures, like a gigantic ant hill.

First, weather would no longer be important, since it is primarily a phenomenon of the atmosphere. Rain, snow, sleet, fog would not trouble the underground world. Even temperature variations are limited to the open surface and would not exist underground. Whether day or night, summer or winter, temperatures in the underground world would remain equable and nearly constant. The vast amounts of energy now expended in warming our surface surroundings when they are too cold, and cooling them when they are too warm, could be saved. The damage done to manmade structures and to human beings by weather would be gone. Transportation over local distances would be simplified. (Earthquakes would remain a danger, of course.)

Second, local time would no longer be important. On the surface, the tyranny of day and night cannot be avoided, and when it is morning in one place, it is noon in another, evening in still another and midnight in yet another. The rhythm of human life therefore varies from place to place. Underground, where there is no externally produced day, but only perpetual darkness, it would be artificial lighting that produces the day and this could be adjusted to suit man's convenience.

The whole world could be on eight-hour shifts, starting and ending on the stroke everywhere, at least as far as business and community endeavors were concerned. This could be important in a freely mobile world. Air transportation over long distances would no longer have to entail "jet lag." Individuals landing on another coast or another continent would find the society they reached geared to the same time of day as at home.

Third, the ecological structure could be stabilized. To a certain extent, mankind encumbers the Earth. It is not only his enormous numbers that take up room; more so, it is all the structures he builds to house himself and his machines, to make possible his transportation and communication, to offer him rest and recreation. All these things distort the wild, depriving many species of plants and animals of their natural habitat—and sometimes, involuntarily, favoring a few, such as rats and roaches.

If the works of man were removed below ground—and, mind you, below the level of the natural world of the burrowing animals—man would still occupy the surface with his farms, his forestry, his observation towers, his air terminals and so on, but the extent of that occupation would be enormously decreased. Indeed, as one imagines the underground world to become increasingly elaborate, one can visualize much of the food supply eventually deriving from hydroponic growth in artificially illuminated areas underground. The Earth's surface might be increasingly turned over to park and to wilderness, maintained at ecological stability.

Fourth, nature would be closer. It might seem that to withdraw underground is to withdraw from the natural world, but would that be so? Would the withdrawal be more complete than it is now, when so many people work in city buildings that are often windowless and artificially conditioned? Even where there are windows, what is the prospect one views (if one bothers to) but sun, sky, and buildings to the horizon—plus some limited greenery?

And to get away from the city now? To reach the real countryside? One must travel horizontally for miles, first across city pavements and then across suburban sprawls.

In an underworld culture, the countryside would be right there, a few hundred yards above the upper level of the cities—wherever you are. The surface would have to be protected from too frequent, or too intense, or too careless visiting, but however carefully restricted the upward trips might be, the chances are that the dwellers of the new caves would see more greenery, under ecologically healthier conditions, than dwellers of surface cities do today.

However odd and repulsive underground living may seem at first thought, there are things to be said for it—and I haven't even said them all.

QUESTIONS

1. Define the following words: *palatable, ecology, jet lag, hydroponic.*

2. Asimov's fourth reason for advocating underground living contains an implied criticism of the way we live today. What areas of life is Asimov commenting on here?

3. Asimov ends his essay by stating that he has not listed all the possible arguments for underground living. Add one argument to Asimov's list.

4. The truth of an argument depends upon the soundness of the evidence presented in its support. What is your evaluation of the soundness of the evidence Asimov presents?

5. What figure of speech* does Asimov use in paragraph four? Is it effective in picturing underground life? Do you think it makes underground life sound appealing?

6. What is your personal reaction to Asimov's argument for underground living? Do you think he is serious? Is his suggestion viable? Given the choice, would you opt for this style of living?

READING AND WRITING SUGGESTIONS

1. A novel by Asimov, *The Caves of Steel,* describes the underground cities of the future. Read his book and write a one-page summary of his arguments.

2. Asimov builds a case in his essay for underground living. In an essay of your own, build a case against underground living. Be sure to counter each of Asimov's four specific points with arguments of your own.

3. There has been considerable discussion in recent years about living in space and about living in underwater dwellings. Do some reading on these two types of environment. How do they compare with underground living? Which of the three life-styles do you see as most desirable? As most practical? Write a brief essay describing the life-style you would prefer and explaining the reasons for your choice.

---

*Definitions for all terms marked with an asterisk may be found in the Glossary.

IS IT TIME TO STOP LEARNING?

Davis S. Saxon

David S. Saxon (1920–) earned a Ph.D. in physics from the Massachusetts Institute of Technology. He has held a number of teaching and administrative positions in higher education and is currently president of the University of California. In the following essay, Saxon argues for a continuing emphasis on higher education in modern American society.

A strange new term has recently crept into our national vocabulary: overeducation. It is a term that would have confounded most Americans in every generation up to this Bicentennial year. For them, education was a social necessity to be provided, an individual good to be sought and an end to be sacrificed for. The only limits were the abilities and aspirations of students and the resources of the community.

What has happened in society today that gives rise to talk of overeducation? Have we actually reached and even passed the socially useful and individually rewarding limits of learning in America? Or have we somehow mislaid our proper measure of the broader values of education in a democratic society?

Let's examine this curious new term, overeducation. Overeducation for *what?* For a full and satisfying life? For a lifetime of changing careers in a rapidly changing world? For active participation in the affairs of a modern democratic government?

No, the term generally means that a person has received more learning, or other learning, than is required for his or her first major job. It may be a perfectly valid description of a person's education in relation to that particular circumstance. But that circumstance, though important, is not the whole of life. And the tendency to measure the value of education against this single, limited yardstick is disastrously shortsighted for both the individual and society.

Measures of Education

Throughout our history, American education has been built to other measures, and the results have had a tremendous influence on the nation's development. One such measure has been the need for leadership based on ability and talent rather than rank. The Pilgrims, after just sixteen years of colonizing the New World wilderness, established Harvard College, declaring that "one of the next things we longed for, and looked after was to advance learning and perpetuate it to posterity; dreading to leave an illiterate ministry to the churches, when our present ministers shall lie in the dust." And Thomas Jefferson called for the education of "youth of talent" without regard for their social or economic status as "the keystone of the arch of our government."

Another measure has been the importance of universal education to a democratic society. Benjamin Franklin wrote that "nothing is of more importance for the public weal, than to firm and train up youth in wisdom and virtue. Wise and good men are, in my opinion, the strength of a state; much more so than riches and arms." A third measure has been the advantage of merging the practical and liberal arts. When Abraham Lincoln signed the land-grant college legislation of 1862, he set America on its course toward a distinctive model of higher education, not for the few but for the many, not as a cloister but as the active partner of agriculture and industry and all the other segments of a developing society.

And when Johns Hopkins University in 1876 joined undergraduate education with the most advanced graduate instruction and research, American education was extending its reach toward the farthest frontiers of scientific and scholarly discovery.

Building to these measures has produced in America an educational system that is in many ways unparalleled in history, and this is a healthy perspective from which to view our present shortcomings and the problems that lie ahead.

Certainly education in the United States is unmatched in its accessibility to the highest levels for the broadest cross-section of the citizenry, though we have much farther to go in this respect. Our total educational structure is unequaled in its diversity—public and private institutions, religious and secular, local and statewide—and this rich diversity is our protection against control or conformity in the realm of ideas. And nowhere else has there been a more rapid transfer of scholarly discoveries through basic research to practical application.

But have we now, finally, reached the useful limits of our educational resources for many of our citizens? Can we now say to some of them, "You won't need any more formal learning for *your* role in society"? And to *which* Americans shall we say that their future working careers or their cultural horizons or their prospects for civic or political leadership don't seem to warrant the cost of a broad education beyond their immediate occupational needs?

Cultivating Potential

I am painfully aware that academic leaders have themselves too often resorted to strictly economic appeals for support because these seemed easier to explain and justify than the less tangible purposes of learning. We have too often promised more than we could deliver on investments in research, and so have invited disappointed expectations and some disillusion with what education can offer in exchange for its considerable cost. But neither education nor society in general will benefit from a continuing rebuff for these sins.

To the extent that the level of education and society's ability to put it to use are out of balance, then what a peculiarly negative solution—what a tragic waste of human potential—to limit education and learning. Wouldn't it make far better sense to concentrate on how to use the full capacity of all of our citizens?

We need that capacity now. I think we are more in need of wisdom today than at most earlier stages of our history. A broad liberal education is not the only ingredient of wisdom, but it is an essential one. We need all the knowledge we can muster to meet our technological and scientific problems. We need all the accumulated experience and understanding of humanity we can absorb to meet our social problems. And I believe we can ill afford the risk of foreclosing the maximum cultivation of that knowledge and understanding simply because it seems not to be required for immediate vocational purposes.

America's vision for 200 years has been longer than that. Over-education is an idea whose time must never come.

QUESTIONS

1. Define the following terms: *confound, perpetuate, keystone, perspective, secular, land-grant college, muster, rebuff.*

2. What is the thesis* of Saxon's essay? Where is it most clearly stated?

3. Saxon quotes three statements which date from the earliest years of this country's history and which embody the nation's early attitudes toward education. What are these statements? Do you agree with them? Why, or why not?

4. Saxon says that we are more in need of wisdom today than at earlier periods in our history, and he then lists some reasons why this is the case. Add a reason of your own to the list.

5. One of the current trends in higher education which Saxon argues against is the move away from liberal, broad-based education to education that is vocational or job-oriented. What is your opinion of this trend?

6. Is our society overproducing highly educated people? Is there a limit to the talent a society can absorb? Saxon says no to these questions, but others feel that highly educated people are made unhappy when they are forced to take jobs that do not take full advantage of their learning and talents. What is your opinion on this issue?

READING AND WRITING SUGGESTIONS

1. Design and then defend your plan for the ideal university. What kinds of students would you want the university to attract? What subjects would be taught there? What methods of teaching would be used?

2. Read John W. Gardner's *Excellence* or a similar book on American education and write a brief essay in which you attack or defend the author's point of view.

3. Write a persuasive essay on the topic, "Every American Has a Right to a College Education."

---

*Definitions for all terms marked with an asterisk may be found in the Glossary.

THE STOCKHOLM ADDRESS

William Faulkner

William Faulkner (1879–1962), one of the greatest of the modern American writers, was born in New Albany, Mississippi. In 1918 he enlisted in the Royal Canadian Air Force, and after the war ended, he enrolled at the University of Mississippi for two years. Faulkner spent most of his life in the small Mississippi town of Oxford, and the fictional Yoknapatawpha County, which served as the setting for much of his writing, is modeled on the area in which he lived. Among Faulkner's best-known works are The Sound and the Fury, Light in August, *and* As I Lay Dying. *In 1949 Faulkner was awarded the Nobel Prize in Literature; on this occasion, he gave the brief but eloquent address that follows.*

I feel that this award was not made to me as a man, but to my work—a life's work in the agony and sweat of the human spirit, not for glory and least of all for profit, but to create out of the materials of the human spirit something which did not exist before. So this award is only mine in trust. It will not be difficult to find a dedication for the money part of it commensurate with the purpose and significance of its origin. But I would like to do the same with the acclaim too, by using this moment as a pinnacle from which I might be listened to by the young men and women already dedicated to the same anguish and travail, among whom is already that one who will some day stand here where I am standing.

Our tragedy today is a general and universal physical fear so long sustained by now that we can even bear it. There are no longer problems of the spirit. There is only the question: When will I be blown up? Because of this, the young man or woman writing today has forgotten the problems of the human heart in conflict with itself which alone can make good writing because only that is worth writing about, worth the agony and the sweat.

He must learn them again. He must teach himself that the basest of all things is to be afraid; and, teaching himself that, forget it forever, leaving no room in his workshop for anything but the old verities and truths of the heart, the old universal truths lacking which any story is ephemeral and doomed—love and honor and pity and pride and compassion and sacrifice. Until he does so, he labors under a curse. He writes not of love but of lust, of defeats in which nobody loses anything of value, of victories without hope and, worst of all, without pity or compassion. His griefs grieve on no universal bones, leaving no scars. He writes not of the heart but of the glands.

Until he relearns these things, he will write as though he stood among and watched the end of man. I decline to accept the end of man. It is easy enough to say that man is immortal simply because he will endure: that when the last ding-dong of doom has clanged and faded from the last worthless rock hanging tideless in the last red and dying evening, that even then there will still be one more sound: that of his puny inexhaustible voice, still talking. I refuse to accept this. I believe that man will not merely endure: he will prevail. He is immortal, not because he alone among creatures has an inexhaustible voice, but because he has a soul, a spirit capable of compassion and sacrifice and endurance. The poet's, the writer's, duty is to write about these things. It is his privilege to help man endure by lifting his heart, by reminding him of the courage and honor and hope and pride and compassion and pity and sacrifice which have been the glory of his past. The poet's voice need not merely be the record of man, it can be one of the props, the pillars to help him endure and prevail.

QUESTIONS

1. Define the following words: *commensurate, pinnacle, travail, ephemeral.*

2. What does Faulkner mean by the last sentence in paragraph three, "He writes not of the heart but of the glands"?

3. There are three key words in Faulkner's address: *immortal, endure,* and *prevail.* Define these words and point out the differences in their meanings.

4. Faulkner's address dwells on two main themes, one concerning young writers and one concerning the fate of humanity. Describe Faulkner's two themes in greater detail and explain how he weaves them together in his address.

5. How does Faulkner support his position that "man will prevail"? Is his argument primarily rational or primarily emotional?

6. How do you respond personally to the message Faulkner conveys in this essay?

READING AND WRITING SUGGESTIONS

1. Write an essay in which you define what the role of the writer should be in today's world.

2. Faulkner says that "our tragedy today is a general and universal physical fear." Do you agree or disagree with Faulkner on this point? Write a brief essay in which you support your position.

3. Imagine that you have won an international prize for something that you have accomplished. Using Faulkner's speech as a model, write an acceptance speech in which you address an issue that you feel is of vital significance to humanity's future.

4. Read Faulkner's *Light in August* and write a brief essay in which you discuss the extent to which Faulkner himself lives up to the goals he advocates for writers in "The Stockholm Address." Use specific details to support your argument.

AGAINST CAPITAL PUNISHMENT

The Marquis of Beccaria

Cesare Bonesana, The Marquis of Beccaria (1738–1794), born in Milan and educated at the Jesuit college in Parma, is numbered among Italy's great philosophers and thinkers. Beccaria's writing style was greatly influenced by the English essayist Joseph Addison, and his first work as an essayist was printed in a small paper called Il Caffé *which was modeled after Addison's periodical, the* Spectator. *The essay below, taken from Beccaria's best-known work,* Crimes and Punishment, *deals with the highly controversial issue of capital punishment.*

Çapital punishment is injurious by the example of barbarity it presents. If human passions, or the necessities of war, have taught men to shed one another's blood, the laws, which are intended to moderate human conduct, ought not to extend the savage example, which in the case of a legal execution is all the more baneful in that it is carried out with studied formalities. To me it seems an absurdity that laws, which are the expression of the public will, which abhor and which punish homicide, should themselves commit one; and that, to deter citizens from private assassination, they should themselves order public manslaughter. What are the true and most useful laws? Are they not those covenants and conditions which all would wish observed and proposed, when the incessant voice of private interest is hushed or is united with the interest of the public? What are every man's feelings about capital punishment? Let us read them in the gestures of indignation and scorn with which everyone looks upon the executioner, who is, after all, an innocent administrator of the public will, a good citizen contributory to the public welfare, an instrument as necessary for the internal security of a state as brave soldiers are for its external. What, then, is the source of this contradiction; and why is this feeling, in spite of reason, ineradicable in mankind? Because men in their most secret hearts, that part of them which more than any other still preserves the original form of their first nature, have never believed that their lives lie at no one's disposal, save in that of necessity alone, which, with its iron sceptre, rules the universe.

What should men think when they see wise magistrates and grave priests of justice with calm indifference causing a criminal to be dragged by their slow procedure to death; or when they see a judge, while a miserable wretch in the convulsions of his last agonies is awaiting the fatal blow, pass away coldly and unfeelingly, perhaps even with a secret satisfaction in his authority, to enjoy the comforts and pleasures of life? "Ah," they will say, "these laws are but the pretexts of force, and the studied, cruel formalities of justice are but a conventional language, used for the purpose of immolating us with greater safety, like victims destined in sacrifice to the insatiable idol of tyranny. That assassination which they preach to us as so terrible a misdeed we see nevertheless employed by them without either scruple or passion. Let us profit by the example. A violent death seemed to us a terrible thing in the descriptions of it that were made to us, but we see it is a matter of a moment. How much less terrible will it be for a man who, not expecting it, is spared all that there is of pain in it."

Such are the fatal arguments employed, if not clearly, at least vaguely, by men disposed to crimes, among whom, as we have seen, the abuse of religion is more potent than religion itself.

If I am confronted with the example of almost all ages and almost all nations who have inflicted the punishment of death upon some crimes, I will reply that the example avails nothing before truth, against which there is no prescription of time; and that the history of mankind conveys to us the idea of an immense sea of errors, among which a few truths, confusedly and at long intervals, float on the surface. Human sacrifices were once common to almost all nations, yet who for that reason will dare defend them? That some few states, and for a short time only, should have abstained from inflicting death, rather favors my argument than otherwise, because such a fact is in keeping with the lot of all great truths, whose duration is but as the lightning flash in comparison with the long and dark night that envelops mankind. That happy time has not yet arrived when truth, as error has hitherto done, shall belong to the majority of men; and from this universal law of the reign of error those truths alone have hitherto been exempt, which supreme wisdom has seen fit to distinguish from others, by making them the subject of a special revelation.

The voice of a philosopher is feeble against the noise and cries of so many followers of blind custom, but the few wise men scattered over the face of the earth will respond to me from their inmost hearts.

QUESTIONS

1. Where does Beccaria state his central theme?*

2. What do you think Beccaria means by the sentence which ends, "the abuse of religion is more potent than religion itself"?

3. In your own words, list the arguments Beccaria makes against capital punishment.

4. This essay was written in the eighteenth century. How well does it portray the thinking of those today who oppose capital punishment? What arguments can you add to those Beccaria presents?

5. Define the following words: *incessant, ineradicable, sceptre, immolating, scruple.*

6. What is Beccaria's purpose in the closing sentence of the essay?

---

*Definitions for all terms marked with an asterisk may be found in the Glossary.

7. Consider the first sentence in the essay. Do you agree with Beccaria that "capital punishment is injurious by the example of barbarity it presents"? Do you think this point of view has general acceptance? If so, why do you think capital punishment continues?

READING AND WRITING SUGGESTIONS

1. Imagine that you have been asked to write an editorial for your local newspaper on the subject of capital punishment. In a brief essay, state your position on this issue and defend it.

2. Do some reading on the ways capital punishment has been carried out in this country and in others, and write a brief essay in which you discuss the relative humaneness of various means of performing capital punishment.

3. Read about three widely publicized capital punishment cases in the recent history of our country. Consult the *Reader's Guide* or other reference sources in the library to find periodicals which have given coverage to the cases. Then write a brief essay in which you discuss whether capital punishment should have been used in each of these three cases.

AWAY WITH THE REALTOR

Frank Lloyd Wright

Frank Lloyd Wright (1869–1959), widely regarded as one of the greatest architectural innovators of the twentieth century, was born in Wisconsin, the son of a preacher. He studied civil engineering at the University of Wisconsin but left the university without graduating. Wright designed over six hundred buildings, some of which are considered remarkable engineering feats. Among the best known are the Larkin Administration Building in Buffalo, New York, the Imperial Hotel in Tokyo, and the Johnson Wax Company Building. Wright was awarded the Royal Gold Medal for Architecture by King George VI of England in 1941 and the Gold Medal of the American Institute of Architecture in 1949. In addition to designing buildings, he wrote a number of books, including The Japanese Print, The Disappearing City, When Democracy Builds, *and* Genius and Mobocracy. *In "Away with the Realtor," Wright criticizes the architecture of American homes and presents a strong plea for more attention to good architectural design.*

To see America with an architecture true to itself, worthy of its new advantages in this new era of the machine—this is my "business."

To profoundly study the nature of good design, design on good terms with Nature, to produce a true, ideal American home, especially for those Americans presently settled in the lower income brackets of our famous "highest standard of living on earth"—a "standard" which may prove to have been only the biggest—this is what we need more than all else.

In other words, what we need is an American architecture.

But American architecture today is not concerned with the study of such design.

Today architecture is becoming an industry; it is no longer great art.

Architecture is becoming a business in league with its own government for housing people wholesale—at retail prices.

Looked at with perspective, the American home we now see spreading wide over the whole country—by way of the realtor, the wholesale house broker, or the "big" developer—is little more than a parody of the old congestion housing in the style of the London dormitory town, crammed with patented gadgetry: packaged ugliness in a choice of old styles or new.

Except for the car, telephone, television, the bathtub, the kitchen and the water closet, there is nothing natural to a free American humanity in any of these houses.

You need only look at the old "front yard" from a "picture window" to see the worst.

Style is and should be the character of what *we* are, not what the house-builder boys would have us be. Style is and should be the expression of our free spirits.

But these so busy all-go-getter boys care too little about the human spirit!

They do not care enough to buy good design. They buy (cheap). They pirate what can be had from the American Institute of Architects' back room or from the market magazines on the newsstands. Why pay for what is on every stand or out there in the gutter now in every city and suburb in America?

These big boys, with the help of duly managed publicity, give us the works on a big scale. They are putting themselves, the producers, in control of us, the consumers.

Because they pay much for publicity, but not much for design (good or bad), they have given to the word *housing* itself the sound of something evil.

These are their crimes: they deny the spirit of man and divorce man from Nature.

The successful ones turn away from that grand and challenging abstraction: design on good terms with Nature!

Instead, some designer (so-called) sits in his office to "turn out" something, anything that will capture the imagination of his boss.

The boss himself is busy out front selling "designs" to the customer, pursuing his chosen profession without benefit of culture or the necessary range of mind or any experience of the integrity of spirit.

And the poor customer, too. Usually he is a prospective homeowner or a government administrator whose only claim to good judgment in architecture is the fact that he has the money.

His culture is usually in his wife's name. He does not know or care much how to live better or how others might live better. Perhaps he—the "customer"—is the chief obstacle to good design, but I won't believe it until he is shown something better.

There are other culprits not so easy to see.

The "realtor" is even more to blame for this packaging of domestic ugliness.

He does not admit that our people should have homes built in the spirit in which our democracy (our freedom) was conceived; does not seem to know that the individual should be integrated and free in his environment, that his environment should be appropriate to new human circumstances, and that the free man and wife should lead a life as beautiful as it can be made in modern times.

He does not allow that the smaller the piece of green earth for this individual, the more unprofitable will be his life, not only for himself but also for humanity.

Rather, the realtor watches the crowd, senses its direction, and gets out to the site before it can arrive.

He gets control of the land, chops it into regular little square pieces side by side and measures success by the smallness of the pieces: the more pieces the better his "success."

In this crowding his profit lies, but never was there any need in America to pack anybody in.

We now have millions of individual building sites available everywhere. Most of them are neglected.

Why, when there is so much idle ideal land, should it be parceled out by realtors to families in tiny strips twenty-five-, fifty-, one-hundred-feet wide?

An acre of ground per family should be the democratic minimum if our country is to survive with its spirit intact. If every family had an acre of ground we should not fill the state of Texas alone. There would be room for playgrounds as well to help solve the teen-ager problem the realtor has helped to create.

The individual realtor is no more to blame than all those bankers (almost all of them) who play it safe and refuse to loan money on a scheme for the house that has good design and sufficient ground.

Bankers, like realtors, are uneducated in good design and are themselves a part of the feudal mass-ignorance which they exploit.

The motto of the banker is "safety first."

Safety means the commonplace to him. Conformity.

Ignorance playing it safe for ignorance.

The education that might have dispelled ignornace and improved the character of life was and is lacking.

In place of the growth of character through education, we have enshrined the old rural maxim: "T'ain't never dangerous to be safe."

Today we have a country full of preachers and teachers advocating it. It is the motto of the average man as he drifts toward conformity, as he becomes the limited-mediocre man, the man we have over-privileged, just as other societies overprivileged royalty.

What we will have done with Democracy is worse than Monarchy.

We placate the mass man, not with grace or style, but "house" him, wholesale at retail.

We play it "safe." We lose our great advantages because we abuse the machine and leave it to such misrepresentatives of the power of machine as the realtor and his big builder.

Every day in every way, we see machine production in control of man's consumption. The machine is imposing ugliness upon our humanity. Machine production is demoralizing the people. Money is used to complete the spiritual degradation of America.

What we are seeing is the disintegration of the integrity essential to Democracy.

We ourselves see: the more money one gets and keeps the more we become stupid standpatters, safety-seekers, defending what the machine has done to us.

Thus, through mass-ignorance and capital "playing it safe," our people get what "housing" they get.

Animals are penned or stabled.

Humans are "housed!"

In this human misery we call "housing," we see, too, the heavy hand of government that should have no business there.

Once politics was the science of human happiness; now it is the imbalance of craftsmanship where getting the most votes lies.

That is why, architecturally speaking, Democratic government has not built a single city of its own in these United States.

I had a chat with the mayor of Philadelphia not long ago.

I found him to be a genuine leader, a lover of his city and fellow man, a perfect mayor. Except in one respect.

Architecturally, he had no conception of what a free city should be. He believed that you could get more culture out of a city by having people step over each other's heads and elbow each other in crowds.

His conception of Philadelphia was the same one that prevailed when that city was first laid out; a carbon copy of the London dormitory town; a congested city built on a plan that predates both the existence of liberty in this country and our new scientific advantages.

We Americans planted here on earth a sweeping assertion of man's spirit—the "sovereignty of the individual"—but our materialism warped us and we put the spirit of man out of business!

The Communists are trying this, too—"by bread alone."

So, are we attempting to beat them at their own game?

Powerful are the forces arrayed against the idea of an architecture worthy of America—the designer, the builder, ignorant customers, sordid banker, the hustling realtor, all cherished by blind mass-government.

Where then does our hope lie?

In all this doghousing of our people, where can we find inspiration for the American life of which our fore-fathers dreamed?

Can our architecture ever contribute to the free man's spirit and his ability to live a "free" life of his own?

Where is a more natural plan and procedure to come from?

Well, first, if it is to come at all, we must be aware of the truth.

My Welsh grandfather's motto was "Truth against the World." When I built my first home, I had carved in the oak slab above the brick fireplace the motto "Truth is Life": a challenge to sentimentality.

Soon after, I thought: Why did I not make it "Life is Truth" and say what I really meant?

I could not alter it; it was built.

If we become aware of the truth, we may live again and take deeper thought on our goal and its problems.

To really "think," Louis Sullivan, *Lieber Meister*,[1] used to say, "is to deal in simples."

Simplicity is a gospel in itself.

So let us start with a house.

What Is a House?

A house is a human circumstance in Nature, like a tree or the rocks of the hills; a good house is a technical performance where form and function are made one; a house is integral to its site, a grace, not a disgrace, to its environment, suited to elevate the life of its individual inhabitants; a house is therefore integral with the nature of the methods and materials used to build it. A house to be a good home has throughout what is most needed in American life today—integrity.

Integrity, once there, enables those who live in that house to take spiritual root and grow.

The real barrier to this new integrity is the lack of good design.

"Good design" is found at the very root of our civilization where now spiritual values are weakened by selfishness and over-privileged ignorance.

---

1. Beloved master teacher.

Is not the nature study of good design our basic necessity?

Truth is, good design has already appeared and is well on the way to individual recognition over the dead bodies of the materialists. New architecture has come from the intelligent use of available machinery for machine prefabrication.

Marshall Erdman is a prefabricator for whom I have designed a standardized three-bedroom house factory-built, erected in the field; this house that would cost without prefabrication $50,000 sells for about $35,000.

The factory has gone to the house; the house is not taken to the factory.

These homes are a start; more and better will follow.

But, first, there must come the *will* to have space—more space on the ground commensurate with the needs of a family growing in the modern spirit of man.

Next to this spacious planning on and of the ground comes better and more natural designs for the prefabrication of buildings to be built upon the ground.

The intricacy of doors and windows and other detailed conveniences of occupation, the appurtenance system (heat and light)—in these matters the factory must finally decide and yet, all these matters must be so designed as to admit of fine varied planning in the design.

All this together amounts to about two-thirds the cost of such an especially designed structure.

So it is important now to take the factory to the house.

Here and there, more or less, by fits and starts, besides the Erdman homes, some of this is going on.

But still lacking is the basic nature study concerning "good design" that can see and use the whole as a unit, serviceable to man's higher ideal of himself and more agreeable not only to his machine methods but to his own love of nature.

How to state this in terms of reality in this whirlpool of selfish, conflicting interests? A statement like this:

Abandon forever the plan of the London-style house, of the dormitory town, of wholesale realtor housing at retail prices and of any participation by government in housing.

For the sake of posterity turn the American home out into more green acreage.

Next: get an over-all plan for the house that not only affords the right to privacy but protects it and affords the charm of living that should be the profit of the individual for living at all in this amazing man-made era of the mighty machine.

Our present drift toward conformity is the illogical betrayal of all for which we became a great nation to present and prove to the world —that is, the right of every man to be true to his better self as himself, free to dream and build, therefore free according to the best and bravest yet known to him; ruled only by the bravest and best.

One more idea: how do we learn where to find the bravest and the best where building is concerned and, when found, how so to use it as to *be* it?

We must learn it from teachers who are qualified by some earned excellence which they are able to impart, but which is so hard to come by. We must reward the teacher as one of first importance.

The realtor and the developer, the banker and the businessman, however activated by altruism, have not qualified themselves for this high service. Their methods need reform or abolition.

Such men as we need should be found capable in the ranks of our American architects—found there, or they will not be found at all.

Call upon our young architects and ourselves to be more careful of their education.

Insist now upon improving the qualifications of the young architect.

Insist upon freedom of life and a fresh new integrity of spirit; the characteristics of true individuality.

Call upon the young with the spirit of youth to help work out these problems of good design, with no interference of any kind by government. In America, government must stay out of culture—it can therefore have no business with housing.

Call upon the young and tell the banker and house broker to reform their many habits.

Disenfranchise wholesale housing at retail prices.

Accomplish this and the *design* for the home-making in America can become as genuine as a work of art in itself.

Recognize the machine as the appropriate magnificent tool of prefabrication to be used *for* man, not *on* him.

QUESTIONS

1. What is the central thesis* of this essay? Is it stated or implied?

2. Wright, who is given to bold assertions, blames a number of people and agencies in addition to the realtor for the ugliness of

---

*Definitions for all terms marked with an asterisk may be found in the Glossary.

housing design. Who are these people and, according to Wright, how are they to blame?

3. Explain the following ideas and show how Wright uses them in his case against modern American architecture.
—"packaging of domestic ugliness"
—"the motto of the banker is 'safety first' "
—"ignorance playing it safe for ignorance"

4. In his essay, does Wright present a sufficient amount of evidence to justify his generalization about American housing? Do you find any examples in the essay of loaded words,* slanted words,* slogans,* or sarcasm? To what end are these devices used? Do you think Wright achieves his purpose in using them?

5. a. Convinced of the connection between architectural excellence and the "free man's spirit," Wright argues that we cannot have the kind of life of which our ancestors dreamed as long as our houses are mean and ugly. Do you agree? Why, or why not?
    b. How do you react to Wright's argument that "an acre of ground per family should be the democratic minimum if our country is to survive with its spirit intact"? Does Wright put too much emphasis on space? Explain your answer.

6. What are the implications of Wright's statement, "powerful are the forces arrayed against the idea of an architecture worthy of America"? Do you think that Wright is justified in criticizing the "ignorant customer," "the sordid banker," "the hustling realtor," and "blind mass-government"? If our architectural style is bad, where do you assign the blame?

7. Explain what you think Wright's reason is for preferring the statement "Life is Truth" to "Truth is Life"? How do these statements relate to the essay as a whole? How do they relate to you in your own life?

READING AND WRITING SUGGESTIONS

1. Write an essay in answer to Wright from the viewpoint of the realtor, responding to the arguments Wright presents in this essay. Then write an answer from the viewpoint of the customer.

---

*Definitions for all terms marked with an asterisk may be found in the Glossary.

2. Write a brief essay about the house or apartment building where you live, defending it—or condemning it—in terms of the arguments set forth in Wright's essay.

3. Write a brief essay describing what you consider to be the perfect house. Explain why you value the architectural elements you describe.

4. Wright mentions the prefabricated houses of Marshall Erdman. Since this essay was written, other builders have attempted to combine excellence of design with mass-produced housing— sometimes with more negative than positive results. Read about some of the current innovations in housing, including the latest trends in prefabrication, solar heating, and general design. In a brief essay, attack or defend these "new houses."

---

from <u>THE RIGHTS OF WOMAN</u>

Mary Wollstonecraft

Mary Wollstonecraft (1759–1797), born near London, England, was a pioneer in the women's rights movement. She began to earn her own living at an early age, working first as a lady's companion, then as a schoolteacher, and later as a governess. Her first published work, Thoughts on the Education of Daughters, *precipitated her introduction to a London circle of literary figures, including William Godwin, an English political philosopher and man of letters whom she married ten years later, in 1797. She died seven months after her marriage, shortly after giving birth to a daughter. Mary Wollstonecraft's major work is* A Vindication of the Rights of Woman. *Many of her ideas on equality of the sexes were shocking to her contemporaries but were prophetic of later developments in women's rights. Some of these ideas are expressed in the essay that follows.*

It is vain to expect virtue from women till they are, in some degree, independent of men; nay, it is vain to expect that strength of natural affection which would make them good wives and mothers. Whilst they are absolutely dependent on their husbands they will be cunning, mean, and selfish; and the men who can be so gratified by the fawning fondness of spaniel-like affection have not much delicacy, for love is not to be bought, in any sense of the words, its silken wings are instantly shrivelled up when any thing beside a return in kind is sought. Yet whilst wealth enervates men, and women live, as it were, by their personal charms, how can we expect them to discharge those ennobling duties which equally require exertion and self-denial. . . .

The private or public virtue of woman is very problematical; for Rousseau and a numerous list of male writers insist that she should all her life be subjected to a severe restraint, that of propriety. Why subject her to propriety—blind propriety—if she be capable of acting from a nobler spring, if she be an heir of immortality? Is sugar always to be produced by vital blood? Is one half of the human species, like the poor African slaves, to be subject to prejudices that brutalize them, when principles would be a surer guard, only to sweeten the cup of man? Is not this indirectly to deny woman reason? for a gift is a mockery if it be unfit for use. . . .

To render her really virtuous and useful, she must not, if she discharge her civil duties, want, individually, the protection of civil laws; she must not be dependent on her husband's bounty for her subsistence during his life or support after his death—for how can a being be generous who has nothing of its own? or virtuous who is not free? The wife, in the present state of things, who is faithful to her husband and neither suckles nor educates her children, scarcely deserves the name of a wife and has no right to that of a citizen. But take away natural rights and duties become null.

Women, then, must be considered as only the wanton solace of men when they become so weak in mind and body that they cannot exert themselves unless to pursue some frothy pleasure or to invent some frivolous fashion. What can be a more melancholy sight to a thinking mind than to look into the numerous carriages that drive helter-skelter about this metropolis in a morning, full of pale-faced creatures who are flying from themselves! I have often wished, with Dr. Johnson, to place some of them in a little shop with half a dozen children looking up to their languid countenances for support. I am much mistaken, if some latent vigor would not soon give health and spirit to their eyes, and some lines drawn by the exercise of reason on the blank cheeks, which before were only undulated by dimples, might restore lost dignity to the character, or rather enable it to attain the true dignity of its nature. Virtue is not to be acquired even by speculation, much less by the negative supineness that wealth naturally generates.

Besides, when poverty is more disgraceful than even vice, is not morality cut to the quick? Still to avoid misconstruction, though I consider that women in the common walks of life are called to fulfill the duties of wives and mothers by religion and reason, I cannot help lamenting that women of a superior cast have not a road open by which they can pursue more extensive plans of usefulness and independence. I may excite laughter by dropping a hint which I mean to pursue some future time, for I really think that women ought to have representatives, instead of being arbitrarily governed without having any direct share allowed them in the deliberations of government. . . .

It is a melancholy truth; yet such is the blessed effect of civilization! The most respectable women are the most oppressed; and, unless they have understandings far superior to the common run of understandings, taking in both sexes, they must, from being treated like contemptible beings, become contemptible. How many women thus waste life away, the prey of discontent, who might have practised as physicians, regulated a farm, managed a shop, and stood erect supported by their own industry, instead of hanging their heads surcharged with the dew of sensibility that consumes the beauty to which it at first gave lustre; nay, I doubt whether pity and love are so near akin as poets feign, for I have seldom seen much compassion excited by the helplessness of females unless they were fair; then, perhaps, pity was the soft handmaid of love, or the harbinger of lust.

How much more respectable is the woman who earns her own bread, by fulfilling any duty, than the most accomplished beauty!—beauty did I say?—so sensible am I of the beauty of moral loveliness or the harmonious propriety that attunes the passions of a well-regulated mind, that I blush at making the comparison; yet I sigh to think how few women aim at attaining this respectability by withdrawing from the giddy whirl of pleasure or the indolent calm that stupefies the good sort of women it sucks in.

QUESTIONS

1. Explain what Wollstonecraft means by the following sentences:
    a. "Is sugar always to be produced by vital blood?"
    b. "The most respectable women are the most oppressed."

2. Was the author's comparison of women to "poor African slaves" a valid comparison in the 1700s, when this essay was written? Is it a valid comparison now?

3. Do you disagree with any of the statements Wollstonecraft makes in this essay? If so, list these statements and explain why you object to them.

4. Define the following words as they are used in this selection: *enervates, propriety, suckles, supineness, harbinger.*

5. a. What two main points is Wollstonecraft making in the last paragraph?
   b. How does this ending relate to the remainder of the essay? Is Wollstonecraft:
     —echoing the introduction?
     —stating the central theme?
     —making suggestions or offering solutions?

6. With what details does Wollstonecraft convey her view of marriage?

7. Do you think this essay is logical or persuasive in its approach? Explain your answer.

READING AND WRITING SUGGESTIONS

1. Wollstonecraft's essay on women's rights was written in the eighteenth century. Write a brief essay in which you discuss the ways her arguments differ from or agree with those a contemporary feminist might use. As you plan your essay, keep in mind that some of the problems Wollstonecraft points out have been resolved and that new problems have arisen since her essay was written.

2. Look at the advertisements and tables of contents in several women's magazines—for example, *Ladies' Home Journal, McCall's* and *Cosmopolitan.* Compare the topics that are being discussed in current issues with the topics of ten years ago, noting the essential ways in which they have changed. Write an essay defending or attacking the new image of women that the contemporary articles reflect.

3. Describe a situation you know of personally in which a woman was discriminated against primarily because of her sex. Use this situation as the focus for a brief essay about a specific problem facing women in today's society.

OF LOQUACITY
AND TEDIOUSNESS
IN DISCOURSE

Owen Felltham

Owen Felltham (1602–1668) was born in Suffolk, England. Not much detail is known about his life. He began writing at an early age, having written one well-known work when he was eighteen. Felltham modeled his writing after that of Francis Bacon, emulating the earlier writer's wit and brevity. These qualities are illustrated in the following persuasive essay, in which Felltham makes a case for brevity and conciseness in speaking.

A prating barber came to trim King Archelaus,[1] and said to him, "How will you please to have me cut your hair?" —Said the king, "Silently." And, certainly, though a man has nothing to do, but to hear and answer, yet a boundless tongue is a strange unbridled beast to be worried with. And the misery is, that those who speak much seldom speak well: it is a sign of ignorance not to know that long speeches, though they may please the speaker, are the torture of the hearer. Horace,[2] I think, was to be pitied when he was put into a sweat, and almost slain in the *Via Sacra*,[3] by the accidental detention of a prating tongue. There is nothing tires one more than words, when they clatter, like a loose window shaken by the wind. A talkative fellow may be compared to an unbraced drum, which beats a wise man out of his wits. Surely, nature did not guard the tongue with the double fence of teeth and lips, without meaning that it should not move too nimbly. When a scholar full of words applied to Isocrates[4] for instruction, the latter demanded of him a double fee:

---

1. A king of Macedon in the fifth century B.C.
2. A Roman poet and satirist who lived from 65 to 8 B.C.
3. The main street in the Roman Forum.
4. An Athenian orator who lived between 436 and 338 B.C.

one, to teach him to speak well; another, to teach him to hold his peace. Those who talk too much to others, I fear, seldom speak enough with themselves; and then, for want of acquaintance with their own bosoms, they may well be mistaken and exhibit foolishness when they think they are displaying wisdom. Loquacity is the fistula of the mind,—ever running and almost incurable. Some are blabbers of secrets, and these are traitors to society; they are vessels unfit for use, for they are bored in their bottoms.

There are others, again, who will cloy you with their own inventions, and this is a fault of poets. He who in his epigram invited his friend to supper made him promise that he

—no verses would repeat.

Some will preamble a tale impertinently, and cannot be delivered of a jest, till they have traveled an hour in trivials; as if they had taken the whole particulars in shorthand, and were reading from their notes: — thus they often spoil a good dish with improper sauce and unsavory farcements. Some are addicted to counseling, and will pour it in, even till they stop the ear. Tedious admonitions stupefy the advised, and make the giver contemptible. It is the short reproof which stays like a stab in the memory, that tells; and oftentimes three words do more good than an idle discourse of three hours. Some have varieties of stories, even to the wearing out of an auditor; and this is frequently the grave folly of old persons, whose unwatched tongues stray into the waste of words, and give us cause to blame their memories, for retaining so much of their youth. There are others also who have a leaping tongue, to jig into the tumult of discourse; and unless you have an Aristius[5] to take you off, you are in great danger of a deep vexation. A rook yard in a spring morning is not a greater nuisance than one of these. Doubtless, the best is to be short, plain, and material. Let me hear one wise man sentence it, rather than twenty fools, garrulous in their lengthened tattle.— *Est tempus quando nihil, est tempus quando aliquid; nullum autem est tempus, in quo dicenda sunt omnia.* (Hug. Vict.)[6] There is a time when we ought to be silent, and there is a time when we may speak; but there is no time in which all things should be spoken.

---

5. A friend of the Roman poet Horace.
6. Hugh of St. Victor's, a Persian scholar of the twelfth century.

QUESTIONS

1. Which sentence in this essay most accurately states its thesis?*

2. Give three examples of the figurative language* Felltham uses in the essay.

3. Do you think this essay is unified* and coherent?* If so, what factors do you think help to achieve this? If not, explain why you think the essay is not coherent.

4. How effective is the first sentence in setting the tone* of the essay?

5. Felltham uses illustrations throughout his essay. Name some of these and discuss how important they are to the development of his argument.

6. Can you think of a situation in which Felltham's advice on loquacity would not apply?

7. Define the following words used in the essay: *prating, fistula, epigram, cloy, impertinent, reproof, vexation, garrulous, rook yard.*

READING AND WRITING SUGGESTIONS

1. Imagine that you have been asked to write an editorial for the school paper on how to speak effectively. In your essay, show how Felltham's admonition relates specifically to public speakers, teachers, trial lawyers, and car salespeople.

2. Find an essay, in this book or in another collection, which you think is excessively wordy. Rewrite it, applying Felltham's advice, "the best is to be short, plain, and material."

3. Read T. S. Eliot's play, *The Cocktail Party,* in which superficial conversation is amply illustrated. In a persuasive essay, defend or attack this type of communication, explaining either its social uses or its lack of usefulness.

---

*Definitions for all terms marked with an asterisk may be found in the Glossary.

DARWIN'S CONCLUSION ON HIS THEORY AND RELIGION

Charles Robert Darwin

Charles Robert Darwin (1809–1882) was born in Shrewsbury, England. Although he ultimately achieved fame as a naturalist and author, he first studied medicine at Edinburgh University and later transferred to Cambridge, where he studied for the ministry. When he was twenty-two, however, he was appointed naturalist on the H.M.S. Beagle, and this five-year sailing expedition prepared him for his lifework in the study of the evolution of species. In 1859, Darwin's great work, The Origin of Species, *was published. Darwin's theory of evolution brought him wide renown, but it also caused a storm of controversy. In the essay that follows, Darwin defends his theory, asserting that no conflict exists between it and religion.*

I see no good reason why the views given in this volume should shock the religious feelings of any one. It is satisfactory, as showing how transient such impressions are, to remember that the greatest discovery ever made by man, namely, the law of the attraction of ·gravity, was also attacked by Leibnitz, "as subversive of natural, and inferentially of revealed, religion." A celebrated author and divine has written to me that "he has gradually learned to see that it is just as noble a conception of the Deity to believe that he created a few original forms, capable of self-development into other and needful forms, as to believe that he required a fresh act of creation to supply the voids caused by the action of his laws."

Why, it may be asked, until recently did nearly all the most eminent living naturalists and geologists disbelieve in the mutability of species? It cannot be asserted that organic beings in a state of nature are subject to no variation; it cannot be proved that the amount of variation in the course of long ages is a limited quantity; no clear distinction has been, or can be, drawn between species and well-marked varieties. It cannot be maintained that species when inter-crossed are invariably sterile, and varieties invariably fertile; or that sterility is a special endowment and sign of creation. The belief that species were immutable productions was almost unavoidable as long as the history of the world was thought to be of short duration; and now that we have acquired some idea of the lapse of time, we are too apt to assume, without proof, that the geological record is so perfect that it would have afforded us plain evidence of the mutation of species, if they had undergone mutation. . . .

Authors of the highest eminence seem to be fully satisfied with the view that each species has been independently created. To my mind it accords better with what we know of the laws impressed on matter by the Creator, that the production and extinction of the past and present inhabitants of the world should have been due to secondary causes, like those determining the birth and death of the individual. When I view all beings not as special creations, but as the lineal descendants of some few beings which lived long before the first bed of the Cambrian system was deposited, they seem to me to become ennobled. Judging from the past, we may safely infer that not one living species will transmit its unaltered likeness to a distant futurity. And of the species now living very few will transmit progeny of any kind to a far distant futurity; for the manner in which all organic beings are grouped shows that the greater number of species in each genus, and all the species in many genera, have left no descendants, but have become utterly extinct. We can so far take a prophetic glance into futurity as to foretell that it will be the common and widely spread species, belonging to the larger and dominant groups within each class, which will ultimately prevail and procreate new and dom-inant species. As all the living forms of life are the lineal descendants of those which lived long before the Cambrian epoch, we may feel certain that the ordinary succession by generation has never once been broken, and that no cataclysm has desolated the whole world. Hence we may look with some confidence to a secure future of great length. And as natural selection works solely by and for the good of each being, all corporeal and mental endowments will tend to prog-ress towards perfection.

It is interesting to contemplate a tangled bank, clothed with many plants of many kinds, with birds singing on the bushes, with various insects flitting about, and with worms crawling through the damp earth, and to reflect that these elaborately constructed forms, so dif-ferent from each other, and dependent upon each other in so complex a manner, have all been produced by laws acting around us. These laws, taken in the largest sense, being growth with reproduction;

inheritance, which is almost implied by reproduction; variability from the indirect and direct action of the conditions of life, and from use and disuse; a ration of increase so high as to lead to a struggle for life, and as a consequence to natural selection, entailing divergence of character and the extinction of less improved forms. Thus, from the war of nature, from famine and death, the most exalted object which we are capable of conceiving, namely, the production of the higher animals, directly follows. There is grandeur in this view of life, with its several powers, having been originally breathed by the Creator into a few forms or into one; and that, whilst this planet has gone cycling on according to the fixed law of gravity, from so simple a beginning endless forms most beautiful and most wonderful have been, and are being evolved.

QUESTIONS

1. What is the central thesis* in this essay? Is it stated or implied?

2. To what use does Darwin put the two quotations in the first paragraph?

3. State Darwin's theory of evolution in your own words. Do you think his defense of this theory is logically developed in this essay, or do you think he relies primarily on persuasion to put across his ideas?

4. Is Darwin optimistic or pessimistic about the future of life forms in general? Of specific life forms?

5. Why do you think that so many people of Darwin's time were offended and outraged by his theory of evolution?

6. Define the following words: *inferentially, mutability, Cambrian, genus.*

7. What is your personal view of Darwin's theory of evolution? Does it challenge your own religious beliefs?

READING AND WRITING SUGGESTIONS

1. Imagine that you have been asked to appear before a church group either to defend or to attack Darwin's theory of evolution. Write an outline of the arguments you would use to support your position.

---

*Definitions for all terms marked with an asterisk may be found in the Glossary.

2. The famous Scopes trial, conducted in 1925, climaxed a controversy over the teaching of the theory of evolution in Tennessee's schools. Read about the events which led up to the trial and review the trial's outcome. Then write a brief essay in which you describe the issues involved in the trial and discuss whether you think a similar controversy could develop today.

PART FOUR

Narration

Narration is the mode of discourse that presents a sequence of events occurring over a period of time. Narrative essays may deal with factual events—ranging from the sinking of the *Titanic* to an episode in the writer's childhood—or they may deal with highly imaginative or fictional events—for example, the arrival on earth of the first extraterrestrial beings. But whether a narrative is factual or imaginative, it is distinguished from the three other modes of discourse in that it expresses its thesis indirectly by showing it rather than directly by telling about it.

Narration may be dramatized, generalized, or summarized. *Dramatized* narration shows characters in action, portraying them as vividly as possible and often presenting dialogue to heighten the immediacy of the scene. In *generalized* narration, the writer maintains a greater distance from the subject, presenting it in a more subdued and contemplative manner. *Summarized* narration condenses generalized narration, presenting a sequence of events both briefly and concisely.

Narrative writing should employ the same sound rhetorical and logical procedures that are essential to the other modes of discourse, and particular attention should be paid to sequential coherence, point of view, and dialogue. To achieve sequential coherence, the writer must decide whether to adopt a strict chronological approach—recounting events as they happened in time—or whether to create a different temporal approach—perhaps giving the story's conclusion first and then showing the events that led up to it. The method used should be determined by the writer's purpose and the nature of the material that is being presented.

To achieve a consistent point of view, the writer must decide whether to give a first-person or a third-person account of an event and must maintain this point of view throughout the essay. Point of view has a great effect on the emphasis of an essay: a first-person narrative is generally more personal, revealing in depth the writer's reactions to an event, whereas a third-person narrative tends to be more objective and allows the writer to explore the private thoughts, feelings, motives, and activities of one or more characters in as much detail as desired.

When presenting dialogue, the writer must demonstrate a good ear, choosing vocabulary and speech patterns to suit the character speaking. No matter how interesting a dialogue may be, no one will find it convincing if the truck driver who is speaking sounds like a teenage girl or if a small child sounds like a college-educated adult.

One further note: each of the essays in this section is essentially a narrative—that is, most of the essay is a story, presented to entertain, to demonstrate an idea, or both. Often writers use stories or anecdotes merely as support for their central thesis, presenting them as examples which point up the truth of their ideas. Such essays are classified elsewhere in this volume in the sections on exposition, description, and argument.

A CHILD'S DREAM OF A STAR

Charles Dickens

Charles Dickens (1812–1870) was born in England to a poor family. When he was twelve his father was taken to debtor's prison, leaving Dickens to support himself. The humiliation associated with his poverty and his father's arrest stayed with him throughout his life, and many of his novels are concerned with unhappy children, as well as social injustice of all kinds. Dickens's vivid portrayal of the poor living conditions endured by the lower classes did much to influence the wealthier classes of Victorian England to examine the social problems of their day. Among his most famous works are the Pickwick Papers, A Christmas Carol, Oliver Twist, The Old Curiosity Shop, David Copperfield, A Tale of Two Cities *and* Great Expectations. *The following essay, "A Child's Dream of a Star," illustrates Dickens's use of overstatement, repetition, imagery, figurative language, and emotional appeal.*

There was once a child, and he strolled about a good deal, and thought of a number of things. He had a sister, who was a child too, and his constant companion. These two used to wonder all day long. They wondered at the beauty of the flowers; they wondered at the height and blueness of the sky; they wondered at the depth of the bright water; they wondered at the goodness and the power of God who made the lovely world.

They used to say to one another sometimes, Supposing all the children upon earth were to die, would the flowers, and the water, and the sky be sorry? They believed they would be sorry. For, said they, the buds are the children of the flowers; and the little playful streams that gambol down the hillsides are the children of the water; and the smallest bright specks playing at hide and seek in the sky all night must surely be the children of the stars; and they would all be grieved to see their playmates, the children of men, no more.

There was one clear, shining star that used to come out in the sky before the rest, near the church spire, above the graves. It was larger and more beautiful, they thought, than all the others, and every night they watched for it, standing hand in hand at a window. Whoever saw it first cried out, "I see the star!" And often they cried out both together, knowing so well when it would rise, and where. So they grew to be such friends with it, that, before lying down in their beds, they always looked out once again to bid it good-night; and when they were turning round to sleep they used to say, "God bless the star!"

But while she was still very young, oh very, very young, the sister drooped, and came to be so very weak that she could no longer stand in the window at night; and then the child looked sadly out by himself, and when he saw the star, turned round and said to the patient, pale face on the bed, "I see the star!" and then a smile would come upon the face, and a little weak voice used to say, "God bless my brother and the star!"

And so the time came all too soon! when the child looked out alone, and when there was no face on the bed; and when there was a little grave among the graves, not there before; and when the star made long rays down toward him, as he saw it through his tears.

Now, these rays were so bright, and they seemed to make such a shining way from earth to heaven, that when the child went to his solitary bed, he dreamed about the star; and dreamed that, lying where he was, he saw a train of people taken up that sparkling road by angels. And the star, opening, showed him a great world of light, where many more such angels waited to receive them.

All these angels, who were waiting, turned their beaming eyes upon the people who were carried up into the star; and soon came out from the long rows in which they stood, and fell upon the people's necks, and kissed them tenderly, and went away with them down avenues of light, and were so happy in their company, that lying in his bed he wept for joy.

But there were many angels who did not go with them, and among them one he knew. The patient face that once had lain upon the bed was glorified and radiant, but his heart found out his sister among all the host.

His sister's angel lingered near the entrance of the star, and said to the leader among those who had brought the people thither:—

"Is my brother come?"

And he said "No."

She was turning hopefully away, when the child stretched out his arms and cried, "O sister, I am here! Take me!" and then she turned her beaming eyes upon him, and it was night; and the star was shining in the room, making long rays down toward him as he saw it through his tears.

From that hour forth, the child looked out upon the star as on the home he was to go to, when his time should come; and he thought that he did not belong to the earth alone, but to the star too, because of his sister's angel gone before.

There was a baby born to be a brother to the child; and while he was so little that he never yet had spoken a word, he stretched his tiny form out on his bed, and died.

Again the child dreamed of the open star, and of the company of angels, and the train of people, and the rows of angels with their beaming eyes all turned upon those people's faces.

Said his sister's angel to the leader:—

"Is my brother come?"

And he said, "Not that one, but another."

As the child beheld his brother's angel in her arms, he cried, "O sister, I am here! Take me!" And she turned and smiled upon him, and the star was shining.

He grew to be a young man, and was busy at his books when an old servant came to him and said:—

"Thy mother is no more. I bring her blessings on her darling son!"

Again at night he saw the star, and all that former company. Said his sister's angel to the leader:—

"Is my brother come?"

And he said, "Thy mother!"

A mighty cry of joy went forth through all the star, because the mother was re-united to her two children. And he stretched out his arms and cried, "O mother, sister, and brother, I am here! Take me!" And they answered him, "Not yet," and the star was shining.

He grew to be a man, whose hair was turning gray, and he was sitting in his chair by his fireside, heavy with grief, and with his face bedewed with tears, when the star opened once again.

Said his sister's angel to the leader:—

"Is my brother come?"

And he said, "Nay, but his maiden daughter."

And the man who had been the child saw his daughter, newly lost to him, a celestial creature among those three, and he said, "My daughter's head is on my sister's bosom, and her arm is around my mother's neck, and at her feet there is the baby of old time, and I can bear the parting from her, God be praised!"

And the star was shining.

Thus the child came to be an old man, and his once smooth face was wrinkled, and his steps were slow and feeble, and his back was bent. And one night as he lay upon his bed, his children standing round, he cried, as he had cried so long ago:—

"I see the star!"

They whispered one another, "He is dying."

And he said, "I am. My age is falling from me like a garment, and I move toward the star as a child. And O my Father, now I thank thee that it has so often opened, to receive those dear ones who await me!"

And the star was shining; and it shines upon his grave.

QUESTIONS

1. List three or four examples of figurative language* in Dickens's essay.

2 What is Dickens's thesis* in this essay?

3. One question is asked several times in the essay. What is it? What is its meaning? At its most specific level, it is simply an inquiry about the brother, but is there another level of meaning?* If so, what is it?

4 Note Dickens's use of dialogue* in the essay. Does it accurately reflect the way people talk? What mood does it create?

5. Is there an implication in the essay that life will triumph over death? Explain your answer.

6. Who is the "leader" mentioned in the essay?

7. Does this essay recall any experiences from your own childhood— a relationship with a brother or sister, or a death in your family? If so, describe the experience and the impression it left on you.

---

*Definitions for all terms marked with an asterisk may be found in the Glossary.

READING AND WRITING SUGGESTIONS

1. Write a narrative essay describing an incident from your own childhood that made a dramatic change in your ideas about life and death. Focus on feelings as much as on facts in your narrative.

2. Read one of Dickens's novels and write a brief narrative essay describing the history of one of the characters in the book.

3. Dickens's essay deals with a sense of loss caused by death, but there are many other factors which can lead to a similar sense of loss. Read Pearl Buck's *The Child Who Never Grew*, the story of a family's reaction to a mentally retarded child, and write a brief essay about the grief and sense of loss that mental retardation or a severe physical handicap can cause.

TERRIER KEPT
A FOURTEEN-YEAR VIGIL

Doane R. Hoag

Doane R. Hoag (1908–) was born in Spokane, Washington, and received his education at Washington State College. He originated the "Passing Parade" radio program, which was made into a series of award-winning documentary films at MGM Studios. He has written motion pictures, television plays, magazine fiction, and a novel, How Vast Is Thy Sea. *Currently, Hoag writes a weekly newspaper column called "The Random Time Machine," which recounts true human interest stories of the past. The following essay, which describes the nearly human devotion of a dog for his master, is taken from that column.*

Edinburgh, Scotland, Sept. 12, 1872—He was a small, curly-haired, bluish-grey Skye Terrier and his name was Bobby. He belonged to an elderly farmer named John Gray, who lived on a farm outside this city. John had no family and few friends. Bobby was his one and only companion.

The two were inseparable. Bobby slept at the foot of his master's bed, sat beside him while he ate his meals, and trotted along beside him as he went about his chores. No one ever saw one without the other.

Once every week, on Wednesdays, John would go into town to do his marketing, and Bobby always went with him. At exactly one o'clock, when the time-gun boomed across the city from the castle on the hill, the two would go into Traill's Restaurant on Drummond Street for their midday meal. John would have a mutton chop while Bobby would have a scone.

This went on for several years until one Wednesday in 1858, Mr. Traill, the restaurant owner, looked in vain for John and Bobby. Inquiring around, he learned that John had died and been buried at Greyfriars Churchyard.

But where was Bobby?

No one seemed to know

Then, on the following Wednesday, at exactly one o'clock, here he came, right up to the door of Traill's Restaurant. Lifting his two front paws, he squealed imploringly until Mr. Traill understood what he wanted and gave him a scone. Bobby took it in his teeth and trotted away.

The next day, again sharp at one o'clock, here he was again. Mr. Traill gave him another scone. This time he followed him. Straight down Drummond Street the little fellow trotted, then north on Bridge Street, west on Chambers, past the University, right out to Greyfriars Churchyard.

"No Dogs Allowed" a sign on the gateway read. Bobby ignored the sign, trotted past it to his master's grave. There he lay down and contentedly chewed on his scone—just as he had while his master was still alive.

All the efforts to lure him away, to find a home for him, failed. Even when it was pouring rain the little dog stayed at his master's grave-side, drenched to the skin and shivering with cold, but still refusing to leave. Taking pity on him, the caretaker of the churchyard built him a little shelter right beside the grave. There Bobby remained. Month after month, year after year, he continued his lonely vigil.

After nine years, some enterprising tax collector discovered that Bobby didn't have a license. The police were dispatched and the dog was hauled into court.

According to the law, unlicensed animals were to be sent to the pound. If no one claimed them, they were either destroyed or turned over to the medical school for experiments. But this was not to be the fate of Bobby. When the news of his arrest spread about the city a mob of enraged citizens quickly gathered and stormed into the court, threatening to tear it apart board by board and stone by stone if Bobby was harmed.

The Lord Provost himself, William Chambers, heard about the riot and hurried to the scene. Not only did he quickly pay for Bobby's license out of his own pocket, but he also had a special brass plate engraved and fastened to Bobby's collar. The inscription read: "Greyfriars' Bobby, from the Lord Provost, 1867."

Bobby was never bothered again, either by law or by the tax collector, but was permitted to keep his vigil undisturbed. Just once each day did he leave his self-appointed post; that was at one o'clock, when the time-gun echoed across the rooftops. Then he would trot down to Drummond Street and Traill's Restaurant for his daily handout of one Scotch scone.

The story of his incredible devotion to a dead master spread all over the world. Famous artists came from afar to paint his picture. A sculptor chiseled his likeness in stone; it stands today outside the churchyard. In America, Henry Bergh, the great humanitarian, heard the story. Partially due to that, he was inspired to form the American Society for the Prevention of Cruelty to Animals.

Bobby continued his graveside vigil until the 12th of September in 1872, when he died at last and was buried beside his master in Greyfriars Churchyard—the only animal in Scottish history to be so honored. The devoted little terrier had maintained his steadfast vigil for no less than fourteen years.

As the poet said:

> My dead old dog, most constant of all my friends,
> He lived out his life but not his love.

There are many mysteries in this world of ours—mysteries for which we find no answers. But surely one of the deepest of all—and one of the most touching—is the love of a dog for a man. And of a man for a dog.

QUESTIONS

1. What is the tone* of this essay?

---

*Definitions for all terms marked with an asterisk may be found in the Glossary.

2. What meaning does Hoag ascribe to Bobby's fourteen-year vigil? Is there sentimentality in the author's final comments? Would many animals show such constancy under similar conditions?

3. Contrast the tax collector's attitude toward Bobby with that of the Lord Provost and the caretaker of the churchyard. What response would our present animal control forces—and our general population—make to a situation like Bobby's?

4. Is extreme devotion, like Bobby's, always a positive attribute? For example, how would you respond to a person who showed similar devotion to a deceased pet? What would you feel about a person who responded as Bobby did to a deceased person?

READING AND WRITING SUGGESTIONS

1. Write a brief narrative essay showing an animal's devotion to a person or to another animal.

2. Read or reread Jack London's novel *The Call of the Wild*. Write a brief essay comparing and contrasting the actions of Bobby and of Buck, the canine protagonist of London's novel.

DIVORCE—
TELEVISION STYLE

Art Buchwald

Art Buchwald (1925–) was born in Mt. Vernon, New York, the son of a curtain manufacturer. He left high school before graduating to join the Marine Corps in World War II. After completing his studies at the University of Southern California, Buchwald worked as a newspaper correspondent in Paris and in a number of other European cities, returning to this country in 1962. Buchwald now writes a nationally syndicated newspaper column and has published several collections of his newspaper articles. Among his books are The Brave Coward, Don't Forget to Write, I Choose Capital Punishment, *and* And Then I Told the President. *The two essays*

that follow represent the kind of humor and sly wisdom which have
made Buchwald famous.

Hello, Mom, is my wife there? . . . What do you mean she won't talk
to me? She's being ridiculous . . . I know she's sore at me, but it's
been almost a week now. How long can she stay mad? . . . Nothing
happened! Nothing at all . . . You only heard her version . . . Saturday, that's when it all started.

I'll admit I agreed to rake the leaves, but that was before I realized
the Pitt-Syracuse game was on TV . . . What's wrong with watching a
football game on TV? . . . I know I also listened to the Notre Dame-
Navy game on the radio, but it was the Game of the Week . . . I did
too talk to her Saturday afternoon. I distinctly remember asking why
she hadn't put any beer on ice.

She said I wouldn't come to dinner? That's not exactly true. I had to
watch the big race at Aqueduct and then there was *Wide World of
Sports* and I said I'd come in after that, but it was just my luck there
was a hockey game on next. You don't see much hockey on television
anymore . . . I told her I'd eat my dinner in the TV room and do you
know what she said? She said, "I'm not running a hotel. You can get
your own dinner!" Now, is that a nice thing to say to somebody
who's watching a hockey game? . . .

Aw, Ma, you know how she exaggerates. The wrestling matches
ended at eleven o'clock. She knew I liked wrestling when I married
her. I came to bed right after *College Scoreboard*.

Sunday? I guess I did say something about raking leaves on Sunday, but first I had to read about the Notre Dame-Navy game and
then the big race at Aqueduct and then the hockey game, and before I
knew it it was time for the Redskin-Eagles kickoff on TV . . . That's
not true. I did let her into the TV room. I only told her to get out after
she asked me what color drapes I wanted in the bedroom just as
Charley Taylor was running for a touchdown . . .

Did she tell you that? . . . Did she also tell you that she wouldn't
give me any lunch unless I brought in the dirty dishes from Saturday
night? Now I ask you what kind of wife is that? . . . I didn't yell at her
. . . I may have raised my voice when it was fourth down, touchdown
to go, and she told me to take all the summer clothes up to the attic,
but I did not use violent language . . . She gets everything wrong . . .
I didn't watch the Detroit-Rams game after that. It was Buffalo against
Houston. And it was a very important game. How many double-
headers do you get on television? . . . Okay, so I forgot we invited the
Winstons over for drinks. I wasn't rude to them. I showed them

where the bar was and said I'd see them in a couple of hours. How did I know they were going to go home before *Great Moments from Pro Football* was over?

Listen, Mom, you talk to her. I'm getting tired of eating TV dinners and there isn't a clean dish left in the house.

And tell her I love her and miss her and the children very much . . . What did she say? She said she'd come back? Great, wonderful. When does she want me to pick her up? . . . Saturday. Gee, I can't Saturday. Illinois is playing Michigan and it could mean an invitation to the Rose Bowl.

HE GAVE THEM UP

Art Buchwald

The trouble with giving up smoking is there never seems to be a right moment to do it. One day I was in Chicago ready to fly back to Washington with a friend, Chuck Grant. Chuck announced on the way to the airport that he was very impressed with the government report and he was giving up smoking as of that day.

"Why didn't you give it up yesterday?" I asked.

"I figured with all that trouble down in Panama it wouldn't be right to give it up on Sunday. But today's the day."

When we got to the airport in Chicago we were informed by American Airlines that our flight to Washington had been canceled as National Airport was closed because of a severe snowstorm. There was a possibility of United Airlines flying to Dulles around noon if the weather cleared up.

We went to the coffee shop to kill three hours. Chuck was very nervous and after three cups of coffee he started eating lumps of sugar.

"Why don't you have a cigarette?" I suggested.

"Well, maybe just one," Chuck said. "I hadn't counted on this cancellation."

Three hours and twelve cigarettes later United announced they were taking off for Dulles and we boarded the plane.

"As of now," said Chuck, "I am not going to smoke another cigarette."

Two hours later the pilot announced over the loudspeaker that we were over Dulles Airport and although the weather was all right, the runway had not been cleared as expected and we would have to circle the field for an hour.

Chuck started chewing on his safety belt.

"You better not do that, Chuck," I said. "Would you like a cigarette?"

"Well, I'll just have one until we get on the ground."

A half hour later the pilot announced that they were still unable to clear the runway and we might have to go to Cleveland or Richmond.

Seventeen planes were stacked above and below us.

Chuck was puffing like a steam engine.

An hour later the pilot said we would still circle over the field but because of fuel considerations we would have to make the decision in a half hour whether to go to an alternate field.

By this time Chuck had run out of cigarettes and started bumming them from other people's lunch trays.

Finally the plane was given the okay to land. We came down to a snow-laden field. It was a fine landing and everyone on the plane broke into applause.

"Now that we're on the ground," Chuck announced, "I've had my last cigarette."

The road from Dulles, which is 30 miles from Washington, was pretty icy and the bus driver had trouble because the wind was whipping up the snow.

Chuck was tearing a newspaper with his fingernails.

"Would you like a cigarette, Chuck?"

"I'll just have one until we get into town."

The ride took over an hour and Chuck bummed cigarettes from everyone on the bus.

We finally got a cab and dropped him off at his house.

The next morning I called and asked him how he was doing with the cigarette situation.

"I had a fight with my wife this morning, I couldn't get the car started, the kids spilled all the salt for the sidewalk in the garage, and I think I just got word I lost a contract I was bidding for. But tomorrow I stop smoking for sure."

QUESTIONS

Divorce—Television Style

1. What adjectives would you use to describe Buchwald's diction:* abstract?* colloquial?* specific? jargon-filled?* metaphorical?* trite?*

2. Consider Buchwald's style.
   a. How does he use exaggeration? Irony?*
   b. How many examples does Buchwald use to make his point? Could he have made his point equally well by using only two examples? Why did he use so many?

3. a. Briefly summarize the events the narrator is describing in the essay.
   b. Does the protagonist have any insight at all into his wife's complaint?
   c. Would the situation really be better if his wife shared his interest in sports?
   d. Whose side are you on—the husband's or the wife's? Why?
   e. What is Buchwald saying about the influence of TV on personal and social relationships?
   f. Recently, *Time* magazine estimated that Americans spend nine billion man-hours watching football each year. The article called the Super Bowl game "The Great American Time Out." Keeping this in mind, decide whether you think the situation Buchwald describes satirically could actually occur.

4. Watching the Redskins on TV obviously gave the protagonist more pleasure than raking the leaves or carrying the summer clothes to the attic. How strong a role does TV play in giving Americans pleasure? Do you think the protagonist is justified in putting off his humdrum chores to watch TV? What would you do in a similar situation?

5. Keeping up with sports events does carry the protagonist outside of himself—giving him an interest as well as something to share with others, if not with his wife. Is this healthy? Does he carry it too far? Do you know anyone this wrapped up in TV sports or some other TV genre? What has happened to that person's relationships with others?

---

*Definitions for all terms marked with an asterisk may be found in the Glossary.

He Gave Them Up

1. What troubles did Chuck have in giving up cigarettes? Do you think that he will kick the habit tomorrow? Ever?

2. What approach do you think would best help Chuck stop smoking cigarettes: substituting another habit, such as chewing gum, when he is under stress, or learning to tolerate stress without a support?

3. Does someone you know respond to stress by falling back on a habit, such as smoking cigarettes, drinking beer, watching TV, or singing? If people must use some psychological supports, which do you recommend? Why?

READING AND WRITING SUGGESTIONS

1. Consider a pastime other than watching TV that helps people escape dull duties and gives them a means of relating to other aficionados. Write a brief narrative essay in the Buchwald manner showing how the pastime could conflict with personal relationships.

2. Identify a habit that you use as a psychological support in times of stress. Using Buchwald's essay as a model, write a brief narrative essay in which you show how you attempt to control your habit in a series of stressful situations.

3. Read some articles on the dangers of smoking cigarettes and write a brief essay exploring the rationalizations a determined smoker might come up with in the face of highly adverse information about his or her habit.

SHAME

Dick Gregory

Dick Gregory (1923–), a well-known comedian and entertainer, was born in St. Louis and attended Southern Illinois University, where he was named an outstanding athlete in 1953. He was a leader in antiwar and civil rights activities during the 1960s. His books include From the Back of the Bus; What's Happening; Dick Gregory's Political Primer; The Myths of American History; *and* Dick Gregory's Natural Diet for Folks Who Eat: Cookin' with Mother Nature. *In this essay, taken from his autobiography,* Nigger, *Gregory explores a humiliating experience he suffered in his childhood.*

I never learned hate at home, or shame. I had to go to school for that. I was about seven years old when I got my first big lesson. I was in love with a little girl named Helene Tucker, a light-complexioned little girl with pigtails and nice manners. She was always clean and she was smart in school. I think I went to school then mostly to look at her. I brushed my hair and even got me a little old handkerchief. It was a lady's handkerchief, but I didn't want Helene to see me wipe my nose on my hand. The pipes were frozen again, there was no water in the house, but I washed my socks and shirt every night. I'd get a pot, and go over to Mister Ben's grocery store, and stick my pot down into his soda machine. Scoop out some chopped ice. By evening the ice melted to water for washing. I got sick a lot that winter because the fire would go out at night before the clothes were dry. In the morning I'd put them on, wet or dry, because they were the only clothes I had.

Everybody's got a Helene Tucker, a symbol of everything you want. I loved her for her goodness, her cleanness, her popularity. She'd walk down my street and my brothers and sisters would yell, "Here comes Helene," and I'd rub my tennis sneakers on the back of my pants and wish my hair wasn't so nappy and the white folks' shirt fit me better. I'd run out on the street. If I knew my place and didn't come too close, she'd wink at me and say hello. That was a good feeling. Sometimes I'd follow her all the way home, and shovel the snow off her walk and try to make friends with her Momma and her aunts. I'd drop money on her stoop late at night on my way back from shining shoes in the taverns. And she had a Daddy, and he had a good job. He was a paper hanger.

I guess I would have gotten over Helene by summertime, but something happened in that classroom that made her face hang in front of me for the next twenty-two years. When I played the drums in high school it was for Helene and when I broke track records in college it was for Helene and when I started standing behind microphones and heard applause I wished Helene could hear it, too. It wasn't until I was twenty-nine years old and married and making money that I finally got her out of my system. Helene was sitting in that classroom when I learned to be ashamed of myself.

It was on a Thursday. I was sitting in the back of the room, in a seat with a chalk circle drawn around it. The idiot's seat, the troublemaker's seat.

The teacher thought I was stupid. Couldn't spell, couldn't read, couldn't do arithmetic. Just stupid. Teachers were never interested in finding out that you couldn't concentrate because you were so hungry, because you hadn't had any breakfast. All you could think about was noontime, would it ever come? Maybe you could sneak into the cloakroom and steal a bite of some kid's lunch out of a coat pocket. A bite of something. Paste. You can't really make a meal of paste, or put in on bread for a sandwich, but sometimes I'd scoop a few spoonfuls out of the paste jar in the back of the room. Pregnant people get strange tastes. I was pregnant with poverty. Pregnant with dirt and pregnant with smells that made people turn away, pregnant with cold and pregnant with shoes that were never bought for me, pregnant with five other people in my bed and no Daddy in the next room, and pregnant with hunger. Paste doesn't taste too bad when you're hungry.

The teacher thought I was a troublemaker. All she saw from the front of the room was a little black boy who squirmed in his idiot's seat and made noises and poked the kids around him. I guess she couldn't see a kid who made noises because he wanted someone to know he was there.

It was on a Thursday, the day before the Negro payday. The eagle always flew on Friday. The teacher was asking each student how much his father would give to the Community Chest. On Friday night, each kid would get the money from his father, and on Monday he would bring it to the school. I decided I was going to buy me a Daddy right then. I had money in my pocket from shining shoes and selling papers, and whatever Helene Tucker pledged for her Daddy I was going to top it. And I'd hand the money right in. I wasn't going to wait until Monday to buy me a Daddy.

I was shaking, scared to death. The teacher opened her book and started calling out names alphabetically.

"Helene Tucker?"

"My daddy said he'd give two dollars and fifty cents."

"That's very nice, Helene. Very, very nice indeed."

That made me feel pretty good. It wouldn't take too much to top that. I had almost three dollars in dimes and quarters in my pocket. I stuck my hand in my pocket and held onto the money, waiting for her to call my name. But the teacher closed her book after she called everybody else in the class.

I stood up and raised my hand.

"What is it now?"

"You forgot me."

She turned toward the blackboard. "I don't have time to be playing with you, Richard."

"My Daddy said he'd . . . "

"Sit down, Richard, you're disturbing the class."

"My Daddy said he'd give . . . fifteen dollars."

She turned around and looked mad. "We are collecting this money for you and your kind, Richard Gregory. If your Daddy can give fifteen dollars you have no business being on relief."

"I got it right now, I got it right now, my Daddy gave it to me to turn in today, my Daddy said . . . "

"And furthermore," she said, looking right at me, her nostrils getting big and her lips getting thin and her eyes opening wide, "we know you don't have a Daddy."

Helene Tucker turned around, her eyes full of tears. She felt sorry for me. Then I couldn't see her too well because I was crying, too.

"Sit down, Richard."

And I always thought the teacher kind of liked me. She always picked me to wash the blackboard on Friday, after school. That was a big thrill, it made me feel important. If I didn't wash it, come Monday the school might not function right.

"Where are you going, Richard?"

I walked out of school that day, and for a long time I didn't go back very often. There was shame there.

Now there was shame everywhere. It seemed like the whole world had been inside that classroom, everyone had heard what the teacher had said, everyone had turned around and felt sorry for me. There was shame in going to the Worthy Boys Annual Christmas Dinner for you and your kind, because everybody knew what a worthy boy was. Why couldn't they just call it the Boys Annual Dinner; why'd they have to give it a name? There was shame in wearing the brown and orange and white plaid mackinaw the welfare gave to three thousand boys. Why'd it have to be the same for everybody so when you walked down the street the people could see you were on relief? It was a nice warm mackinaw and it had a hood, and my Momma beat me and called me a little rat when she found out I stuffed it in the bottom of a pail full of garbage way over on Cottage Street. There was shame in running over to Mister Ben's at the end of the day and asking for his rotten peaches, there was shame in asking Mrs. Simmons for a spoonful of sugar, there was shame in running out to meet the relief truck. I hated that truck, full of food for you and your kind. I ran into the house and hid when it came. And then I started to sneak through alleys, to take the long way home so the people going into White's Eat Shop wouldn't see me. Yeah, the whole world heard the teacher that day, we all know you don't have a Daddy.

It lasted for a while, this kind of numbness. I spent a lot of time feeling sorry for myself. And then one day I met this wino in a restaurant. I'd been out hustling all day, shining shoes, selling newspapers, and I had goo-gobs of money in my pocket. Bought me a bowl of chili for fifteen cents, and a cheeseburger for fifteen cents, and a Pepsi for five cents, and a piece of chocolate cake for ten cents. That was a good meal. I was eating when this old wino came in. I love winos because they never hurt anyone but themselves.

The old wino sat down at the counter and ordered twenty-six cents worth of food. He ate it like he really enjoyed it. When the owner, Mister Williams, asked him to pay the check, the old wino didn't lie or go through his pocket like he suddenly found a hole.

He just said: "Don't have no money."

The Owner yelled: "Why in hell you come in here and eat my food if you don't have no money? That food cost me money."

Mister Williams jumped over the counter and knocked the wino off his stool and beat him over the head with a pop bottle. Then he stepped back and watched the wino bleed. Then he kicked him. And he kicked him again.

I looked at the wino with blood all over his face and I went over. "Leave him alone, Mister Williams. I'll pay the twenty-six cents."

The wino got up, slowly, pulling himself up to the stool, then up to the counter, holding on for a minute until his legs stopped shaking so bad. He looked at me with pure hate. "Keep your twenty-six cents. You don't have to pay, not now. I just finished paying for it."

He started to walk out, and as he passed me, he reached down and touched my shoulder. "Thanks, sonny, but it's too late now. Why didn't you pay it before?"

I was pretty sick about that. I waited too long to help another man.

QUESTIONS

1. Suppose Gregory had *only* written these words instead of his essay: "Even as a young child, I really cared and I really tried hard; I was shamed by many circumstances in my deprived environment." Would this sentence have the same impact that his story has? What means does Gregory use to make you feel his hope and his humiliation?

2. How does the closing anecdote about the wino relate to the rest of the narrative? What purpose does it serve?

3. Gregory states that "everybody's got a Helene Tucker, a symbol of everything you want."
   a. Would this essay have the same impact if Gregory had not used the figure of Helene Tucker? What was Helene a symbol of for Gregory? What did he want in his childhood that he did not have?
   b. Why was he so upset by being shamed in front of Helene and by the fact that she felt sorry for him?
   c. How long did Helene remain a symbol for Gregory?

4. Why did Gregory finally get over the shame? Was it because he finally attained all of the things he wanted or because he gained more self-respect? Could Gregory have written this essay if he wasn't more secure now—if he still felt the shame? Think back to an event that made you feel shame. Could you write about it and publish it for everyone to see?

5. We do not know all of the reasons why people are willing to pay the price of high achievement, but we do know some. One reason is that people often work to fulfill needs they first felt during a deprived childhood. Another reason is that people sometimes copy role models provided by adults they admire.
   a. What are some of Gregory's achievements as an adult? Can you relate them to his childhood experiences?
   b. Gregory suffered a major trauma when he tried to buy himself a daddy and was humiliated by his teacher. Might he still have achieved as much in adulthood if Helene's father had been his,

if he had used her father as a role model, and if he had not experienced the deprivation that he did?

c. The important leadership Gregory exerted in the struggle for civil rights may have been influenced by the trauma and need he experienced as a child. If this were the case, would the good he has done be worth the price he paid?

READING AND WRITING SUGGESTIONS

1. Consider Gregory's account of the way he tried to be like Helene and his descriptions of his hunger, his poverty, and the humiliations that some people receiving welfare have to endure. Write a brief narrative essay showing what would have occurred if his teacher had responded the way a truly sensitive person would: recognizing the child's real wish—to buy a sense of worth in his own and other people's eyes—and granting the child recognition, love, understanding, and respect. Describe how the child might have felt and acted subsequently if the teacher had reacted in this way.

2. Read a book about deprived childhoods, such as Jonathan Kozol's *Death at an Early Age*, which illustrates Gregory's powerful image of "a kid who made noises because he wanted someone to know he was there." Write a brief essay describing what humiliation can do to a child already uncertain of his or her own self-worth.

WHO SHALL LIVE?
WHO SHALL DIE?

Hallam Tennyson

Hallam Tennyson (1921–) is a writer for the British Broadcasting Corporation, where he has been Assistant Head of Radio Drama for thirteen years. This essay, which grew out of a radio program developed by Tennyson, appeared in The Listener, *an English newspaper. It concerns a remarkable woman, Dr. Adelaide Hautval, who maintained her moral integrity in the face of the psychological and physical pressures of the concentration camp at Auschwitz.*

In 1964 Dr. Wladislaw Dering, a Polish GP with a practice in Finsbury Park [London], brought an action for libel against the author and publishers of the novel *Exodus*. He claimed that he would be identified with the "Dr. Dehring" mentioned in the novel, who was described as having carried out 17,000 experimental operations on Jewish inmates of Auschwitz concentration camp "without anesthetics." Although the number of operations had been grossly exaggerated, it was shown—through the able defense led by Lord Gardiner—that Dr. Dering (himself a prisoner in the camp through his connections with the Polish underground) *had* carried out about 130 of these operations at the request of the SS, and that, when young Jewish men and women were the patients involved, he had been careless to the point of brutality. The doctor's main plea of justification in the witness box was that to have refused the Nazis' orders to operate would have been to risk almost certain death, and it was over this question of justification through fear that the testimony of a certain French Protestant, Dr. Adelaide Hautval, was to have a crucial effect. Dr. Hautval reached Auschwitz in 1943, because while in prison in Bourges for an infringement of the permit regulations in crossing into the occupied zone of France, she had insisted on wearing the yellow star as a protest against the Gestapo's treatment of French Jews who were thrown into prison with her. She was branded *amie des juifs*[1] and told that as she liked Jews so much she had better share their fate. In Auschwitz she was asked on at least five occasions to help with the experiments in the notorious Block 10, and each time refused to do so. On one occasion when Dr. Wirths of the SS asked her how it was that as a psychiatrist she could not see that Jews were different from herself, she replied: "I can see several people who are different from me, beginning with you." Earlier in the trial, a Polish Jewish doctor, Dorota Lorska, spoke of having met Dr. Hautval shortly after her own arrival at Auschwitz. "She explained to me as a doctor what was happening in Block 10," said Dr. Lorska. "At the end of that conversation she told me that it was impossible that we should ever get out of the camp alive. "The Germans will not allow people who know what is going on here to get in touch with the outside world. So the only thing that is left is to behave for the rest of the short time that remains as human beings.'"

Dr. Hautval's evidence made a deep impression. The judge himself described her reply to Wirths as "devastating" and "likely to live in the minds of the jury for many years." And there is no doubt that she did much to damage Dr. Dering's case. The jury brought in a verdict of guilty but awarded Dr. Dering damages to the value of only a halfpenny. In other words, although he had been libeled (for one thing through the exaggeration of the number of experimental operations), his reputation could not be said to have suffered severely since the facts established during the trial were damaging enough.

Ever since reading about the trial I had wanted to meet Dr. Hautval, but it was not till Dering died that I felt ready to think of building a radio program which would take the trial as its starting point. So in 1969 I embarked on a protracted correspondence with Dr. Hautval, whom I discovered to be a health inspector in schools 30 kilometers north of Paris. For over a year she displayed extreme reluctance to meet me: she was opposed to the war crimes trials, had taken part in the Dering libel action against her will and only agreed in the end because she thought it would have been unfair if he had got heavy damages. Most important of all, she expressed a deep-rooted antipathy to personal publicity. In June of this year, I went to my first meeting with *Mlle. le docteur* (Women's Lib will have a high old time over the problems set by French genders) in considerable trepidation. I need not have worried.

Adelaide Hautval, now a woman of 65, has a clear musical voice that belies her years, a manner that is relaxed and friendly yet can

---

1. Friend of the Jews.

suddenly blaze into indignation when matters of principle are in question (it was soon noticeable that she spoke of Auschwitz with complete detachment, but got extremely worked up over problems of contemporary medical ethics), and an aquiline profile whose severity is quickly dissolved in a flashing eager smile. She carries her Auschwitz number branded proudly on her forearm (Dr. Dering admitted to having his erased), but she was never still long enough for me to be able to read the digits.

The daughter of a Protestant pastor in Alsace, Dr. Hautval remembered from a very early age her family's intense concern for and interest in "the Jewish problem." Not only did her father reverence the Jews as "the people of the Book," and feel a greater affinity with them than he did with many of his Catholic neighbors, but there was also the strong identification with the sorrows of the exiled Hebrews of an Alsatian family cut off from its French homeland since the Franco-Prussian War. "This reverence for the Jews has never left me. I can never forget that they have suffered more than any other people in history. . . ."

That Dr. Hautval's sympathies were not confined to the Judeo-Christian tradition was soon amply demonstrated. She saw me looking at an appliqué hanging covering the whole length of the sitting-room wall: I wondered if it was a design by Paul Klee. Multicolored scrolls and disks and ferns danced on an orange background. When I saw Chinese ideograms, I could not forbear asking what the hanging represented. "Oh, that's my 'tapestry,' " she said. "I've been working on it for years. It's supposed to show the aspirations of humanity, all reaching upward toward the light. That's a Taoist quotation and there's the cross of Christianity floating above the Tao. And down in the corner, those marks represent the African faiths. We mustn't forget them." On my next visit, the large hanging had been taken down—it was "being worked on"—and in its place was a much smaller affair. "Those are the evil tendencies in humanity," Dr. Hautval explained, and she looked at it quizzically. "I've only just begun it." A cloud of jagged spirochete-like objects was gathering to the right-hand side. They looked at little forlorn and purposeless—proof that in Dr. Hautval's cosmogony the devil does *not* have all the best tunes.

In the Dering trial great play was made with the fact that she was never "punished" as a result of her refusal to take part in the Nazi experiments. In fact, she fully expected to be punished after her confrontation with Wirths. A German political prisoner, who was in charge of the allocation of work, advised her strongly to accept Wirths' order that she should work for him, since an execution squad instructed to deal with special offenders was coming to the camp the next day and she would almost certainly be on their list. Dr. Hautval said that she could not work for Wirths whatever the consequences, and awaited the arrival of the squad in as calm a frame of mind as possible. However, during the night, this German colleague managed to arrange for her to be smuggled to Birkenau, a subsidiary part of Auschwitz. To Dr. Hautval this "escape" was merely a sign of the relative unimportance of her gesture of defiance and she had never before talked of it to anyone. That her own courage could ever be sufficient to influence others still seems to her highly improbable.

QUESTIONS

1. Tennyson's essay moves backward and forward in time rather than progressing in a linear sequence. Do you think that this technique is more effective than a linear narration would have been? Why, or why not?

2. What is the significance in the essay of the two tapestries? What do they reveal about Adelaide Hautval's character?

3. What is Dr. Hautval's opinion of war crimes trials? Judging from what you learned about her in this essay, why do you think she holds this opinion?

4. Consider the character of Dr. Dering.
   a. Why do you think he brought a lawsuit against the author and publishers of the novel *Exodus* when he knew of the incidents in his past that might be brought out in the course of the trial?
   b. Dr. Dering was confined at Auschwitz because of his connections with the Polish underground. What does this tell you about his character?
   c. In an essay of her own, Hautval has described the progressive process of degradation that erodes the character of basically good people in situations such as Dering's. She says, "You agree with a certain principle, you let it take hold of you: next comes a second principle and you carry on in the same way without even letting yourself see where it's leading you. I'm sure that all the terrible things done in the world begin with small acts of cowardice." Discuss how such a process can lead a person like Dr. Dering to commit progressively more immoral acts.

5. Hautval has written that she doesn't think "anyone in the world has the right to judge or decide what he himself would do in the

quite extraordinary conditions that had to be faced in places like Auschwitz." Do you think you can judge how you would act in the face of extreme danger when you have not had to face that danger yet?

READING AND WRITING SUGGESTIONS

1. Reflect on the fact that many people who have committed immoral or criminal acts have later said that they did so in the name of obedience. Write a brief narrative essay about a person in recent history who has applied this explanation to his or her actions and discuss the moral implications of this kind of self-justification.

2. Read a book about a person, whether fictional or real, who has displayed great courage in the face of adversity (Ernest J. Gaines's *Autobiography of Miss Jane Pittman* and John F. Kennedy's *Profiles in Courage* are two excellent books you might consider reading). Write a brief narrative essay describing one courageous action of the person you read about.

A DIARY OF A WINNER

Liv Ullmann

Liv Ullmann (1939–) is an internationally acclaimed actress. (For more detailed biographical information, see page 16.) In the following excerpt from her book, Changing, *Ullmann records and reflects on some of the experiences she had during a single week in 1972.*

At the end of 1972 an American film magazine printed a long article about me, and on the cover under my smiling face you could read: "THE STORY OF A WINNER."

Here is a week chosen at random from that time:

Monday

The most incredible things can happen in Hollywood. One can become a star overnight. Jewels and furs can suddenly appear on the doormat. But I think only I have *nine* Christmas trees.

One of them is for Linn, but she is going home to her grandmother and cousins and a white Christmas in Norway.

Friends are sitting on the floor in my hotel corridor decorating a tree that will be waiting for me when I get back from taking Linn to the airport. They have bought colored balls and long strings of Swedish flags—but that is not an uncommon mistake in Hollywood, where Norway is thought to be some province in Scandinavia.

My friends are waiting by my door when I return and I take their lovely present into the room, which they had envisioned empty and desolate after my daughter's departure.

They gasp with admiration, because along the walls and in the corners there are Christmas trees of every shape and color glistening and shining with big and little magical lights. One of them even rotates and sings carols.

The famous Movie Hero fetches me for dinner. He brings an enormous fir tree covered with artificial silver and imitation pearls. Unfortunately, he resembles my first love and when anyone does that, red warning lights switch on inside me. It is very difficult in America when those lights start blinking—because American men say "I love you" as part of the conversation.

And when the man is one of the Famous you cannot laugh it off; because they have such sensitive egos, and think they never give better performances than when they half-close their velvet eyes over a glass of wine and whisper lines from the films in which they have acted.

The next day all the papers proclaim that the famous Movie Hero and I are lovers.

Tuesday

I am invited to dinner at Hugh Hefner's, publisher of *Playboy*. Upon our arrival we have to pass through several electric gates with built-in television cameras. Pictures of all who pass through are flashed onto a screen in the guardhouse, scrutinized by three private detectives with loaded revolvers in their belts. There have been several attempted burglaries and crimes of violence. Only a few weeks previously in this same neighborhood bestial murders were committed without any other prupose or motive than the murderer's delight in killing those who, in his eyes, were too rich and successful.

The Playboy king is wearing terry-cloth pajamas. Some girls walk about with long furry rabbits' ears fastened to their heads and little round tails on their bottoms.

We look at films: A dog makes love to a girl. I think of Pet[1] and hope she will not discover what I am doing.

Afterward we sit in small groups, not knowing what to talk about because our host is asleep on the sofa and the rest of us don't know each other that well. The rabbit girls show some of the guests around the house.

I walk through the grounds. An artificial mountain in the garden. Inside it a subterranean grotto with swirling warmed waves. Two people are doing things in the water under red and blue spotlights.

Wednesday

A long working day. In the early morning, dress rehearsal for *40 Carats*, after an endless drive with a chauffeur who used to play cowboy roles and does not realize that he keeps clicking the false teeth in his mouth all the time.

Later there is skating practice. Ten men, headed by the director, the photographer and the producer, follow me to see what I can do. Even though in the film I am meant to appear clumsy and out of practice (just as a woman of forty is believed to be), they now want to see if I can stay on my feet at all.

I haven't skated since I was a child. Memories of fiascos on cold skating rinks in Trondhjem when I was awkward and thirteen years old, with wobbly knees and ankles that buckled. Evening after evening, hoping to learn the art—so that one day I could glide through the soft darkness accompanied by caressing music, hand in hand with James Stewart.

Now, years later, the only difference is the applause from my ten attendants. Then they ask if I would like a stand-in.

Lunch. A Swedish journalist sits waiting for me on the lawn outside the canteen. Not having read this week's papers, he thinks I am still going with last week's Film Hero. Fifteen minutes of the precious lunch break are spent on him, so the papers at home will not report that I have become "stuck up."

In the dining room wait an agent and a producer. They want to consult with me about who is to have the male lead in my next film. I am delighted at being asked, even though I know that it is all a

---

1. Ullmann's dog.

pretense laid on to please me. I suspect that somewhere is an actor with a signed contract being consulted in the same way about me.

In the afternoon I try on hats. The same crowd as in the morning gathers in the producer's office to learn from me how far down over my forehead I want the brims. *I*, who am so unsure about taste in clothes that I will change a dress if my daughter sends me a critical look.

Then an interview: "You were so sad in that article in the *Los Angeles Times*," they tell me. "Could you give us an amusing version?"

I have just been through the opening of my first Hollywood film, which no one liked.

"You were wonderful," they say, and embrace me.

In the evening I attend a ball. The most famous of the guests are placed on a stage, where they are to eat. There we sit in tiers, one above the other, turned toward the hall so that those who have paid for their food can watch us chew ours and see that we chat and behave like ordinary, simple people.

Mae West is borne in between two strong men with long hair and open-necked shirts with masses of muscles underneath. They whisper in my ear that these are her lovers. She has yellow corkscrew curls and her face is heavily made up, and she has false eyelashes that are coming loose. They ask me to come and meet her. She so wants to know me. Dumbly we grasp each other's hands.

As I walk away, I hear her hiss to one of the lovers, "Who the hell was that?"

Thursday

Call Linn in Norway. She says she is busy watching television, so could I please be brief. I tell her about the tree she has been given. It is big; the branches are caramel and chocolate, the trunk made of candies in every color, and the whole tree is covered with little lights that twinkle and twinkle and twinkle.

Later in the day I fly to New York. The trip lasts five and a half hours and I sleep the whole way. That is what I love about flying: there are no telephone calls. It is like a gift of time—time that I have all to myself.

At the airport, there are photographers, cars, and people I ought to recognize. At the hotel I have been given the best suite, overloaded with flowers and fruit. I long for all the people I don't recognize to leave my room! Who are they? What do they want? And why?

I stand looking out at New York from the thirtieth floor. Enormous buildings for human beings, almost touching the sky. The cars below so closely packed you cannot see the street.

Then I walk through the enormous spaces that are my rooms, my home for a few days. On the wall is posted a list telling me what to do if I want a pleasant stay: never be in the room without putting the chain on the door; never let anyone in who says he has come to repair the television; never speak to strangers in the lobby.

A sudden memory of Linn. Linn at a grownups' party the day before she left: all the guests have been given musical instruments. And we sit on the floor and sing and play our instruments and laugh.

Linn asks if she may sing a solo, and we are all silent for her. Very serious, she sings "London Bridge Is Falling Down."

Somewhere inside me an old dream awakens—a vision: the rightness of having several generations gathered in mutual pleasure in the same room, enjoying each other.

Linn later that evening: I see her through the veranda window. She is sitting on a sofa with an old man. Her head is moving. I see only their backs and her gesticulating hands. She is living her own life out there.

For a few years still, she will be the center of her own universe, as *I* once was in mine—until she was born and I experienced it as a gift to see *her* take my place in me.

Friday

Formal lunch with *Time* magazine. The senior executives have invited me to meet with them in their most private dining room. They want to do a cover story about me and I am to be examined to find out if I am enough of a personality for such an honor. During a barrage of questions and provocations across the large round table, I try to eat something as well. I still have a long day's work ahead of me. *They* are tough men, but *I* am a woman from Trondhjem.

For the last two weeks a reporter from *Time* has been with me while I filmed in Greece, and then on the plane to Los Angeles for endless hours—so that I didn't dare go to sleep in case my mouth fell open. Some secrets must be kept from the press. We became good friends and parted like brother and sister after a week in Hollywood.

Now I am told that another writer is to be with me in New York. Over the coffee I ask the new one why he has suddenly appeared on the scene. He tells me it is because he is tough and level-headed and not easily fooled. *Time* wants to counterbalance the positive information it has gathered, and is now looking for the negative side of Miss Ullmann.

And he is there to reveal it.

I willingly share with him my weaknesses, ladle out how bad I really am, yet in a way that I hope will charm the boots off him.

By evening I am dead tired and longing for home. On my bedside table is a kind of tree I always have with me. It is a little twisted plant, and on its branches hang various brass objects, each with its own significance. I imagine it brings me luck. It was given to me by a great actress when I left the National Theatre and set forth into the world.

I telephone to say I am unable to keep a dinner appointment. Give instructions for no calls to be put through. Pull the blankets over my head. Wake up in the middle of the night with troubling thoughts provoked by the *Time* interview.

Saturday

Filming in the streets of New York. Wearing tailor-made suits and smart hats in the middle of the world's largest city. People gathering to look. Cars and skyscrapers and faces merging. Autograph hunters moving about in a clump, glued together by their common interest.

Hairdresser, make-up man, dresser—the three are never more than a few steps away. They adjust me: pluck at my hair, dab at my face, pull at my clothes, showing their friendliness; and all the while I must maintain my concentration. Smile and be friendly back.

I think of the time when Mamma, Bitten and I were here some years ago. We wanted to have a drink in the Plaza Hotel, but were not allowed in because we were wearing slacks. Mamma indignantly explaining in agitated Trondhjem English that she was out with her daughters and such treatment was insolent. It could never have happened in the America *she* lived in thirty years before.

Now, in the afternoon, I am here again, am filming in the heart of the Plaza Hotel, working in its elegant red and golden vestibule.

There are so many people wanting to watch that they look like a great chorus lining the walls.

Television, radio and journalists.

A fat, officious woman asks who the star is.

"Liv Ullmann," I say modestly.

"I don't know her. It can't be a good film."

When we have finished for the day, I meet the journalist from *Time*. He gives me a copy of his book about Vietnam—he was a correspondent there for a year. I like him. We talk about war and pollution, about children and love, discover a quick, spontaneous agreement that

colors our conversations, turns our meeting into a feast of thoughts and ideas.

At least this is how I experience it.

He may write about me as nastily as he likes; at least we *talked* together.

In the evening Max von Sydow visits me. He is one of my best working companions and a close friend as well, ever since *Hour of the Wolf,* the film where we met, when I was very pregnant with Linn.

We have a picnic on the floor of my suite. Potted plants we transform into trees, and the silk cushions are grass and flowers.

The Plaza Hotel is so elegant that the waiter's expression never changes: just a slight quiver of the nostrils when he goes down on his knees and serves us dinner on the wall-to-wall carpet.

Sunday

Back in Los Angeles. Christmas. Christmas trees in all the streets. Lights in the windows and colorful decorations on the doors. So different from Norway:

The white silence in the woods. The snow and the spruce and the tracks of skis.

Here the sun is shining and I go out in a thin jacket. I cannot stand being in the hotel room with all the Christmas trees glinting at me.

Seven o'clock on Christmas Eve and I am on my way back from the studio. At home everyone will be sitting eating spare ribs and sauerkraut.

Four young girls—very young—in a window we drive past. They are happy, they lean out, laugh to the cars and the people in them. They are slim, have tousled hair.

A stab in the heart of yearning and fear because those days will never come again.

I bring two of my Christmas trees into my bedroom.

One is from Linn. She has decorated it with angels and Santas she made herself.

The other is from a close friend. It is stuck in a pot of earth.

"So that you can plant it in America when you leave," he says, "then you will have a root here as well."

QUESTIONS

1. What adjective would you use to describe the tone* of this essay: amused? proud? ironical?* bittersweet?

---

*Definitions for all terms marked with an asterisk may be found in the Glossary.

2. Name four of the experiences described by Ullmann that you would like to have. Name four that you would not like to have.

3. During Christmas week of 1972, when these excerpts from Ullmann's diary were written, do you think she saw herself as a winner or a loser? Do you think she was a winner or a loser?

4. In another part of her book, *Changing,* Ullmann wrote: "I met an athlete who had reached the top. Heard him talking of his record race when there were tenths of a second between him and the next man. What had he sacrificed for those moments? What did the reverse side of his medal look like? Had he not paid for his few seconds of triumph with days and months and years during which he had had to say no to everything else?"
   a. On the basis of her diary excerpts, how do you think Ullmann would answer these questions if they were directed to her? How would you answer them for her?
   b. Can great achievers be total winners? Explain your answer.
   c. Would you be willing to lose a great deal in order to win a great deal? Why, or why not?

READING AND WRITING SUGGESTIONS

1. Write a narrative essay showing what Ullmann's diary might have been like if she had viewed herself as an unquestionable winner.

2. Read a biography which attempts to reveal the real feelings and private experiences of someone who was portrayed as a glamorous hero when he was alive—for example, John F. Kennedy or Clark Gable. Decide whether you consider the person to be a winner or a loser and write a brief narrative essay supporting your judgment.

SHOOTING AN ELEPHANT

George Orwell

George Orwell (1903–1950) was the pseudonym of Eric Blair, an English writer who was born the son of a minor customs official in India. Orwell was educated in England, but he returned to southern Asia as a young man and served with the Imperial Police in Burma. Both as a man and as a writer, he strongly criticized totalitarian societies. His questioning of totalitarianism can be seen in his books Animal Farm, *a political satire, and* 1984, *a grim vision of what the future might be like in a highly regimented society. In "Shooting an Elephant," Orwell explores the internal conflicts of a man caught between private conviction and public pressure.*

In Moulmein, in Lower Burma, I was hated by large numbers of people—the only time in my life that I have been important enough for this to happen to me. I was sub-divisional police officer of the town, and in an aimless, petty kind of way anti-European feeling was very bitter. No one had the guts to raise a riot, but if a European woman went through the bazaars alone somebody would probably spit betel juice over her dress. As a police officer I was an obvious target and was baited whenever it seemed safe to do so. When a nimble Burman tripped me up on the football field and the referee (another Burman) looked the other way, the crowd yelled with hideous laughter. This happened more than once. In the end the sneering yellow faces of young men that met me everywhere, the insults hooted after me when I was at a safe distance, got badly on my nerves. The young Buddhist priests were the worst of all. There were several thousands of them in the town and none of them seemed to have anything to do except stand on street corners and jeer at Europeans.

All this was perplexing and upsetting. For at that time I had already made up my mind that imperialism was an evil thing and the sooner I chucked up my job and got out of it the better. Theoretically—and secretly, of course—I was all for the Burmese and all against their oppressors, the British. As for the job I was doing, I hated it more bitterly than I can perhaps make clear. In a job like that you see the dirty work of Empire at close quarters. The wretched prisoners huddling in the stinking cages of the lock-ups, the grey, cowed faces of the long-term convicts, the scarred buttocks of the men who had been flogged with bamboos—all these oppressed me with an intolerable sense of guilt. But I could get nothing into perspective. I was young and ill-educated and I had had to think out my problems in the utter silence that is imposed on every Englishman in the East. I did not even know that the British Empire is dying, still less did I know that it is a great deal better than the younger empires that are going to supplant it. All I knew was that I was stuck between my hatred of the empire I served and my rage against the evil-spirited little beasts who tried to make my job impossible. With one part of my mind I thought of the British Raj[1] as an unbreakable tyranny, as something clamped down, *in saecula saeculorum*,[2] upon the will of prostrate peoples; with another part I thought that the greatest joy in the world would be to drive a bayonet into a Buddhist priest's guts. Feelings like these are the normal by-products of imperialism; ask any Anglo-Indian official, if you can catch him off duty.

One day something happened which in a round-about way was enlightening. It was a tiny incident in itself, but it gave me a better glimpse than I had had before of the real nature of imperialism—the real motives for which despotic governments act. Early one morning the sub-inspector at a police station the other end of the town rang me up on the 'phone and said that an elephant was ravaging the bazaar. Would I please come and do something about it? I did not know what I could do, but I wanted to see what was happening and I got on to a pony and started out. I took my rifle, an old .44 Winchester and much too small to kill an elephant, but I thought the noise might be useful *in terrorem*.[3] Various Burmans stopped me on the way and told me about the elephant's doings. It was not, of course, a wild elephant, but a tame one which had gone "must."[4] It had been chained up, as tame elephants always are when their attack of "must" is due, but on the previous night it had broken its chain and escaped. Its mahout,[5] the only person who could manage it when it was in that state, had set out in pursuit, but had taken the wrong direction and

---

1. Reign.
2. A Latin phrase meaning "forever and ever" or "for all eternity."
3. Latin for "as a means of provoking flight; an instrument of terror."
4. A period of frenzy occurring in elephants during the mating season.
5. Trainer and rider.

was now twelve hours' journey away, and in the morning the elephant had suddenly reappeared in the town. The Burmese population had no weapons and were quite helpless against it. It had already destroyed somebody's bamboo hut; killed a cow and raided some fruit-stalls and devoured the stock; also it had met the municipal rubbish van, and, when the driver jumped out and took to his heels, had turned the van over and inflicted violences upon it.

The Burmese sub-inspector and some Indian constables were waiting for me in the quarter where the elephant had been seen. It was a very poor quarter, a labyrinth of squalid bamboo huts, thatched with palm-leaf, winding all over a steep hillside. I remember that it was a cloudy, stuffy morning at the beginning of the rains. We began questioning the people as to where the elephant had gone, and, as usual, failed to get any definite information. That is invariably the case in the East; a story always sounds clear enough at a distance, but the nearer you get to the scene of events the vaguer it becomes. Some of the people said that the elephant had gone in one direction, some said that he had gone in another, some professed not even to have heard of an elephant. I had almost made up my mind that the whole story was a pack of lies, when we heard yells a little distance away. There was a loud, scandalized cry of "Go away, child! Go away this instant!" and an old woman with a switch in her hand came round the corner of a hut, violently shooing away a crowd of naked children. Some more women followed, clicking their tongues and exclaiming; evidently there was something that the children ought not to have seen. I rounded the hut and saw a man's dead body sprawling in the mud. He was an Indian, a black Dravidian coolie, almost naked, and he could not have been dead many minutes. The people said that the elephant had come suddenly upon him round the corner of the hut, caught him with its trunk, put its foot on his back and ground him into the earth. This was the rainy season and the ground was soft, and his face had scored a trench a foot deep and a couple of yards long. He was lying on his belly with arms crucified and head sharply twisted to one side. His face was coated with mud, the eyes wide open, the teeth bared and grinning with an expression of unendurable agony. (Never tell me, by the way, the the dead look peaceful. Most of the corpses I have seen looked devilish.) The friction of the great beast's foot had stripped the skin from his back as neatly as one skins a rabbit. As soon as I saw the dead man I sent an orderly to a friend's house nearby to borrow an elephant rifle. I had already sent back the pony, not wanting it to go mad with fright and throw me if it smelled the elephant.

The orderly came back in a few minutes with a rifle and five cartridges, and meanwhile some Burmans had arrived and told us that
the elephant was in the paddy fields below, only a few hundred yards
away. As I started forward practically the whole population of the
quarter flocked out of the houses and followed me. They had seen the
rifle and were all shouting excitedly that I was going to shoot the
elephant. They had not shown much interest in the elephant when he
was merely ravaging their homes, but it was different now that he
was going to be shot. It was a bit of fun to them, as it would be to an
English crowd; besides they wanted the meat. It made me vaguely
uneasy. I had no intention of shooting the elephant—I had merely
sent for the rifle to defend myself if necessary—and it is always
unnerving to have a crowd following you. I marched down the hill,
looking and feeling a fool, with the rifle over my shoulder and an
ever-growing army of people jostling at my heels. At the bottom,
when you got away from the huts, there was a metalled road and
beyond that a miry waste of paddy fields a thousand yards across, not
yet ploughed but soggy from the first rains and dotted with coarse
grass. The elephant was standing eight yards from the road, his left
side towards us. He took not the slightest notice of the crowd's
approach. He was tearing up bunches of grass, beating them against
his knees to clean them and stuffing them into his mouth.

I had halted on the road. As soon as I saw the elephant I knew with
perfect certainty that I ought not to shoot him. It is a serious matter to
shoot a working elephant—it is comparable to destroying a huge and
costly piece of machinery—and obviously one ought not to do it if it
can possibly be avoided. And at that distance, peacefully eating, the
elephant looked no more dangerous than a cow. I thought then and I
think now that his attack of "must" was already passing off; in which
case he would merely wander harmlessly about until the mahout
came back and caught him. Moreover, I did not in the least want to
shoot him. I decided that I would watch him for a little while to make
sure that he did not turn savage again, and then go home.

But at that moment I glanced round at the crowd that had followed
me. It was an immense crowd, two thousand at the least and growing
every minute. It blocked the road for a long distance on either side. I
looked at the sea of yellow faces above the garish clothes—faces all
happy and excited over this bit of fun, all certain that the elephant
was going to be shot. They were watching me as they would watch a
conjurer about to perform a trick. They did not like me, but with the
magical rifle in my hands I was momentarily worth watching. And
suddenly I realized that I should have to shoot the elephant after all.
The people expected it of me and I had got to do it; I could feel their

two thousand wills pressing me forward, irresistibly. And it was at this moment, as I stood there with the rifle in my hands, that I first grasped the hollowness, the futility of the white man's dominion in the East. Here was I, the white man with his gun, standing in front of the unarmed native crowd—seemingly the leading actor of the piece; but in reality I was only an absurd puppet pushed to and fro by the will of those yellow faces behind. I perceived in this moment that when the white man turns tyrant it is his own freedom that he destroys. He becomes a sort of hollow, posing dummy, the conventionalized figure of a sahib.[6] For it is the condition of his rule that he shall spend his life in trying to impress the "natives," and so in every crisis he has got to do what the "natives" expect of him. He wears a mask, and his face grows to fit it. I had got to shoot the elephant. I had committed myself to doing it when I sent for the rifle. A sáhib has got to act like a sahib; he has got to appear resolute, to know his own mind and do definite things. To come all that way, rifle in hand, with two thousand people marching at my heels, and then to trail feebly away, having done nothing—no, that was impossible. The crowd would laugh at me. And my whole life, every white man's life in the East, was one long struggle not to be laughed at.

But I did not want to shoot the elephant. I watched him beating his bunch of grass against his knees, with that preoccupied grandmotherly air that elephants have. It seemed to me that it would be murder to shoot him. At that age I was not squeamish about killing animals, but I had never shot an elephant and never wanted to. (Somehow it always seems worse to kill a *large* animal.) Besides, there was the beast's owner to be considered. Alive, the elephant was worth at least a hundred pounds; dead, he would only be worth the value of his tusks, five pounds, possibly. But I had got to act quickly. I turned to some experienced-looking Burmans who had been there when we arrived, and asked them how the elephant had been behaving. They all said the same thing: he took no notice of you if you left him alone, but he might charge if you went too close to him.

It was perfectly clear to me what I ought to do. I ought to walk up to within, say, twenty-five yards of the elephant and test his behavior. If he charged I could shoot, if he took no notice of me it would be safe to leave him until the mahout came back. But also I knew that I was going to do no such thing. I was a poor shot with a rifle and the ground was soft mud into which one would sink at every step. If the elephant charged and I missed him, I should have about as much

---

6. Master; an Indian form of respect used when addressing a Britisher.

chance as a toad under a steam-roller. But even then I was not thinking particularly of my own skin, only of the watchful yellow faces
behind. For at that moment, with the crowd watching me, I was not
afraid in the ordinary sense, as I would have been if I had been alone.
A white man mustn't be frightened in front of "natives"; and so, in
general, he isn't frightened. The sole thought in my mind was that if
anything went wrong those two thousand Burmans would see me
pursued, caught, trampled on and reduced to a grinning corpse like
that Indian up the hill. And if that happened it was quite probable
that some of them would laugh. That would never do. There was only
one alternative. I shoved the cartridges into the magazine and lay
down on the road to get a better aim.

The crowd grew very still, and a deep, low, happy sigh, as of
people who see the theatre curtain go up at last, breathed from innumerable throats. They were going to have their bit of fun after all.
The rifle was a beautiful German thing with cross-hair sights. I did
not then know that in shooting an elephant one would shoot to cut an
imaginary bar running from ear-hole to ear-hole. I ought, therefore,
as the elephant was sideways on, to have aimed straight at his ear-
hole; actually I aimed several inches in front of this, thinking the
brain would be further forward.

When I pulled the trigger I did not hear the bang or feel the kick—
one never does when a shot goes home—but I heard the devilish roar
of glee that went up from the crowd. In that instant, in too short a
time, one would have thought, even for the bullet to get there, a
mysterious, terrible change had come over the elephant. He neither
stirred nor fell, but every line on his body had altered. He looked
suddenly stricken, shrunken, immensely old, as though the frightful
impact of the bullet had paralyzed him without knocking him down.
At last, after what seemed a long time—it might have been five
seconds, I dare say—he sagged flabbily to his knees. His mouth
slobbered. An enormous senility seemed to have settled upon him.
One could have imagined him thousands of years old. I fired again
into the same spot. At the second shot he did not collapse but
climbed with desperate slowness to his feet and stood weakly upright, with legs sagging and head drooping. I fired a third time. That
was the shot that did for him. You could see the agony of it jolt his
whole body and knock the last remnant of strength from his legs. But
in falling he seemed for a moment to rise, for as his hind legs collapsed beneath him he seemed to tower upwards like a huge rock
toppling, his trunk reaching skywards like a tree. He trumpeted, for
the first and only time. And then down he came, his belly towards
me, with a crash that seemed to shake the ground even where I lay.

I got up. The Burmans were already racing past me across the mud. It was obvious that the elephant would never rise again, but he was not dead. He was breathing very rhythmically with long rattling gasps, his great mound of a side painfully rising and falling. His mouth was wide open—I could see far down into the caverns of pale pink throat. I waited a long time for him to die, but his breathing did not weaken. Finally I fired my two remaining shots into the spot where I thought his heart must be. The thick blood welled out of him like red velvet, but still he did not die. His body did not even jerk when the shots hit him, the tortured breathing continued without a pause. He was dying, very slowly and in great agony, but in some world remote from me where not even a bullet could damage him further. I felt that I had got to put an end to that dreadful noise. It seemed dreadful to see the great beast lying there, powerless to move and yet powerless to die, and not even to be able to finish him. I sent back for my small rifle and poured shot after shot into his heart and down his throat. They seemed to make no impression. The tortured gasps continued as steadily as the ticking of a clock.

In the end I could not stand it any longer and went away. I heard later that it took him half an hour to die. Burmans were bringing dahs[7] and baskets even before I left, and I was told they had stripped his body almost to the bones by the afternoon.

Afterwards, of course, there were endless discussions about the shooting of the elephant. The owner was furious, but he was only an Indian and could do nothing. Besides, legally I had done the right thing, for a mad elephant has to be killed, like a mad dog., if its owner fails to control it. Among the Europeans opinion was divided. The older men said I was right, the younger men said it was a damn shame to shoot an elephant for killing a coolie, because an elephant was worth more than any damn Coringhee coolie. And afterwards I was very glad that the coolie had been killed; it put me legally in the right and it gave me a sufficient pretext for shooting the elephant.I often wondered whether any of the others grasped that I had done it solely to avoid looking a fool.

QUESTIONS

1. Explain the meaning of the following phrases in the context of the essay as a whole.
   "He wears a mask, and his face grows to fit it."
   Seeing "the dirty work of Empire at close quarters."

---

7. Crude litters much in use for transport throughout the East.

2. What is the tone* of the narrative? Does the author sound more like a member speaking in the House of Commons or like one civil servant talking to another over drinks in a club? How does Orwell achieve this effect?

3. a. Summarize the events in the story from the first report of the rampaging elephant to the end.
   b. Did the protagonist think he *ought* to shoot the elephant? What reasons did he give for his conclusion?
   c. Why did the protagonist think that he *had* to shoot the elephant?

4. a. What does Orwell mean by the sentence, "They had not shown much interest in the elephant when he was merely ravaging their homes, but it was different now that he was going to be shot"?
   b. Is this sentence an exaggeration? If so, why might Orwell exaggerate his description of the people's thoughts?
   c. Is Orwell suggesting the same thing that Eldridge Cleaver suggests in his essay on p. 52—that people are motivated by a blood lust?

5. Consider the last sentence of the essay.
   a. Does the sentence express a sound reason for killing the elephant? Explain your answer.
   b. Have you ever done something you didn't want to do in order to avoid looking foolish? If so, what was it you did? How did you feel afterward?

READING AND WRITING SUGGESTIONS

1. Consider Orwell's sentence, "When a white man turns tyrant it is his own freedom that he destroys." Although Orwell is referring specifically to white men in a colonial context, the sentence can be generalized to apply to all people. Write a narrative essay about a person to whom this generalization applies.

2. Read about a fictional character, such as Captain Vere in Herman Melville's *Billy Budd,* who acts from a sense of duty even when that duty conflicts with what he or she thinks is right. Write a narrative essay in which you describe the internal tensions such a person experiences.

---

*Definitions for all terms marked with an asterisk may be found in the Glossary.

A SKINNY DAKOTA KID WHO MADE GOOD

Will Rogers

Will Rogers (1879–1935), an American humorist, was born in Oologah, Indian Territory, which is now Oklahoma. Early in his career, he worked in a Wild West show and twirled a lariat on the vaudeville stage. Later he developed a monologue style that combined satire with homespun philosophy; this style made him one of the most popular American humorists of all time. Besides appearing in motion pictures and on the radio, Rogers wrote a syndicated newspaper column. He was also the author of a number of books, including The Cowboy Philosopher on Prohibition, Illiterate Digest, *and* Ether and Me. *In this essay, Rogers uses the history of a young jockey as a means of exploring the nature of honor, of greatness, and of meaningful work.*

Out of the west came a little skinny runt kid, born out in the hills of South Dakota. On Sundays the Cowpunchers and Ranchers would meet and have Cow Pony races. On account of his being small he was lifted up and a surcingle was strapped around over his legs and around the horse. He was taken to the starting line on a straightaway and was "lapped and tapped" off. He had the nerve and he seemed to have the head. So they cut the surcingle and he got so he could sit up there on one of those postage stamp things they call a Jockey's saddle. He kept riding around these little Country Shooting Gallery meets, and Merry-Go-Round Gatherings, until he finally got good enough to go to a real race track at New Orleans. There he saw more Horses in one race than he had ever seen at one track before.

His first race he ran 2nd. Then he said to himself, "Why run second? Why not run first?" And he did. They began to notice that this kid really *savied* a Horse. He spoke their language. Horses seemed to know when the kid was up. He carried a Bat (Jockey's term for a whip) but he never seemed to use it. Other Jocks would come down the stretch whipping a Horse out when the best he could finish would be 4th or 5th. But not this kid. When he couldn't get in the money he never punished them. He hand rode them. He could get more out of a Horse with his hands than another Jock could get with the old Battery up both sleeves.

He got to be recognized as one of the best, and he passed from one Stable to another until he landed with the biggest, a real Trainer and a Real Sportsman-Owner. How many thousands of People in every line come to New York every year that want to make good, get ahead and be recognized! They come by the millions. How many, if anything happened to them, would get even a passing Notice in the busy and overcrowded New York Press. If some Millionaire died, the best he could get would be a column. Then perhaps it wouldn't be read through by a dozen. But what blazoned across the front pages of every Metropolitan daily a few days ago, in bigger headlines than a Presidential Nomination, bigger than the Prince of Wales will get on his arrival? In a race at Saratoga Springs, N. Y., a Horse had fallen and carried down with him a little skinny Kid (that had slept in his youth not in a 5th Avenue Mansion but in Box Stalls all over the Country with Horses, the Horses he knew how to ride and the Horses that loved to run their best for him).

Here was the Headline: "SANDE IS HURT. He may never ride again." They don't have to give even his first name; few know it. They don't have to explain who he is. They don't have to tell which Rockefeller or Morgan it was. It was just Sande. There is only one. Our Sande! The boy who had carried America's colors to Victory over England's great Papyrus and their Premier Jockey Steve Donohue.

The Ambulance rushes on the track and picks him up; it is followed by hundreds afoot, running. The entire grand stands of people rush to the temporary Track Hospital to see how Sande is, and hoping and praying that it's not serious. He revives long enough to tell his Wife he is all right. Game kid that. Then he faints again. Mrs. Vanderbilt and the elite of Society are assisting and doing all they can to help. A personal Physician to a President of the United States is working over him. He could not have shown any more anxiety over the President than he did over this kid. When the thousands of pleasure seekers and excitement hunters rushed from the stands and saw them lifting that frail lifeless looking form from the track Ambulance there was not one that wouldn't have given an Arm off their body if they had thought it would save his Life, and that goes for Touts, and Grooms, and Swipes, as well as the Public.

Some western people who don't know are always saying Easterners have no Heart, everything is for themselves and the Dough. Say, don't tell me that! Geography don't change Human Nature. If you are

Right, people are for you whether it's in Africa or Siberia. A wire was sent by Mr. Widener, a millionaire Racing Official, to Dr. Russell the great Specialist of Roosevelt Hospital, New York, "Come at once. Spare no expense. SANDE is Hurt!" That's all Secretary Slemp could do if President Coolidge was hurt.

Mr. Sinclair withdrew all Horses from the remaining Races. He would withdraw them for Life if he knew it would restore this Kid who worked for him, back to normal again.

Now what made this One Hundred and Ten Pounds (half portion of physical manhood) beloved by not only the racing Public but by the masses who never bet a cent on a Horse race in their lives? The same thing that will make a man great in any line—his absolute HONESTY. The racing public are very fickle and when they lose they are apt to lay blame on almost any quarter. But win or lose, they knew it was not Sande. To have insinuated to one of them that he ever pulled a Horse, would have been taking your Life in your hands. What do you suppose he could have gotten out of some bunch of betting Crooks to have pulled Zev in the big International Race? Why, enough to retire on and never have to take another chance with his Life by riding. He could have done it on the back stretch and no one would have ever known.

Ability is all right but if it is not backed up by Honesty and Public confidence you will never be a Sande. A man that don't love a Horse, there is something the matter with him. If he has no sympathy for the man that does love Horses then there is something worse the matter with him. The best a Man can do is to arrive at the top of his chosen profession. I have always maintained that one Profession is deserving of as much honor as another provided it is honorable.

Through some unknown process of reasoning we have certain things that are called Arts, and to be connected with them raises you above your fellow Man. Say, how do they get that way? If a Man happens to take up Painting and becomes only a mediocre painter, why should he be classed above the Bricklayer who has excelled every other Bricklayer? The Bricklayer is a true Artist in his line or he could not have reached the top. The Painter has not been acclaimed the best in his line hence the Bricklayer is superior. Competition is just as keen in either line. In fact there are more good bricklayers than Painters. If you are the best Taxi Driver you are as much an Artist as Kreisler. You save lives by your skilful driving. That's a meritorious profession, is it not?

A Writer calls himself a Literary Man or an Artist. There are thousands of them, and all, simply because they write, are termed Artists.

Is there a Sande among them? Caruso was great, but he had only to show ability. He didn't have to demonstrate any honesty. Nobody tried to keep him from singing his best by bribery.

Now if you think the Racing Public and millions of well wishers are hoping for this Kid's recovery, what about the Horses? They knew him better than the Humans did. Why, that Horse would have broke his own neck rather than hurt Sande. Who is going to ride him in the next race and make him win and not whip him?—not Sande. Who is going to sit on him just where he will be the easiest to carry? Not Sande. Who is going to lean over and whisper in his ear and tell him when to go his best? Not Sande. Who is going to carry a Bat and not use it? Not Sande. Who is going to watch the hand on that starting Barrier and have him headed the right way just when the starter springs it? Not Sande. No, the Horses are the ones who are going to miss him.

If we could speak their language like he can, here are a few conversations that you will hear through the cracks in the Box Stalls: "Gee, I can't run; I don't seem to get any help. I wish Sande were back."

A three year old replies, "I wish there was something we could do. If they would just let us go up to the Hospital and talk to him he would savy," "I wish we had him here in a Box Stall. I would stand up the rest of my life and give him my bed. I would fix him some Clean Hay to lay on. He don't want those White Caps and Aprons running around. He wants to lay on a Horse Blanket, and have his busted Leg wrapped up with Bandages like he knows how to use on ours. I bet they ain't even got Absorbine up there. That Kid would rather have a Bran Mash than all that Goo they will feed him with up there."

The Old Stake Horse 4 stalls down the line overhears and replies: "Sure, I bet they have one of them Bone Specialists. What that Kid needs is a good Vet."

The old Selling Plater butts in: "Sure, we could cheer him up if he was here. Them Foreigners up there don't speak his Tongue. That kid is part Horse. Remember how he used to kid wid us when he would be working us out at daylight when the rest of the Star Jocks was in feathers. One morning I told him if he didn't quit waking me up so early in the morning I was going to buck him off. He got right back at me; he said, 'If you do I will get you left at the Post your next race.' Gee, he sure did throw a scare into me. And, say, you couldn't loaf on that Bird either. He knew when you was loafing and when you was trying. I threw up my tail one hot day to make him think I was all through. He give me one cut with the Bat and I dropped that tail and left there so fast I could have run over Man of War. Gee, those were great days; Do youse reckon Zev knows anything about it? I hope they don't tell him; it would break his heart. He sure did love that kid."

Patient readers, Lincoln went down in History as "HONEST Abe," BUT HE NEVER WAS A JOCKEY. If he had been a Jockey he might have gone down as just "Abe."

QUESTIONS

1. Identify at least three words or slang expressions in the essay that suggest the racing world. What do these words contribute to the essay's atmosphere?

2. Examine Rogers's grammar and writing style and his practice of capitalizing certain common nouns. What impression is he trying to convey? Why?

3. Why was Sande so widely admired by people and, according to Rogers, by horses?

4. Is one profession more honorable than another? What standards, if any, should we use in judging the relative value of various professions? How can we tell if someone has reached the top of his or her profession?
    a. Answer these questions as you think Rogers would answer them.
    b. Give your own opinions on these questions.
    c. Judging from your reading and your experience, answer the questions as you think most people would.

5. Sande's career as a jockey was quite possibly finished by his injuries. He could have been rich, retired, and uninjured if he had thrown some races, but he kept his honor. Was he really better off for having stayed honest, or would he have been better off if he had thrown a race or two?

READING AND WRITING SUGGESTIONS

1. Write a brief narrative essay describing someone who would meet Rogers's standard for a successful professional.

2. Read *Blind Ambition*, John Dean's account of his involvement in the Watergate scandal. Write a brief narrative essay showing how Dean's life might have been today if he had acted differently.

MARY DUFF'S LAST HALF-CROWN

John Brown

John Brown (1810–1882) was born in Biggar, Scotland. He was a practicing physician throughout most of his life, but he also found time to write a large number of essays, many of which are collected in Rab and His Friends, Horae Subsecivae *("Leisure Hours"), and* John Leech and Other Papers. *His literary style is characterized by its humor, its tenderness, and its simplicity. Brown's faith in God and his capacity for seeing the best in human nature are revealed in the following account of Mary Duff.*

Hugh Miller, the geologist, journalist, and man of genius, was sitting in his newspaper office late one dreary winter night.

The clerks had all left and he was preparing to go, when a quick rap came to the door. He said "Come in," and in looking towards the entrance, saw a little ragged child all wet with sleet. "Are ye Hugh Miller?" "Yes." "Mary Duff wants ye." "What does she want?" "She's deeing." Some misty recollection of the name made him at once set out, and with his well-known plaid and stick he was soon striding after the child, who trotted through the now deserted High Street into the Canongate. By the time he got to the Old Playhouse Close, Hugh had revived his memory of Mary Duff; a lively girl who had been bred up beside him in Cromarty. The last time he had seen her was at a brother mason's marriage, where Mary was "best maid" and he "best man." He seemed still to see her bright, young, careless face, her tidy short-gown, and her dark eyes, and to hear her bantering, merry tongue.

Down the close went the ragged little woman, and up an outside stair, Hugh keeping near her with difficulty. In the passage she held out her hand and touched him; taking it in his great palm, he felt that she wanted a thumb. Finding her way like a cat through the darkness, she opened a door, and saying, "That's her!" vanished. By the light of a dying fire he saw lying in the corner of the large, empty room something like a woman's clothes, and on drawing nearer became aware of a thin, pale face and two dark eyes looking keenly but helplessly up at him. The eyes were plainly Mary Duff's, though he could recognize no other feature. She wept silently, gazing steadily at him. "Are you Mary Duff?" "It's a' that's o' me, Hugh." She then tried to speak to him, something plainly of great urgency, but she couldn't; and seeing that she was very ill, and was making herself worse, he put half a crown into her feverish hand and said he would call again in the morning. He could get no information about her from the neighbors; they were surly or asleep.

When he returned next morning, the little girl met him at the stairhead, and said, "She's deid." He went in and found that it was true; there she lay, the fire out, her face placid, and the likeness of her maiden self restored. Hugh thought he would have known her now, even with those bright black eyes closed as they were, *in aeternum*. [1]

Seeking out a neighbor, he said he would like to bury Mary Duff, and arranged for a funeral with an undertaker in the close. Little seemed to be known of the poor outcast, except that she was a "licht," or as Solomon would have said, a "strange woman." "Did she drink?" "Whiles."

On the day of the funeral one or two residents in the close accompanied him to the Canongate churchyard. He observed a decent-looking little old woman watching them, and following at a distance, though the day was wet and bitter. After the grave was filled, and he had taken off his hat, as the men finished their business by putting on and slapping the sod, he saw this old woman remaining; she came up and curtsying, said, "Ye wad ken that lass, sir?" "Yes; I knew her when she was young." The woman then burst into tears, and told Hugh that she "keepit a bit shop at the close-mooth, and Mary dealt wi' me, and aye paid reglar, and I was feared she was dead, for she had been a month awin' me half a crown"; and then with a look and voice of awe, she told him how on the night he was sent for, and immediately after he had left, she had been awakened by some one in her room; and by her bright fire—for she was a bein well-to-do body —she had seen the wasted dying creature, who came forward and said, "Wasn't it half a crown?" "Yes." "There it is," and putting it under the bolster, vanished!

Poor Mary Duff, her life had been a sad one since the day when she had stood side by side with Hugh at the wedding of their friends. Her father died not long after, and her mother supplanted her in the affections of the man to whom she had given her heart. The shock

---

1. For eternity.

made home intolerable. She fled from it blighted and embittered, and, after a life of shame and misery, crept into the corner of her room to die alone.

"My thoughts are not your thoughts, neither are your ways my ways, saith the Lord. For as the heavens are higher than the earth, so are my ways higher than your ways, and my thoughts than your thoughts."

QUESTIONS

1. Define the following words: *bantering, surly, placid, bolster, "licht."*

2. What different images of Mary Duff are presented at various points in the essay? How does Brown use the narrative form to add interest to his characterization?

3. What overall image does this essay give of Mary Duff? Does Brown present her favorably or unfavorably?

4. What is the meaning of the biblical quotation in the final paragraph? How does it relate to the picture Brown has painted of Mary Duff?

5. Brown's essay presents both Mary Duff's strengths and her weaknesses. Would you say that she is essentially a strong person or a weak one?

READING AND WRITING SUGGESTIONS

1. Write a brief narrative essay describing a person you believe has a strong sense of social justice. Describe the person in a variety of situations, showing how he or she demonstrated this quality in each situation.

2. Write a brief narrative essay describing a friend or family member whose behavior seems to you to be self-destructive.

3. Read Erich Fromm's book, *The Art of Loving*, and write a brief narrative essay about someone you know who has the "capacity to love" which Fromm describes in his book.

A DISSERTATION
UPON ROAST PIG

Charles Lamb

Charles Lamb (1775–1834), an English essayist, critic, and poet, overcame many obstacles to pursue his career as a writer. After receiving only seven years of formal education, he became a clerk at age fifteen. He was confined to an insane asylum for a brief period when he was twenty-one, and, a few months after his release, his sister was committed for life to an insane asylum for the murder of their mother. Lamb obtained his sister's release by pledging to care for her, and from that time onward he spent much of his time tending to her needs. Working together, Lamb and his sister produced Tales from Shakespeare *and* Poetry for Children. *Despite Lamb's fear that his sister's psychotic episodes would recur, his writing is often cheerful and humorous. "A Dissertation upon Roast Pig," one of the most highly praised of Lamb's many fine essays, provides an excellent example of his use of humor and satire.*

Mankind, says a Chinese manuscript, which my friend M. was obliging enough to read and explain to me, for the first seventy thousand ages ate their meat raw, clawing or biting it from the living animal, just as they do in Abyssinia to this day. This period is not obscurely hinted at by their great Confucius in the second chapter of his "Mundane Mutations," where he designates a kind of golden age by the term Cho-fang, literally the Cooks' holiday. The manuscript goes on to say that the art of roasting, or rather broiling (which I take to be the elder brother) was accidentally discovered in the manner following. The swineherd, Ho-ti, having gone out into the woods one morning, as his manner was, to collect mast for his hogs, left his cottage in the care of his eldest son Bo-bo, a great lubberly boy, who being fond of playing with fire, as younkers of his age commonly are, let some sparks escape into a bundle of straw, which kindling quickly spread the conflagration over every part of their poor mansion, till it was reduced to ashes. Together with the cottage (a sorry antediluvian makeshift of a building, you may think it), what was of much more importance, a fine litter of new-farrowed pigs, no less than nine in number, perished. China pigs have been esteemed a luxury all over the East from the remotest periods that we read of. Bo-bo was in the utmost consternation, as you may think, not so much for the sake of the tenement, which his father and he could easily build up again with a few dry branches, and the labor of an hour or two, at any time, as for the loss of the pigs. While he was thinking what he should say to his father, and wringing his hands over the smoking remnants of one of those untimely sufferers, an odor assailed his nostrils, unlike any scent which he had before experienced. What could it proceed from?—not from the burnt cottage—he had smelt that smell before— indeed this was by no means the first accident of the kind which had occurred through the negligence of this unlucky young firebrand. Much less did it resemble that of any known herb, weed, or flower. A premonitory moistening at the same time overflowed his nether lip. He knew not what to think. He next stooped down to feel the pig, if there were any signs of life in it. He burnt his fingers, and to cool them he applied them in his booby fashion to his mouth. Some of the crumbs of the scorched skin had come away with his fingers, and for the first time in his life (in the world's life indeed, for before him no man had known it) he tasted—crackling! Again he felt and fumbled at the pig. It did not burn him so much now, still he licked his fingers from a sort of habit. The truth at length broke into his slow under- standing that it was the pig that smelt so, and the pig that tasted so delicious; and, surrendering himself up to the newborn pleasure, he feel to tearing up whole handfuls of the scorched skin with the flesh next it, and was cramming it down his throat in his beastly fashion, when his sire entered amid the smoking rafters, armed with a retri- butory cudgel, and, finding how affairs stood, began to rain blows upon the young rogue's shoulders as thick as hailstones, which Bo- bo heeded not any more than if they had been flies. The tickling pleasure which he experienced in his lower regions had rendered him quite callous to any inconveniences he might feel in those remote quarters. His father might lay on, but he could not beat him from his pig till he had fairly made an end of it, when, becoming a little more sensible of his situation, something like the following dialogue en- sued:—

"You graceless whelp, what have you got there devouring? Is it not enough that you have burnt me down three houses with your dog's tricks, and be hanged to you, but you must be eating fire, and I know not what—what have you got there, I say?"

"Oh, father, the pig, the pig, do come and taste how nice the burnt pig eats!"

The ears of Ho-ti tingled with horror. He cursed his son, and he cursed himself that ever he should beget a son that should eat burnt pig.

Bo-bo, whose scent was wonderfully sharpened since morning, soon raked out another pig, and fairly rending it asunder, thrust the lesser half by main force into the fists of Ho-ti, still shouting out, "Eat, eat, eat the burnt pig, father, only taste—O Lord!"—with such like barbarous ejaculations, cramming all the while as if he would choke.

Ho-ti trembled in every joint while he grasped the abominable thing, wavering whether he should not put his son to death for an unnatural young monster, when the crackling scorching his fingers, as it had done his son's, and applying the same remedy to them, he, in his turn, tasted some of its flavor, which, make what sour mouths he would for a pretense, proved not altogether displeasing to him. In conclusion (for the manuscript here is a little tedious) both father and son fairly sat down to the mess, and never left off till they had despatched all that remained of the litter.

Bo-bo was strictly enjoined not to let the secret escape, for the neighbors would certainly have stoned them for a couple of abominable wretches, who could think of improving upon the good meat which God had sent them. Nevertheless, strange stories got about. It was observed that Ho-ti's cottage was burnt down now more frequently than ever. Nothing but fires from this time forward. Some would break out in broad day, others in the nighttime. As often as the sow farrowed, so sure was the house of Ho-ti to be in a blaze; and Ho-ti himself, which was the more remarkable, instead of chastising his son, seemed to grow more indulgent to him than ever. At length they were watched, the terrible mystery discovered, and father and son summoned to take their trial at Pekin, then an inconsiderable assize town. Evidence was given, the obnoxious food itself produced in court, and verdict about to be pronounced, when the foreman of the jury begged that some of the burnt pig, of which the culprits stood accused, might be handed into the box. He handled it, and they all handled it, and burning their fingers as Bo-bo and his father had done before them, and nature prompting to each of them the same remedy, against the face of all the facts, and the clearest charge which judge had ever given—to the surprise of the whole court, townsfolk, strangers, reporters, and all present—without leaving the box, or any manner of consultation whatever, they brought in a simultaneous verdict of Not Guilty.

The judge, who was a shrewd fellow, winked at the manifest iniquity of the decision; and, when the court was dismissed, went privily, and bought up all the pigs that could be had for love or money. In a few days his lordship's town house was observed to be on fire. The thing took wing, and now there was nothing to be seen but fires in every direction. Fuel and pigs grew enormously dear all over the district. The insurance offices one and all shut up shop. People built slighter and slighter every day, until it was feared that the very science of architecture would in no long time be lost to the world. Thus this custom of firing houses continued, till in process of time, says my manuscript, a sage arose, like our Locke, who made a discovery that the flesh of swine, or, indeed, of any other animal, might be cooked (burnt as they called it) without the necessity of consuming a whole house to dress it. Then first began the rude form of a gridiron. Roasting by the string, or spit, came in a century or two later, I forget in whose dynasty. By such slow degrees, concludes the manuscript, do the most useful, and seemingly the most obvious arts, make their way among mankind.

Without placing too implicit faith in the account above given, it must be agreed that if a worthy pretext for so dangerous an experiment as setting houses on fire (especially in these days) could be assigned in favor of any culinary object, that pretext and excuse might be found in roast pig.

Of all the delicacies in the whole *mundus edibilis,*[1] I will maintain it to be the most delicate—*princeps obsoniorum.*[2]

I speak not of your grown porkers—things between pig and pork—those hobbydehoys—but a young and tender suckling—under a moon old—guiltless as yet of the sty—with no original speck of the *amor immunditiae,*[3] the hereditary failing of the first parent, yet manifest—his voice as yet not broken, but something between a childish treble and a grumble—the mild forerunner, or *praeludium,*[4] of a grunt.

He must be roasted. I am not ignorant that our ancestors ate them seethed, or boiled—but what a sacrifice of the exterior tegument!

There is no flavor comparable, I will contend, to that of the crisp, tawny, well-watched, not over-roasted crackling, as it is well called—the very teeth are invited to their share of the pleasure at this banquet in overcoming the coy, brittle resistance—with the adhesive oleaginous—oh, call it not fat—but an indefinable sweetness growing

---

1. World of eating.

2. Prince of delight.

3. Love of filth.

4. Prelude.

up to it—the tender blossoming of fat—fat cropped in the bud—taken in the shoot—in the first innocence—the cream and quintessence of child-pig's yet pure food—the lean, no lean, but a kind of animal manna—or, rather, fat and lean (if it must be so) so blended and running into each other that both together make but one ambrosian result, or common substance.

Behold him, while he is doing—it seemeth rather a refreshing warmth than a scorching heat that he is so passive to. How equably he twirleth round the string!—Now he is just done. To see the extreme sensibility of that tender age, he hath wept out his pretty eyes—radiant jellies—shooting stars!

See him in the dish, his second cradle, how meek he lieth!—wouldst thou have had this innocent grow up to the grossness and indocility which too often accompany maturer swinehood? Ten to one he would have proved a glutton, a sloven, an obstinate, disagreeable animal—wallowing in all manner of filthy conversation! From these sins he is happily snatched away—

> Ere sin could blight, or sorrow fade,
> Death came with timely care—

his memory is odoriferous—no clown curseth, while his stomach half rejecteth, the rank bacon—no coal heaver bolteth him in reeking sausages—he hath a fair sepulchre in the grateful stomach of the judicious epicure—and for such a tomb might be content to die.

He is the best of sapors. Pineapple is great. She is, indeed, almost too transcendent—a delight, if not sinful, yet so like to sinning, that really a tender-conscienced person would do well to pause—too ravishing for mortal taste, she woundeth and excoriateth the lips that approach her—like lovers' kisses, she biteth—she is a pleasure bordering on pain from the fierceness and insanity of her relish—but she stoppeth at the palate—she meddleth not with the appetite—and the coarsest hunger might barter her consistently for a mutton chop.

Pig—let me speak his praise—is no less provocative of the appetite than he is satisfactory to the criticalness of the censorious palate. The strong man may batten on him, and the weakling refuseth not his mild juices.

Unlike to mankind's mixed characters, a bundle of virtues and vices, inexplicably intertwisted, and not to be unraveled without hazard, he is—good throughout. No part of him is better or worse than another. He helpeth, as far as his little means extend, all around. He is the least envious of banquets. He is all neighbors' fare.

I am one of those who freely and ungrudgingly impart a share of the good things of this life which fall to their lot (few as mine are in this kind) to a friend. I protest I take as great an interest in my friend's pleasures, his relishes, and proper satisfactions, as in mine own. "Presents," I often say, "endear Absents." Hares, pheasants, partridges, snipes, barn-door chickens (those "tame villatic fowl"), capons, plovers, brawn, barrels of oysters, I dispense as freely as I receive them. I love to taste them, as it were, upon the tongue of my friend. But a stop must be put somewhere. One would not, like Lear, "give everything." I make my stand upon pig. Methinks it is an ingratitude to the Giver of all good flavors, to extra-domiciliate, or send out of the house, slightingly (under pretext of friendship, or I know not what), a blessing so particularly adapted, predestined, I may say, to my individual palate. It argues an insensibility.

I remember a touch of conscience in this kind at school. My good old aunt, who never parted from me at the end of a holiday without stuffing a sweetmeat, or some nice thing into my pocket, had dismissed me one evening with a smoking plum cake, fresh from the oven. On my way to school (it was over London Bridge) a gray-headed old beggar saluted me (I have no doubt at this time of day that he was a counterfeit). I had no pence to console him with, and in the vanity of self-denial, and the very coxcombry of charity, schoolboy-like, I made him a present of—the whole cake! I walked on a little, buoyed up, as one is on such occasions, with a sweet soothing of self-satisfaction; but before I had got to the end of the bridge my better feelings returned and I burst into tears, thinking how ungrateful I had been to my good aunt, to go and give her good gift away to a stranger that I had never seen before, and who might be a bad man for aught I knew; and then I thought of the pleasure my aunt would be taking in thinking that I—I myself, and not another—would eat her nice cake—and what should I say to her the next time I saw her—how naughty I was to part with her pretty present—and the odor of that spicy cake came back upon my recollection, and the pleasure and the curiosity I had taken in seeing her make it, and her joy when she sent it to the oven, and how disappointed she would feel that I had never had a bit of it in my mouth at last—and I blamed my impertinent spirit of almsgiving, and out-of-place hypocrisy of goodness, and, above all, I wished never to see the face again of that insidious, good-for-nothing, old gray imposter.

Our ancestors were nice in their method of sacrificing the tender victims. We read of pigs whipped to death with something of a shock, as we hear of any other obsolete custom. The age of discipline is gone by, or it would be curious to inquire (in a philosophical light merely) what effect this process might have towards intenerating and dulcifying a substance, naturally so mild and dulcet as the flesh of young pigs. It looks like refining a violet. Yet we should be cautious, while we condemn the inhumanity, how we censure the wisdom of the practice. It might impart a gusto.

I remember an hypothesis, argued upon by the young students, when I was at St. Omer's, and maintained with much learning and pleasantry on both sides, "Whether supposing that the flavor of a pig who obtained his death by whipping (*per flagellationem extremam*)[5] superadded a pleasure upon the palate of a man more intense than any possible suffering we can conceive in the animal, is man justified in using that method of putting the animal to death?" I forget the decision.

His sauce should be considered. Decidedly, a few bread crumbs, done up with his liver and brains, and a dash of mild sage. But, banish, dear Mrs. Cook, I beseech you, the whole onion tribe. Barbecue your whole hogs to your palate, steep them in shallots, stuff them out with plantations of the rank and guilty garlic; you cannot poison them, or make them stronger than they are—but consider, he is a weakling—a flower.

QUESTIONS

1. Consult your dictionary for the following words: *mast, lubberly, younkers, antediluvian, farrowed, consternation, premonitory, nether, crackling, retributory, cudgel, chastise, assize, hobbydehoys, tegument, oleaginous, quintessence, odoriferous, sepulchre, epicure, sapors, excoriate, censorious, batten, villatic, coxcombry, impertinent, insidious, intenerating, dulcify.*

2. Give the central thesis of Lamb's essay.
   a. To what purpose does Lamb include the experience involving his aunt, the gray-headed beggar, and the plum cake? How does this account from his own experience relate to his thesis? Could it have been omitted without weakening the essay?
   b. How does Lamb make the transitions* between the different parts of the essay? Do you think the essay works effectively as a whole? Why, or why not?
   c. What is your opinion of the essay's closing paragraph? Compare the introduction of the essay with its conclusion and

---

5. Through extreme whipping.

*Definitions for all terms marked with an asterisk may be found in the Glossary.

decide whether this beginning and ending would lead you to predict that the essay as a whole would be well organized.

3. Give the meaning of the following sentences and explain how they are used in the essay.
   —"She is a pleasure bordering on pain."
   —" 'Presents,' I often say, 'endear Absents.' "
   —"He is a weakling—a flower."
   —"It looks like refining a violet."

4. Lamb uses a number of methods to create humor in his essay. Examine some of the passages you found most amusing and describe how Lamb has made them humorous.

5. Lamb compares the pig and mankind as follows: "Unlike to mankind's mixed characters, a bundle of virtues and vices, inexplicably intertwisted, and not to be unraveled without hazard, he is—good throughout." Look beyond the humor in this sentence and decide what it suggests about Lamb's attitude towards people. Find other places in the essay where Lamb criticizes humanity either openly or by implication.

READING AND WRITING SUGGESTIONS

1. Using the first part of Lamb's essay as a model, write a brief narrative essay about a lucky experience that you or someone you know has had. Arrange the events surrounding the experience in chronological order, and relate the incident so that it builds to a climax.

2. Read in an encyclopedia or another source about how Charles Goodyear accidentally discovered the process of vulcanization after long years of fruitless experimentation. Write a narrative essay on the workings of chance or luck which focuses on this incident in Goodyear's life.

PART FIVE

ESSAYS FOR
INDEPENDENT ANALYSIS

SURRENDER AS THE
NOBLE COURSE

Andrew M. Greeley

Andrew M. Greeley (1928–), a Roman Catholic priest, is a so-ciologist, educator, and writer. He is currently director of the Center for the Study of American Pluralism in Chicago, lecturer in sociology at the University of Chicago, and professor of higher education at the University of Illinois in Chicago. Greeley is the author of more than twenty books, many of them commentaries on current Ameri-can life. One of his special concerns is young people. His book Strangers in the House: Catholic Youth in America *is a collection of essays in which he examines factors in the American culture which lead to apathy among youth. And* the Young Shall See Visions *and* Letters to Nancy *deal with problems of religious belief, love and marriage, and other questions common to young people. In the essay that follows, Greeley discusses the vulnerability that is an inevitable part of close relationships.*

The trouble with intimacy is that it means vulnerability. Everyone wants intimacy but few of us are very good at vulnerability. We pay lip service to "openness" and "trust," but usually these are mask words which we use to hide ourselves and to keep others at bay. Get too close to me and I'll beat you over the head with my openness and trust.

With the vocabulary provided by Freud and his followers, and the time provided by increased leisure and life expectancy, our gener-ation is the first in history to set out self-consciously and in massive numbers to search for the joys of intimacy. But there is no evidence that we have much progressed over our predecessors in our skills at vulnerability. We attempt to make bricks, despite the biblical lesson on the subject, without straw.

How much authentic vulnerability—as opposed to the synthetic kind acquired on encounter weekends—have you observed on the expressway to intimacy?

The vulnerable person is strong enough to risk getting hurt—not pointlessly, not irrationally, not as an inverted defense mechanism; but as a part of a reasonable if not altogether rational risk. He can give himself to another human being not like a dive bomber crashing into an aircraft carrier or like a Mack truck crumpling a Volkswagen, but rather in a gentle and subtle process by which the other is invited, indeed seduced, to give himself in return.

How many such people do you know?

The vulnerable person takes a chance on having his heart broken. He strips himself of his defenses (not completely, not suddenly, not traumatically, but slowly, like an accomplished burlesque dancer) in the hope that when the other sees him as he is, the other will find him irresistible. In such a defenseless position, he can very easily be hurt, badly hurt.

Furthermore, he *will* be hurt. The lesson of all our experience is that the vulnerable person does indeed have his heart broken, he is indeed ridiculed, rejected, made a fool of. Sometimes the pain of such a heartbreak is healed as reconciliation restores the violated intimacy. But only the most naive believe that all stories have happy endings (though only the most cynical believe that none do). Some broken hearts remain broken.

Yet the deadly paradox of intimacy is that either we strip away our defenses in a continuing process or we will build them up in a similar process. We either let the other get closer to us and thus get closer to him or we push each other away. There is no middle ground. When push comes to shove, most of us push instead of surrendering.

In our pseudosophistication we try to persuade ourselves that we are no longer troubled by the shame of physical nudity. It is an act that normally does not work. But physical nakedness is a symbol— indeed a "sacrament" (in the old sense of a revealing insight)—of psychological nakedness. We are "shamed" when we take off our clothes because we have nothing left under which to hide, nothing to protect our weaknesses and deficiencies, we are defenseless, easily hurt. Psychic nakedness is much more terrifying—and hence much less frequently attempted. For if the other can see us as we are, then we are open to being destroyed by him.

So we hedge our bets and protect our own apparent worthlessness. The cynical "Why take the chance?"—rarely spoken but more rarely ignored—dominates our emotional life. We cover our fear with a barrage of words claiming that we are not afraid. It is all the other people who claim to be "open and trusting" who are kidding themselves.

The theologians used to call this fear of the other "original sin." The name may be out of fashion, but the reality is not. Blessed be he who does not take chances for he will not be hurt. Woe to him who risks giving his whole self, for he surely will be hurt.

But then it may be worth it. And the name of that thought, according to the old theologians, was Grace.

A DEBT TO DICKENS

Pearl S. Buck

Pearl S. Buck (1892–1973) is one of America's best-known authors. The daughter of Presbyterian missionaries, she was taken to China as a young child and spent most of her early years there. After graduating from Randolph-Macon Woman's College in Virginia, she returned to China and married a missionary. Buck won international fame and a Pulitzer Prize for her book The Good Earth, *the story of a Chinese peasant and his wife struggling for land and security. Other works by Buck include* Sons, A House Divided, Fighting Angel, *and* The Exile. *She received the Nobel Prize in literature in 1938. The following essay is a moving account of Pearl Buck's early life in China and of the comfort and companionship she found at that time in the works of Charles Dickens.*

I have long looked for an opportunity to pay a certain debt which I have owed since I was seven years old. Debts are usually burdens, but this is no ordinary debt, and it is no burden, except as the feeling of warm gratitude may ache in one until it is expressed. My debt is to an Englishman, who long ago in China rendered an inestimable service to a small American child. That child was myself and that Englishman was Charles Dickens. I know no better way to meet my obligation than to write down what Charles Dickens did in China for an American child.

First, you must picture to yourself that child, living quite solitary in a remote Chinese countryside, in a small mission bungalow perched upon a hill among the rice fields in the valleys below. In the near distance wound that deep, treacherous, golden river, the Yangtse, and some of the most terrifying and sinister, as well as the most delightful and exciting moments of that child's life, were spent beside the river. She loved to crawl along its banks upon the rocks or upon the muddy flats and watch for the lifting of the huge four-square nets that hung into the moving yellow flood, and see out of that flood come perhaps again and again an empty net, but sometimes great flashing, twisting silver bodies of fish. She lingered beside villages of boat folk, and saw them live, the babies tied to a rope and splashing in the shallower waters. But she saw babies dead thrown into the deep waters. She wandered small and alien among the farm folk in the earthen houses among the fields. She accepted a bowl of rice and cabbage often at meal time and sat among the peasants on the threshing floor about the door and ate, usually in silence, listening and listening, answering their kindly, careless questions, bearing with shy, painful smiles their kind, teasing laughter at her yellow curls and unfortunate blue eyes, which they thought so ugly. She was, she knew, very alien. Upon the streets of the great city where sometimes she went she learned to accept the cry of foreign devil, and to realize she was a foreign devil. Once when she was very, very small, before she knew better, she turned as worms will, and flung back a word she had learned among the boat folk when they quarrelled. It was a word so wicked that the youth who called her foreign devil ran howling with terror, and thereafter she went more contentedly, not using the word any more because of its great wickedness, but knowing she had it to use if she needed it very much.

She grew from a very tiny child into a bigger child, still knowing she was alien. However kindly the people about her might be, and they were much more often kind than not, she knew that she was foreign to them. And she wondered very much about her own folk and where they were and how they looked and at what they played. But she did not know. In the bungalow were her parents, very busy, very, very busy, and when she had learned her lessons in the morning quickly, they were too busy to pay much heed to her and so she wandered about a great deal, seeing and learning all sorts of things. She had fun. But very often she used to wonder, "Where are the other children like me? What is it like in the country where they live?" She longed very much, I can remember, to have some of them to play with. But she never had them.

To this small, isolated creature there came one day an extraordinary accident. She was an impossibly voracious reader. She would like to have had children's books, but there were none, and so she read everything—Plutarch's *Lives* and Fox's *Martyrs*, the Bible, church history, and the hot spots in Jonathan Edwards's sermons, and conversations out of Shakespeare, and bits of Tennyson and Browning which she could not understand at all. Then one day she looked doubtfully at a long row of somber blue books on a very high shelf. They were quite beyond her reach. Later she discovered this was because they were novels. But being desperate she put a three-cornered bamboo stool on top of a small table and climbed up and stared at the bindings and in faded black titles she read *Oliver Twist*, by Charles Dickens. She was then a little past seven years old. It was a very hot August day, in the afternoon about three o'clock, when the household was asleep, all except the indefatigable parents, and they were very, very busy. She took *Oliver Twist* out of his place—it was fat and thick, for *Hard Times* was bound with it—and in great peril descended, and stopping in the pantry for a pocket full of peanuts, she made off to a secret corner of the veranda into which only a small, agile child could squeeze, and opened the closely printed pages of an old edition, and discovered her playmates.

How can I make you know what that discovery was to that small, lonely child? There in that corner above the country road in China, with vendors passing beneath me, I entered into my own heritage. I cannot tell you about those hours. I know I was roused at six o'clock by the call to my supper, and I looked about dazed, to discover the long rays of the late afternoon sun streaming across the valleys. I remember twice I closed the book and burst into tears, unable to bear the tragedy of Oliver Twist, and then opened it quickly again, burning to know more. I remember, most significant of all, that I forgot to touch a peanut, and my pocket was still quite full when I was called. I went to my supper in a dream, and read as late as I dared in my bed afterward, and slept with the book under my pillow, and woke again in the early morning. When *Oliver Twist* was finished, and after it *Hard Times*, I was wretched with indecision. I felt I must read it all straight over again, and yet I was voracious for that long row of blue books. What was in them? I climbed up again, finally, and put *Oliver Twist* at the beginning, and began on the next one, which was *David Copperfield*. I resolved to read straight through the row and then begin at the beginning once more and read straight through again.

This program I carried on consistently, over and over, for about ten years, and after that I still kept a Dickens book on hand, so to speak, to dip into and feel myself at home again. Today I have for him a feeling which I have for no other human soul. He opened my eyes to people, he taught me to love all sorts of people, high and low, rich and poor, the old and little children. He taught me to hate hypocrisy and pious mouthing of unctuous words. He taught me that beneath gruffness there may be kindness, and that kindness is the sweetest thing in the world, and goodness is the best thing in the world. He taught me to despise money grubbing. People today say he is obvious and sentimental and childish in his analysis of character. It may be so, and yet I have found people surprisingly like those he wrote about—the good a little less undiluted, perhaps, and the evil a little more mixed. And I do not regret that simplicity of his, for it had its own virtue. The virtue was of a great zest for life. If he saw everything black and white, it was because life rushed out of him strong and clear, full of love and hate. He gave me that zest, that immense joy in life and in people, and in their variety.

He gave me, too, my first real glimpse of a kindly English God, a sort of father, to whom the childlike and the humble might turn. There was no talk of hell in his books. He made Christmas for me, a merry, roaring English Christmas, full of goodies and plum puddings and merriment and friendly cheer. I went to his parties over and over again, for I had no others. I remember one dreadful famine winter the thing that kept me laughing and still a child was *Pickwick Papers*. I read it over and over, and laughed, as I still laugh, over the Wellers and the widow and Mr. Pickwick and all his merry company. They were as real to me as the sad folk outside the compound walls, and they saved me.

And he made me love England. I have no drop of English blood in my veins. I have German and Dutch and French ancestors, I was born in the United States of American parents, and I have spent my life in China. But part of me is English, for I love England with a peculiar, possessing love. I do possess something of England. When I went there years later, London was my city and the countryside I knew. I was not strange. The people were my own people, too. England is the mother of a certain part of my spirit. I can never take sides against England or the English. It is not only that we speak a common tongue and that we are the same race. There is far more than that. I know English people. I love English people. I have grown up among them. I am used to them. They have been my companions for many years. They are forever my friends. When several years ago in China there was a period of misunderstanding of certain British policies, I steadfastly refused to agree with the distrust expressed by some of my Chinese friends toward England. I was sure of the quality of the English people and of their integrity. What they said they would do, they would do. And they did. Their armies were peacefully withdrawn when the necessity of protection was over, they did not proceed to the conquest the Chinese thought was inevitable, and more than any Western power they have steadily shown their honesty of purpose toward the Chinese. After it was over, my Chinese friends said wondering, "You were right." And I replied, "I knew I was."

This is what Charles Dickens did for me. His influence I cannot lose. He has made himself a part of me forever.

SCIENCE: NO LONGER A SACRED COW

Frank Trippett

Frank Trippett (1926–) is a feature writer for Time *Magazine and teaches part-time at the State University of New York at Purchase. He has also been a writer for* Look *and* Newsweek *magazines and for the St. Petersburg* Florida Times. *In this essay, Trippett focuses on the risks that accompany scientific and technological progress and on the need for society to set up safeguards to minimize these risks.*

The technologic euphoria which began about 1600 with Francis Bacon and was continued by the 18th century philosophers of the enlightenment achieved its most extreme expression among the 20th century futurologists, who took it for granted that the year 2000 would see the dawn of a technologic utopia.
—René Dubos; *Beast or Angel?*

America's euphoric awe of science began to ebb with the Pandoran gift to mankind of the atomic bomb. Yet the most extreme expression of the nation's continued reverence for science and technology—dramatized in the tendency to call products "wonders" (as in drugs) or "miracles" (as in fabrics) or "magic" (as in electronics)—awaited the moment that a human foot first touched the moon. That feat, the President of the U.S. assured his countrymen, was to be ranked as the greatest thing since—*Creation.* After that exaltation, there was only one way, by the law of psychological gravity, for Sci-Tech's prestige to go.

Sure enough, down it went. And in its place has risen a new public attitude that seems the antithesis of the former awe. That awe has given way to a new skepticism, the adulation to heckling. To the bewilderment of much of the scientific community, its past triumphs have been downgraded, and popular excitement over new achievements, like snapshots from Mars, seems to wane with the closing words of the evening news. Sci-Tech's promises for the future, far from being welcomed as harbingers of utopia, now seem too often to be threats. Fears that genetic tinkering might produce a Doomsday Bug, for example, bother many Americans, along with dread that the SST's sonic booms may add horrid racket to the hazards (auto fumes, fluorocarbons, strontium 90) that already burden the air.

Increasingly this new skepticism is spreading even among professionals in the world of Sci-Tech. Indeed, it could be heard conspicuously last week as 4,200 members of the American Association for the Advancement of Science gathered in Denver for their annual brainstorming. Arthur Kantrowitz, head of Avco Everett Research Laboratory Inc. in Everett, Mass., came plugging, once again, for the creation of a "science court" that might help sort out "facts from values" in controversies that have been multiplying in the atmosphere of question and dispute. One of the speakers in Denver, Science Historian June Goodfield, a visiting professor at New York's Rockefeller University, welcomed public skepticism as a healthy development that is basically "a call for science to turn a human face toward society." The new spirit, said Goodfield, marks the end of "mutual myths" long held by society (about the scientist as hero) and science (about its freedom from obligation to society).

The new skepticism can be seen, as well as heard, in the emergence of a fresh willingness to challenge the custodians of arcane technical knowledge on their own ground. It is most conspicuously embodied in the environmental crusade and the consumers' rebellion, but is also at play across a far wider field. It applies public light and political heat to Detroit's automotive engineers, who for generations had dispatched their products to an acquiescent public. It encompasses protests against the location of dams massively certified by science, opposition to the erection of nuclear power plants declared to be safe and sound, open disputes about the real values of scientifically approved medicines, and the increasing willingness of patients to sue physicians to make them account for mistakes in treatment. Sci-Tech, in a sense, has been demoted from its demigodhood. The public today rallies, in its untidy way, around the notion that Hans J. Morgenthau put into words in *Science: Servant or Master?* "The scientist's monopoly of the answers to the questions of the future is a myth."

The fading of this mythology is the result of Americans' gradual realization that science and technology's dreamy wonders sometimes turn out to be nightmarish blunders. Detergents that make dishes gleam may kill rivers. Dyes that prettify the food may cause cancer. Pills that make sex safe may dangerously complicate health. DDT, cyclamates, thalidomide and estrogen are but a few of the mixed blessings that, all together, have taught the layman a singular lesson: the promising fruits of science and technology often come with hidden worms.

The public's anxiety, anger and skepticism have been reinforced by the exposure of many remarkably human frailties within the halls of science. Biologist Barry Commoner's *Science and Survival,* documenting an erosion of scientific integrity and denouncing official secrecy and lying about nuclear fallout, came in 1966 as merely an early ripple in a wave of muckraking that has washed away the glowing image of the scientist as some kind of superman. Scientists now appear to be as fallible as the politicians with whom they increasingly consort. In *Advice and Dissent: Scientists in the Political Arena,* two academic scientists, Physics Teacher Joel Primack of the University of California and Environmentalist Frank von Hippel of Princeton, present case histories documenting the tendency of many scientists to "look the other way" when the Government wants to lie about technical matters. A scholarly polemic by Lewis Mumford, *The Pentagon of Power,* scathes not the scientists but their intimacy with governmental powers. The identification is so complete that scientists, Mumford charges, have until lately "been criminally negligent in anticipating or even reporting what has actually been taking place."

Scientists themselves, like many of those at Denver, have been increasingly questioning their own role. Protesting science's callous use of human guinea pigs for experimentation, Dr. Richard M. Restak, a Washington neurologist, decries the fact that the prestigious National Institutes of Health refused to establish a code governing such experiments until its sponsored researchers were found guilty of injecting live cancer cells into uninformed subjects. Writing on the Op-Ed page of the New York *Times,* Restak voiced "a creepy realization that when left to their own devices, biomedical scientists are capable of some rather nasty mischief indeed." Then he put a central, if often asked, question: "Do we need yet more horrors to bring home the truth that science is too important to be left to the scientsts?"

America's current spirit of skepticism toward Sci-Tech is, above all, the popular response to that question. The answer is a note so resounding that when it came, it was mistaken for a mortal war on science. So alarmed was Philip Handler, president of the National

Academy of Sciences, that in 1972 he preached publicly on the urgent need to stave off the "crumbling of the scientific enterprise." Today, with that enterprise clearly waxing (federal funding for science this year: $24.7 billion, up 67% in eight years), Handler's excessive reaction may seem like that of a pampered sacred cow at the approach of a foot-and-mouth inspector. The fact is that the new skepticism, at bottom, is not antiscience at all. It is only at war with the once prevalent assumption that science and technology should be allowed utter freedom, with little or no accounting to those who have to live with the bad results as well as the good. If the layman on the street has discovered that science is fallible, that hardly makes him its permanent enemy. After all, everybody has forgiven Newton for thinking that the sun was populated.

So the new skepticism, in its present maturity, turns out to be essentially political in its aspiration. Its successes include the very existence of the Environmental Protection Agency and, as a particular example, the EPA's recent action obliging the Ford Motor Co. to recall 54,000 cars to make sure that they meet emission standards. Skepticism can be credited with last year's California referendum on nuclear power; the fact that the voters did not veto nuclear expansion misses the point, which is that an arcane subject hitherto considered the sole province of the scientist and engineer was submitted to ordinary citizens. And only a remarkably awakened citizenry could have inspired the self-criticism of the recent Senate committee report that chastised the Senate for laxness in overseeing the agencies that oversee the industries that are conduits of Sci-Tech.

Perhaps the most significant result so far of the new skepticism might be called the Case of the Nonexistent Doomsday Bug. The scene: a session of the Cambridge, Mass., city council, with delegations from Harvard, M.I.T. and the National Institutes of Health in nervous attendance. The issue: Should Harvard and M.I.T. be permitted to go ahead with experiments in so-called recombinant DNA —experiments involving the implantation, in cells of a common bacterium, of alien DNA-born genes? The crucial question: Do the risks of research that could engender a hypothetical Doomsday Bug—some new strain of bacteria that might find its invisible way into the bodies of the people—outweigh whatever knowledge might be gained?

There was a sobering question. Here is another, just as intriguing and much easier to answer: How on earth did an issue like that wind up in the hands of a political body whose analytical resources are usually tested by questions of stop-light placement? Answer: three years ago, while contemplating the very first recombinant DNA experiments, many researchers themselves grew worried about the unfathomable risks. Instead of merely fretting among themselves, as scientists have usually done, they decided to make their fears public —and more. In a step unprecedented in the history of science, a group of them associated with the discoverer of DNA, James Watson, publicly asked colleagues around the world to suspend recombinant DNA experiments until the risks could be assessed and adequate safeguards established.

Without that, the public might never have heard of the risks— until, perhaps, too late. Nor, last summer, would the Cambridge city council have got word that Harvard and M.I.T. were about to launch the controversial research. The council did hear, though. It thereupon put the experiments under a moratorium until the issue of risk could be studied by a committee of eight citizens—not a scientist among them. When the committee report emerged, it was greeted as a model of brevity, intelligence and balance. The upshot, approved by the council: the experiments could proceed, but only under safeguards a bit more strict that those recommended by the National Institutes of Health.

So the case was closed—but with surprisingly little attention to the transcendent issue that had been settled. It was the issue of science's sovereignty, its traditional right to pursue research in the lab with neither guidance nor intervention from laymen. That sovereignty, in the Cambridge case, yielded to the public's claim to safety and well-being.

After that, the new skeptics are entitled to feel, so far so good. But their very success has raised, in some minds, the question of how far society should go in exercising control over science. The answer must weigh the obvious danger that society might stifle or thwart the key profession on which it must rely for solutions to inescapably technical problems. One non-scientist at last week's A.A.A.S. convention —New York Lawyer George Ball, former Under Secretary of State— thinks that such a danger is already at hand. Ball sees the Cambridge council's monitoring of DNA experiments as an "ominous opening wedge" of a movement that might end up demanding "a bureaucratic preview of all scientific research to ascertain whether it meets some loosely defined test of social desirability."

Such an outcome would plainly be bad news for science and society. But the good news, so far, is that nobody appears to be either demanding or expecting such a result. Even the most skeptical of the skeptics seem perfectly willing to let science go its way in the pursuit of knowledge. Still, if there is no sign that Americans fear what scientists may discover, there is also little expectation that any of their discoveries will provide answers to the enduring human mysteries that are impelling people these days on many a mystical and spiritual pilgrimage. All the new spirit of skepticism really asks is that science and society together take thoughtful stock when there seems a clear risk, as in the DNA experiments, that the pursuit of knowledge might damage, endanger or even exterminate human life. That seems little enough to ask.

ARE THE KILLER BEES HERE?

Keith Coulbourn

Keith Coulbourn (1928–) was a writer and reporter for a number of newspapers in Florida, Louisiana, and Tennessee prior to joining the Atlanta Journal and Constitution, where he has worked for nine years. Interested in the accounts of killer bees that have been appearing in the press and concerned about the potential dangers the bees pose for this country, Coulbourn attended a state meeting of beekeepers where killer bees were a topic for discussion. This essay was written following that meeting.

One of Georgia's biggest beekeepers recently packed up a batch of 1,500 queens with their attendant drones and workers and shipped them off to a beekeeper in Canada. Everything worked fine for a while. The bees went from flower to flower collecting pollen and making their honey. Then when winter came, the bees took off one day and never came back. Disappeared.

And mean? Most bees are easy to get along with. You can putter around their hive all you want if you stay out of their way. But some of them have the nastiest temper this side of a woman scorned. You can't come within 20 feet of them before the guards spot you and come on a beeline, so to speak, to dive bomb you.

Could it be, some of Georgia's 5,000 or so beekeepers wonder, that this is the African bee influence? They think so. They say that the African bee, which is sometimes called the Killer Bee, is already here.

This is that nasty-tempered bee that was brought to Brazil from Africa in 1957 for genetic experiments and that got loose and took over the whole country. In fact, according to news accounts, the killer bee has been heading toward the United States at about 200 miles a year and should arrrive here by about 1984.

Most people are appalled. It's like a plague of locusts, except that these bees are much worse. Early reports had them moving up Central America, country by country. The Panama Canal might hold them up a little, it was speculated, but nothing would really stop their northward movement. They were unstoppable.

So they would move up Central America like a buzzing juggernaut, stinging people and animals alike to death, through Costa Rica in the first year, Nicaragua the next, then Honduras, Guatemala and finally into Mexico. Two or three years later they would cross the border into Texas, appearing at the same time somehow in lower Florida and the Keys, then working themselves up to the Dallas-Macon parallel within a few more years.

Where would it all end? According to news accounts, nobody knew.

But more important, perhaps, was what it meant. Is this some terrible retribution invoked by Nature? Is it like creeping kudzu? Like the strangling water hyacinths? The vicious piranha? The inexorable fire ant, mysterious swine flu, inscrutable Japanese snails and ghoulish walking catfish?

And is there a pattern here?

Many people will never get within 20 feet of a beehive during their whole lives, so they couldn't care less about what happens to the bees. If they saw a bee roaming around in their backyard, they're as likely as not to run inside for the spray gun. But the idea of an invasion of bees from below the border—African mau-maus, at that —captures the imagination of everyone in an uncanny way and probably should be put in perspective.

In short, it follows the familiar pattern of a gothic tale. All ghost stories and tales of the mysterious are gothic, and so is most science fiction. The one about the killer bees happens to follow in the well-worn path of 10,000 stories in the "Frankenstein" mold.

Here you have an obscure doctor in a jungle laboratory messing around with things that are—and he should have known this to begin with—completely beyond his or anyone else's ability to comprehend: genes and all that.

Oh, he has the best of intentions. He wants to improve the lot of mankind by producing a super bee, but there are some things we simply shouldn't fiddle around with. Critics say that it's a piece of arrogance to mess with God's creation because it invariably produces not a scientific miracle but a monster.

People didn't always think that way, of course. Back in the 1600s and up to about the mid-1700s when it was the lot of everyone to struggle first-hand with nature, the world was considered basically evil. Lucifer had charge of earth not only in Biblical doctrine but in fact. God's instrument here on earth, however, was man, who could win important battles in this behind-the-scenes war by extending civilization, for instance, and bringing form upon the face of the earth.

Styles of thought, like everything else, change mainly because they become a bore. When the romantics took over, plugging into very primitive emotional juices, all this imagery was reversed and the modern gothic style was born. This style always opposes good and evil but not always the same way. Nature is good, say the romantics, and so is man in nature. But when man presumes to improve on nature, look out, for she can bring forth all manner of hellish retribution.

Much of the current back-to-nature movement is romantically inspired, as well as probably most of the opposition to scientific technology like space travel and nuclear power. It's all part of the horrified throng running through the mountains with firebrands to track down and destroy the monster created by Dr. Frankenstein.

The multiplex of gothic themes has so deeply settled in our archetypal memory bank and so often seems to be verified wherever we look that when innocent members of the media go junketing for something to write about bees, they find material aplenty for the headline already buzzing in their brains: KILLER BEES HEADING NORTH!

One of the big television networks flew its crew down to see Dr. Warwick E. Kerr in Brazil and interviewed him for two hours, then extracted three sentences from it to broadcast in which Dr. Kerr expressed his regrets about the experiment.

Dr. Roger A. Morse, professor of apiculture at Cornell University in Ithaca, N.Y., laughed about it the other day when he came to Atlanta to address some 200 members of the Georgia Beekeepers Association. He laughed not about Dr. Kerr's "regrets," but about the way the media reduces very complex events to the morality play it feeds the public.

Regrets? Dr. Kerr doesn't regret his experiments or his decision to do them in the least. He might regret the slip-up in which some of the African bees got loose because that was not supposed to happen, but that's about it. And certainly he's not doing penance for what happened, as TV viewers might have assumed.

To Brazilians—at least the commercial beekeepers of Brazil—he's a hero, according to Dr. Morse. By bringing in the African bees, honey production in Brazil has increased 25 to 30 percent. They now produce as much honey per hive as bees in this country do.

In fact, Dr. Kerr's experiments in 1957 were on the same order as the somewhat cruder experiments that probably occurred in this country back in the 1800s.

Dr. Morse says that his students have found ads in the old bee journals of those days offering African queens for sale. There were known as vigorous honey makers, aggressive and quite mean. Were any of them actually shipped over? Dr. Morse says he doesn't know that, but almost certainly some were brought in and they also likely mixed with the local stock.

Apparently there are no native honeybees in this country, according to V. Rodney Coleman, extension entomologist at the University of Georgia. When bees were brought in, Indians called them "the white man's flies." Now Europe had several kinds of bees at the time —some just as mean as the Africans—but American settlers brought the best honey makers they could find with the gentlest temper. That was the Italians.

The most important qualification, though, was that they could adapt to the climate over here. That means in part that when it gets cold, they know how to cluster together and keep warm. Bees can't function under about 60 degrees. There was bound to be some genetic mixing with other varieties, of course, both when the bees were first brought to this continent and later during the experiments of the 1800s, but the Italians still make up the overwhelming majority of American honeybees.

Except for the queen, bees live a very brief time. Queens can live for several years, but the workers, who gather the pollen, live about three weeks, and drones, who eat honey and mate with the queen, die on sexual contact. Queens are obviously the most important personage in the hive because they contribute half of the genetic characteristics their progeny have. If the queen happens to be an African, the hive is quickly Africanized. She lays thousands of eggs a day.

But it can also happen if the drone that mates with her is an African. And because the African bee is generally more aggressive, this may happen more often than one would expect by chance.

One afternoon in early spring, the virgin queen bee saunters to the front stoop of her hive, flutters her wings experimentally for a moment, then buzzes off, ascending in a slow, sensual circle some 40 feet in the air, there to fly around like a common hussy.

At the same time, the drones take off in a wave of good-fellowship, leveling off at 40 feet with drones from all the other nearby hives. These drones, sometimes thousands of them, will fly for five miles around their hive just having a good old time till they meet the queen; then sex rears its ugly head, contact is made, the drone falls dead and the queen returns to lay more thousands of eggs. Matriarchies are all alike.

The African bee, at least the variety that everyone is so concerned with, evolved in tropic latitudes. It doesn't know how to cluster, for instance, because it never gets cold enough where it grew up for that to be important. But it is a hustler. It wakes up an hour earlier than most other varieties and starts scrounging around for pollen; it also works an hour later in the day. This is how it produces so much honey.

This willingness to work is part of what people mean when they refer to the African bee's aggressiveness. They also include its hair-trigger inclination to attack. In addition to that, it happens to be genetically dominant. If an African and Italian bee mate, the baby bee is an African.

Now the psychological profile of the African bee falls easily into place. A bee that drives itself as the African does has got to be a little fanatic. With that explosive temper and genetic dominance, it can be only one kind: paranoia. He has illusions of grandeur, in other words, and is bent on conquering the world. When an African drone is flying around at 40 feet with all the other consorts, it's not just a good time he's after; he's got something to prove. So the moment he spots the queen—zap!—he takes her.

The only fly in the ointment, so to speak, is that the African bee can really expect to conquer only part of the world. The tropics and some of the subtropics. Brazil, lying largely in the tropic zone (the equator runs through its northern bulge) was a perfect place for the African bee, especially since the honeybees there were too civilized for their own good.

But the African bee won't spread to this country and take over, according to Dr. Morse, because of the climate. They wouldn't improve the honeymaking capability of the bees already here, incidentally, so there's no reason for their being imported, he says, but they may spread on their own to some hives on the Texas-Mexico border and south Florida.

Not all bee experts project such a sanguine future. Troy H. Fore Jr. of Jesup, editor and publisher of the Speedy Bee, reports that one USDA entomologist links disappearing disease with the spread of African genes in the American honeybees. It's called Wilson's Hypothesis.

Dr. William T. Wilson, researcher at the USDA's Laramie, Wyo., Bee Lab, says it's not a disease so much as it is a syndrome sometimes called autumn collapse and spring and winter dwindle. This is a result, he says, of importing the African bees from Dr. Kerr for experiments at the Bee Lab in Baton Rouge, La., in the early 1960s. Fifteen colonies were established, Dr. Wilson says, and only one or two were destroyed when it was realized how how vicious they were; the others got loose and joined local swarms or, in some cases, might have been used to impregnate queens in California.

Disappearing disease was first reported in the Sacramento Valley of California in 1961-62, in Louisiana and Texas in 1963-64. And last year "virtually every state" reported disappearing bees.

Lee Russell, secretary-treasurer of the Georgia Beekeepers Assn., says she expects "a lot of hives in Georgia to be empty when they're opened up this spring."

Nobody's worried about the pure-bred African in this country, in other words. He'll disappear in the cold and won't come back. But it's also possible, they say, that the genetically dominant African could mix with the Italians to produce a bad-tempered Italian that can live in the cold. And the way things are going, that's what'll happen.

NEW SCHOOLS

Eric Hoffer

Eric Hoffer (1902–), the self-taught waterfront philosopher, was born in New York, the son of a cabinet maker. He has labored as a factory worker, a migrant farm worker, and a dishwasher, and since 1943, he has worked as a longshoreman on the Pacific Coast. Though his formal education ended in grammar school, he is one of America's most popular thinkers and is a frequent writer and lecturer on current issues. He holds weekly seminars at the University of California. Hoffer is probably best known for his first book, The True Believers. *Other works include* The Ordeal of Change, The Temper of Our Time, *and* Reflections on the Human Condition. *"New schools" is an essay excerpted from his latest book,* In Our Time.

Some time ago, while writing an essay on the young, I was surprised by the discovery that the young at present do not constitute a higher percentage of the population than they did in the past. The percentage of the young has remained remarkably constant through many decades. What has changed is the percentage of teen-agers.

We used to count as teen-agers those between the ages of 13 and 19. Now the teen-age group includes those between the ages of 10 and 30. Television is giving 10-year-olds the style of life of juveniles, while the post-Sputnik education explosion has been keeping students in their late twenties on the campuses in a state of prolonged adolescence. There are no children any more. Our public schools are packed with mini-men hungering for the prerogatives and probably the responsibilities of adults.

The poet W. H. Auden said that what America needs are puberty rites and a council of elders—which are probably beyond our reach. What this country needs and can have is child labor. The mini-men, bored by meaningless book learning, are hungry for action, hungry to acquire all kinds of skills. There will be no peace in the schools and no effective learning until the curriculum is reformed to meet the needs of the new type of students.

There is evidence that a student in his early twenties, when he is eager to learn, can master in less than a year all the book learning that teachers try to force into unwilling, bored minds through grammar and high school. There is also evidence that forced book learning in public schools, rather than preparing students for a fuller mastery of subjects later in college, often makes them unfit for it. When the great British physicist Sir Joseph Thomson was asked why England produced great scientists, he answered: "Because we hardly teach science at all in schools. Over here the minds that come to physics arrive in the laboratory with a freshness untarnished by routine." Reading and writing are a different matter—if these are not thoroughly mastered early in life, we will continue to have what we have now: college students who can do neither.

I propose, then, that half of the school day be given to book learning—reading and writing, elementary mathematics, a familiarization with the geography of the planet, and a bird's-eye view of history—and the other half to the mastery of skills. Retired skilled carpenters, masons, plumbers, electricians, mechanics, gardeners, architects, city planners, etc., could teach the young how to build houses and roads, how to landscape and garden, how to operate all sorts of machines. Retired bankers, manufacturers, merchants, and politicians could familiarize the young with finance and management.

In small towns where there is only one school it would be easy to set aside a hundred acres or so on which generations of students could build a model neighborhood, plant gardens, and raise crops. In large cities the work would have to be done on the outskirts or on land made available by slum clearance. By the time they graduated from high school, the young would be equipped to earn a living and to run the world.

There is no reason to believe that adults will soon regain their lost nerve and be able to impose their values on the young. But there is nothing to prevent adults from transmitting their skills. It is also becoming evident that a society that does not know how to cope with juveniles can maintain the measure of stability and continuity requisite for civilized living only by abolishing adolescence—by giving the young the skills, opportunities, responsibilities, and rewards of grown-ups.

CONCERNING GOOD AND BAD FORTUNE

Francesco Petrarch

Francesco Petrarch (1304–1374), born in Italy, was one of the greatest scholars of the Middle Ages. In 1341 he was crowned at Rome as the Poet Laureate of the Holy Roman Empire, and he is ranked with Dante among Italian poets. His Treatise on the Remedies of Good and Bad Fortune, *from which the selection below is taken, was dedicated to a friend, Azon da Correggio. In this essay, Petrarch discusses the vagaries of fortune and recommends the means by which we can rise above the uncertainties of life.*

When I consider the instability of human affairs, and the variations of fortune, I find nothing more uncertain or restless than the life of man. Nature has given to animals an excellent remedy under disasters, which is the ignorance of them. We seem better treated in intelligence, foresight, and memory. No doubt these are admirable presents; but they often annoy more than they assist us. A prey to unuseful or distressing cares, we are tormented by the present, the past, and the future; and, as if we feared we should not be miserable enough, we join to the evil we suffer the remembrance of a former distress and the apprehension of some future calamity. This is the Cerberus with three heads we combat without ceasing. Our life might be gay and happy if we would; but we eagerly seek subjects of affliction to render it irksome and melancholy. We pass the first years of this life in the shades of ignorance, the succeeding ones in pain and labor, the latter part in grief and remorse, and the whole in error; nor do we suffer ourselves to possess one bright day without a cloud.

Let us examine this matter with sincerity, and we shall agree that our distresses chiefly arise from ourselves. It is virtue alone which can render us superior to Fortune; we quit her standard, and the combat is no longer equal. Fortune mocks us; she turns us on her wheel: she raises and abases us at her pleasure, but her power is founded on our weakness. This is an old-rooted evil, but it is not

306

incurable: there is nothing a firm and elevated mind cannot accomplish. The discourse of the wise and the study of good books are the best remedies I know of; but to these we must join the consent of the soul, without which the best advice will be useless. What gratitude do we not owe to those great men who, though dead many ages before us, live with us by their works, discourse with us, are our masters and guides, and serve us as pilots in the navigation of life, where our vessel is agitated without ceasing by the storms of our passions! It is here that true Philosophy brings us to a safe port, by a sure and easy passage; not like that of the schools, which, raising us in its airy and deceitful wings, and causing us to hover on the clouds of frivolous dispute, lets us fall without any light or instruction in the same place where she took us up.

Dear friend, I do not attempt to exhort you to the study I judge so important. Nature has given you a taste for all knowledge, but Fortune has denied you the leisure to acquire it; yet, whenever you could steal a moment from public affairs, you sought the conversation of wise men; and I have remarked that your memory often served you instead of books. It is therefore unnecessary to invite you to do what you have always done; but, as we cannot retain all we hear or read, it may be useful to furnish your mind with some maxims that may best serve to arm you against the assaults of misfortune. The vulgar, and even philosophers, have decided that adverse fortune was most difficult to sustain. For my own part I am of a different opinion, and believe it more easy to support adversity than prosperity; and that fortune is more treacherous and dangerous when she caresses than when she dismays. Experience has taught me this, not books or arguments. I have seen many persons sustain great losses, poverty, exile, tortures, death, and even disorders that were worse than death, with courage; but I have seen none whose heads have not been turned by power, riches, and honors. How often have we beheld those overthrown by good fortune, who could never be shaken by bad! This made me wish to learn how to support a great fortune. You know the short time this work has taken. I have been less attentive to what might shine than to what might be useful on this subject. Truth and virtue are the wealth of all men; and shall I not discourse on these with my dear Azon? I would prepare for you, as in a little portable box, a friendly antidote against the poison of good and bad fortune. The one requires a rein to repress the sallies of a transported soul; the other a consolation to fortify the overwhelmed and afflicted spirit.

Nature gave you, my friend, the heart of a king, but she gave you not a kingdom, of which therefore Fortune could not deprive you. But

I doubt whether our age can furnish an example of worse or better treatment from her than yourself. In the first part of your life you were blessed with an admirable constitution and astonishing health and vigor: some years after we beheld you thrice abandoned by the physicians who despaired of your life. The heavenly Physician, who was your sole resource, restored your health, but not your former strength. You were then called iron-footed, for your singular force and agility; you are now bent, and lean upon the shoulders of those whom you formerly supported. Your country beheld you one day its governor, the next an exile. Princes disputed for your friendship, and afterwards conspired your ruin. You lost by death the greatest part of your friends; the rest, according to custom, deserted you in calamity. To these misfortunes was added a violent disease, which attacked you when destitute of all succors, at a distance from your country and family, in a strange land, invested by the troops of your enemies; so that those two or three friends whom fortune had left you could not come near to relieve you. In a word, you have experienced every hardship but imprisonment and death. But what do I say? You have felt all the horrors of the former, when your faithful wife and children were shut up by your enemies; and even death followed you, and took one of those children, for whose life you would willingly have sacrificed your own.

In you have been united the fortunes of Pompey and Marius; but you were neither arrogant in prosperity as the one, nor discouraged in adversity as the other. You have supported both in a manner that has made you loved by your friends and admired by your enemies. There is a peculiar charm in the serene and tranquil air of virtue, which enlightens all around it, in the midst of the darkest scenes, and the greatest calamities. My ancient friendship for you has caused me to quit everything for you to perform a work, in which, as in a glass, you may adjust and prepare your soul for all events; and be able to say, as Aeneas did to the Sibyl, "Nothing of this is new to me; I have foreseen, and am prepared for it all." I am sensible that, in the disorders of the mind, as well as those of the body, discourses are not thought the most efficacious remedies; but I am persuaded also that the malady of the soul aught to be cured by spiritual applications.

If we see a friend in distress, and give him all the consolation we are able, we perform the duties of friendship, which pays more attention to the disposition of the heart than the value of the gift. A small present may be the testimony of a great love. There is no good I do not wish you, and this is all I can offer toward it. I wish this little treatise may be of use to you. If it should not answer my hopes, I shall, however, be secure of pardon from your friendship. It presents you with the four great passions: Hope and Joy, the daughters of Prosperity; Fear and Grief, the offspring of Adversity; who attack the soul, and launch at it all their arrows. Reason commands in the citadel to repulse them; your penetration will easily perceive which side will obtain the victory.

CHANNELLED WHELK

Anne Morrow Lindbergh

Anne Morrow Lindbergh (1906–) was born in Englewood, New Jersey. While her father, Dwight Morrow, was the American ambassador to Mexico, Charles Lindbergh visited Mexico City on a goodwill tour following his solo flight across the Atlantic. He and Anne Morrow met at this time and were later married. The Lindberghs were the central figures in a highly publicized family tragedy involving the kidnapping and death of their baby. Anne Morrow Lindbergh has written several best-sellers, both in prose and poetry. Among her best-known works are North to the Orient, Listen! The Wind, *and* Gift from the Sea, *an introspective study of the problems of women. In this essay, she discusses the difficulty of attaining inner harmony in the midst of the distractions and complexities of daily life.*

The shell in my hand is deserted. It once housed a whelk, a snail-like creature, and then temporarily, after the death of the first occupant, a little hermit crab, who has run away, leaving his tracks behind him like a delicate vine on the sand. He ran away, and left me his shell. It was once a protection to him. I turn the shell in my hand, gazing into the wide open door from which he made his exit. Had it become an encumbrance? Why did he run away? Did he hope to find a better home, a better mode of living? I too have run away, I realize, I have shed the shell of my life, for these few weeks of vacation.

But his shell—it is simple; it is bare, it is beautiful. Small, only the size of my thumb, its architecture is perfect, down to the finest detail. Its shape, swelling like a pear in the center, winds in a gentle spiral to the pointed apex. Its color, dull gold, is whitened by a wash of salt from the sea. Each whorl, each faint knob, each criss-cross vein in its egg-shell texture, is as clearly defined as on the day of creation. My eye follows with delight the outer circumference of that diminutive winding staircase up which this tenant used to travel.

My shell is not like this, I think. How untidy it has become! Blurred with moss, knobby with barnacles, its shape is hardly recognizable any more. Surely, it had a shape once. It has a shape still in my mind. What is the shape of my life?

The shape of my life today starts with a family. I have a husband, five children and a home just beyond the suburbs of New York. I have also a craft, writing, and therefore work I want to pursue. The shape of my life is, of course, determined by many other things; my background and childhood, my mind and its education, my conscience and its pressures, my heart and its desires. I want to give and take from my children and husband, to share with friends and community, to carry out my obligations to man and to the world, as a woman, as an artist, as a citizen.

But I want first of all—in fact, as an end to these other desires—to be at peace with myself. I want a singleness of eye, a purity of intention, a central core to my life that will enable me to carry out these obligations and activities as well as I can. I want, in fact—to borrow from the language of the saints—to live "in grace" as much of the time as possible. I am not using this term in a strictly theological sense. By grace I mean an inner harmony, essentially spiritual, which can be translated into outward harmony. I am seeking perhaps what Socrates asked for in the prayer from the *Phaedrus* when he said, "May the outward and inward man be at one." I would like to achieve a state of inner spiritual grace from which I could function and give as I was meant to in the eye of God.

Vague as this definition may be, I believe most people are aware of periods in their lives when they seem to be "in grace" and other periods when they feel "out of grace," even though they may use different words to describe these states. In the first happy condition, one seems to carry all one's tasks before one lightly, as if borne along on a great tide; and in the opposite state one can hardly tie a shoe-string. It is true that a large part of life consists in learning a technique of tying the shoe-string, whether one is in grace or not. But there are techniques of living too; there are even techniques in the search for grace. And techniques can be cultivated. I have learned by some experience, by many examples, and by the writings of countless others before me, also occupied in the search, that certain environments, certain modes of life, certain rules of conduct are more conducive to inner and outer harmony than others. There are, in fact, certain roads that one may follow. Simplification of life is one of them.

I mean to lead a simple life, to choose a simple shell I can carry easily—like a hermit crab. But I do not. I find that my frame of life does not foster simplicity. My husband and five children must make their way in the world. The life I have chosen as wife and mother entrains a whole caravan of complications. It involves a house in the suburbs and either household drudgery or household help which wavers between scarcity and non-existence for most of us. It involves food and shelter; meals, planning, marketing, bills, and making the ends meet in a thousand ways. It involves not only the butcher, the baker, the candlestickmaker but countless other experts to keep my modern house with its modern "simplifications" (electricity, plumbing, refrigerator, gas-stove, oil-burner, dish-washer, radios, car, and numerous other labor-saving devices) functioning properly. It involves health; doctors, dentists, appointments, medicine, cod-liver oil, vitamins, trips to the drugstore. It involves education, spiritual, intellectual, physical; schools, school conferences, car-pools, extra trips for basketball or orchestra practice; tutoring; camps, camp equipment and transportation. It involves clothes, shopping, laundry, cleaning, mending, letting skirts down and sewing buttons on, or finding someone else to do it. It involves friends, my husband's, my children's, my own, and endless arrangements to get together; letters, invitations, telephone calls and transportation hither and yon.

For life today in America is based on the premise of ever-widening circles of contact and communication. It involves not only family demands, but community demands, national demands, international demands on the good citizen, through social and cultural pressures, through newspapers, magazines, radio programs, political drives, charitable appeals, and so on. My mind reels with it. What a circus act we women perform every day of our lives. It puts the trapeze artist to shame. Look at us. We run a tight rope daily, balancing a pile of books on the head. Baby-carriage, parasol, kitchen chair, still under control. Steady now!

This is not the life of simplicity but the life of multiplicity that the wise men warn us of. It leads not to unification but to fragmentation. It does not bring grace; it destroys the soul. And this is not only true of my life, I am forced to conclude; it is the life of millions of women in America. I stress America, because today, the American woman more than any other has the privilege of choosing such a life. Woman in large parts of the civilized world has been forced back by war, by poverty, by collapse, by the sheer struggle to survive, into a smaller circle of immediate time and space, immediate family life, immediate problems of existence. The American woman is still relatively free to choose the wider life. How long she will hold this enviable and precarious position no one knows. But her particular situation has a significance far above its apparent economic, national or even sex limitations.

For the problem of the multiplicity of life not only confronts the American woman, but also the American man. And it is not merely the concern of the American as such, but of our whole modern civilization, since life in America today is held up as the ideal of a large part of the rest of the world. And finally, it is not limited to our present civilization, though we are faced with it now in an exaggerated form. It has always been one of the pitfalls of mankind. Plotinus was preaching the dangers of multiplicity of the world back in the third century. Yet, the problem is particularly and essentially woman's. Distraction is, always has been, and probably always will be, inherent in woman's life.

For to be a woman is to have interests and duties, raying out in all directions from the central mother-core, like spokes from the hub of a wheel. The pattern of our lives is essentially circular. We must be open to all points of the compass; husband, children, friends, home, community; stretched out, exposed, sensitive like a spider's web to each breeze that blows, to each call that comes. How difficult for us, then, to achieve a balance in the midst of these contradictory tensions, and yet how necessary for the proper functioning of our lives. How much we need, and how arduous of attainment is that steadiness preached in all rules for holy living. How desirable and how distant is the ideal of the contemplative, artist, or saint—the inner inviolable core, the single eye.

With a new awareness, both painful and humorous, I begin to understand why the saints were rarely married women. I am convinced it has nothing inherently to do, as I once supposed, with chastity or children. It has to do primarily with distractions. The bearing, rearing, feeding and educating of children; the running of a house with its thousand details; human relationships with their myriad pulls—woman's normal occupations in general run counter to creative life, or contemplative life, or saintly life. The problem is not merely one of *Woman and Career, Woman and the Home, Woman and Independence*. It is more basically: how to remain whole in the midst of the distractions of life; how to remain balanced, no matter what centrifugal forces tend to pull one off center; how to remain strong, no matter what shocks come in at the periphery and tend to crack the hub of the wheel.

What is the answer? There is no easy answer, no complete answer. I have only clues, shells from the sea. The bare beauty of the channelled whelk tells me that one answer, and perhaps a first step, is in simplification of life, in cutting out some of the distractions. But how? Total retirement is not possible. I cannot shed my responsibilities. I cannot permanently inhabit a desert island. I cannot be a nun in the midst of family life. I would not want to be. The solution for me, surely, is neither in total renunciation of the world, nor in total acceptance of it. I must find a balance somewhere, or an alternating rhythm between these two extremes; a swinging of the pendulum between solitude and communion, between retreat and return. In my periods of retreat, perhaps I can learn something to carry back into my worldly life. I can at least practice for these two weeks the simplification of outward life, as a beginning. I can follow this superficial clue, and see where it leads. Here, in beach living, I can try.

One learns first of all in beach living the art of shedding; how little one can get along with, not how much. Physical shedding to begin with, which then mysteriously spreads into other fields. Clothes, first. Of course, one needs less in the sun. But one needs less anyway, one finds suddenly. One does not need a closet-full, only a small suitcase-full. And what a relief it is! Less taking up and down of hems, less mending, and—best of all—less worry about what to wear. One finds one is shedding not only clothes—but vanity.

Next, shelter. One does not need the airtight shelter one has in winter in the North. Here I live in a bare sea-shell of a cottage. No heat, no telephone, no plumbing to speak of, no hot water, a two-burner oil stove, no gadgets to go wrong. No rugs. There were some, but I rolled them up the first day; it is easier to sweep the sand off a bare floor. But I find I don't bustle about with unnecessary sweeping and cleaning here. I am no longer aware of the dust. I have shed my Puritan conscience about absolute tidiness and cleanliness. Is it possible that, too, is a material burden? No curtains. I do not need them for privacy; the pines around my house are enough protection. I want the windows open all the time, and I don't want to worry about rain. I begin to shed my Martha-like anxiety about many things. Washable slipcovers, faded and old—I hardly see them; I don't worry about the impression they make on other people. I am shedding pride. As little furniture as possible; I shall not need much. I shall ask into my shell only those friends with whom I can be completely honest. I find I am shedding hypocrisy in human relationships. What a rest that will be! The most exhausting thing in life, I have discovered, is being insincere. That is why so much of social life is exhausting; one is wearing a mask. I have shed my mask.

I find I live quite happily without those things I think necessary in winter in the North. And as I write these words, I remember, with some shock at the disparity in our lives, a similar statement made by a friend of mine in France who spent three years in a German prison camp. Of course, he said, qualifying his remark, they did not get enough to eat, they were sometimes atrociously treated, they had little physical freedom. And yet, prison life taught him how little one can get along with, and what extraordinary spiritual freedom and peace such simplification can bring. I remember again, ironically, that today more of us in America than anywhere else in the world have the luxury of choice between simplicity and complication of life. And for the most part, we, who could choose simplicity, choose complication. War, prison, survival periods, enforce a form of simplicity on man. The monk and the nun choose it of their own free will. But if one accidentally finds it, as I have for a few days, one finds also the serenity it brings.

Is it not rather ugly, one may ask? One collects material possessions not only for security, comfort or vanity, but for beauty as well. Is your sea-shell house not ugly and bare? No, it is beautiful, my house. It is bare, of course, but the wind, the sun, the smell of the pines blow through its bareness. The unfinished beams in the roof are veiled by cobwebs. They are lovely, I think, gazing up at them with new eyes; they soften the hard lines of the rafters as grey hairs soften the lines on a middle-aged face. I no longer pull out grey hairs or sweep down cobwebs. As for the walls, it is true they looked forbidding at first. I felt cramped and enclosed by their blank faces. I wanted to knock holes in them, to give them another dimension with pictures or windows. So I dragged home from the beach grey arms of driftwood, worn satin-smooth by wind and sand. I gathered trailing green vines with floppy red-tipped leaves. I picked up the whitened skeletons of conchshells, their curious hollowed-out shapes faintly reminiscent of abstract sculpture. With these tacked to walls and propped up in corners, I am satisfied. I have a periscope out to the world. I have a window, a view, a point of flight from my sedentary base.

I am content. I sit down at my desk, a bare kitchen table with a blotter, a bottle of ink, a sand dollar to weight down one corner, a clam shell for a pen tray, the broken tip of a conch, pink-tinged, to finger, and a row of shells to set my thoughts spinning.

I love my sea-shell of a house. I wish I could live in it always. I wish I could transport it home. But I cannot. It will not hold a husband, five children and the necessities and trappings of daily life. I can only carry back my little channelled whelk. It will sit on my desk in Connecticut, to remind me of the ideal of a simplified life, to encourage me in the game I played on the beach. To ask how little, not how much, can I get along with. To say—is it necessary?—when I am tempted to add one more accumulation to my life, when I am pulled toward one more centrifugal activity.

Simplification of outward life is not enough. It is merely the outside. But I am starting with the outside. I am looking at the outside of a shell, the outside of my life—the shell. The complete answer is not to be found on the outside, in an outward mode of living. This is only a technique, a road to grace. The final answer, I know, is always inside. But the outside can give a clue, can help one to find the inside answer. One is free, like the hermit crab, to change one's shell.

Channelled whelk, I put you down again, but you have set my mind on a journey, up an inwardly winding spiral staircase of thought.

WHY I WRITE

Joan Didion

Joan Didion (1935–) was born in California and began her career when she won Vogue *magazine's Prix de Paris award in her senior year of college. She later became an associate editor of* Vogue. *She is the author of a book of essays,* Slouching Towards Bethlehem, *and of three novels–*Run River, Play It As It Lays, *and* A Book of Common Prayer. *In this essay, Didion describes the characteristics of mind and personality that have made her a writer.*

Of course I stole the title for this talk, from George Orwell. One reason I stole it was that I like the sound of the words: *Why I Write*. There you have three short unambiguous words that share a sound, and the sound they share is this: *I   I   I*

In many ways writing is the act of saying *I*, of imposing oneself upon other people, of saying *listen to me, see it my way, change your mind*. It's an aggressive, even a hostile act. You can disguise its aggressiveness all you want with veils of subordinate clauses and qualifiers and tentative subjunctives, with ellipses and evasions— with the whole manner of intimating rather than claiming, of alluding rather than stating—but there's no getting around the fact that setting words on paper is the tactic of a secret bully, an invasion, an imposition of the writer's sensibility on the reader's most private space.

I stole the title not only because the words sounded right but because they seemed to sum up, in a no-nonsense way, all I have to tell you. Like many writers I have only this one "subject," this one "area": the act of writing. I can bring you no reports from any other front. I may have other interests: I am "interested," for example, in marine biology, but I don't flatter myself that you would come out to hear me talk about it. I am not a scholar. I am not in the least an intellectual, which is not to say that when I hear the word "intellectual" I reach for my gun, but only to say that I do not think in abstracts. During the years when I was an undergraduate at Berkeley I tried, with a kind of hopeless late-adolescent energy, to buy some temporary visa into the world of ideas, to forge for myself a mind that could deal with the abstract.

In short I tried to think. I failed. My attention veered inexorably back to the specific, to the tangible, to what was generally considered, by everyone I knew then and for that matter have known since, the peripheral. I would try to contemplate the Hegelian dialectic and would find myself concentrating instead on a flowering pear tree outside my window and the particular way the petals fell on my floor. I would try to read linguistic theory and would find myself wondering instead if the lights were on in the bevatron up the hill. When I say that I was wondering if the lights were on in the bevatron you might immediately suspect, if you deal in ideas at all, that I was registering the bevatron as a political symbol, thinking in shorthand about the military-industrial complex and its role in the university community, but you would be wrong. I was only wondering if the lights were on in the bevatron, and how they looked. A physical fact.

I had trouble graduating from Berkeley, not because of this inability to deal with ideas—I was majoring in English, and I could locate the house-and-garden imagery in *The Portrait of a Lady* as well as the next person, "imagery" being by definition the kind of specific that got my attention—but simply because I had neglected to take a course in Milton. For reasons which now sound baroque I needed a degree by the end of that summer, and the English department finally agreed, if I would come down from Sacramento every Friday and talk about the cosmology of *Paradise Lost,* to certify me proficient in Milton. I did this. Some Fridays I took the Greyhound bus, other Fridays I caught the Southern Pacific's City of San Francisco on the last leg of its transcontinental trip. I can no longer tell you whether Milton put the sun or the earth at the center of his universe in *Paradise Lost,* the central question of at least one century and a topic about which I wrote 10,000 words that summer, but I can still recall the exact rancidity of the butter in the City of San Francisco's dining car, and the way the tinted windows on the Greyhound bus cast the oil refineries around Carquinez Straits into a grayed and obscurely sinister light. In short my attention was always on the periphery, on what I could see and taste and touch, on the butter, and the Greyhound bus. During those years I was traveling on what I knew to be a very shaky passport, forged papers: I knew that I was no legitimate resident in any world of ideas. I knew I couldn't think. All I knew then was what I couldn't do. All I knew then was what I wasn't, and it took me some years to discover what I was.

Which was a writer.

By which I mean not a "good" writer or a "bad" writer but simply a writer, a person whose most absorbed and passionate hours are spent arranging words on pieces of paper. Had my credentials been in order I would never have become a writer. Had I been blessed with even limited access to my own mind there would have been no reason to write. I write entirely to find out what I'm thinking, what I'm looking at, what I see and what it means. What I want and what I fear. Why did the oil refineries around Carquinez Straits seem sinister to me in the summer of 1956? Why have the night lights in the bevatron burned in my mind for twenty years? *What is going on in these pictures in my mind?*

When I talk about pictures in my mind I am talking, quite specifically, about images that shimmer around the edges. There used to be an illustration in every elementary psychology book showing a cat drawn by a patient in varying stages of schizophrenia. This cat had a shimmer around it. You could see the molecular structure breaking down at the very edges of the cat: the cat became the background and the background the cat, everything interacting, exchanging ions. People on hallucinogens describe the same perception of objects. I'm not a schizophrenic, nor do I take hallucinogens, but certain images do shimmer for me. Look hard enough, and you can't miss the shimmer. It's there. You can't think too much about these pictures that shimmer. You just lie low and let them develop. You stay quiet. You don't talk to many people and you keep your nervous system from shorting out and you try to locate the cat in the shimmer, the grammar in the picture.

Just as I meant "shimmer" literally I mean "grammar" literally. Grammar is a piano I play by ear, since I seem to have been out of school the year the rules were mentioned. All I know about grammar is its infinite power. To shift the structure of a sentence alters the meaning of that sentence, as definitely and inflexibly as the position of a camera alters the meaning of the object photographed. Many people know about camera angles now, but not so many know about sentences. The arrangement of the words matters, and the arrangement you want can be found in the picture in your mind. The picture dictates the arrangement. The picture dictates whether this will be a sentence with or without clauses, a sentence that ends hard or a dying-fall sentence, long or short, active or passive. The picture tells you how to arrange the words and the arrangement of the words tells you, or tells me, what's going on in the picture. *Nota bene:*

It tells you.

You don't tell it.

Let me show you what I mean by pictures in the mind. I began *Play It As It Lays* just as I have begun each of my novels, with no notion of "character" or "plot" or even "incident." I had only two pictures in my mind, more about which later, and a technical intention, which was to write a novel so elliptical and fast that it would be over before you noticed it, a novel so fast that it would scarcely exist on the page at all. About the pictures: the first was of white space. Empty space. This was clearly the picture that dictated the narrative intention of the book—a book in which anything that happened would happen off the page, a "white" book to which the reader would have to bring his or her own bad dreams—and yet this picture told me no "story," suggested no situation. The second picture did. This second picture was of something actually witnessed. A young woman with long hair and a short white halter dress walks through the casino at the Riviera in Las Vegas at one in the morning. She crosses the casino alone and picks up a house telephone. I watch her because I have heard her paged, and recognize her name: she is a minor actress I see around Los Angeles from time to time, in places like Jax and once in a gynecologist's office in the Beverly Hills Clinic, but have never met. I know nothing about her. Who is paging her? Why is she here to be paged? How exactly did she come to this? It was precisely this moment in Las Vegas that made *Play It As It Lays* begin to tell itself to

me, but the moment appears in the novel only obliquely, in a chapter
which begins:

"Maria made a list of things she would never do. She would never:
walk through the Sands or Caesar's alone after midnight. She would
never: ball at a party, do S-M unless she wanted to, borrow furs from
Abe Lipsey, deal. She would never: carry a Yorkshire in Beverly
Hills."

That is the beginning of the chapter and that is also the end of the
chapter, which may suggest what I meant by "white space."

I recall having a number of pictures in my mind when I began the
novel I just finished, *A Book of Common Prayer*. As a matter of fact one
of these pictures was of that bevatron I mentioned, although I would
be hard put to tell you a story in which nuclear energy figured.
Another was a newspaper photograph of a hijacked 707 burning on
the desert in the Middle East. Another was the night view from a
room in which I once spent a week with paratyphoid, a hotel room on
the Colombian coast. My husband and I seemed to be on the Colombian coast representing the United States of America at a film
festival (I recall invoking the name "Jack Valenti" a lot, as if its
reiteration could make me well), and it was a bad place to have fever,
not only because my indisposition offended our hosts but because
every night in this hotel the generator failed. The lights went out. The
elevator stopped. My husband would go to the event of the evening
and make excuses for me and I would stay alone in this hotel room, in
the dark. I remember standing at the window trying to call Bogotá
(the telephone seemed to work on the same principle as the generator) and watching the night wind come up and wondering what I
was doing eleven degrees off the equator with a fever of 103. The
view from that window definitely figures in *A Book of Common
Prayer*, as does the burning 707, and yet none of these pictures told
me the story I needed.

The picture that did, the picture that shimmered and made these
other images coalesce, was the Panama airport at 6 A.M. I was in this
airport only once, on a plane to Bogotá that stopped for an hour to
refuel, but the way it looked that morning remained superimposed
on everything I saw until the day I finished "A Book of Common
Prayer." I lived in that airport for several years. I can still feel the hot
air when I step off the plane, can see the heat already rising off the
tarmac at 6 A.M. I can feel my skirt damp and wrinkled on my legs. I
can feel the asphalt stick to my sandals. I remember the big tail of a
Pan American plane floating motionless down at the end of the tarmac. I remember the sound of a slot machine in the waiting room. I
could tell you that I remember a particular woman in the airport, an

American woman, a *norteamericana*, a thin *norteamericana* about 40 who wore a big square emerald in lieu of a wedding ring, but there was no such woman there.

I put this woman in the airport later. I made this woman up, just as I later made up a country to put the airport in, and a family to run the country. This woman in the airport is neither catching a plane nor meeting one. She is ordering tea in the airport coffee shop. In fact she is not simply "ordering" tea but insisting that the water be boiled, in front of her, for twenty minutes. Why is this woman in this airport? Why is she going nowhere, where has she been? Where did she get that big emerald? What derangement, or disassociation, makes her believe that her will to see the water boiled can possibly prevail?

"She had been going to one airport or another for four months, one could see it, looking at the visas on her passport. All those airports where Charlotte Douglas's passport had been stamped would have looked alike. Sometimes the sign on the tower would say 'Bienvenidos' and sometimes the sign on the tower would say 'Bienvenue,' some places were wet and hot and others dry and hot, but at each of these airports the pastel concrete walls would rust and stain and the swamp off the runway would be littered with the fuselages of cannibalized Fairchild F-227's and the water would need boiling.

"I knew why Charlotte went to the airport even if Victor did not.

"I knew about airports."

These lines appear about halfway through *A Book of Common Prayer*, but I wrote them during the second week I worked on the book, long before I had any idea where Charlotte Douglas had been or why she went to airports. Until I wrote these lines I had no character called "Victor" in mind: the necessity for mentioning a name, and the name "Victor," occurred to me as I wrote the sentence. *I knew why Charlotte went to the airport* sounded incomplete. *I knew why Charlotte went to the airport even if Victor did not* carried a little more narrative drive. Most important of all, until I wrote these lines I did not know who "I" was, who was telling the story. I had intended until that moment that the "I" be no more than the voice of the author, a 19th-century omniscient narrator. But there it was:

"I knew why Charlotte went to the airport even if Victor did not.

"I knew about airports."

This "I" was the voice of no author in my house. This "I" was someone who not only knew why Charlotte went to the airport but also knew someone called "Victor." Who was Victor? Who was this narrator? Why was this narrator telling me this story? Let me tell you one thing about why writers write: had I known the answer to any of these questions I would never have needed to write a novel.

EARLY PURITANS REPLACED BY PURSUERS OF PLEASURE

Douglas Dunkel

Douglas Dunkel (1946–) was born in Michigan. In 1968 he earned a bachelor's degree in art, and in 1973 he received a master's degree in rural sociology from Ohio State University. Dunkel served with the Peace Corps in India from 1969 to 1971. He also taught sociology for two years at the Federal University in Vicosa, Brazil. While working part-time in West Virginia with the American Civil Liberties Union, Dunkel wrote this essay, one of a series called American Issues Forum, *which was carried over television and in newspapers in West Virginia during America's bicentennial year. The series dealt with issues that have been important to America and which promise to be with us for some time. In this selection, Dunkel makes some interesting observations about America's conversion to the pleasure ethic.*

The American Revolution did not terminate with Cornwallis' surrender at Yorktown. That was only the beginning of an American cultural revolution and we in the last quarter of the 20th century are certainly more different from our founding fathers and mothers than they were from their British adversaries. How dour and straightlaced do our Puritan predecessors appear next to the Pepsi generation!

Puritan society was organized on the principles of Calvinism, which led to the Protestant Work Ethic. Proponents of Calvinism believed that hard work, self-discipline and clean living were necessary for salvation. The profits that resulted from such dedicated work were not to be enjoyed in this life. This left the alternatives of saving or reinvesting and consequently created more profits. This doctrine is often credited as being the catalyzing agent in developing the capitalistic economic system since it focused on the importance of work as almost the sole reason for existence.

Eventually, popular sayings such as "All work and no play make Jill a dull girl" developed to serve as a counter-balance when Calvinism began to be modified in the 19th century. But the Protestant work ethic was reinforced during the Victorian age by the pervasive acceptance of Social Darwinism and its basic tenet, "survival of the fittest." If America's resources were bountiful, it was still an austere life. Scarcity and not affluence was the mode.

Thus, during a major part of American history, the pursuit of pleasure was considered perverse, an evil temptation to be avoided. How then have we arrived at today's preoccupation with "the good life" and our Disneyland fantasy world of perpetual happiness? What accounts for our shift in orientation from work to leisure? Have the American people suddenly been transformed by a hedonistic value system?

Transformed, definitely, but probably not so suddenly. If we look at other societies, an almost universal human proclivity toward play seems to exist. As with most basic human activities, its forms are tempered by the curtural context. Since play and work are not always mutually compatible, our play is generally reserved for leisure periods. With the standardization of the 40-hour work week, almost every American has become a member of the "leisure class." While daily work has become less creative and more routinized, greater periods of leisure have afforded opportunities to seek satisfaction.

Martha Wolfenstein, a social scientist, cites the emergence of a "fun morality." No longer are attitudes toward fun, play, and amusement tainted by puritanical hang-ups of wickedness. Comfort has become a national priority.

In a well-known experiment, rats could press a lever that stimulated "pleasure centers" in their brains. Once they learned how to stimulate themselves, the animals pressed the lever almost continuously and had no desire to do anything else. Human beings also possess "pleasure centers" and react in similar fashion. But does this mean that we are only pleasure machines?

The pursuit of happiness is an unalienable right, according to the Declaration of Independence. Ironically, people who live in developing countries jokingly comment that Americans can not relax and enjoy life. We pursue pleasure with the same relentless intensity of our work. Unlike some cultures that define leisure as doing nothing, Americans must be doing something. During leisure periods we play sports, take vacations and take up hobbies.

If active pursuit does not result in the realization of sufficient pleasure, we turn to artificial stimulation. Dr. Joel Fort estimates that the average middle class medicine cabinet contains somewhere around 40 drugs, a goodly number of which are mind-altering substances. Consumption is encouraged by the spending of between one and two million dollars a day both in the alcoholic beverage industry and the tobacco industry. Is it any wonder that 10 million people in the United States are classified as alcoholics?

With respect to those Americans who still consider themselves happy, social critics contend that this is a false satisfaction derived from attaining false needs, or as one described it, "euphoria in unhappiness."

If there has been any dominant factor contributing to our conversion to the pleasure ethic, perhaps the threat of mass extermination from nuclear war deserves the award. The destruction wreaked by our use of the atomic bomb at the end of World War II traumatized the American psyche. When the cold war heated up we built bomb shelters to survive the possible holocaust. Happiness was subterranean security.

The popularity of disaster movies may be a latent consequence of our fear of World War III. It is far better to succumb to earthquakes and sharks on a limited scale than total extinctions.

Regardless of the reason, Calvinism is being replaced with hedonism; instead of leading a life that will save us in the future, we are enjoying ourselves before we disappear.

THE EMOTIONAL COMMITMENT TO ORGANIC GARDENING

Arthur W. Galston

Arthur William Galston (1920–) was born in New York. He took his bachelor's degree at Cornell University and his master's degree and doctorate at the University of Illinois. He has been a university professor for most of his career, and he currently teaches in the biology department at Yale University. An authority in plant physiology, Galston has been the recipient of many awards for his work, including an NSF Fellowship to the University of London, a Guggenheim Fellowship to the University of Stockholm, and a Fulbright Fellowship to Australia. He is listed in American Men and Women of Science. *In the following essay, which grew out of Galston's experiences with some of his students at Yale, he discusses the growing cynicism with which society regards scientific data.*

Several years ago, in response to the then strong student pressures for "relevance" in education and moved by a desire to consider certain social problems in the framework of the newer knowledge of biology, several colleagues and I initiated a course entitled "Biology and Human Affairs." Designed for nonscientists (it inevitably became known as "Biology for Poets"), the course has attracted relatively large numbers of students. It has met with moderate success in its effort to provide some biological background against which one can consider such topics as population growth, pollution, genetics and intelligence, organ transplantation, biological engineering and chemical and biological warfare. Teaching such a course is a challenge because of the great diversity of student backgrounds in biology (How much basic science should I teach?) and because of the inadequate grounding in social science of most biologists, compared with the occasionally great sophistication of some students (Am I out of my depth?). These difficulties have resulted in a constant modification of the course, both in subject matter and approach, a situation that is likely to continue for some years.

Interacting with the students in informal discussions has made several instructors in the course aware of the extent to which many students have become disillusioned with science—as a method of arriving at an understanding of man and the universe in which he lives and as a means of improving the quality of life. To many of the "poets" in the course, scientists are otherworldly people, content to fiddle in their laboratories while the world—for which they are at least partly responsible—burns in napalm, decays into pollution and becomes dehumanized into mechanical, computerized, assembly-line work routines.

The scientist is also held responsible for the antisocial uses to which many of his discoveries are put by the military (bombs, chemical and biological weapons, flamethrowers, automated battlefields), by government (electronic "bugging" devices, computerized data banks for politcal dissidents) and industry (shoddy mass-produced automobiles, chemical products that pollute the environment, useless and expensive gadgetry). Many students seem unwilling to agree that the findings of the scientist are ethically neutral and that it is society that must determine whether they shall be used for good or evil. Because of his special insight and knowledge, the scientist is expected to give guidance to the decision-making agencies of government and business (which frequently do not respect his testimony) and to maintain constant surveillance over the new technology his research discoveries have spawned. Since, with relatively minor exceptions, scientists have not performed this watchdog role adequately, both society in general and students in particular have recently given much less approval to the aspirations and accomplishments of science than heretofore. In addition, some students have reacted with cynical disbelief to some of the data of science, which they would not have questioned several years ago. Let me illustrate with one case history.

As a reaction to the recent exposés concerning the deleterious effects of various pesticides on animal life and the ecosystem, the possible damage to babies from inordinately high quantities of nitrates in their foodstuffs—a result of the application of high quantities of chemical fertilizers—and the known toxic effects of certain common chemicals used as food preservatives, some people, including many students, have become devotees of "organic gardening." Produce grown by organic gardeners is ostensibly never subjected to potentially toxic pesticidal sprays, is fertilized only by manure, leaf mold or other organic materials and is never artifically perserved by chemicals. Materials so produced are often more expensive than the usual commercially available foods and frequently must be purchased in special stores.

In the course of my lectures on botany, I had occasion to point out that the green plant is a complete autotroph for organic materials; that is, given only carbon dioxide from air, sunlight and water, plus inorganic minerals from the soil, it is capable of synthesizing the thousands of organic compounds out of which it is constructed. Under favorable soil conditions, it has absolutely no need for any external sources of organic compounds; and the harvest produced from crops supplied with purely inorganic fertilizers will be just as rich in vitamins, amino acids and other key nutritional requirements for man as one produced from heavily manured crops. This has been demonstrated many times, not only by analyzing for such components in the laboratory, but also by feeding test animals with both kinds of product. In the absence of evidence to the contrary, almost all scientists would conclude that there is no demonstrable difference, either chemical or nutritional, between inorganically and organically grown plants.

Why, then, the students want to know, is it beneficial to apply manure, leaf mold, peat moss, compost and other organic materials to the soil? The answer lies, not in the plant, but in the soil itself. Soil is comprised of various-sized particles of degraded rock wetted by a solution containing organic and inorganic materials, together with organic remains of various kinds of creatures, large numbers of living bacteria, fungi and algae, occasional small animals and a system of air spaces permeating the entire mass. This elaborate mixture of components is not static; on the contrary, it is constantly undergoing transformation. As the organisms grow, the available nutrients in the soil solution and the organic remains are used up. In compensation, these organisms secrete materials that solubilize the rock particles, making new minerals available for plants, and also glue soil particles together into large crumbs, keeping the soil well aerated and in good "tilth" for plant growth.

If the organic matter of the soil is depleted, then the activity of soil microorganisms diminishes and soil quality may deteriorate. Soils poor in organic matter characteristically have poor water-holding capacity, deficient mineral nutrients in the soil solution and a compacted texture so deficient in air spaces that roots cannot respire properly. Plants growing in such a soil may be mineral deficient for any one of these reasons, and it is to be expected that the addition of chemical fertilizers would only partially alleviate their mineral deficiencies, while manure or other organic additives would do a more complete job.

If, however, the soil has adequate organic matter to sustain its population of microorganisms and to maintain its proper structure, then the addition of chemical fertilizers is sufficient to produce optimal growth and chemical composition of the plants growing in the soil. The best proof of this statement is that plants can be grown from seed to seed in synthetic chemical solutions, entirely without organic addenda of any kind, and without even the physical support furnished by soil. Such plants are as capable of supporting the growth of the animals that eat them as are "organically grown plants."

These are facts, as certain (and as tentative) as any I know in science. Yet, I think it is fair to say that they were not really believed by some students in the class who are emotionally committed to "organic gardening." This is true partially because they are in revolt against "the establishment" and the synthetic, plastic world it has created. This leads them to propose impossible additional conditions before they will believe the facts cited above. "How do you know that there aren't undiscovered vitamins or growth factors that you can't analyze for?" Of course, scientists don't know, but point to the fact that synthetic diets made of known growth factors will support normal growth of test organisms, including man, and will support reproduction of test animals, such as mice and rats, over several generations. This puts the burden of proof for other growth factors squarely in the skeptics' court, but many of them feel no necessity to prove anything; they are content to reiterate the possibility that there is more to know about diet than we now know, without being more specific and without paying regard to the usual rules of evidence.

My advice to devotees of organic food is to pay the extra cost of such foods if they wish to avoid some pesticide residues and preservatives, but not to do so under the illusion that plants grown on organic media are necessarily any better than plants grown with an optimum mixture of chemical fertilizers. It is doubtful whether such advice will be taken.

In a follow-up discussion, I asked how many students regularly consume vitamin pills. About one-third of the class raised their hands. I then pointed out that the body needs only minute quantities of vitamins, that a typical Yale College diet more than adequately provides the quantities needed, that excess vitamins are merely excreted and that massive quantities of certain vitamins could actually produce harmful effects. The students listened respectfully, but later queries revealed that practically none had changed their habits and continued, often at great personal expense, to pop useless and perhaps harmful pills as part of their daily routine. They did not really counter the evidence I advanced, nor did they change their way of thinking. They continued a daily practice that was demonstrably illogical, yet somehow comfortable to them. I conclude that the Yale undergraduate, like others in the community, does not behave like a completely logical animal, cherishes his prejudices dearly and treats science and scientists with interested attention, but not with complete trust.

THE CASE FOR OPTIMISM

Maurice Strong

Maurice F. Strong (1929–) was born in Manitoba, Canada, and became an outdoorsman at an early age. At one time he worked as a fur trader with the Hudson Bay Company and learned to speak the Eskimo language. Later, Strong toured the world for two years, spending over a year in East Africa, where he learned Swahili. In 1970 the Secretary General of the United Nations asked him to become an undersecretary, with responsibility for environmental affairs. Strong participated in the first UN Conference on the Human Environment, and he maintains that we have reason to hope that planetary doomsday can be headed off. In this essay, he lists ten steps we can take to prevent catastrophe.

Are we headed for planetary doomsday? Is the human prospect as bleak and unpromising as the prophets of doom suggest? I believe that there is a *case for hope*, that doomsday is not inevitable.

• There is hope in the dawning realization of our basic interdependence in caring for and sharing the world's precious resources.

• There is hope in the attitudes of young people, in their questioning of the competitive, materialistic values of our society, in their awakened sensitivities to its inequities and injustices.

• There is hope in the courageous experimentation of some people, particularly youth, with new, simpler, more human life-styles, which are pioneering new concepts of growth and alternatives to traditional development patterns.

• There is hope in the growing number of positive examples of the way the creative uses of technology, combined with political will, can indeed produce a better and more livable environment.

• There is hope in many parts of the developing world where traditional values and cultures have been harmonized with modern technology to permit the achievement of a quality of life that is in no way inferior to that enjoyed by the wealthier societies and in many ways has much to teach them.

• There is hope in the nature of man himself, man at his best, and in the evidence in our past that we can and do respond to appeals to our higher values and our larger concepts of enlightened self-interest.

I am fully persuaded that the case for hope must begin with a realistic acknowledgment of the fact that we do indeed face risks to our survival and, perhaps more importantly, to the survival of the qualities and values which endow human life with its higher purposes and meaning. Doomsday is possible—even probable—if we continue on our present course, but it is not inevitable. It is possible to opt for a future of unparalleled promise and opportunity for the human species. But this future can come about only if we make a radical change in our present course.

The same science and technology that has given us the power to effect such a destructive impact on our natural environment and resources can help provide the means not only to control that impact but also to give all people access to at least the basic requirements for a decent life.

Let me set out 10 major steps that I believe we must take to achieve this end.

A New Approach to Societal Decision-Making   Our present dilemma points up serious deficiencies in societal decision-making processes. Clearly, our past decisions have not been producing the results we expected. No one consciously decided to pollute our air or waters, to produce the urban squalor that afflicts so many of our cities, to destroy so much of our natural endowment of plant and animal life, and to produce the glaring disparities between rich and poor that characterize our global society. But, nevertheless, these conditions now confronting us are the products of our past actions—the unforeseen results of decisions taken to meet other narrower, short-term objectives.

It is evident that we must develop better methods of evaluating the full consequences of those decisions which significantly affect both the physical and the social environment—before such decisions are made.

Societal management in the environmental age requires prime emphasis on the management of the whole system of relationships of the individual activities that combine to affect man's own development and well-being. This approach will assume even more importance than the management of any individual activity within the system. It also will require that we develop better techniques of allocating the real costs of activities to those who benefit from them, of assigning real value to such traditionally free goods as water and air. It means drastically revising our concepts and methods of evaluating the future. If we continue to value the future by means of present methods of discounting future values at current interest rates, it would not be good economics to preserve the oceans, the atmosphere, and the other precious resources of our "only one earth."

Stabilizing World Population   This goal should be achieved quickly in the industrialized countries that are already moving in that direction —and at the earliest feasible date in most other countries. The timing of population stabilization will vary considerably from country to country, reflecting the very different situations that exist in the balance among population, resources, and development goals. But it is essential that on a global basis the goal must be to stabilize population growth by the first quarter of the next century. Stabilization will be difficult to achieve in the developing countries in particular. Some of them are already facing the prospect of population limitation through famine and disease, and these forbidding prospects will undoubtedly accelerate if efforts to limit population in more humane ways prove too little or too late. Zero growth can be brought about only by increasing the incentives for reducing family size by spreading the benefits of development more widely and by evolving improved techniques of family planning for those thus motivated to use them.

In an era when the borders of the world are closed to large-scale immigration, the population growth of each nation is first and foremost a matter of its own responsibility; the economic and social pressures it creates and the effect on development goals primarily affect its own national situation. The population of individual nations becomes a world concern when its activities and needs begin to impinge on the resources and rights of others, whether as a result of increased population growth or the increased demands of existing populations. This situation is clearly going to happen in many cases —in some cases it is already happening. Therefore, to say that population is first and foremost a national responsibility does not relieve us of the need to see it as a global concern.

Reducing Demand on Natural Resources and Environment—A New Commitment to Conservation   The consumption habits and production methods, particularly in the industrialized societies, must be significantly altered to reduce the demand on scarce resources and pressures on the natural environment. It must go far beyond the development of "add on" pollution-control technologies to the redesign of industrial systems and a much broader distribution of industrial capacity. Energy conservation in particular is a high priority. The fact that Sweden, whose standard of living is comparable to that of the United States, has a per capita energy use only about half that of the United States illustrates the fact that significant reductions can be effected in energy use without materially affecting living standards. Indeed better use of resources and care of the environment can be accompanied by significant increases in the real quality of life. Consumers must be prepared to modify their demands, particularly for the kind of variety in consumer products that represents differences in packaging and presentation more than in substance. Consumers must also be prepared to accept the higher prices that will be necessary for assuring that product costs incorporate fully the cost of the environmental protection to which they give rise.

The ethic of abundant resources must give way to the ethics of scarcity and conservation. Higher costs provide greater incentives for the development of more efficient methods of using and reusing natural resources. Greater emphasis must be placed on the development of less-energy-intensive technologies, more closed-system methods, low-entropy and recycling technologies.

Increasing World Food Supply Without Destroying the Ecological Basis for Sustained Production   Feeding the world's growing population and achieving adequate nutritional standards is one of the most urgent issues of our generation. But this goal must be accomplished without destroying the ecological basis on which sustained production of food depends. Ecologically sound management of productive agricultural land is absolutely indispensable to meeting the world's food-supply problems on a long-term basis. Use of fertilizers and chemical pesticides should be carefully controlled to assure a maximum contribution to increased food production and a minimum of risks of secondary consequences that could largely offset or wholly negate the benefits of such increases. We must arrest the tragic loss of productive agricultural land through the march of the deserts, massive soil erosion, and salination caused by the mismanagement of man's activities. We must make more effective use of human, animal, and other organic wastes as fertilizers and develop more effective non-chemical methods of pest control. We must drastically reduce large-scale losses of food grains during storage, processing, and handling, which approach one-third of the total harvested in some developing countries. We should maintain reserves, stocks of food, and other vital resources in quantities sufficient for meeting foreseeable emergencies. This should be done, as is being proposed with respect to food in relation to the World Food Conference, under a system of shared international responsibility, both for costs and resource use.

Redirecting the Urban Revolution   The industrialized countries first made the fundamental transition from a primarily rural to a largely urbanized society, and now the developing countries are doing so. This transition is both a product of our new technological civilization and the focus of many of its dilemmas. Urban areas have, on the whole, been growing at rates about double those of overall population growth. In 1950 there were 75 cities with a million or more inhabitants and a total population of 174 million; in 1970 there were 162 such cities, including four that had 10 million or more inhabitants, and the total population was 416 million; it is estimated that by the year 1985 there will be 273 cities with 1 million or more inhabitants, including 17 with over 10 million, and the total population will be 805 million. In some areas eco-disasters of major proportions are shaping up as cities are faced with the prospects of being overwhelmed by the virtually unmanageable problems of meeting the basic needs of their exploding populations.

Some countries, notably China, have succeeded in limiting the growth of their cities and in achieving a workable balance between rural and urban growth patterns. This is a balance that all countries must ultimately achieve, because present rates of urban growth are simply not sustainable in the long term.

Urban growth, which depends on a high degree of concentration and centralization, must give way to the development of networks of sustainable urban "ecosystems," which are in harmony with the resource base on which they depend. The sharp distinctions between rural and urban life will have to disappear as rural life acquires many of the advantages and attributes now found in urban areas and as the advantages of rural life become more accessible to inhabitants of urban areas. These new developments will entail a wholly new and integrated approach to the planning and management of human settlements.

Organization and Reorientation of Science and Technology   Just as man's mastery of science and technology has helped to produce many of his present difficulties, the power of science and technology must now be consciously evoked if he is to deal effectively with these difficulties. A large-scale reduction of research and development expenditures and a reorientation of the priorities of science and technology is essential. That will involve a reshaping of policies and incentives to harness the resources of industrial corporations, which are the leading repositories and practitioners of the world's technology, and to assure that they are directed to the achievement of the social goals of society.

There must also be a much more effective relationship between scientists and technologists on the one hand and political decision-makers on the other. Specifically, better means must be provided for advising and guiding scientists and technologists concerning decisions that shape our environmental future. Scientists and technologists must play a major part in reshaping the societal decision-making processes to which I have already referred.

A shift of some of the very large expenditures now being made on resource and development for military purposes to a budget favoring technologies for environmental control and betterment would improve, not diminish, our basic security. For the pursuit of narrow concepts of military security at the expense of the environmental security on which the future of all depends is surely illusory.

A New Approach to Growth   New concepts of growth must be elaborated that give primacy to man's social goals and aspirations and assure that economic development is clearly designed to achieve these goals. This means that new models for economic and social progress must be designed. In the industrialized world this will involve alternative lifestyles and patterns of consumption oriented more to quality and non-material satisfactions and less to sheer quantity.

Economic incentives and penalties must be reoriented to make it more attractive to engage in those activities that are socially desirable, and less attractive to undertake those that impinge on or contradict social goals. The highly industrialized societies should generally forgo the temptation for ever greater growth measured in traditional material terms. Most new industrial development should take place in underdeveloped regions, not in the already heavily industrialized areas.

New directions for growth in the developing nations should be designed to bypass the errors and excesses of societies that were industrialized earlier. The need for diversity in patterns of development should be recognized and respected as well as each nation's right to self-reliance in choosing its own development goals and means of achieving them.

Management and Care of the Oceans   One of the greatest challenges of all time and certainly one of the greatest facing this generation is the task of bringing the 70 percent of the globe represented by the oceans out of national jurisdiction and under the rule of law and management. And the way in which we meet this challenge will do much to determine the future prospects for world peace and order. Within the foreseeable future many of the activities of man that have traditionally been carried out on land will be capable of being carried out on the oceans—some of them amounting in effect to the creation of man-made territory.

This great new source of wealth must not become the object of a new round of fierce competition among the wealthy countries with the technologies to exploit them, nor the basis of a new form of exploitation in which the wealthy extract a disproportionate share of the benefits at the expense of the poor. Resources of the oceans, and particularly of those that lie beyond national jurisdictions, must be subjected to effective international management and control so as to assure that the majority living in the developing world are the principal beneficiaries of these resources.

Creation of a New International Economic Order   The technological civilization is characterized by a network of interdependencies that is global in scale. The cooperation of the poor is clearly necessary for the effective functioning of this society. At the same time, the rich are most acutely vulnerable to the kinds of disruption of the technological society that can now be effected by relatively small groups of desperate people. Thus enlightened self-interest reinforces basic moral and ethical considerations in dictating that the benefits of the technological society be more widely and equitably shared.

In effect, we must extend into international life the principles of distributive justice and minimum opportunities for all that are accepted as the basis for relations between rich and poor in most national societies today. This means a vast increase in the flow of resources between rich and poor countries, not merely on the basis of charity, but as a precondition to the kind of basic economic security which is essential to the health and stability of a functioning world system. And it will mean replacement of traditional development aid programs with more automatic and impersonal methods of transferring resources, such as use of special drawing rights and levies, tolls, or user charges on the use of the global commons of oceans and atmosphere and possibly on the utilization of non-renewable resources.

Revolution in Values and Behavior   It must be evident that all the foregoing proposals will require significant changes in our present system of values and patterns of behavior. The principal changes must be made in the industrial world, which today commands such a disproportionate share of the wealth and power that this technological society has made possible. The Western world needs its own form of "cultural revolution"—and it needs it urgently.

I am well aware that most of the proposals I have just advanced seem incompatible with present political realities. But let us be reminded that political realities are not immutable; there are times when practical needs must be shaped to match political realities, but on occasion these needs are such as to compel existing political realities to give way to new and larger realities.

We must believe that it is possible to build a new foundation of political will based on the combination of man's higher moral precepts and enlightened awareness of his larger self-interest. If the task is monumental, the stakes are even more so. At risk is the human future. I believe we still have the capacity to shape that future. But I am equally convinced that it will be determined largely by what we decide or fail to decide in the next decade.

ON THE MEANING
OF WORK

Robert Coles

*Robert Coles (1918–) was born in Kansas City, Missouri. He re-
ceived his B.A. and M.A. from the University of Illinois and his
Ph.D. from the University of North Carolina. His work in marketing
research at the Westinghouse Electric Corporation and as an industrial economist with the Federal Reserve Bank has led to his writing a
number of booklets and articles on merchandising, advertising, and
management. In this essay, Coles presents some characteristics we
need to consider when we define work.*

In early December of 1934 a serious and scholarly young French lady,
about to turn twenty-six, took a job in a factory at the outskirts of
Paris. Day after day she operated a drill, used a power press, and
turned a crank handle. From doing so Simone Weil became tired and
sad, but she persisted—and all the while kept a "factory journal." In
time she moved to another factory, there to pack cartons under distinctly unfavorable circumstances. She felt cramped, pushed, and in
general badly used, even as her co-workers did; eventually she was
fired. Still undaunted, she found employment in the well-known
Renault works, the pride of industrial France. She lived in a world of
machines and shop stewards and intense heat and long working
days. She saw men and women hurt and insulted, men and women
grow weak and bitter and weary. She also saw men and women
struggle hard to find what joy and humor they could amid those long
stretches of dangerous and exhausting work. Enraged, at a loss to
know what she thought and believed to be true, she kept at her job.
She also kept asking her co-workers to share their thoughts with her.
  Simone Weil was a moral philosopher, a theologian, some would
say. She had no interest in studying factory life sociologically or
analyzing the psychological "adjustment" of workers to their jobs.
Nor was she trying to see how "the other half" lives for one or
another reason. She had in mind no shocking news stories as she

worked week after week, month after month. She was not out to prove that the modern worker is "exploited" or on the verge of joining some "revolution"—or alternatively, happy beyond anyone's comprehension but his own. Though her mind was capable of constructing its fair share of abstractions, she sensed the danger of doing so. An intellectual, she profoundly distrusted, even scorned, the dozens and dozens of writers and scholars and theorists who wrote with assurance about the workingman and his lot. Instead she wanted to place herself in the very midst of what interested her, there to learn from concrete experience—and only later would she stop and ask herself what she *believed*, what she had to *say*, about subjects like "the effect of work on the worker," subjects that she well knew a mind like hers was tempted to seize and probe and dissect without the slightest exposure to a Renault factory building, let alone those who work inside it.

Eventually she would carry her experiences to the countryside; she learned to pick crops, plow the land, tend animals, and in general live the life of a peasant—to the point that she unnerved her hosts. She was no snob, no condescending "observer" bent on picking up a few facts, establishing a reputation of sorts, then hurrying off so as to cash in on the time spent "out there." The people with whom she stayed (at Bourges, about 100 miles due south of Paris) later remarked upon their guest's ability to cut through the barriers that naturally went to separate her from them—"and put herself at our level."

In fact Simone Weil wanted to do more than "understand" others, or make them feel that she was stooping ever so gracefully. She saw factory workers and field hands as her brothers and sisters, out of a deep and certainly religious need to do so, a longing she described (for herself and for the rest of us) in *The Need for Roots,* written toward the end of her short yet intense life. (She died in 1943 at the age of thirty-three.) In the book she emphasizes that we need desperately—indeed die spiritually if we do not have—a community, one whose life, whose values and customs and traditions, whose *sanction*, a person doesn't so much think about as take for granted. If that is not very original and surprising, Miss Weil's notion of what a "community" is, or ought to be, goes much further; she sees us as always wanting to be in touch with others, not only our immediate families or more distant kin or our neighbors but those we work with, with whom we spend well over half our waking hours. For her, economists and political scientists (not to mention politicians), as well as psychologists and sociologists, all too often fail to grasp the true rhythms in life. True, they point out how much money we have or don't have, how much power one or another "class" has; or else they emphasize the lusts and rages we feel and try to express or subdue. Meanwhile, all over the world millions and millions of men and women (yes, and children) mark their lives by working, resting from work as best they can, and going back to work—until they die. And for Simone Weil it is with such day-to-day experiences that one who wants to comprehend man's nature and society's purposes ought to start.

Though she got on well with her fellow workers in several factories and on a farm, and though she held off at all times from extending cheap pity to those men and women, or condescension masked as moral outrage, or contempt dressed up as radical theory, she had to set down what she saw and heard. That is to say, she had to list the various kinds of suffering she saw among France's workers:

> We must change the system concerning concentration of attention during working hours, the types of stimulants which make for the overcoming of laziness or exhaustion—and which at present are merely fear and extra pay—the type of obedience necessary, the far too small amount of initiative, skill and thought demanded of workmen, their present exclusion from any imaginative share in the work of the enterprise as a whole, their sometimes total ignorance of the value, social utility, and destination of the things they manufacture, and the complete divorce between working life and family life. The list could well be extended.

She went on to do so; she extended her list and spelled out how life goes for millions of workmen in what she called "our industrial prisons"—where (she well knew) men are glad to be, rather than go hungry or be idle. But she was not primarily a social critic; perhaps more than anything else she was a visionary, hence easily written off as impractical—but uncannily able to say things starkly and prophetically and with apparent naiveté, which more cautious and "realistic" men only in time would come to see as indeed significant. So she noted how frightened and sullen her co-workers became, how drained they felt by the end of the day, how tempted they were to make minor mistakes, slow down, even at times cause considerable damage to the plant in which they worked or to the products they were turning out. Why is it so, she asked—why must men (in both American and Russia—that is, under capitalism and Communism alike) work in such huge, cold, impersonal places, and feel so fortunate (such is their vulnerability, their fear, their insecurity) for having even that kind of opportunity? The answer, no doubt, is that efficiency demands it; in a modern industrial nation mass production has to take place in large factories. Yet, in the France of the 1930s,

Miss Weil saw what we in America are now beginning to notice and worry about: the dangers which a cult of efficiency and productivity, unqualified by ethical if not spiritual considerations, can present us with. She saw how much her worker friends needed one another, how hard they tried to enjoy one another's company, notwithstanding all the factory rules and regulations. She saw how tempted they were to stay off the job, to feign illness or offer some other excuse that enabled them to take at least this day off. She saw how greedy and thoughtless an industrial empire can become: land, water, air, raw materials, the lives of people—everything is grist for those modern mills of ours, which in turn are defended as necessary for our "advanced civilization," while all the while we cough and hold our noses and our ears and see about us an increasingly bleak and contaminated land, and feel upset as well, at a loss, and more than a little angry. The words and phrases are familiar, indeed have become clichés: absenteeism, ecological disaster, alienation, dehumanization, the loss of a sense of community.

Simone Weil sensed in her intuitive way that something was wrong, that a new order of attention must be given to the ordinary working man—whether he wears a blue collar or a white one—to his need for fellowship and dignity as well as money, to his struggle for meaning as well as possessions.

Working people with whom I have talked make quite clear the ways they feel cornered, trapped, lonely, pushed around at work, and, as Simone Weil kept on emphasizing, confused by a sense of meaninglessness. These feelings, I have noticed, often take the form of questions—and I will take the liberty of paraphrasing some of them that I have heard: What am I doing that *really matters?* What is the point to it all—not life, as some philosophers say, but the specific, tangible things I do or make? What would I do if I had a real choice— something which I doubt I ever will have? Is there some other, some better way to work? Might we not break up these large factories and offices, work closer to our homes, closer to one another as workers— and work together on something that is not a fragment of this, a minor part of that, but is whole and significant and recognizable as important in our lives?

If those were "romantic" inquiries for a much-troubled and fussy and brilliant French religious philosopher and political essayist in the 1930s, they may not be altogether impractical for us today. The workers I have heard may not speak as Simone Weil did; but like her they are able to be obsessed by the riddles and frustrations that life presents—and like her, they can spot trouble when it is in front of them, literally in the air, the dangerously contaminated air. As never before, our industrial societies are now being forced to look inward, so to speak, to become aware of the implications of our policies, among them those followed by the thousands of businesses which employ millions of workers. No doubt in the 1930s a skeptic could easily have made light of Simone Weil's concern that the French landscape outside various giant factories was in several ways being defaced. No doubt today what she (and over the decades many, many workers) wanted done inside those factories can still seem impractical. But that word "impractical" is one that history has taught us to think twice about. One generation's impracticality has a way of becoming another's urgent necessity.

WHERE I LIVED, AND WHAT I LIVED FOR

Henry David Thoreau

Henry David Thoreau (1817–1862), the great American philosopher, poet, and naturalist, was born in Concord, Massachusetts. After graduating from Harvard, Thoreau worked for a while as a teacher. But, uncertain as to what he wanted to do with his life, he resigned his position and took on a series of odd jobs. From 1845 to 1847 Thoreau lived in a small cabin that he built for himself on the shores of Walden Pond near Concord, Massachusetts. He recorded his experiences in his best-known work, Walden, *a classic in American literature. The selection below, taken from* Walden, *highlights Thoreau's spirit of individualism and his lifelong passion for freedom.*

At a certain season of our life we are accustomed to consider every spot as the possible site of a house. I have thus surveyed the country on every side within a dozen miles of where I live. In imagination I have bought all the farms in succession, for all were to be bought, and I knew their price. I walked over each farmer's premises, tasted his wild apples, discoursed on husbandry with him, took his farm at his price, at any price, mortgaging it to him in my mind; even put a higher price on it,—took every thing but a deed of it—took his word for his deed, for I dearly love to talk,—cultivated it, and him too to some extent, I trust, and withdrew when I had enjoyed it long enough, leaving him to carry it on. This experience entitled me to be regarded as a sort of real-estate broker by my friends. Wherever I sat, there I might live, and the landscape radiated from me accordingly. What is a house but a *sedes*, a seat?—better if a country seat. I discovered many a site for a house not likely to be soon improved, which some might have thought too far from the village, but to my eyes the village was too far from it. Well, there I might live, I said; and there I did live, for an hour, a summer and a winter life; saw how I could let the years run off, buffet the winter through, and see the spring come in. The future inhabitants of this region, wherever they may place their houses, may be sure that they have been anticipated. An afternoon sufficed to lay out the land into orchard, woodlot, and pasture, and to decide what fine oaks or pines should be left to stand before the door, and whence each blasted tree could be seen to the best advantage; and then I let it lie, fallow perchance, for a man is rich in proportion to the number of things which he can afford to let alone.

My imagination carried me so far that I even had the refusal of several farms,—the refusal was all I wanted,—but I never got my fingers burned by actual possession. The nearest that I came to actual possession was when I bought the Hollowell Place, and had begun to sort my seeds, and collected materials with which to make a wheelbarrow to carry it on or off with; but before the owner gave me a deed of it, his wife—every man has such a wife—changed her mind and wished to keep it, and he offered me ten dollars to release him. Now, to speak the truth, I had but ten cents in the world, and it surpassed my arithmetic to tell, if I was that man who had ten cents, or who had a farm, or ten dollars, or all together. However, I let him keep the ten dollars and the farm too, for I had carried it far enough; or rather, to be generous, I sold him the farm for just what I gave for it, and, as he was not a rich men, made him a present of ten dollars, and still had my ten cents, and seeds, and materials for a wheelbarrow left. I found thus that I had been a rich man without any damage to my poverty. But I retained the landscape, and I have since annually carried off what it yielded without a wheelbarrow. With respect to landscapes,—

> I am monarch of all I *survey*,
> My right there is none to dispute.

I have frequently seen a poet withdraw, having enjoyed the most valuable part of a farm, while the crusty farmer supposed that he had got a few wild apples only. Why, the owner does not know it for many years when a poet has put his farm in rhyme, the most admirable kind of invisible fence, has fairly impounded it, milked it, skimmed it, and got all the cream, and left the farmer only the skimmed milk.

The real attractions of the Hollowell farm, to me, were: its complete retirement, being about two miles from the village, half a mile from the nearest neighbor, and separated from the highway by a broad field; its bounding on the river, which the owner said protected it by its fogs from frosts in the spring, though that was nothing to me; the gray color and ruinous state of the house and barn, and the dilapidated fences, which put such an interval between me and the last occupant; the hollow and lichen-covered apple trees, gnawed by rabbits, showing what kind of neighbors I should have; but above all, the recollection I had of it from my earliest voyages up the river, when the house was concealed behind a dense grove of red maples, through which I heard the house-dog bark. I was in haste to buy it, before the proprietor finished getting out some rocks, cutting down the hollow apple trees, and grubbing up some young birches which had sprung up in the pasture, or, in short, had made any more of his improvements. To enjoy these advantages I was ready to carry it on; like Atlas,[1] to take the world on my shoulders,—I never heard what compensation he received from that,—and do all those things which had no other motive or excuse but that I might pay for it and be unmolested in my possession of it; for I knew all the while that it would yield the most abundant crop of the kind I wanted if I could only afford to let it alone. But it turned out as I have said.

All that I could say, then, with respect to farming on a large scale, (I have always cultivated a garden), was, that I had had my seeds ready. Many think that seeds improve with age. I have no doubt that time discriminates between the good and the bad; and when at last I shall plant, I shall be less likely to be disappointed. But I would say to my fellows, once for all, As long as possible live free and uncommitted. It makes but little difference whether you are committed to a farm or the county jail.

Old Cato,[2] whose "De Re Rustica" is my "Cultivator," says,—and the only translation I have seen makes sheer nonsense of the passage,

---

1. A Greek god who carried the world and sky on his shoulders.
2. Marcus Porcius Cato, a Roman philosopher.

—"When you think of getting a farm, turn it thus in your mind, not to buy greedily; nor spare your pains to look at it, and do not think it enough to go round it once. The oftener you go there the more it will please you, if it is good." I think I shall not buy greedily, but go round and round it as long as I live, and be buried in it first, that it may please me the more at last.

The present was my next experiment of this kind, which I purpose to describe more at length; for convenience, putting the experience of two years into one. As I have said, I do not propose to write an ode to dejection, but to brag as lustily as chanticleer in the morning, standing on his roost, if only to wake my neighbors up.

When first I took up my abode in the woods, that is, began to spend my nights as well as days there, which, by accident, was on Independence Day, or the Fourth of July, 1845, my house was not finished for winter, but was merely a defence against the rain, without plastering or chimney, the walls being of rough, weather-stained boards, with wide chinks, which made it cool at night. The upright white hewn studs and freshly planed door and window casings gave it a clean and airy look, especially in the morning, when its timbers were saturated with dew, so that I fancied that by noon some sweet gum would exude from them. To my imagination it retained throughout the day more or less of this auroral character, reminding me of a certain house on a mountain which I had visited the year before. This was an airy and unplastered cabin, fit to entertain a travelling god, and where a goddess might trail her garments. The winds which passed over my dwelling were such as sweep over the ridges of mountains, bearing the broken strains, or celestial parts only, of terrestrial music. The morning wind forever blows, the poem of creation is uninterrupted; but few are the ears that hear it. Olympus[3] is but the outside of the earth everywhere.

The only house I had been the owner of before, if I except a boat, was a tent, which I used occasionally when making excursions in the summer, and this is still rolled up in my garret; but the boat, after passing from hand to hand, has gone down the stream of time. With this more substantial shelter about me, I had made some progress toward settling in the world. This frame, so slightly clad, was a sort of crystallization around me, and reacted on the builder. It was suggestive somewhat as a picture in outlines. I did not need to go outdoors to take the air, for the atmosphere within had lost none of its freshness. It was not so much within doors as behind a door where I

---

3. The mythological home of the Greek gods.

sat, even in the rainiest weather. The Harivansa[4] says, "An abode without birds is like a meat without seasoning." Such was not my abode, for I found myself suddenly neighbor to the birds; not by having imprisoned one, but having caged myself near them. I was not only nearer to some of those which commonly frequent the garden and the orchard, but to those wilder and more thrilling songsters of this forest which never, or rarely, serenade a villager,—the woodthrush, the veery, the scarlet tanager, the field-sparrow, the whippoorwill, and many others.

I was seated by the shore of a small pond, about a mile and a half south of the village of Concord and somewhat higher than it, in the midst of an extensive wood between that town and Lincoln; and about two miles south of that our only field known to fame, Concord Battle Ground; but I was so low in the woods that the opposite shore, half a mile off, like the rest, covered with wood, was my most distant horizon. For the first week, whenever I looked out on the pond it impressed me like a tarn high up on the side of a mountain, its bottom far above the surface of other lakes, and, as the sun arose, I saw it throwing off its nightly clothing of mist, and here and there, by degrees, its soft ripples or its smooth reflecting surface was revealed, while the mists, like ghosts, were stealthily withdrawing in every direction into the woods, as at the breaking up of some nocturnal conventicle. The very dew seemed to hang upon the trees later into the day than usual, as on the sides of mountains.

This small lake was of most value as a neighbor in the intervals of a gentle rain-storm in August, when, both air and water being perfectly still, but the sky overcast, mid-afternoon had all the serenity of evening, and the wood-thrush sang around, and was heard from shore to shore. A lake like this is never smoother than at such a time; and the clear portion of the air above it being shallow and darkened by clouds, the water, full of light and reflections, becomes a lower heaven itself so much the more important. From a hill-top near by, where the wood had been recently cut off, there was a pleasing vista southward across the pond, through a wide indentation in the hills which form the shore there, where their opposite sides sloping toward each other suggested a stream flowing out in that direction through a wooded valley, but stream there was none. That way I looked between and over the near green hills to some distant and higher ones in the horizon, tinged with blue. Indeed, by standing on tiptoe I could catch a glimpse of some of the peaks of the still bluer and more distant mountain ranges in the northwest, those true-blue

---

4. A fifth-century Hindu religious epic.

coins from heaven's own mint, and also of some portion of the village. But in other directions, even from this point, I could not see over or beyond the woods which surrounded me. It is well to have some water in your neighborhood, to give buoyancy to and float the earth. One value even of the smallest well is, that when you look into it you see that earth is not continent but insular. This is as important as that it keeps butter cool. When I looked across the pond from this peak toward the Sudbury meadows, which in time of flood I distinguished elevated perhaps by a mirage in their seething valley, like a coin in a basin, all the earth beyond the pond appeared like a thin crust insulated and floated even by this small sheet of intervening water, and I was reminded that this on which I dwelt was but *dry land*.

Though the view from my door was still more contracted, I did not feel crowded or confined in the least. There was pasture enough for my imagination. The low shrub-oak plateau to which the opposite shore arose stretched away toward the prairies of the West and the steppes of Tartary, affording ample room for all the roving families of men. "There are none happy in the world but beings who enjoy freely a vast horizon,"—said Damodara,[5] when his herds required new and larger pastures.

Both place and time were changed, and I dwelt nearer to those parts of the universe and to those eras in history which had most attracted me. Where I lived was as far off as many a region viewed nightly by astronomers. We are wont to imagine rare and delectable places in some remote and more celestial corner of the system, behind the constellation of Cassiopeia's Chair, far from noise and disturbance. I discovered that my house actually had its site in such a withdrawn, but forever new and unprofaned, part of the universe. If it were worth the while to settle in those parts near to the Pleiades or the Hyades, to Aldebaran or Altair,[6] then I was really there, or at an equal remoteness from the life which I had left behind, dwindled and twinkling with as fine a ray to my nearest neighbor, and to be seen only in moonless nights by him. Such was that part of creation where I had squatted:—

> There was a shepherd that did live,
>   And held his thoughts as high
> As were the mounts whereon his flocks
>   Did hourly feed him by.

---

5. A Hindu god.

6. Constellations and stars.

What should we think of the shepherd's life if his flocks always wandered to higher pastures than his thoughts?

Every morning was a cheerful invitation to make my life of equal simplicity, and I may say innocence, with Nature herself. I have been as sincere a worshipper of Aurora[7] as the Greeks. I got up early and bathed in the pond; that was a religious exercise, and one of the best things which I did. They say that characters were engraven on the bathing tub of King Tching-thang[8] to this effect: "Renew thyself completely each day; do it again, and again, and forever again." I can understand that. Morning brings back the heroic ages. I was as much affected by the faint hum of a mosquito making its invisible and unimaginable tour through my apartment at earliest dawn, when I was sitting with door and windows open, as I could be by any trumpet that ever sang of fame. It was Homer's requiem; itself an Iliad and Odyssey in the air, singing its own wrath and wanderings. There was something cosmical about it; a standing advertisement, till forbidden, of the everlasting vigor and fertility of the world. The morning, which is the most memorable season of the day, is the awakening hour. Then there is least somnolence in us; and for an hour, at least, some part of us awakes which slumbers all the rest of the day and night. Little is to be expected of that day, if it can be called a day, to which we are not awakened by our Genius, but by the mechanical nudgings of some servitor, are not awakened by our own newly acquired force and aspirations from within, accompanied by the undulations of celestial music, instead of factory bells, and a fragrance filling the air—to a higher life than we fell asleep from; and thus the darkness bear its fruit, and prove itself to be good, no less than the light. That man who does not believe that each day contains an earlier, more sacred, and auroral hour than he has yet profaned, has despaired of life, and is pursuing a descending and darkening way. After a partial cessation of his sensuous life, the soul of man, or its organs rather, are reinvigorated each day, and his Genius tries again what noble life it can make. All memorable events, I should say, transpire in morning time and in a morning atmosphere. The Vedas[9] say, "All intelligences awake with the morning." Poetry and art, and the fairest and most memorable of the actions of men, date from such an hour. All poets and heroes, like Memnon, are the children of Aurora, and emit their music at sunrise. To him whose elastic

---

7. The goddess of the dawn.

8. Another name for Confucius.

9. Hindu religious scriptures.

and vigorous thought keeps pace with the sun, the day is a perpetual morning. It matters not what the clocks say or the attitudes and labors of men. Morning is when I am awake and there is a dawn in me. Moral reform is the effort to throw off sleep. Why is it that men give so poor an account of their day if they have not been slumbering? They are not such poor calculators. If they had not been overcome with drowsiness, they would have performed something. The millions are awake enough for physical labor; but only one in a million is awake enough for effective intellectual exertion, only one in a hundred millions to a poetic or divine life. To be awake is to be alive. I have never yet met a man who was quite awake. How could I have looked him in the face?

We must learn to reawaken and keep ourselves awake, not by mechanical aids, but by an infinite expectation of the dawn, which does not forsake us in our soundest sleep. I know of no more encouraging fact that the unquestionable ability of man to elevate his life by a conscious endeavor. It is something to be able to paint a particular picture, or to carve a statue, and so to make a few objects beautiful; but it is far more glorious to carve and paint the very atmosphere and medium through which we look, which morally we can do. To affect the quality of the day, that is the highest of arts. Every man is tasked to make his life, even in its details, worthy of the contemplation of his most elevated and critical hour. If we refused, or rather used up, such paltry information as we get, the oracles would distinctly inform us how this might be done.

I went to the woods because I wished to live deliberately, to front only the essential facts of life, and see if I could not learn what it had to teach, and not, when I came to die, discover that I had not lived. I did not wish to live what was not life, living is so dear; nor did I wish to practise resignation, unless it was quite necessary. I wanted to live deep and suck out all the marrow of life, to live so sturdily and Spartan-like as to put to rout all that was not life, to cut a broad swath and shave close, to drive life into a corner, and reduce it to its lowest terms, and, if it proved to be mean, why then to get the whole and genuine meanness of it, and publish its meanness to the world; or if it were sublime, to know it by experience, and be able to give a true account of it in my next excursion. For most men, it appears to me, are in a strange uncertainty about it, whether it is of the devil or of God, and have *somewhat hastily* concluded that it is the chief end of man here to "glorify God and enjoy him forever."

Still we live meanly, like ants; though the fable tells us that we were long ago changed into men; like pygmies we fight with cranes; it is error upon error, and clout upon clout, and our best virtue has for its

occasion a superfluous and evitable wretchedness. Our life is frit-
tered away by detail. An honest man has hardly need to count more
than his ten fingers, or in extreme cases he may add his ten toes, and
lump the rest. Simplicity, simplicity, simplicity! I say, let your affairs
be as two or three, and not a hundred or a thousand; instead of a
million count half a dozen, and keep your accounts on your thumb
nail. In the midst of this chopping sea of civilized life, such are the
clouds and storms and quicksands and thousand-and-one items to be
allowed for, that a man has to live, if he would not founder and go to
the bottom and not make his port at all, by dead reckoning, and he
must be a great calculator indeed who succeeds. Simplify, simplify.
Instead of three meals a day, if it be necessary eat but one; instead of a
hundred dishes, five; and reduce other things in proportion. Our life
is like a German Confederacy, made up of petty states, with its
boundary forever fluctuating, so that even a German cannot tell you
how it is bounded at any moment. The nation itself, with all its so-
called internal improvements, which, by the way, are all external and
superficial, is just such an unwieldly and overgrown establishment,
cluttered with furniture and tripped up by its own traps, ruined by
luxury and heedless expense, by want of calculation and a worthy
aim, as the million households in the land; and the only cure for it, as
for them, is in a rigid economy, a stern and more than Spartan
simplicity of life and elevation of purpose. It lives too fast. Men think
that it is essential that the *Nation* have commerce, and export ice, and
talk through a telegraph, and ride thirty miles an hour, without a
doubt, whether *they* do or not; but whether we should live like
baboons or like men, is a little uncertain. If we do not get out sleepers, and forge rails, and devote days and nights to the work, but go to
tinkering upon our *lives* to improve *them*, who will build railroads?
And if railroads are not built, how shall we get to heaven in season?
But if we stay at home and mind our business, who will want railroads? We do not ride on the railroad; it rides upon us. Did you ever
think what those sleepers are that underlie the railroad? Each one is a
man, an Irishman, or Yankee man. The rails are laid on them, and
they are covered with sand, and the cars run smoothly over them.
They are sound sleepers, I assure you. And every few years a new lot
is laid down and run over; so that, if some have the pleasure of riding
on a rail, others have the misfortune to be ridden upon. And when
they run over a man that is walking in his sleep, a supernumerary
sleeper in the wrong position, and wake him up, they suddenly stop
the cars, and make a hue and cry about it, as if this were an exception.
I am glad to know that it takes a gang of men for every five miles to

keep the sleepers down and level in their beds as it is, for this is a sign that they may sometime get up again.

Why should we live with such hurry and waste of life? We are determined to be starved before we are hungry. Men say that a stitch in time saves nine, and so they take a thousand stitches to-day to save nine to-morrow. As for *work*, we haven't any of any consequence. We have the Saint Vitus' dance, and cannot possibly keep our heads still. If I should only give a few pulls at the parish bell-rope, as for a fire, that is, without setting the bell, there is hardly a man on his farm in the outskirts of Concord, notwithstanding that press of engagements which was his excuse so many times that morning, nor a boy, nor a woman, I might almost say, but would forsake all and follow that sound, not mainly to save property from the flames, but, if we will confess the truth, much more to see it burn, since burn it must, and we, be it known, did not set it on fire,—or to see it put out, and have a hand in it, if that is done as handsomely; yes, even if it were the parish church itself. Hardly a man takes a half hour's nap after dinner, but when he wakes he holds up his head and asks, "What's the news?" as if the rest of mankind had stood his sentinels. Some give directions to be waked every half hour, doubtless for no other purpose; and then, to pay for it, they tell what they have dreamed. After a night's sleep the news is as indispensable as the breakfast. "Pray tell me any thing new that has happened to a man anywhere on this globe,"—and he reads it over his coffee and rolls, that a man has had his eyes gouged out this morning on the Wachito River; never dreaming the while that he lives in the dark unfathomed mammoth cave of this world, and has but the rudiment of an eye himself.

For my part, I could easily do without the post-office. I think that there are very few important communications made through it. To speak critically, I never received more than one or two letters in my life—I wrote this some years ago—that were worth the postage. The penny-post is, commonly, an institution through which you seriously offer a man that penny for his thoughts which is so often safely offered in jest. And I am sure that I never read any memorable news in a newspaper. If we read of one man robbed, or murdered, or killed by accident, or one house burned, or one vessel wrecked, or one steamboat blown up, or one cow run over on the Western Railroad, or one mad dog killed, or one lot of grasshoppers in the winter,—we never need read of another. One is enough. If you are acquainted with the principle, what do you care for a myriad instances and applications? To a philosopher all *news*, as it is called, is gossip, and they who edit and read it are old women over their tea. Yet not a few are greedy after this gossip. There was such a rush, as I hear, the other day at one of the offices to learn the foreign news by the last arrival, that several large squares of plate glass belonging to the establishment were broken by the pressure,—news which I seriously think a ready wit might write a twelvemonth, or twelve years, beforehand with sufficient accuracy. As for Spain, for instance, if you know how to throw in Don Carlos and the Infanta, and Don Pedro[10] and Seville and Granada, from time to time in the right proportions, —they may have changed the names a little since I saw the papers,— and serve up a bull-fight when other entertainments fail, it will be true to the letter, and give us as good an idea of the exact state or ruin of things in Spain as the most succinct and lucid reports under this head in the newspapers: and as for England, almost the last significant scrap of news from that quarter was the revolution of 1649; and if you have learned the history of her crops for an average year, you never need attend to that thing again, unless your speculations are of a merely pecuniary character. If one may judge who rarely looks into the newspapers, nothing new does ever happen in foreign parts, a French revolution not excepted.

What news! how much more important to know what that is which was never old! "Kieou-he-yu (great dignitary of the state of Wei) sent a man to Khoung-tseu to know his news. Khoung-tseu caused the messenger to be seated near him, and questioned him in these terms: What is your master doing? The messenger answered with respect: My master desires to diminish the number of his faults, but he cannot come to the end of them. The messenger being gone, the philosopher remarked: What a worthy messenger! What a worthy messenger!" The preacher, instead of vexing the ears of drowsy farmers on their day of rest at the end of the week,—for Sunday is the fit conclusion of an ill-spent week, and not the fresh and brave beginning of a new one,—with this one other draggle-tail of a sermon, should shout with thundering voice,—"Pause! Avast! Why so seeming fast, but deadly slow?"

Shams and delusions are esteemed for soundest truths, while reality is fabulous. If men would steadily observe realities only, and not allow themselves to be deluded, life, to compare it with such things as we know, would be like a fairy tale and the Arabian Nights' Entertainments. If we respected only what is inevitable and has a right to be, music and poetry would resound along the streets. When we are unhurried and wise, we perceive that only great and worthy

---

10. Nineteenth-century Spanish nobles.

things have any permanent and absolute existence,—that petty fears and petty pleasures are but the shadow of the reality. This is always exhilarating and sublime. By closing the eyes and slumbering, and consenting to be deceived by shows, men establish and confirm their daily life of routine and habit everywhere, which still is built on purely illusory foundations. Children, who play life, discern its true law and relations more clearly than men, who fail to live it worthily, but who think that they are wiser by experience, that is, by failure. I have read in a Hindoo book, that "there was a king's son, who, being expelled in infancy from his native city, was brought up by a forester, and, growing up to maturity in that state, imagined himself to belong to the barbarous race with which he lived. One of his father's ministers having discovered him, revealed to him what he was, and the misconception of his character was removed, and he knew himself to be a prince. So soul," continues the Hindoo philosopher, "from the circumstances in which it is placed, mistakes its own character, until the truth is revealed to it by some holy teacher, and then it knows itself to be *Brahme*."[11] I perceive that we inhabitants of New England live this mean life that we do because our vision does not penetrate the surface of things. We think that that *is* which *appears* to be. If a man should walk through this town and see only the reality, where, think you, would the "Mill-dam"[12] go to? If he should give us an account of the realities he beheld there, we should not recognize the place in his description. Look at a meeting-house, or a court-house, or a jail, or a shop, or a dwelling-house, and say what that thing really is before a true gaze, and they would all go to pieces in your account of them. Men esteem truth remote, in the outskirts of the system, behind the farthest star, before Adam and after the last man. In eternity there is indeed something true and sublime. But all these times and places and occasions are now and here. God himself culminates in the present moment, and will never be more divine in the lapse of all the ages. And we are enabled to apprehend at all what is sublime and noble only the perpetual instilling and drenching of the reality that surrounds us. The universe constantly and obediently answers to our conceptions; whether we travel fast or slow, the track is laid for us. Let us spend our lives in conceiving then. The poet or the artist never yet had so fair and noble a design but some of his posterity at least could accomplish it.

---

11. Brahma, the Hindu creator.
12. Shopping area of Concord.

Let us spend one day as deliberately as Nature, and not be thrown off the track by every nutshell and mosquito's wing that falls on the rails. Let us rise early and fast, or break fast, gently and without perturbation; let company come and let company go, let the bells ring and the children cry,—determined to make a day of it. Why should we knock under and go with the stream? Let us not be upset and overwhelmed in that terrible rapid and whirlpool called a dinner, situated in the meridian shallows. Weather this danger and you are safe, for the rest of the way is downhill. With unrelaxed nerves, with morning vigor, sail by it, looking another way, tied to the mast like Ulysses. If the engine whistles, let it whistle till it is hoarse for its pains. If the bell rings, why should we run? We will consider what kind of music they are like. Let us settle ourselves, and work and wedge our feet downward through the mud and slush of opinion, and prejudice, and tradition, and delusion, and appearance, that alluvion which covers the globe, through Paris and London, through New York and Boston and Concord, through Church and State, through poetry and philosophy and religion, till we come to a hard bottom and rocks in place, which we can call *reality*, and say, This is, and no mistake; and then begin, having a *point d'appui*,[13] below freshet and frost and fire, a place where you might found a wall or a state, or set a lamp-post safely, or perhaps a gauge, not a Nilometer,[14] but a Realometer, that future ages might know how deep a freshet of shams and appearances had gathered from time to time. If you stand right fronting and face to face to a fact, you will see the sun glimmer on both its surfaces, as if it were a cimeter,[15] and feel its sweet edge dividing you through the heart and marrow, and so you will happily conclude your mortal career. Be it life or death, we crave only reality. If we are really dying, let us hear the rattle in our throats and feel cold in the extremities; if we are alive, let us go about our business.

Time is but the stream I go a-fishing in. I drink at it; but while I drink I see the sandy bottom and detect how shallow it is. Its thin current slides away, but eternity remains. I would drink deeper; fish in the sky, whose bottom is pebbly with stars. I cannot count one. I know not the first letter of the alphabet. I have always been regretting that I was not as wise as the day I was born. The intellect is a cleaver; it discerns and rifts its way into the secret of things. I do not wish to be any more busy with my hands than is necessary. My head is hands

---

13. Base.
14. A gauge used to measure the rise of the Nile River.
15. An outmoded spelling of *scimitar*, a sword with a curved blade.

and feet. I feel all my best faculties concentrated in it. My instinct tells me that my head is an organ for burrowing, as some creatures use their snout and fore-paws, and with it I would mine and burrow my way through these hills. I think that the richest vein is somewhere hereabouts; so by the divining-rod and thin rising vapors I judge; and here I will begin to mine.

GENERAL GUIDE
TO ANALYZING ESSAYS

An essay is more than a random collection of ideas; it is a literary work in which the author combines form and style to express ideas as forcefully and compellingly as possible. In analyzing an essay, then, it is important that you examine the way the ideas are expressed as well as the nature of the ideas themselves.

In a good essay, the title, introduction, thesis, supporting ideas, transitional devices, and closing are integrated in a unified and coherent structure. The tone and diction of the essay are free from problems and appropriate to the essay's organization and purposes. And the ideas proposed in the essay are supported by reliable evidence and logical reasoning. In short, a good essay's structure conveys its meaning clearly and eloquently.

This guide has been formulated to help you examine in detail the essays you read and write. It provides questions that you can use to examine the rhetoric, evaluate the logic, and explore the ideas in an essay. Literary terms used in this guide are defined in detail in the Glossary.

Examining Rhetoric

Organization

1. What mode of discourse is used?
   —Argument? Logical argument? Persuasive argument?
   —Description? Objective description? Impressionistic description?
   —Narration? Dramatized narration? Generalized narration? Summarized narration?
   —Exposition?

2. Is the title general or specific? Are metaphors, alliteration, or other devices used in the title? If so, for what purpose?

   Are there subtitles? If so, what purpose do they serve?

3. Is there an introduction? Does the essay begin with a quotation? An anecdote? A straw man? General information? Statistics? An allusion? A rhetorical question? An unusual statement? A statement about the significance of the essay's thesis?

355

What is the purpose of the introduction? How does it relate to the essay's thesis? How is the transition made between the introduction and the body of the essay?

4. Is the essay's thesis implied, or is it directly stated? Where is it most clearly expressed? What does this location suggest about the essay's emphasis?

   Is the thesis repeated in the course of the essay? If so, why do you think the author has done this?

5. What is the main pattern of development used to present supporting ideas? Classification? Example? Definition? Analysis? Process analysis? Comparison and contrast? Analogy? Cause and effect?

   Is there sufficient unity in the essay? Do all of the supporting ideas pertain to the thesis? Are enough ideas presented to support the thesis? Are too many ideas presented?

   Is there sufficient coherence? Are the ideas presented in an appropriate sequence? Is this sequence chronological, spatial, logical, or is some other form of organization used?

   Are ideas linked by appropriate transitional structures? What transitional methods are used? Parallel structures? Coordinating conjunctions? Subordinating conjunctions? Repetition of essential ideas? Enumeration of ideas?

   Is there foreshadowing? Flashback? If so, how is each device used?

6. How does the essay close? With a reassertion of proof? A summary of the points made in the essay? A statement of deeper meaning? A statement of the implications of the thesis?

Style and Tone

1. Is figurative language used in the essay? If so, what kinds are used? Metaphors? Personification? Similes? Idioms? Hyperbole? Others?

   For what purpose are the figures of speech used? Do they contribute to the beauty and tone of the essay? Do they enhance or obscure the essay's meaning?

2. Does the essay contain highly technical or difficult language? Could simpler synonyms be used with greater effectiveness?

3. Does the essay contain many general or abstract words? Do they obscure meaning? Could specific or concrete words be substituted to express more clearly the essay's meaning?

4. Are there diction problems in the essay? Do you find examples of jargon, triteness, pretentious words, or slang? What effect does this use of language have on the essay as a whole?

5. What is the tone of the essay? Humorous? Angry? Informal? Scholarly? Ironic? Matter-of-fact? Other? Does the tone coordinate well with the purpose of the essay?

6. Are the sentences in the essay long and complex? Brief and simple? What does the style of the sentences contribute to the essay as a whole? Does the style of the sentences detract in any way from the essay?

7. Are there any sentence problems? Do you find examples of wordiness or deadwood? Undue repetition of words, sounds, or meanings? Inappropriate cuteness? Other problems?

Evaluating Logic

Evidence

1. What are the author's qualifications? Does he or she have the education and experience necessary to write about the topic? What else has the author written? Is he or she known to have a particular bias toward the subject?

2. What magazine or book does the essay appear in? What is the reputation of that source? Can you depend on it for honesty and accuracy?

3. What is the publication date of the essay? If timeliness is important, is the material up to date? Have there been important developments in the area discussed since the essay was published? Is the issue discussed in the essay still important, or is it outdated?

4. Has the essay been cut? If so, do you think the deleted material could provide important clues as to the honesty and accuracy of the essay as a whole?

5. Are the facts accurate? Is the number of facts cited sufficient to prove the author's point?

6. Do the opinions and quotations cited come from qualified authorities?

7. Does the author use any deceptive devices to strengthen the essay's argument? Does the author use misleading statements? Loaded or slanted words? Slogans? A misleading writing style? Bandwagon appeal? Sentimental appeal? Appeals based on misleading authority? Any other devices?

Reasoning

1. Is the major proposition (thesis) stated clearly? Is it stated in an unbiased, unslanted way? Is it arguable?

2. Are all of the relevant minor (supporting) propositions stated?

3. Are all difficult or problematical terms defined?

4. Are all counter-arguments anticipated and answered?

5. If inductive reasoning is used, are generalizations based on sufficient evidence and are hasty generalizations avoided?

6. If reasoning by analogy is used, is the analogy based on a sufficient number of characteristics shared by the things being compared? Are both weak and false analogies successfully avoided?

7. If deductive reasoning is used, has the major premise (generalization about the class) been arrived at inductively from sufficient evidence? Does the major premise ignore any significant fact? Is the fact stated in the minor premise (application to a specific member of the class) true? Does the conclusion follow logically?

8. Are there logical fallacies in the essay? Do you find examples of overgeneralization? Unsupported inferences? Assumption of proof by failure to find the opposite case? Special pleading? Avoiding the question with a non sequitur or an ad hominem attack. Begging the question? False dilemmas? False sequences? Other fallacies?

Comprehending and Interpreting Ideas

1. What is the title? How can it be paraphrased? What does it suggest about the essay's thesis? The tone of the essay? The viewpoint from which the essay is written? The essay's emphasis?

2. What does the introduction tell you? Is it aimed simply at attracting the reader's interest? If not, what does it suggest about the essay's thesis? Its tone? The author's viewpoint? The emphasis of the essay?

3. What is the essay's central thesis?

4. What supporting ideas are used to develop the thesis? What do the transitional structures show about relationships among ideas in the essay?

5. What ideas are presented in the closing? What do they tell you about the essay's emphasis? Its meaning? Its implications?

6. What levels of meaning lie behind the ideas given? What do the ideas suggest about what our world and our behavior are like at present? About what they should be like?

Applying Ideas

1. How do the ideas in the essay apply to your current activities and ideas?

2. Does the essay suggest any changes you might make in your life in the future?

GLOSSARY

Abstract Words/Concrete Words

A concrete word has a referent that can be touched or seen (book, cloud, car, baby), whereas an abstract word has an idea as a referent—something which cannot be touched or seen (peace, need, anger, freedom).

Ad Hominem Attack

A method of avoiding the issue in argument by presenting negative information about a person's character instead of dealing directly with the person's ideas.

Alliteration

The repetition of sounds at the beginning of words.

Analogy

See the introduction to Comparison and Contrast in Part I, Exposition.

Analysis

See the introduction to Analysis in Part I, Exposition.

Antonyms

Words which have directly opposite meanings—for example, "love" and "hate."

Appeals Based on Misleading Authority

Used in this sense, an authority can be someone who knows a great deal about a subject, or it can be a source of information, such as statistics, the encyclopedia, or the U.S. Constitution. Quoting an authority is common practice in legal and scholarly writings, but it can be misused in at least two ways: when the writer does not tell exactly who or what the authority is and how the evidence was obtained, and when the authority cited is not qualified to comment on the subject. The statement "Research reveals that children like baseball better than swimming," for example, invites the reader to ask what research is being alluded to and where it was obtained.

Argument

See the introduction to Part III, Argument.

Assumption of Proof by Failure to Find an Opposite Case

The assertion that something is true because there is no evidence that it is not true. Positive evidence is necessary to prove something; a mere demonstration that there is no evidence against a proposition does not prove that the proposition is true.

Avoiding the Question

Distracting the reader from the case in point by presenting material which is not relevant. Two devices commonly used in avoiding the question are the non sequitur and the ad hominem attack, each of which is defined in a separate entry in this glossary.

Bandwagon Appeal

A method of encouraging a person to take a specific course of action on the grounds that everyone else is doing it.

Cause and Effect

See the introduction to Cause and Effect in Part I, Exposition.

Chronological Order

A method of organization in which a narrative or the stages in process are presented in the order in which they occurred in time.

Circular Argument

A method of arguing the truth of a premise by restating the premise rather than giving evidence to show why it is true—for example, "You need a sense of humor to be happy because happiness depends on being able to see the funny side of things."

Classification

See the introduction to Classification in Part I, Exposition.

Clichés

> *See* Trite Expressions.

Closing

> The conclusion of an essay. Some devices commonly used in closings are the reassertion of proof given in support of the thesis, a summary of the points made in the essay, a presentation of the implications or significance of the points made, and a statement of some deeper meaning hitherto undiscussed in the essay.

Coherence

> The arrangement of supporting ideas in such a way that they flow smoothly and logically. Some arrangements commonly used to achieve coherence are chronological order, spatial order, order or importance, order needed for comparison and contrast, induction, and deduction. Coherence may be increased through the use of transitional structures which help the reader follow the line of thought from one idea to the next.

Colloquial English or *Colloquialism*

> *See* Informal English.

Comparison

> *See* the introduction to Comparison and Contrast in Part I, Exposition.

Concrete Words

> *See* Abstract Words/Concrete Words.

Connotation

> The meanings associated with a word apart from its explicit meaning, or denotation. For example, the word "yellow" *denotes* a color, but it also *connotes* cowardice.

Context

> The setting in which an idea develops or an event occurs.

Contrast

> *See* the introduction to Comparison and Contrast in Part I, Exposition.

Coordinating Conjunctions

> Conjunctions, such as *and*, *but*, and *yet*, which are used to connect words and phrases of equal importance.

Deadwood

> Words which do not contribute to meaning or clarity. For example, "He teaches in the area of English" has no clearer meaning than "He teaches English."

Definition

> *See* the introduction to Definition in Part I, Exposition.

Deduction

> *See* the introduction to Part III, Argument.

Denotation

> The exact, literal meaning of a word.

Description

> *See* the introduction to Part II, Description.

Dialogue

> Passages in written material representing conversation between two or more people.

Diction

> The choice of words used in talking or writing.

Dramatized Narration

> *See* the introduction to Part IV, Narration.

Emphasis

The amount of stress given to specific ideas. There are five main ways to give an idea emphasis:
— Position: In most essays, the ending is the most emphatic position, the beginning is the second most emphatic position, and the middle is the least emphatic position.
— Proportion: The greatest amount of space is generally given to the most important ideas.
— Repetition: Ideas to be emphasized are often repeated in order to establish their importance in the reader's mind.
— Typography: Italics, capital letters, and exclamation points may be used to show emphasis.
— Headnotes and titles: Headnotes and titles are sometimes used to highlight ideas.
— Tagging: Phrases like "the most important" and "the crux of the matter" signal emphasis.

Euphemisms

Less direct or milder words substituted for words considered distasteful or offensive. For example, "sanitary landfill" is a euphemism for "garbage dump."

Example

See the introduction to Example in Part I, Exposition.

Exposition

See the introduction to Part I, Exposition.

False Analogy

See the introduction to Comparison and Contrast in Part I, Exposition.

False Dilemma

A logical fallacy that involves two elements: the dilemma— equally unwanted choices—and falseness—choices that are not the only ones possible. An example of false dilemma is the question "Does my suit look better than you expected it to look or does it look worse?"

False Sequence

Sometimes called *post hoc, ergo propter hoc reasoning,* this fallacy suggests that if one event follows another, the second event necessarily must be caused by the first event. An example of this type of reasoning is: "Most accidents happen within fifty miles of people's homes. Therefore, it is safer to drive on long trips than it is to drive around town." Logically, of course, most accidents happen near people's homes because people spend more time driving near home; there is no basis for the belief that it is safer to drive far from home.

Figurative Language

Language that carries a meaning different from the denotative meaning of the words. Figurative language is used to convey the sense or feeling of a situation rather than the objective facts. Some of the more commonly used kinds of figurative language are metaphors, similes, idioms, and personification. (Each type of figurative language is defined in a separate entry.)

Figures of Speech

See Figurative Language.

Flashback

The interruption of the chronological sequence of a narrative in order to portray an event which occurred at a previous point in time.

Foreshadowing

Giving a clue to an event which will occur later in a narrative.

General Language/Specific Language

General language is loose and imprecise, whereas specific language pinpoints meaning more exactly. For example, "The quarterback broke his ankle" is more specific than "The football player suffered an injury."

Generalized Narration

See the introduction to Part IV, Narration.

Hyperbole

Deliberate overstatement or exaggeration which is used to heighten the effect of a statement.

Idiom

An expression that has come to have a specific meaning through long usage. An idiom's meaning is not readily understandable from its grammatical structure or from the meanings of its parts. To "give in" to someone, for example, is an idiom.

Impressionistic Description

See the introduction to Part II, Description.

Induction

See the introduction to Part III, Argument.

Informal English

The level of language that is used in ordinary conversation and in most books, articles, and newspapers.

Introduction

The beginning of an essay, often used to establish common ground with readers, to attract their interest, or to serve as a keynote or setting for an essay. The introduction should relate directly to the thesis. Some devices commonly used in introductions are headnotes, anecdotes, straw men, statistics, allusions, rhetorical questions, and quotations.

Irony

The use of an expression in a humorous or sarcastic way which implies the exact opposite of the expression's literal meaning.

Jargon

Technical language used by specialists.

Left-out information

Relevant information which an author deliberately withholds because it contradicts his or her thesis.

Levels of Meaning

The various levels at which the sense and implications of a literary work may be read. All works have a literal meaning—the actual sense of the words on the page—but beyond this, the characters, objects, and actions in a work often reflect a more general meaning—political, moral, spiritual, etc.—which applies beyond the specific case described in the work.

Loaded Words

Words associated with strong feelings which are used to appeal to readers' emotions.

Logic

The science of correct thinking based on established criteria and methods for reasoning.

Logical Argument

See the introduction to Part III, Argument.

Logical Fallacy

An error in reasoning. Some common fallacies are overgeneralization, assumption of proof by failure to find an opposite case, special pleading, avoiding the question, circular argument, the false dilemma, the false sequence, and the false analogy. (Each type of fallacy is defined in a separate entry.)

Main Idea

See Thesis.

Major Proposition

See Proposition.

Metaphor

A comparison between things that are essentially unlike. The comparison is implied rather than directly stated, and, unlike a simile, it is not introduced by "like" or "as." (*See* the introduction to Part II, Description.)

Methods of Reasoning

Procedures that are used in argument for organizing and weighing information. Three major methods of reasoning are induction, deduction, and analogy. (For a definition of these three methods, see the introduction to Part III, Argument.)

Minor Proposition

See Proposition.

Misleading Statements

Statements that seem to say one thing when they really say a less desirable thing. For example, the statement "These fine limited editions have been presented to the Duke of Edinburgh" suggests that the Duke appreciates these items, and, therefore, that we should do so as well. However, the sentence only states that the editions were given to the Duke; it does not actually comment on his opinion of them.

Misleading Writing Style

A style deliberately used by an author to confuse readers or to divert their attention from a deficiency in the author's argument. Some devices commonly used to mislead readers are double negatives, irrelevant material, highly complex sentences and paragraphs, and difficult or extremely technical vocabulary.

Mixed Metaphor

A metaphor in which one figure of speech is combined incongruously with another—for example, "The *ship of state* is traveling a *rocky road.*"

Mode of Discourse

See the Preface to this volume.

Monologue

A written passage representing the speech of a single person.

Narration

See the introduction to Part IV, Narration.

Non Sequitur

A statement which does not follow from the evidence given or which does not relate to the question asked.

Objective Description

See the introduction to Part II, Description.

Overgeneralization

A *generalization* is a statement that applies to all cases in a specific class. An *overgeneralization* is a generalization which is not true for all cases, even though it may sound true. "All men were once boys" is a generalization because it applies to all cases in the class "men." "All men like to eat" is an overgeneralization because some men do not enjoy eating, even though they *must* eat in order to survive.

Paradox

A statement that is true even though it seems contradictory, unbelievable, or absurd.

Parallelism

The expression of ideas that are equally important in the same grammatical form. For example, in the sentence "He enjoyed only two things: food and sleep," the words "food" and "sleep" are both nouns and, therefore, parallel in structure. In the sentence "He enjoyed only two things: eating and sleep," however, the parallelism is destroyed.

Patterns (Methods) of Development

See the introduction to Part I, Exposition.

Personification

The attribution of human qualities to animals or inanimate objects—for example, "She's a great ship."

Persuasive Argument

See the introduction to Part III, Argument.

Point of View

The vantage point from which an author discusses a topic or relates a narrative. (For a more detailed discussion of point of view, see the introduction to Part IV, Narration.)

Post Hoc Ergo Propter Hoc Reasoning

See False Sequence.

Pretentious Writing

Writing which is more excessive or learned than the situation demands. For example, "Prolixity simulates erudition" is a pretentious way of saying "Wordiness gives the appearance of high education."

Process Analysis

See the introduction to Analysis in Part I, Exposition.

Proposition

The point to be argued. A proposition may be an idea or a suggested course of action. The *major proposition* is the thesis—the main point to be considered—and the minor propositions are the points used to support the major proposition.

Rhetorical Question

A question to which no answer is expected—for example, "Who would not prefer freedom to slavery?"

Satire

A literary method which uses wit, irony, or sarcasm to ridicule human failings.

Sentimental Appeal

A method of argument in which the author attempts to convince readers of the truth of a proposition by appealing strictly to their emotions.

Simile

A figure of speech in which the words "like" or "as" are used to make direct comparisons between things that are essentially dissimilar.

Slang

Informal colloquial language—for example, the words "ain't" and "cop."

Slanted words

See Loaded Words.

Slogans

Brief, striking phrases which are sometimes used in argument to arouse the reader's enthusiasm. They are often used to camouflage a lack of logical reasoning.

Special Pleading

The use of one set of standards to judge the author's side of the argument and another, often more exacting, set to judge the opposing point of view.

Specific Language

See General Language/Specific Language.

Straw Man

A logical fallacy in which the author introduces an easily demolished argument opposing his or her own point of view and then points out the errors in that argument.

Style

An author's individual way of writing—of using words, constructing sentences, and organizing ideas.

Subordinating Conjunctions

Conjunctions, such as *although* and *because*, which are used to connect unequal ideas.

Summarized Narration

See the introduction to Part IV, Narration.

Synonyms

Words which have the same or similar meanings.

Theme

See Thesis.

Thesis

The main idea or central point of the essay. It may be stated directly or implied.

Title

A word, phrase, or sentence set off at the beginning of a literary work and used to convey its main idea. A title may be explicit or general, and it may be accompanied by a subtitle which either extends or restricts its meaning.

Tone

The feeling or attitude an author conveys in a work. The tone of an essay may be humorous, angry, informal, scholarly, sarcastic, or matter of fact, among others.

Transitional Structures

Structures that are used to give coherence and to show relationships among ideas in literary works. Five frequently used types of transitional structures are conjunctions, parallel structures, enumeration, ordered headings, and repetition of content.
— Conjunctions: *See* Coordinating Conjunctions and Subordinating Conjunctions.
— Parallel structures: Words, phrases, clauses, or sentences which are given the same grammatical form to show that they are of equal importance. (*See* Parallelism.)
— Enumeration: The numbering or orderly listing of ideas.
— Ordered headings: Headings which illustrate by means of position, type size, or type style the relative importance of various ideas. First-order headings subsume ideas designated by second-order headings; in turn, second-order headings subsume ideas designated by third-order headings, and so on.
— Repetition of Content: The restatement of important ideas throughout an essay to establish a sense of continuity and to remind the reader of the essay's focus.

Trite Expressions

Sometimes called clichés, trite expressions are those which have grown stale through frequent use.

Understatement

Use of language that is deliberately gentler, milder, weaker, or less sensational than the situation merits. For example, it is an understatement to call a civil war an "unpleasant situation."

Unity

The achievement of integrity in an essay by using supporting ideas directly related to the thesis and by eliminating all irrelevant ideas.

Unsupported Inferences

Inferences are conclusions derived logically from specific given information. Authors make *unsupported* inferences when they draw conclusions from insufficient evidence.

Weak Analogy

An anology in which the similarities between two things do not fully justify the comparison being drawn. (*See* the introduction to Comparison and Contrast in Part I, Exposition.)

BIBLIOGRAPHY

Arendt, Hannah. *The Human Condition.* Chicago: University of Chicago Press, 1958.

Asimov, Isaac. *The Caves of Steel.* Garden City, N.Y.: Doubleday, 1954.

————. *Pebble in the Sky.* Garden City, N.Y.: Doubleday, 1950.

Beccaria, Cesare Bonesana. *An Essay on Crimes and Punishments.* London: J. Almon, 1767.

Benson, Herbert. *The Relaxation Response.* New York: Morrow, 1975.

Blatty, William Peter. *The Exorcist.* New York: Harper & Row, 1971.

Brown, Barbara. *New Mind, New Body—Biofeedback: New Directions for the Mind.* New York: Harper & Row, 1974.

Brown, John. *Horae Subsecivae.* Edinburgh: D. Douglas, 1890.

————. *John Leech and Other Papers.* Edinburgh: D. Douglas, 1882.

————. *Rab and His Friends.* Freeport, N.Y.: Books for Libraries Press, 1972.

Buchwald, Art. *And Then I Told the President.* New York: Putnam, 1965.

————. *The Brave Coward.* New York: Harper, 1957.

————. *Don't Forget to Write.* Cleveland: World, 1960.

————. *I Choose Capital Punishment.* Cleveland: World, 1963.

Buck, Pearl S. *The Child Who Never Grew.* New York: John Day, 1950.

————. *The Exile.* New York: Reynal & Hitchcock, 1936.

————. *Fighting Angel.* New York: Reynal & Hitchcock, 1936.

————. *The Good Earth.* New York: Grosset & Dunlap, 1944.

————. *A House Divided.* New York: Collier & Son, 1935.

————. *Sons.* New York: Collier & Son, 1932.

Burnford, Sheila. *The Incredible Journey.* Boston: Little, Brown, 1961.

Chisholm, Shirley. *Unbought and Unbossed.* Boston: Houghton Mifflin, 1970.

Cleaver, Eldridge. *Eldridge Cleaver's Post-Prison Writings and Speeches*. New York: Random House, 1969.

———. *Soul on Ice*. New York: McGraw-Hill, 1967.

Darwin, Charles. *The Origin of Species*. New York: Dutton, 1928.

Dean, John Wesley. *Blind Ambition*. New York: Simon & Schuster, 1976.

Defoe, Daniel. *Robinson Crusoe*. New York: Doubleday, 1946.

Dickens, Charles. *A Christmas Carol*. New York: Heineman, 1967.

———. *David Copperfield*. New York: Collier & Son, 1917.

———. *Great Expectations*. New York: Dutton, 1971.

———. *The Old Curiosity Shop*. New York: Scribner, 1914.

———. *Oliver Twist*. Oxford: Clarendon Press, 1966.

———. *The Posthumous Papers of the Pickwick Club*. New York: Harper, 1873.

———. *A Tale of Two Cities*. New York: Crowell, 1904.

Dickey, James. *Deliverance*. Boston: Houghton Mifflin, 1970.

Didion, Joan. *A Book of Common Prayer*. New York: Simon & Schuster, 1977.

———. *Play It As It Lays*. New York: Farrar, Straus & Giroux, 1970.

———. *Run River*. New York: Astor-Honor, 1961.

———. *Slouching Towards Bethlehem*. New York: Farrar, Straus & Giroux, 1968.

Eliot, T. S. *The Cocktail Party*. London: Faber & Faber, 1950.

Faulkner, William. *As I Lay Dying*. New York: J. Cape, 1930.

———. *Light in August*. New York: Random House, 1967.

———. *The Sound and the Fury*. New York: Random House, 1966.

Fielding, William John. *Strange Customs of Courtship and Marriage*. New York: Hart, 1967.

Franklin, Benjamin. *Poor Richard's Almanack*. New York: Century, 1898.

Friedan, Betty. *The Feminine Mystique*. New York: Norton, 1963.

Fromm, Erich. *The Art of Loving*. New York: Bantam Books, 1963.

Gaines, Ernest J. *The Autobiography of Miss Jane Pittman*. New York: Dial Press, 1971.

Galsworthy, John. *The Forsyte Saga*. New York: Scribner, 1933.

Gardner, John W. *Excellence: Can We Be Equal and Excellent Too?* New York: Harper, 1961.

Gellius, Aulus. *The Attic Nights of Aulus Gellius*. Cambridge: Harvard University Press, 1946–52.

Gibson, William. *The Miracle Worker*. New York: Knopf, 1957.

Godwin, Gail. *Glass People*. New York: Knopf, 1972.

———. *The Perfectionists*. New York: Harper & Row, 1970.

Goldsmith, Oliver. *The Deserted Village*. New York: Harper, 1902.

———. *She Stoops to Conquer*. New York: F. A. Stokes, 1899.

———. *The Vicar of Wakefield*. New York: Dutton, 1909.

Gould, Lois. *Final Analysis*. New York: Random House, 1974.

———. *Necessary Objects*. New York: Dell, 1973.

———. *A Sea-Change*. New York: Simon & Schuster, 1976.

———. *Such Good Friends*. New York: Random House, 1970.

Greeley, Andrew M. *And Young Men Shall See Visions*. New York: Sheed & Ward, 1964.

———. *Letters to Nancy*. New York: Sheed & Ward, 1964.

———. *Strangers in the House: Catholic Youth in America*. New York: Sheed & Ward, 1961.

Greenburg, Dan. *How to Be a Jewish Mother*. Los Angeles: Price, Stern, Sloane, 1965.

———. *Scoring*. New York: Dell, 1973.

———. *Something's There*. New York: Doubleday, 1976.

Gregory, Dick. *Dick Gregory's Natural Diet for Folks Who Eat: Cookin' with Mother Nature*. New York: Harper & Row, 1964.

———. *Dick Gregory's Political Primer*. New York: Harper & Row, 1972.

————. *From the Back of the Bus.* New York: Avon Books, 1962.

————. *Nigger: An Autobiography.* New York: Dutton, 1964.

————. *No More Lies: The Myths of American History.* New York: Harper & Row, 1971.

Gunther, John. *Death Be Not Proud.* New York: Harper, 1949.

Haley, Alex. *Roots.* Garden City, N.Y.: Doubleday, 1976.

Hemingway, Ernest. *For Whom the Bell Tolls.* New York: Scribner, 1940.

————. *A Moveable Feast.* New York: Scribner, 1964.

————. *The Old Man and the Sea.* New York: Scribner, 1952.

————. *The Sun Also Rises.* New York: Scribner, 1970.

Hobson, Laura K. *Gentlemen's Agreement.* New York: Simon & Schuster, 1947.

Hoffer, Eric. *In Our Time.* New York: Harper & Row, 1976.

————. *The Ordeal of Change.* New York: Harper & Row, 1963.

————. *Reflections on the Human Condition.* New York: Harper & Row, 1973.

————. *The Temper of Our Time.* New York: Harper & Row, 1967.

————. *The True Believers.* New York: Harper, 1951.

Huxley, Aldous. *After Many a Summer Dies the Swan.* New York: Harper, 1939.

James, Henry. *The Turn of the Screw.* New York: Macmillan, 1898.

Katz, Stanley N. *Colonial America.* Boston: Little, Brown, 1971.

Keller, Helen. *The Story of My Life.* New York: Doubleday, Page, 1903.

————. *The World I Live In.* New York: Appleton-Century, 1938.

Kennedy, John F. *Profiles in Courage.* New York: Harper & Row, 1964.

Keyes, Daniel. *Flowers for Algernon.* New York: Harcourt Brace & World, 1966.

King, Martin Luther. *Strength to Love.* New York: Harper & Row, 1963.

————. *Stride Toward Freedom*. New York: Harper, 1958.

————. *Why We Can't Wait*. New York: Harper & Row, 1964.

Klobuchar, Jim, and Tarkenton, Fran. *Tarkenton*. New York: Harper & Row, 1976.

Kozol, Jonathan. *Death at an Early Age*. Boston: Houghton Mifflin, 1967.

Lamb, Charles, and Lamb, Mary. *Poetry for Children*. Freeport, N.Y.: Books for Libraries Press, 1970.

————. *Tales from Shakespeare*. New York: Macmillan, 1958.

Langer, Lawrence. *The Holocaust and the Literary Imagination*. New Haven: Yale University Press, 1975.

Lash, Joseph. *Eleanor and Franklin*. New York: Norton, 1971.

Laurents, Arthur. *The Way We Were*. New York: Harper & Row, 1972.

Levin, Ira. *Rosemary's Baby*. New York: Random House, 1967.

Lindbergh, Anne Morrow. *Gift from the Sea*. New York: Pantheon, 1955.

————. *Listen! The Wind*. New York: Harbrace, 1940.

————. *North to the Orient*. New York: Harcourt Brace, 1935.

London, Jack. *The Call of the Wild*. New York: Macmillan, 1903.

MacKenzie, Henry. *The Man of Feeling*. New York: Garland, 1974.

————. *The Man of the World*. New York: Garland, 1974.

Mead, Margaret. *Coming of Age in Samoa*. New York: Blue Ribbon Books, 1932.

Melville, Herman. *Billy Budd*. Cambridge: Harvard University Press, 1948.

Newman, Edwin. *Strictly Speaking: Will America Be the Death of English?* Indianapolis: Bobbs-Merrill, 1974.

Orwell, George. *Animal Farm*. New York: Harcourt Brace, 1954.

————. *1984*. New York: Harcourt Brace, 1949.

Packard, Vance. *The Hidden Persuaders*. New York: McKay, 1957.

Rogers, Will. *The Cowboy Philosopher on Prohibition*. New York: Harper, 1919.

———. *Ether and Me*. New York: Putnam, 1929.

———. *The Illiterate Digest*. New York: A. & C. Boni, 1936.

Ross, Elizabeth K. *On Death and Dying*. New York: Macmillan, 1969.

St. John, Christopher. *Ellen Terry and George Bernard Shaw: A Correspondence*. New York: Putnam, 1931.

Sigourney, Lydia H. *Letters to Young Ladies*. London: Jackson & Walford, 1841.

———. *Lucy Howard's Journal*. New York: Harper, 1858.

Skinner, B. F. *Walden Two*. New York: Macmillan, 1962.

Stanat, Kirby W. *Job Hunting Secrets and Tactics*. Milwaukee: Westwind Press, 1977.

Sterne, Laurence. *A Sentimental Journey*. New York: Dutton, 1926.

———. *Tristram Shandy*. New York: Liveright, 1942.

Thoreau, Henry David. *Walden*. New York: Norton, 1951.

Toffler, Alvin. *Future Shock*. New York: Random House, 1970.

Turgenev, Ivan. *A Sportsman's Notebook*. London: Cresset Press, 1950.

Turner, Ernest S. *A History of Courting*. New York: Dutton, 1955.

Twain, Mark. *Huckleberry Finn*. New York: Harcourt Brace & World, 1961.

Ullman, Liv. *Changing*. New York: Knopf, 1977.

Wright, Frank Lloyd. *The Disappearing City*. New York: Horizon Press, 1969.

———. *Genius and Mobocracy*. New York: Horizon Press, 1971.

———. *The Japanese Print*. New York: Horizon Press, 1967.

———. *When Democracy Builds*. Chicago: University of Chicago Press, 1945.

Wollstonecraft, Mary. *Thoughts on the Education of Daughters*. Clifton, N.J.: A. M. Kelley, 1972.

———. *A Vindication of The Rights of Women*. New York: Norton, 1975.